LITTLE AMERICA

*Two famous Soviet humourists
survey the United States*

by

ILYA ILF and EUGENE PETROV

ISHI PRESS INTERNATIONAL

Little Golden America

two famous Soviet humourists survey the United States

by Ilya Ilf and Eugene Petrov

Одноэтажная Америка

Odnoetazhnya Amerika (One-Storied America) First published in the U.S.S.R. 1936. Little Golden America. First published in England in 1944. Translated from the Russian by Charles Malamuth

This printing in December, 2010 by Ishi Press in New York and Tokyo

with a new Foreword by Sam Sloan

ISBN 4-87187-674-8
978-4-87187-674-2

Ishi Press International
1664 Davidson Avenue, Suite 1B
Bronx NY 10453-7877
USA
1-917-507-7226

Printed in the United States of America

Foreword by Sam Sloan

Little Golden America
two famous Soviet humorists survey the United States
by Ilya Ilf and Eugene Petrov

Odnoetazhnya Amerika (One-Storied America) First published in the U.S.S.R. 1936. Little Golden America. First published in England in 1944. Translated from the Russian by Charles Malamuth

This is one of the most popular books ever published in the Soviet Union. It remains popular in Russia today. We Americans cannot figure out what makes it so popular. It is a good book, interesting and well written, but does not contain anything so outstanding as to make it the most popular book ever written. Yet almost every Russian seems to have read or to be familiar with "Little Golden America".

The book is virtually unknown in America. I first learned of it while attending the World Chess Olympiad in Khanty-Mansiysk in Siberia in Russia, held September 23 to October 4, 2010. One of the great things the organizers did for the chess players was they hired 124 English speaking Siberian girls they called "tutors". Most of them were college students, around age 20. Every team in the Olympiad was assigned a tutor, who was given the job of taking care of us. Anything our little hearts desired, we had only to ask our tutor for it and it would be provided!!!

What was especially remarkable about this is that all of these tutors were beautiful. This remarkable fact was the subject of much discussion amongst the chess players. Had they screened the tutors so that only the beautiful ones were selected? Or, is it simply the fact that all Siberian girls are beautiful?

In either case, it seemed that all of them had read or were familiar with "*Little Golden America*". That is how I learned about this book. They told me they like this book, "Because this book about different world for us, and to be honest we don't know what is life in the USA".

It describes the adventures of the two authors, **Ilya Ilf** and **Eugene Petrov**, who arrived in **New York City** on the passenger ship *Normandie*. After one month in New York, they bought a car and started traveling around the United States. They went to Chicago and San Francisco and then swept back through the Southern States. When they arrived back in New York to return to Europe, they said that they had traveled ten thousand miles:

> "OUR JOURNEY came to an end. Within two months we had been in twenty-five states and several hundred towns, we had breathed the dry air of deserts and prairies, and crossed the Rocky Mountains, had seen Indians, had talked with the young unemployed, with the old capitalists, with radical intellectuals, with revolutionary workers, with poets, with writers, with engineers. We had examined factories and parks, had admired roads and bridges, had climbed up the Sierra Nevadas and descended into the Carlsbad Caves. We had traveled ten thousand miles. And throughout that entire journey we never once stopped thinking of the Soviet Union.

> "We had traveled over American highways but in our thoughts were Soviet highways. We spent nights in American hotels, but we thought about Soviet hotels. We examined Ford's factories, but in our thoughts w□saw ourselves in our own automobile factories, and while conversing with Indians we thought of Kazakstan. Through the tremendous distance that separated us from

Soviet soil we envisioned it with especial incisiveness. It is necessary to see the capitalist world in order to appreciate in a new way the world of socialism. All the attributes of the socialist arrangement of our life, which man ceases to notice because of daily contact with them, seem especially significant at a distance."

The book seems very factual. It is certainly not what I would call propaganda. It is probably one of the few books that Soviet readers were allowed to read to learn about America that were not propaganda.

The same two authors were already famous for their previous works. They always wrote together, never as individuals. They do not explain where they got all the money from to do the things that they did. They probably worked during the initial month they spent in New York, as they seemed to have arrived with little money.

Ilya Ilf (Ilya Arnoldovich Faynzilberg (Russian: Илья Арнольдович Файнзильберг, Ukrainian Ієхієл-Лейб Арнóльдович Файнзільберг , Ukrainian: ; 1897–1937) and Evgeny or Yevgeni Petrov (Yevgeniy Petrovich Kataev or Katayev (Russian: Евгений Петрович Катаев , Ukrainian: Євген Петрович Катаєв ; 1903–1942) were two Soviet prose authors of the 1920s and 1930s. They did much of their writing together, and are almost always referred to as "Ilf and Petrov". They became popular for their two satirical novels: *The Twelve Chairs* and its sequel, *The Little Golden Calf*. The two texts are connected by their main character, Ostap Bender, a con man in pursuit of elusive riches.

They were written and are set in the relatively liberal era in Soviet history, the New Economic Policy of the 1920s. The main characters generally avoid contact with the apparently lax law enforcement. Their position outside the organized, goal-driven, productive Soviet society is emphasized. It also gives the authors a convenient platform from which to look at this society and to make fun of its less attractive and less Socialist aspects. These are among the most widely read and quoted books in Russian culture. The Twelve Chairs was adapted for popular films both in the USSR and in the U.S. (by Mel Brooks in the latter).

The two writers traveled across the Depression-era USA. Ilf took many pictures throughout the journey, and the authors produced a photo essay entitled "American Photographs," published in Ogonyok magazine. Shortly after that they published the book Одноэтажная Америка ; literally: "One-storeyed America", translated as Little Golden America (an allusion to The Little Golden Calf). The first edition of the book did not include Ilf's photographs. Both the book documents their adventures with their characteristic humor and playfulness. Notably, Ilf and Petrov were not afraid to praise many aspects of the American lifestyle in these works. The title comes from the following description.

"America is primarily a one-and two-story country. The majority of the American population lives in small towns of three thousand, maybe five, nine, or fifteen thousand inhabitants."

Ilf died of tuberculosis shortly after the trip to America; Petrov died in a plane crash in 1942 while he was covering the Eastern Front.

A minor planet 3668 Ilfpetrov, discovered by Soviet astronomer Lyudmila Georgievna Karachkina in 1982 is named after them. 3668 Ilfpetrov (1982 UM7) is a main-belt asteroid discovered on October 21, 1982 by Karachkina, L. G. at Nauchnyj. The asteroid is named for Ilf and Petrov, two collaborative Soviet satirists best known for their novel, The Twelve Chairs.

Одноэтажная Америка (literally: "One-storeyed America") Translation: Little Golden America (1937)

An interesting question worthy of study is: Why was this book able to escape the censors, assuming that it was?

Although not propaganda, there is a pro-Soviet anti-Capitalist tilt throughout the book. For example, it says that while Americans think of themselves as being patriotic, just as Soviets are, the Americans achieve this by ignoring the lynchings of Negros in the South. (This ignores the fact that the Soviet Union did not have any Negros, thus avoiding the problem.)

The authors make the point that a Soviet man will never let it be far from his consciousness that he is a Soviet Man, whereas the American rarely thinks of himself as an American. Here it is noteworthy that the word "Russian" is never used, only "Soviet".

The authors wrote novels that made them famous and thus gave them the freedom to write what they wished while conforming with the Marxist and thereby the Soviet view of society.

Their two satirical novels, The Twelve Chairs and its sequel The Little Golden Calf are connected by their main character, Ostap Bender, a con man in pursuit of elusive riches. Portraying the typical capitalist as a con man trying to cheat and swindle poor people so that he can greedily gain riches in a fruitless pursuit of happiness conforms to the Soviet ideal of all men working together in a harmonious common goal for the benefit society.

With the benefit of history, we know how the Soviet dream

of a "workers paradise" eventually turned out, but that does not stop this from being a good book.

The title "Little Golden America" seems odd. America was certainly a little country compared to the Soviet Union which was more than triple the size, especially since Alaska was not yet part of America when this book was written.

The word "Golden" probably pertained to the fact that even in the Soviet Union it was realized that America was a far richer country. However, the real reason for the title seems to be more related to the themes of the previous books by the two authors and to have little to do with whether America was either "little" or "golden".

As to the statement *"America is primarily a one-and two-story country. The majority of the American population lives in small towns of three thousand",* this was certainly true in 1935 when this book was written. My mother grew up in Creston, Iowa, a town of 3,000. I suppose that what makes this statement noteworthy is in 1935 most Soviets were living on collective farms and not even in towns of 3,000. Nowadays most Americans have moved off of the farms and live in cities.

It is remarkable that the entire text of their original 202 page book in Russian in RTF format and can be downloaded at

http://lib.ru/ILFPETROV/amerika.txt

By the way, I now live in Bronx New York near the home of our great leader, Trotsky. I picked this spot so as to be inspired by the great man and also because it is near the subway.

Sam Sloan
Bronx, New York
15 December 2010

CONTENTS

PART I

FROM A TWENTY-SEVENTH-STORY WINDOW

PART II

THROUGH THE EASTERN STATES

PART III

TOWARD THE PACIFIC OCEAN

PART IV

THE GOLDEN STATE

PART V

BACK TO THE ATLANTIC

PART I

FROM A TWENTY-SEVENTH-STORY WINDOW

I

The *Normandie*

AT NINE o'clock a special train leaves Paris for Le Havre with passengers for the *Normandie*. This train makes no stops. Three hours after its departure it rolls into the large structure which is in the Havre maritime station. Here the passengers descend to a shut-in platform, are lifted by escalators to the upper floor of the station, walk through halls and along passageways, all completely enclosed, and finally find themselves in a large vestibule where they take their places in elevators and depart for their various decks. At last they are on the *Normandie*. They have not the slightest idea what it looks like, for throughout this journey they had not even caught a glimpse of its outer contours.

We, too, walked into an elevator. A lad in a red tunic with gold buttons gracefully lifted his arm and pressed a knob. The shining new elevator rose a little, stopped and suddenly moved down, paying no heed whatever to the uniformed operator who desperately continued to press the knob. After falling three floors instead of rising two, we heard the painfully familiar phrase—on this occasion pronounced in impeccable French: "The elevator is out of order!"

We took the stairway to our cabin, a stairway covered throughout with a non-inflammable rubber carpet of bright green. The corridors and vestibules of the ship were covered with the same carpeting, which makes each footfall soft and soundless. But one does not fully appreciate the merits of rubber carpeting until the ship begins to roll in earnest. Then the carpeting seems to grip the soles. True, that does not save one from being seasick, but it does keep one from falling.

The stairway was not at all of the steamship type. It was broad, slanting, with runs and landings of dimensions generous enough for a mansion.

The cabin was likewise quite unsteamerlike. A spacious room with two ample windows, two broad wooden beds, easy-chairs, wall closets, tables, mirrors—in fact, all the blessings of a communal dwelling, even unto a telephone.

Only in a storm does the *Normandie* resemble a ship. But in good

7

weather it is a large hotel, with a sweeping view of the ocean, which, having suddenly torn loose from its moorings in a modern seaside health resort, is floating away at the rate of thirty-odd knots an hour.

Down below, from the platforms of the various floors of the station people who were seeing the passengers off shouted their final good wishes and farewells. They shouted in French, in English, in Spanish. They also shouted in Russian. A strange chap in a black seafaring uniform with a silver anchor and a shield of David on one sleeve, a beret on his head and a sad little beard on his chin, was shouting something in Jewish. Later we learned that he was the ship's rabbi; the General Transatlantic Company had engaged him to minister to the spiritual needs of a certain portion of its passengers. Other passengers had at their disposal Catholic and Protestant priests. Moslems, fire worshippers, and Soviet engineers travelled without benefit of clergy; on that score the General Transatlantic Company left them entirely to their own devices.

The *Normandie* has a spacious church with dim electric lights; it is designed primarily for Catholic services, but may be adjusted to suit other denominational needs. Thus, the altar and the icons may be covered with special shields designed for that purpose and the Catholic church converted automatically into a Protestant house of worship. As for the rabbi of the sad little beard, there being no available room for him, the children's nursery was assigned for the performance of his rites. Whereupon the company provided him with a *tallith* and even with special drapery for covering temporarily the mundane representations of bunnies and kittens.

The ship left the harbour. On the pier, at the mole, everywhere were crowds of people. The *Normandie* was still a novelty to the citizens of Le Havre. They forgathered from all corners of the city to greet the transatlantic titan and bid it *bon voyage.*

But the French shore was finally lost in the smoky mists of the murky day. Toward evening we saw the lights of Southampton. For an hour and a half the *Normandie* stood in its roadstead there, taking on passengers from England, surrounded on three sides by the distant and mysterious lights of a strange city. Then again she put out to sea, and again began the seething tumult of unseen waves aroused by tempestuous winds.

In the stern, where we were located, everything trembled. The deck and the walls and the lights and the easy-chairs and the glasses on the washstand and the washstand itself trembled. The ship's vibration was so pronounced that even objects from which one did not expect any sound made a noise. For the first time we heard the sound of towels, soap, the carpet on the floor, the paper on the table, the electric bulb, the curtain, the collar thrown on the bed. Everything in the cabin resounded, and some things even thundered. If a passenger became thoughtful for a moment and relaxed his facial muscles, his teeth at once began to chatter of their own free will. All through the night it seemed to us that someone was trying to break down the door of our cabin and someone else was constantly rapping at our window-pane and laughing ominously. We discovered no less than a hundred different sounds inside our cabin.

The *Normandie* was on its tenth voyage between Europe and America. It was scheduled to go into dry dock after its eleventh trip, when its stern would be taken apart and the structural deficiencies that caused vibration eliminated.

In the morning a sailor came into our cabin and closed its windows with metal shutters. A storm was rising. A small freighter was having a difficult time making its way to the French shore. At times it disappeared in the waves, only the tips of its masts remaining visible.

We had always expected to find the ocean roadway between the Old and New Worlds quite lively with traffic. Now and then, we imagined, we would come across ships blaring music and waving flags. But we found the ocean a grandiosely deserted expanse. The little boat that we saw bucking the storm four hundred miles from Europe was the only ship we passed during the entire *five* days of our crossing. The *Normandie* rolled with slow and dignified deliberateness. It steamed ahead, never decreasing its accustomed speed, nonchalantly flinging aside the high waves that attacked it on all sides. Rarely would it dip—and then in even tenor with the ocean. Here was no unequal struggle between some miserable contraption fashioned by man's hand and the unbridled forces of nature. It was rather a contest between well-matched titans.

In a semicircular smoking saloon three famous wrestlers with cauliflower ears were sitting with their coats off, playing cards. Shirts bulged out from under their vests. They were in the throes of painful thinking. Huge cigars dangled from their mouths. At another table two men played chess, every minute adjusting the chessmen that kept sliding off the board. Two others, their chins cupped in the palms of their hands, watched the chess game. Who but Soviet folk would ever think of playing the queen's gambit in such weather? We guessed it: the charming Botvinniks proved to be Soviet engineers.

In time people met one another and formed congenial groups. A printed list of passengers was distributed. There we found a very amusing surname: Sandwich—a whole family of Sandwiches, Mr. Sandwich, Mrs. Sandwich, and young Master Sandwich.

We entered the Gulf Stream. A warm rain drizzled. In the oppressive hothouse atmosphere hung the heavy sediment of the oily smoke that the *Normandie's* smokestacks belched forth.

We set out to inspect the ship. A third-class passenger does not see much of the boat on which he travels. He is not allowed either into the first or into the tourist class. Nor does the tourist-class passenger see much more of the *Normandie*, for he likewise is not permitted to trespass certain limits. But the first-class passenger *is* the *Normandie*

A*

He occupies no less than nine-tenths of the entire ship. Everything is immense in the first class—the promenade decks, the lounges, the saloons for smoking and the saloons for playing cards, and the saloons especially for ladies, and a hothouse where fat little French swallows swing on glass branches and hundreds of orchids hang from the ceiling, and the theatre with its four hundred seats, and the swimming-pool full of water illuminated through its bottom with green electric lights, and the marketing square with its department store, and the saloons for sport where elderly bald-headed gentlemen, flat on their backs, play ball with their feet, and other saloons where the same bald-headed men, tired of tossing balls and jumping up and down on a cinder-path platform, dream in embroidered easy-chairs; above all immense is the carpet that covers the main saloon, for surely it weighs more than half a ton.

Even the smokestacks of the *Normandie*, which one might think would belong to the entire ship, are reserved exclusively for the first class. In one of them the dogs of the first-class passengers are kept. Beautiful pedigree dogs, bored to the verge of madness, stand in their cages. Most of the time they are rocked to dizziness. Now and then they are led out on a leash for a walk on a special deck reserved for them. Then they bark uncertainly and regard the tossing ocean sadly.

We went into the galley. Scores of chefs were at work around a huge electric stove. Scores of others were dressing fowl, carving fish, baking bread, rearing tortes. In a special department kosher food was being prepared. Occasionally the steamship's rabbi would come down here to make sure that the gay French chefs did not throw bits of the unorthodox *trefa* into this sequestered food.

The *Normandie* is reputed to be a masterpiece of French technique and art. Its technique is indeed splendid. Admirable are its speed, its fire-fighting system, the bold and elegant lines of its body, its radio station. But as for art, surely the French have known better days. There were, of course, the faultlessly executed paintings on the glass walls; but the paintings themselves were not in any way distinguished. The same might be said of the bas-relief, the mosaic, the sculpture, the furniture. There was a profusion of gold, of coloured leather, of beautiful metals, silks, expensive wood, fine glass. There was much wealth but little real art. As a whole, it was what French artists, helplessly shrugging their shoulders, called "stile triomphe." Not long ago in Paris, on the Champs-Elysées, was opened a Café Triomphe, sumptuously upholstered in the boudoir manner. A pity! We should like to have seen as partners of the remarkable French engineers who created the *Normandie* equally remarkable French artists and architects. All the more is the pity since France has such people.

Certain defects in technique—for example, the vibration in the stern, which threw the elevator out of commission for half an hour—and other annoying trifles must be charged not against the engineers who built this first-rate ship, but rather against the impatient orders of their clients who were in a hurry to begin exploiting the ship under any circumstances in order to secure a blue ribbon for record speed.

On the eve of the ship's arrival in New York there was a gala banquet and an evening of amateur entertainment managed by the passengers themselves. The dinner was the same as ever, except that a spoonful of Russian caviare was added. Besides that, the passengers were given pirate hats of paper, rattles, badges with blue ribbons on which "Normandie" was inscribed, and wallets of artificial leather, also with the trade-mark of the company. Gifts are distributed to prevent pilfering of the ship's property. The point is, the majority of travellers are victims of the psychosis of collecting souvenirs. During the *Normandie's* first voyage the passengers stole as mementoes a huge quantity of knives, forks, and spoons. Some even carried away plates, ash-trays, and pitchers. So, it proved more convenient to make a gift of a badge for a buttonhole rather than lose a spoon needed in the ménage. The passengers were overjoyed with these toys. A fat lady, who throughout the five days of the journey had sat in a corner of the dining saloon all alone, suddenly in a most businesslike manner put the pirate hat on her head, discharged her popgun, and attached the badge to her bosom. Evidently she regarded it as her duty to take advantage conscientiously of all the blessings she was entitled to by virtue of her ticket.

The petty-bourgeois amateur entertainment began in the evening. The passengers gathered in the saloon. The lights were put out, and a spotlight was trained on a small stage. There, her entire body trembling, appeared a haggard young woman in a silver dress. The orchestra, made up of professional musicians, regarded her with pity. The audience applauded encouragingly. The young lady opened her mouth convulsively and shut it at once. The orchestra patiently repeated the introduction. Sensing forebodings of something frightful, the audience tried not to look at each other. Suddenly the young lady trembled and began to sing. She sang that famous song, "Parlez-moi d'amour," but she sang it so quietly and so badly that her tender call was not heard by anyone. In the middle of the song she quite unexpectedly ran off the stage, hiding her face in her hand. Another young lady appeared, and she was even more haggard. She was in an all-black dress, yet bare-footed. Sheer fright was written all over her face. She was a bare-foot amateur dancer. The audience began to glide out of the hall stealthily. None of this was at all like our buoyant, talented, vociferous amateur entertainments.

On the fifth day the decks of the steamer were filled with suitcases and trunks unloaded out of the cabins. The passengers moved to the right side, and, holding on to their hats, avidly peered into the horizon. The shore was not yet visible, but New York's skyscrapers were already rising out of the water like calm pillars of smoke. An astounding contrast, this—after the vacant ocean, suddenly the largest city in the world. In the sunny smoke dimly gleamed the steel extremities of the hundred-and-two-storied Empire State Building. Beyond the stern of the *Normandie* seagulls swirled. Four powerful little tugboats began to turn the enormous body of the ship, pulling it up and pushing it toward the pier. On the left side was the small green statue of liberty. Then suddenly it was on the right side. We were being turned around, and the city turned around us, showing us first one and then another of its sides. Finally, it stopped in its tracks, impossibly huge, thunderous, and quite incomprehensible as yet.

The passengers walked down covered passageways into the customs shed, went through all the formalities, and emerged into the streets of the city, without having once seen the ship on which they had come.

2

The First Evening in New York

THE CUSTOMS shed at the docks of the French Line is immense. Under the ceiling hang large iron letters of the Latin alphabet. Each passenger stops under the letter with which his surname begins. Here his luggage will be brought to him from the ship and here it will be examined.

The voices of the arrivals and of those meeting them, laughter and kisses, resounded hollowly throughout the shed, the bare structural parts of which made it seem rather like a shop where turbines were being manufactured.

We had not informed anyone of our impending arrival, and no one met us. We waited under our letters for the customs clerk. Finally he came. He was a calm and unhurried man. He was in no way affected by our having just crossed an ocean in order to show him our suitcases. He politely touched the upper layer of our belongings and did not look any further. Then he stuck out his tongue, a most ordinary, moist tongue, a tongue devoid of all gadgets whatsoever, wetted the huge labels with it and pasted them on our travelling-bags.

When we finally freed ourselves it was already evening. A white taxi-cab with three gleaming lanterns on its roof, looking like an old-fashioned carriage, took us to the hotel. At first we were tormented by the thought that because of our inexperience we had got into the wrong taxi, into some antiquated vehicle, and that we were funny and provincial. But, having fearfully looked out the window, we saw that automobiles with just as silly little lamps as ours were going in all directions back and forth. We quieted down a little. Later we were told that these little lamps are placed on the roof, so that the taxi may be more noticeable among a million other automobiles. For the same reason taxis in America are painted in the most garish colours—orange, canary, white.

Our attempt to take a look at New York from an automobile failed. We drove through quite dark and dreary streets. From time to time something rumbled hellishly under our feet or something else thundered overhead. Whenever we stopped before the traffic lights the sides of the automobiles that stood beside us hid everything from view. The chauffeur turned back several times and asked again for the address. It seemed that he was somewhat anxious about our English. Now and then he would look at us patronizingly, and his face seemed to say: "Never mind, you won't get lost! Nobody ever got lost in New York."

The thirty-two brick stories of our hotel merged with the rufous nocturnal sky.

While we were filling up short registration cards, two men of the hotel service stood lovingly over our baggage. On the neck of one of them hung a shining ring with the key of the room we had selected. The elevator lifted us up to the twenty-seventh story. This was the commodious and calm elevator of a hotel that was not very old and not very new, not very expensive and, to our regret, not very cheap.

We liked the room, but we did not pause to explore it. Hurry into the street, the city, the tumult! The curtains of the windows crackled under the fresh sea wind. We threw our overcoats on the couch, ran out into the narrow corridor covered with a patterned carpet, stepped into the elevator, and the elevator, clicking softly, flew down. We looked at each other significantly. After all, this really was a great event! For the first time in our lives we were about to walk in New York.

A thin, almost transparent national flag with stars and stripes hung over the entrance to our hotel. Only a short distance away stood the polished cube of the Hotel Waldorf-Astoria. In prospectuses it is called the best hotel in the world. The windows of the "best hotel in the world" sparkled blindingly, and over its entrance hung two national flags. Right on the sidewalk, by the wall of the building, lay tomorrow's newspapers. Passers-by bent down, took a New York *Times* or *Herald Tribune* and placed two cents on the ground beside the newspapers. The newsdealer had gone somewhere. The newspapers were held down with a broken piece of brick, quite as it is done in Moscow by our old women newsvendors as they sit in their plywood kiosks. Cylindrical garbage cans stood at each corner of the street crossings. A considerable flame spouted out of one of the cans. Someone had evidently thrown a lighted cigarette-end there, and so the New York refuse, which consists mostly of newspapers, caught fire. An alarming red light illumined the polished walls of the Waldorf-Astoria. Passers-by smiled and dropped remarks as they walked by. A policeman, his face set, was already moving toward the eventful spot. Having decided that our hotel was in no danger of catching fire, we went on.

At once a slight misfortune befell us. We thought we would walk slowly, looking around attentively in order to study, to observe, to take in, and so forth. But New York is not one of those cities where people move slowly. The people who passed us did not walk, they ran. And so we, too, ran. From that moment on we could not stop. We spent a whole month in New York, and throughout that time we were constantly racing somewhere at top-speed. Simultaneously, we acquired such a businesslike and preoccupied air that John Pierpont Morgan, Jr., himself might have envied us. At our rate of speed *he* would have earned approximately sixty million dollars during that month. *We* earned somewhat less.

In a word, we started off at a trot. We sped by signs on which in lights were outlined the words: "Cafeteria" or "United Cigars" or "Drugs—Soda" or something else equally enticing yet so far utterly incomprehensible. Thus we ran to Forty-second Street, and there we stopped.

In the store windows of Forty-second Street winter was in full swing. In one window stood seven elegant wax ladies with silver faces. They all wore wonderful astrakhan fur coats, and regarded each other quizzically. In another window stood twelve ladies in sports costumes, leaning on ski poles. Their eyes were blue, their lips red, their ears pink. In other windows stood young mannikins with grey hair, or dapper gentlemen in inexpensive, and hence suspiciously resplendent, suits. But we were really not impressed by all this store munificence. It was something else that astonished us.

In all the large cities of the world one can always find a place where people look at the moon through a telescope. Here, on Forty-second Street, we also found a telescope. But it was mounted on an automobile.

The telescope pointed at the sky. In charge of it was an ordinary mortal, just like the men at the telescopes in Athens, in Naples, or in Odessa. And his was the joyless manner peculiar to all exploiters of street telescopes throughout the world.

The moon showed itself in the interstice between two sixty-storied buildings. However, the curious onlooker, applying himself to the tube, gazed not at the moon but considerably higher: he looked at the top of the Empire State Building and its hundred and two stories. In the light of the moon, the steel eminence of the Empire State seemed to be covered with snow. The heart turned cold at the sight of this chaste and noble building glistening like a sliver of artificial ice. We stood there long, silently gazing up. The skyscrapers of New York make one proud of all the people of science and of labour who build these splendid edifices.

The newsvendors roared hoarsely. The earth trembled underfoot, and through the grates in the sidewalk came a sudden gust of heat as if from an engine-room. That was because down there passed a train of the New York métro—the subway, as it is called here.

Through vents, placed in the pavement and covered with round

metallic covers, steam broke out. For a long time we could not understand where that steam came from. The red lights of the advertisements
cast an operatic light upon it. Almost at any moment one expected
the vents to open, Mephistopheles spring out of one of them, and,
after clearing his throat, begin to sing in deep bass, right out of *Faust*:
"A sword at my side, on my hat a gay feather; a cloak o'er my shoulder
—and altogether, why, got up quite in the fashion!"

We again rushed forward, deafened by the cries of the newsvendors.
They shout with such desperation that, to use Leskov's expression, it is
afterwards necessary for a whole week to dig the voice out with a shovel.

It cannot be said that the lighting of Forty-second Street was mediocre.
And yet Broadway, lighted by millions and perhaps even by billions of
electric lamps, filled with swirling and jumping advertisements constructed out of kilometres of coloured neon tubes, appeared before us
just as unexpectedly as New York itself rears up out of the limitless
vacancy of the Atlantic Ocean.

We stood at the most popular corner in the States, at the corner of
Forty-second and Broadway. The "Great White Way," as Americans
call Broadway, stretched before us.

Here electricity has been brought down (or brought up, if you like)
to the level of a trained circus animal. Here it has been forced to make
faces, to hurdle over obstacles, to wink, to dance. Edison's sedate
electricity has been converted into Durov's [1] trained seal. It catches
balls with its nose. It does sleight-of-hand tricks, plays dead, comes to
life, does anything it is ordered to do. The electric parade never stops.
The lights of the advertisements flare up, whirl around, go out, and
then again light up: letters, large and small, white, red, and green,
endlessly run away somewhere, only to return a second later and renew
their frantic race.

On Broadway are concentrated the theatres, cinemas, and dance halls
of the city. Tens of thousands of people move along the pavements.
New York is one of the few cities of the world where the population
promenades on a definite street. The approaches to the cinemas are so
brightly lighted that, it seems, if anyone were to add one more little
lamp the whole thing would blow up from excessive light, all of it
would go to the devil. But it would be impossible to squeeze in
another little lamp; there is no room for it. The newsvendors raise
such a howl that digging the voice out of it would require more than

[1] Vladimir Leonidovich Durov (1863-1934), scion of a Russian family of circus clowns
and animal trainers, was primarily an animal trainer himself who claimed to have established a unique method of training circus animals, based on the principles of conditioning
reflexes (Professor Pavlov) and "establishing mutual confidence." This mélange of science
and sentimentality Durov called "zoopsychology." Since some of his clowning acts had
been suppressed by tsarist censorship because of their allegedly dangerous political satire,
Durov was regarded as a "revolutionary" circus performer—and in 1919 was granted a
subsidy by the Soviet government for a Zoopsychological Laboratory, which he founded in
Moscow. He published several books on zoopsychology and animal tales for children, by
whom he was affectionately known as "Grandpa Durov."—C. M.

a week, more likely years of persistent toil. High in the sky, on some uncounted story of the Paramount Building, flared the face of an electric clock. Neither star nor moon was visible. The light of the advertisements eclipsed everything else. In the display windows, among simple crisscross neckties, small illuminated price tags turn around and go into a balancing act. These are the micro-organisms in the cosmos of Broadway's electricity. In the tumultuous uproar a calm beggar plays his saxophone. A gentleman in a top-hat walks into a theatre, and with him is the inevitable lady, whose evening-gown has a train. A blind man led by a dog moves like a sleep-walker. Certain young men walk without hats. That is fashionable. Their neatly combed hair glistens under the street lamps. The odour of cigars, nasty ones and expensive ones.

At that very moment, when it occurred to us that we were so far from Moscow, before us floated the lights of the Cameo motion-picture theatre. The Soviet film, *The New Gulliver*, was being exhibited there.

The surge of Broadway carried us several times back and forth, and flung us into a side street.

We knew nothing yet about the city. Therefore, we cannot mention the streets here. We remember only that we stood under the trestle of an elevated railway. An autobus passed, and without much ado we boarded it.

Even several days later, when we began to orient ourselves in the New York whirlpool, we could not remember where the autobus took us that first evening. It seems to us that it was the Chinese section, but it is quite possible that it was an Italian or a Jewish section.

We walked along narrow, smelly streets. No, the electricity here was ordinary, not like a trained animal. It shone rather dimly, and it did not indulge in any hurdles. A large policeman stood against the wall of a house. On the cap over his broad, imperious face gleamed the silver shield of the City of New York. Having noticed the uncertainty with which we walked down the street, he came to us; but, receiving no inquiry, again returned to his vantage-point at the wall, ever the stiff and stately minion of the law.

From one shabby little house came dull singing. The man who stood at the entrance to the house told us that this was the night lodging of the Salvation Army.

"Who may sleep here?"

"Anyone. No one is asked his name. No one is asked about his occupation or his past. Here night lodgers receive bed, coffee, and bread free of charge. In the morning they also get coffee and bread. Then they are free to go away. The sole condition is that they must take part in the evening and morning prayers."

The singing that reached us from the house gave evidence of the fact that at this very moment this sole condition was being fulfilled. We went in.

Previously, about twenty-five years ago, there was a Chinese opium smoking den in this dwelling. It had been a dirty and dismal den of iniquity. Since then it had become cleaner, but, while losing its erstwhile exoticism, it did not become less dismal. The upper part of the former den of iniquity was devoted to prayer meetings, while below, the sleeping quarters consisted of bare walls, a bare stone floor, and canvas folding cots. That odour of coffee and dampness, which is always a part of hospital and charity cleanliness, permeated all. In a word, this was an American staging of Gorky's *Lower Depths*.

In this bedraggled hall the night lodgers sat stiffly on benches that came down in an amphitheatre toward a small stage. As soon as the singing stopped, the next number on the programme began.

Between an American national flag, which stood on the stage, and Biblical texts, which hung all over the walls, a pinkish old man in a black suit jumped like a clown. He talked and gesticulated with such passion that he gave the impression of selling something. Yet he was merely telling the instructive history of his life, telling about the beneficent crisis when he turned his heart back to God.

He had been a tramp ("as frightful a tramp as you, old devils!"), he had carried on horribly, had used profane language ("remember your own habits, my friends"), he stole—yes, all of that happened, too, alas! But now it was all done with. Now he owned his own home and lived like a decent man ("Hasn't God created us in his own image, in his own manner?"). Not long ago he had even bought himself a radio receiving set. And all this he had received directly with the help of God.

The old man talked with extraordinary facility; it seemed therefore that he was now appearing for at least the thousandth time. He clicked his fingers, laughed hoarsely, sang religious ditties, and ended up with great enthusiasm, shouting:

"Let's sing, brothers!"

Again the dull, humdrum singing began.

The night lodgers were appalling. Almost all of them were no longer young. Unshaven, with lustreless eyes, they swayed on their crude benches. They sang submissively and lazily. Some of them could not overcome the fatigue of the day, and slept.

We vividly imagined to ourselves the wanderings through the frightful places of New York, the days passed at bridges and warehouses, in the midst of garbage, in the everlasting nebulousness of human degeneration. To sit after that in a night lodging and sing hymns was sheer torture.

Then before the audience appeared a fellow as hale and healthy as a policeman. He had a lilac-coloured vaudevillian nose and the voice of a skipper. He was as bold and jaunty as anyone could possibly be. Again began a tale about the benefits of turning to God. The skipper, it seemed, had also been quite a sinner at one time. His fantasy was not great, however, and he soon ended up with the declaration that now, thanks to God's help, he, too, had a radio receiving set.

Again they sang. The skipper waved his arms, displaying considerable experience as an orchestra leader. Two hundred men ground to powder by life again listened to this conscienceless twaddle. These poor people were not offered work, they were offered only God—a God as spiteful and exacting as the Devil.

The night lodgers did not object. Any god with a cup of coffee and a slice of bread was fairly acceptable. Let us sing then, brothers, to the glory of the coffee god!

And the throats, which for half a century had belched forth only horrible oaths, drowsily began to blare now the glory of the Lord.

We again walked through some slums and again did not know where we were. With thunder and lightning, trains raced overhead along the rail-road stockades of the elevated railway. Young men in light-coloured hats crowded around drug-stores, exchanging curt phrases. Their manner was exactly like that of the young men who in Warsaw populate Krakhmalnaya Street. In Warsaw a gentleman from Krakhmalnaya is not considered exactly God's precious little ewe lamb. It is sheer luck if he turns out to be merely a thief, for he might be something much worse than that.

Late at night we returned to our hotel, not yet disappointed with New York nor elated over it, but rather disturbed by its hugeness, its wealth, and its poverty.

3
What Can Be Seen From a Hotel Window

OUR FIRST hours in New York—the walk through the city at night and then the return to the hotel—will always remain with us as a memorable event.

Yet, as a matter of fact, nothing unusual had occurred.

We walked into the very ordinary marble vestibule of the hotel. To the right, behind a smooth wooden railing, worked two young clerks. Both of them had pale, smoothly shaven cheeks and black little narrow moustaches. Beyond them sat a girl cashier at a calculating machine. On the left was located the tobacco stand. In its glass case open wooden boxes of cigars stood next to each other. On the white gleaming surface of the inside covers of the boxes were displayed old-fashioned handsome men with thick moustaches and pink cheeks, gold and silver medals, scutcheons, green palms and Negresses gathering tobacco. In the corners stood the prices: 5, 10, or 15 cents apiece, or 15 cents for two, or 10 cents for three. Even more tightly than the cigars lay small packages of cigarettes in soft covers, also wrapped in cellophane. Americans seem to smoke mostly "Lucky Strike," a dark green package with a red circle in the middle; "Chesterfield," a white package with a gold inscription; and "Camel," a yellowish package bearing the picture of a brown camel.

The entire wall opposite the entrance to the vestibule was occupied by spacious elevators with gilded doors. The doors opened on the right, on the left, or in the middle, disclosing inside the elevator the Negro who held on with his hand to the iron steering-gear and who was dressed in bright coloured trousers with gold braid and in a green jacket with ornate twisted shoulder straps. Just as at the Northern Railway Station in Moscow the train announcer loudly informs people going to summer resorts that the next train is bound without stops for Mytishchi, but beyond that will make all the stops, so here the Negroes announced that the elevator was going to the sixteenth floor, or to the thirty-second floor, with the first stop likewise at the sixteenth floor. Eventually we fathomed this little ruse of the management's—on the sixteenth floor was located its restaurant and cafeteria.

We walked into the elevator, and it rushed up. On the way the elevator stopped, the Negro opened the door, cried "Up!" and the passengers called out the numbers of their floors. A woman entered. All the men removed their hats and travelled on without hats. We followed suit. That was the first American custom we learned. But acquaintance with the customs of a foreign country is not so easy and is almost always accompanied by confusion. Several days later we were going up in an elevator to our publishers. A woman entered, and with the expeditiousness of old experienced New Yorkers we took off our hats. The other men did not follow our knightly example, however, and even regarded us with curiosity. We learned that hats should be taken off only in private and hotel elevators; whereas, in buildings where people transact business one may keep one's hat on.

At the twenty-seventh story we left the elevator and walked along a narrow corridor to our rooms. The large second-rate New York hotels in the centre of the city are built very economically. Their corridors are narrow, their rooms, although expensive, are small, and their ceilings are of standard height—that is, rather low. The client poses before the builder the problem of squeezing into a skyscraper as many rooms as possible. These small rooms, however, are clean and comfortable. They always have hot and cold water, a shower, stationery, telegraph blanks, postcards with views of the hotel, laundry bags, and printed laundry blanks on which you merely place figures indicating the number of pieces of soiled laundry being sent out. Laundering is done quickly and unusually well in America. The ironed shirts look better than new ones on display in a store window. And each one of them is placed in a paper pocket, around which is a paper ribbon with the trade-mark of the laundry, and all of it is neatly pinned together, with pins even around the sleeves. Moreover, the laundry is brought back mended and the socks darned. In America such comforts are not at all a sign of luxury. They are standardized and accessible.

Upon entering the room we began to look for the switch, and for a long time could not understand how electricity is turned on here. At first we wandered through the rooms in the dark, then we struck matches, felt our way along the walls, investigated the doors and windows, but there was no switch anywhere. Several times in sheer desperation we would sit down to rest in the darkness. At last we found it. Near every lamp hung a short thin chain with a little ball on the end. A pull on the little chain and the electricity is lighted. Another pull and it is out. The beds had not been made up for the night, so we began to look for the button of the bell to summon the maid. But there was no button. We looked everywhere. We pulled all the likely strings, but that did us no good. Then we understood that the servants must be called by telephone. We rang for the porter and called for the maid.

In the room was furniture which subsequently we saw in all the hotels of America without exception—in the East, the West, and the South. We did not visit the North. But there is every reason to suppose that even there we would have found exactly the same furniture as in New York: a brown commode with a mirror, metal bedsteads trickily painted to look like wood, several soft easy-chairs, a rocking-chair, portable plug lamps (bridge lamps), on high thin legs with large cardboard lampshades.

On the commode we found a fat little book in a black cover. On the book was the gold trade-mark of the hotel. The book proved to be a Bible. This ancient composition had been adapted for business people whose time is limited. On the first page was a table of contents especially composed by the solicitous management of the hotel:

"For allaying spiritual doubts—page so-and-so, text so-and-so.

"For family troubles—page so-and-so, text so-and-so.

"For financial troubles—page . . ., text . . .

"For success in business—page . . ., text . . ."

That page was somewhat greasy.

We opened the windows. They had to be opened in a peculiar American way, not at all as in Europe. They had to be raised, like windows in a railway carriage.

The windows of our little rooms looked out on three sides. Below lay New York at night.

What can be more alluring than a strange city's lights thickly sown throughout that immense and foreign world which had gone to sleep on the shores of the Atlantic Ocean! From over there, from the side of the ocean, a warm wind wafted. Quite close rose several skyscrapers. It seemed as though one could touch them with one's hand. Their lighted windows could be counted. Farther away the lights became more and more dense. Among them were especially bright ones, which stretched out in straight and in bent chains (these must have been street lamps). Beyond gleamed a sheer gold dust of tiny lights, and then a dark unlighted swath. (The Hudson? Or was that the East River?) And again the gold mists of boroughs, constellations of unknown streets and squares. In that world of lights, which at first seemed stationary, one could note a certain movement. Now down the river slowly floated the red light of a cutter. A tiny automobile passed down the street. At times, suddenly, somewhere on the other shore of the river, a light as little as a tiny particle of dust would flash and go out. Surely one of the seven million denizens of New York had turned off the light and gone to bed! Who was he? A clerk? An employee of the elevated railroad? Perhaps a lonely girl had gone to sleep—some salesgirl (there are so many of them in New York). And at this very moment, lying under two thin blankets, stirred by the steamer whistles of the Hudson, was she seeing in her dreams a million dollars?

New York was asleep, and a million Edison lamps were guarding its slumber. Immigrants from Scotland, from Ireland, from Hamburg and Vienna, from Kovno and Bialystok, from Naples and Madrid, from Texas, Dakota, and Arizona, were asleep. Asleep were also immigrants from Latin America, from Australia, from Africa and China. Black, white, and yellow people were asleep. Looking at the scarcely trembling lights, we wanted to find out as soon as possible how these people work, how they amuse themselves, what they dream of, what they hope for, what they eat.

Finally, utterly exhausted, we, too, went to bed. We had had altogether too many impressions for the first day. New York cannot be taken in such large doses. It is a frightful, yet at the same time pleasant, experience to have one's body lie in a comfortable American bed, in a state of complete rest, while the mind continues to rock on the *Normandie*, to ride in a wedding-carriage taxi, to run along Broadway, to travel.

In the morning, having awakened on our twenty-seventh story and having looked out of the window, we saw New York in a pellucid morning mist.

We beheld what might be called a peaceful pastoral scene. A few white threads of smoke rose to the sky, while to the spire of a small twenty-story hut was even attached an idyllic and all-metal cockerel. Sixty-storied skyscrapers, which yesterday evening seemed so close, were separated from us by at least ten red iron roofs and a hundred high stacks and skylights, among which laundry hung and the most ordinary cats wandered about. On the walls could be seen advertisements. The walls of the skyscrapers were full of brick dullness. Most of the buildings in New York are made of red brick.

New York opened at once on several planes. The upper plane was occupied by the tops of those skyscrapers which were higher than ours. They were crowned with spires—glass or gold cupolas gleaming in the sun, or towers with large clocks. The towers themselves were the height of a four-story house. On the next plane, open in its entirety to our gaze, in addition to stacks, skylights, and tomcats one could see flat roofs on which were small one-storied houses with gardens, skimpy trees, little brick paths, a small fountain, and even rattan chairs. Here one could pass the time of day to perfection, almost as at Klyazma, inhaling the petrol perfume of flowers, and listening to the melodic baying of the elevated railway. That monstrosity was on the next plane of New York City. The railway lines of the elevated rest on iron poles and pass on the level of the second and third stories, and only in certain parts of the city do they rise to the fifth or sixth story. This antiquated structure discharges from time to time a horrible clatter that numbs the brain. It causes healthy people to become nervous and the nervous to lose their minds, while the insane jump at the sound in their padded cells and roar like lions. In order to see the last and fundamental plane, the plane of the street, one had to bend out of the window and look down at a right angle. There, as in reversed binoculars, one could see a tiny crossing with tiny automobiles, pedestrians, newspapers strewn on the pavement, and even two rows of shining buttons attached to the lanes where pedestrians are allowed to cross the street.

From the other window one could see the Hudson River, which separates the State of New York from the State of New Jersey. The houses that go down to the Hudson are in New York, while the houses on the other side of the river are in Jersey City. We were told that what at first glance seems a strange administrative division has its compensations. One can, for example, live in one State and work in another. One could also indulge in speculations in New York while paying taxes in Jersey. There, by the way, the taxes are not so high. This seems to add colour to the grey monotonous life of a stockbroker. Or one can get married in New York and get divorced in New Jersey, or the other way around. It all depends upon where the divorce laws are easier and where the marriage-breaking process is cheaper. We, for example, when buying the automobile for our journey through the country, insured it in New Jersey, which charges a few dollars less than New York.

4
Appetite Departs While Eating

THE NEWCOMER need have no fear about leaving his hotel and plunging into the New York jungle. Despite the amazing sameness of its streets, it is well-nigh impossible to get lost there.

Yet the secret is simple. The thoroughfares are divided into two types: the perpendicular ones, or avenues; and the horizontal, or streets. Thus the island of Manhattan has been laid out. Parallel to each other are First, Second, and Third avenues. Then parallel to them is Lexington Avenue, Fourth Avenue, a continuation of which from the central railway station bears the name of Park Avenue (that is the street of the wealthy), Madison Avenue, beautiful (shopping district) Fifth Avenue, Sixth, Seventh, and so forth. Fifth Avenue divides the city into two parts, the East and West. All these avenues (and they are many) are crossed by streets, of which there are several hundred. And if the avenues have certain distinguishing attributes (some are wider, others are narrower; there is an elevated over Second, Third, Sixth, and Ninth; in the middle of Park Avenue is a grass plot; on Fifth Avenue tower the Empire State Building and Radio City), the streets are quite indistinguishable, and even old New Yorkers cannot tell one street from another by any outward signs. The geometry of New York is violated only by meandering Broadway, which crosses the city diagonally on its run of a score of miles.

The main shoals of pedestrians and automobiles advance along the wide avenues. Under them like coal-mines lie the black and damp, four-track tunnels of subways. Over them is the iron thunder of the elevated. Here are all the types of transport—even several old-fashioned, double-deck autobuses and street-cars. Doubtless, in Kiev, where street-car traffic has been removed from the main street, people would be amazed to hear that down Broadway, the liveliest street in the world, a street-car still hobbles along. Woe to the man who must cross the city, not lengthwise but crosswise, and who would be stricken with the insane idea of taking a taxi-cab for that purpose! His taxi will turn into a street and head straight into a chronic cul-de-sac. While policemen drive the snorting automobile flocks down the length of the avenues, hordes of indignant *schlemiehls* and maniacs congregate in the dirty narrow lanes that cut the city—no, not lengthwise but crosswise. The queues stretch for several blocks, chauffeurs fidget in their seats, passengers impatiently stick their heads out of windows and, falling back in anguish, open their newspapers.

It is hard to believe, yet it is a fact that some seventy years ago on the corner of Fifth Avenue and Forty-second Street, on the very spot where more automobiles can flock together in five minutes than there are in all of Poland, stood a wooden inn which had the following two significant notices posted for the benefit of American travellers:

IT IS FORBIDDEN TO GO TO BED IN BOOTS

and

IT IS FORBIDDEN FOR MORE THAN SIX
GUESTS TO SLEEP IN ONE BED

We left the hotel to lunch somewhere, and soon found ourselves on Forty-second Street. During our first days in New York, no matter where we were bound for, we invariably landed on Forty-second Street.

In the crowd, which carried us along, we heard shreds of that quick New York speech which surely must be as strange to the ear of a Londoner as it is to the ear of a Muscovite. Along the walls sat boys—bootblacks, who drummed their brushes on their crudely fashioned wooden boxes, touting for customers. Street photographers aimed their cameras at the passers-by, choosing usually ladies with escorts or tourists from the sticks. After clicking his camera, the photographer would approach the object of his attack and press on him the printed address of his studio. For twenty-five cents the photographed pedestrian may have a candid photograph of himself, a splendid photograph, in the uninhibited act of raising his leg.

Under the sooty spans of a bridge, in the shadow of which gleamed mud left over from last night's rain, a man with hat aslant and an open shirt was delivering a speech. About a score of the curious gathered around him. He was a propagandist for the ideas of the recently assassinated United States senator from Louisiana, Huey P. Long. He spoke on distribution of wealth. His listeners asked him questions. He replied. His chief task seemed to be to amuse his audience. Not far from him, on the sunflecked sidewalk, stopped a fat Negress of the Salvation Army. She wore an old-fashioned bonnet and run-down shoes. She took a bell out of her suitcase and rang it loudly. The suitcase she placed on the sidewalk at her feet. After waiting for a few disciples of the late-lamented senator to desert to her side, squinting against the sun, she began to bellow something, rolling her eyes and banging her own fat bosom. We went several blocks, but the shouting of the Negress was still distinctly heard in the component noise of this restless city.

In front of a ready-to-wear store a man walked calmly back and forth. On his back and on his chest he carried two identical placards: "This Place Is On Strike." In the next street were a few more pickets. Over the large show window of a corner store, despite the sunny morning, gleamed the blue letters "Cafeteria" in electric lights. The cafeteria was large, bright, and clean. Along the walls were glass cases filled with beautiful, appetizing edibles. To the left of the entrance was the cashier's booth. On the right was a metal stand with small slot athwart as in a coin bank. From the opening emerged the end of a blue pasteboard stub. Those who entered tugged at this end. We also tugged. The melodic clang of a bell resounded. One stub was in our hand, and through the slot of the coin bank another blue stub popped out. Then we did what all New Yorkers do when they dash into a cafeteria for a hurried bite. From a special table we each took a light brown tray, placed on it forks, spoons, knives, and paper napkins; and, feeling extremely awkward in our heavy overcoats and hats, went to the right end of a glass-enclosed counter. Down the entire length of this counter ran three rows of nickelled pipes on which we conveniently placed our trays and slid them along after placing each dish upon them. The counter itself was a tremendous camouflaged electric plate. Soups, chunks of roast, sausages of various lengths and thicknesses, legs of pork and lamb, meat loaves and roulades, mashed, fried, baked, and boiled potatoes and potatoes curiously shaped in pellets, globules of Brussels sprouts, spinach, carrots, and numerous other side dishes were kept warm here. White chefs in starched nightcaps, aided by neat but heavily rouged and marcelled girls in pink headdresses, were busy placing on the glass cover of the counter plates of food and punching that figure on the stub which indicated the cost of each dish. Then came salads and vinaigrettes, various hors d'œuvres, fish in cream sauces and fish in jellied sauces. Then came bread, rolls, and traditional round pies with apple, strawberry, and pineapple fillings. Here coffee and milk were issued. We moved down the counter, pushing our trays. On the thick layer of chipped ice were plates of compotes and ice-cream, oranges and grapefruit cut in half, large and small glasses with various juices. Persistent advertising has taught Americans to drink juices before break-fast and lunch. In the juices are vitamins which are presumably beneficial to the customers, while the sale of juices is indubitably of benefit to fruit merchants. We soon succumbed to this American custom. At first we drank the thick yellow orange juice. Then we passed to the translucent green juice of the grapefruit. Then before eating we began to take the grapefruit itself (it is covered with sugar and is eaten with a spoon; its taste reminds one somewhat of the taste of an orange with a dash of lemon in it, although it is juicier than both these fruits). Finally, with some trepidation and not all at once, we began to imbibe the mundane tomato juice, peppering it a bit beforehand. That proved to be the tastiest of all and the most refreshing, and it best suited our South Russian stomachs. The one thing we did not learn to do in America was to eat melon before dinner. Yet that takes the place of honour among American hors d'œuvres.

In the middle of the cafeteria stood polished wooden tables without tablecloths, and beside them coat-racks. Those who wished could put their hats under their chairs, where there was a special shelf for that purpose. On the tables were stands with bottles of oil, vinegar, catsup, and various other condiments. There was also granulated sugar in a glass flagon wrought in the manner of a pepper-shaker with holes in its metal stopper.

The settling of accounts with the customers was simple. No one could leave the cafeteria without sooner or later passing the cashier's booth and presenting the stub with the total punched in it. Here also cigarettes were sold and one was free to take a toothpick.

The process of eating was just as superbly rationalized as the pro-duction of automobiles or of typewriters.

The automats have progressed farther along this road than the cafeterias. Although they have approximately the same outward appear-ance as the cafeterias, they differ from the latter in that they have carried the process of pushing food into American stomachs to the point of virtuosity. The walls of the automats are occupied throughout with little glass closets. Near each one of them is a slit for dropping a "nickel" (a five-cent coin). Behind the glass stands a dour sandwich or a glass of juice or a piece of pie. Despite the shining glass and metal, the sausages and cutlets deprived of liberty somehow produce a strange impression. One pities them, like cats at a show. A man drops a nickel, acquires the right to open the little door, takes out his sandwich, carries it to his table and there eats it, again putting his hat under his chair on the special shelf. Then the man goes up to a tap, drops his "nickel," and out of the tap into the glass drips exactly as much coffee and milk as is supposed to drip. One feels something humiliating, something insulting to man in that. One begins to suspect that the owner of the automat has outfitted his establishment, not in order to present society with a pleasant surprise, but in order to discharge from service poor marcelled girls with pink headdresses and thereby earn a few more dollars.

But automats are not over popular in America. Evidently the bosses themselves feel that there must be some limit to rationalization. Hence, the normal little restaurants, for people of modest means, belonging to mighty trusts are always full. The most popular of these—Childs—has become in America a standard for inexpensive food of good quality. "He dines at Childs": that means that the man earns $30 a week. In any part of New York one can say: "Let's have dinner at Childs," and it would not take him more than ten minutes to reach Childs. At Childs one receives the same clean handsome food as in a cafeteria or an automat. Only there one is not deprived of the small satisfaction of looking at a menu, saying "H'm," asking the waitress whether the veal is good, and receiving the answer: "Yes, sir!"

Generally speaking, New York is remarkable because it has everything. There you can find the representatives of any nation, secure any dish, any object from an embroidered Ukrainian shirt to a Chinese stick with a bone handle in the shape of a hand, which is used for back-scratching, from Russian caviare and vodka to Chilean soup and Italian macaroni. There are no delicacies in the world that New York cannot offer. But for all of it one must pay in dollars. And we want to talk about the preponderant majority of Americans who can pay only cents and for whom exist Childs, cafeterias, and automats. When describing the latter establishments, we can boldly declare that this is how the average American is fed. Under this concept of the average American is presupposed a man who has a decent job and a decent salary and who from the point of view of capitalism is an example of the healthy prospering American, happy and optimistic, who receives all the blessings of life at a comparatively low price.

The splendid organization of the restaurant business seems to confirm that. Model cleanliness, good quality of produce, an extensive choice of dishes, a minimum of time lost in dining. All that is so. But here is the trouble. All this beautifully prepared food is quite tasteless—

colourless in taste. It is not injurious to the stomach. It is most likely even of benefit to it. But it does not present man with any delights, any gustatory satisfaction. When you select in the closets of the automat or on the counter of the cafeteria an attractive piece of roast, and then eat it at your table, having shoved your hat under your chair, you feel like a buyer of shoes which proved to be more handsome than substantial. Americans are used to it. They eat fast, without wasting a single extra minute at the table. They do not eat; they fill up on food, just as an automobile is filled with petrol. The French gourmet who can sit four hours at a dinner, chewing each piece of meat in exultation, washing it down with wine and then smacking every mouthful of coffee with cognac—he is, of course, no model man. But the cold American eater, bereft of the natural human desire to get some satisfaction out of food, evokes amazement.

For a long time we could not understand why American dishes, so appetizing in appearance, are so unappealing in taste. At first we thought the Americans simply do not know how to cook. But then we learned that that alone is not the point: the crux of the matter is in the organization itself, in the very essence of the American economic system. Americans eat a blindingly white but utterly tasteless bread, frozen meat, salty butter, unripe tomatoes, and canned goods.

How does it happen that the richest country in the world, a country of grain growers and cattle raisers, of gold and remarkable industry, a country which has sufficient resources to create a paradise, cannot give the people tasty bread, fresh meat, real butter, and ripe tomatoes?

Near New York we saw waste places overgrown with weeds, forsaken plots of earth. No one sowed grain there, no one raised cattle there. We saw there neither setting hens with chicks nor truck gardens.

"You see," we were told, "it simply would not pay. We cannot compete here with the monopolists from the West."

Somewhere in Chicago, in the slaughter-houses, they kill cattle and transport the meat throughout the country in frozen form. From somewhere in California they ship frozen chickens, and green tomatoes which are supposed to ripen in transit. And no one dares to challenge the mighty monopolists to a fight.

Sitting in a cafeteria, we read Mikoyan's speech, which said that food in a socialist country must be palatable—that it must bring joy to people—and it sounded like poetry to us.

While in America the business of feeding people, as any other business, is built on this single consideration: does it pay or does it not pay? It does not pay to raise cattle and to have truck gardens in New York. Therefore, people eat frozen meat, salty butter, and unripe tomatoes. Some business man discovers that it pays to sell chewing gum, so people are taught to chew this cud. Cinema pays better than theatre; therefore, cinema develops while the theatre is neglected, although from a cultural standpoint the American theatre is much more important than the cinema. The elevated brings an income to certain companies; therefore, New Yorkers become martyrs. Along Broadway, through all the crowded traffic, with a hellish screeching, a street-car hobbles along— only because it pays one man, the owner of an ancient street-car company.

All the time we were there we felt an irresistible desire common to all Soviet people to complain and to offer suggestions. We wanted to write to the Soviet control and to the party control and to the Central Committee and to *Pravda*, but there was no one to complain to, and there is no such thing in America as "a book of suggestions."

5
We Seek an Angel Without Wings

TIME PASSED. We were still in New York and did not know when or whither we should proceed. Yet, our plan included a journey across the entire continent, from ocean to ocean.

That was a fine, but essentially a quite indefinite, plan. We had made it up in Moscow and had discussed it ardently all the way to America.

We paced scores of kilometres over the decks of the *Normandie* damp with ocean spray, arguing about the details of that journey and dousing each other with geographic nomenclature. At dinner, drinking the pure but weak wine from the cellars of the General Transatlantic Company, we muttered almost senselessly, "Kahleeforneeya," "Tyekhas," or something equally beautiful and enticing.

The plan was astounding because of its simplicity. We were to arrive in New York, buy an automobile, and ride, ride, ride until we arrived in California. Then we would turn around and ride, ride, ride until we arrived in New York. It was all simple and wonderful, like an Andersen fairy-tale. "Tra-ta-ta" sounds the klaxon, "tru-tu-tu" sounds the motor, we ride across the prairie, we swing over mountain chains, we quench the thirst of our trusty machine with the icy water of the Cordilleras, and the great Pacific sun casts its blinding brilliance on our tanned faces.

In short, you can see for yourself that we were a bit "touched," and roared at each other like chained dogs: "Sierra Nevada," "Rocky Mountains," and the like.

But when we stepped on American soil everything proved not so simple and not so romantic.

In the first place, Tyekhas is not called Tyekas, but Texas. But that was only half the trouble.

None of our new friends in New York offered any objections to our purchasing an automobile. Travel in one's own automobile is the cheapest and most interesting means of transportation in the States. Railroad travel would cost several times as much. Besides, you cannot see America from a train window. It is not a writer's business to do anything of the kind. So, as for the automobile idea, our suppositions met with approval. The difficulty was in finding a man who could go with us. We could not go by ourselves. We knew the English language well enough to engage a room in a hotel, to order a dinner in a restaurant, to go to a cinema and understand the meaning of a picture—knew it even to the extent of conversing about this or that or the other thing with some indulgent person who was not in a hurry to go anywhere—but we knew no more. Yet more was precisely what we needed. Besides, there was one other consideration. The American automobile highway is the kind of place where, as the winged word of the chauffeur has it, you ride straight into the open grave. Here you need an experienced guide.

And so, quite unexpectedly, there opened before us an abyss. And we stood on its very edge. We actually needed a man, who:

could drive a machine to perfection;

knew America to perfection, in order to show it to us properly;

spoke English well;

spoke Russian well;

had sufficient cultural background;

had a good character, otherwise he would spoil the journey; and

did not like to make money.

The last point was obligatory, because we did not have much money. We lacked it to such an extent that, to tell the truth, we had very little of it.

Thus, as a matter of fact, we needed an ideal creature, a rose without thorns, an angel without wings. We needed a complex hybrid: a guide-chauffeur-interpreter-altruist. Michurin himself would have given up. It would have taken scores of years to breed this hybrid.

There was no sense in buying an automobile until we found the appropriate hybrid, yet the longer we stayed in New York the less money we had left for an automobile. We solved this complex problem daily, and yet we could not solve it. Besides, there was almost no time for thinking about it.

On the way to America we did not take into consideration one thing: hospitality, American hospitality. It is limitless and far outstrips everything possible or conceivable of its kind, including Russian, Siberian, and Georgian hospitality. The first American you meet will not fail to invite you to his house or to a restaurant to drink a cocktail with him. At each cocktail party you will find ten friends of your new acquaintance. Each one of them will not fail to invite you to a cocktail party of his own, and each one of these will have ten or fifteen friends. In two days you suddenly acquire a hundred new acquaintances, and within a week several thousand. It is simply dangerous to spend a year in America, because you will be a confirmed drunkard and a kind of Gleb Uspensky tramp.

All the several thousands of our new friends were filled with one desire: to show us everything that we would want to see, to go with us wherever we'd like to go, to explain everything to us that we did not understand. Remarkable people are these Americans. It is pleasant to be friends with them, and it is easy to do business with them.

We were almost never alone. The telephone of our hotel began to ring in the morning, and it rang as regularly as that in an information bureau. In the rare and brief intervals between meetings with necessary and interesting people we dreamed of this ideal creature still out of our reach. Even our amusements were most businesslike, spurred on by such advice as:

"You must see it; otherwise, you will never know America!"

"What? You haven't been in a burlesque? Well, but then you haven't seen America! Why, that is the most vulgar spectacle in the world! You can see it only in America!"

"What? You haven't been to the automobile races? Excuse me, but you don't know what America is!"

It was on a bright October morning that we made our way by automobile out of New York to an agricultural exhibit in the little town of Danbury, in the state of Connecticut.

We will say nothing here about the roads on which we travelled. That would take time, inspiration, a special chapter.

The red autumnal landscape stretched on both sides of the road. The leafage was red-hot, and when it seemed that nothing in the world could be redder there appeared another grove of maddeningly Indian colour. That was not the design of the forest around Moscow, to which our eyes were accustomed, where you will find red and bright yellow and soft brown. Here everything flamed as in a sunset, and this amazing conflagration around New York, this Indian sylvan gorgeousness, continued all through October.

A roar and a clatter was heard as we approached Danbury. The flock of automobiles rested on the slopes of a little valley that was still green. There the exhibit was laid out. Policemen stretched out their arms forbiddingly, chasing us from one place to another. We finally found a place for the automobile and went to the stadium.

At the round tribune the roar was heart-rending, and over the high walls of the stadium flew small stones and hot sand, thrown up by machines around the sharp turn. It would have been easy to lose an eye or a tooth. We hastened our footsteps, shielded ourselves with our arms, just as the Pompeians must have done when their native city was perishing in a volcanic eruption.

We had to wait in a small queue to buy tickets. Around us was the clatter of a drab, provincial fair. The vendors, who have been described more than once by O. Henry, loudly praised their wares: strange aluminium whistles, carved swagger sticks, sticks crowned with dolls, all the trash found at a fair. A cow with beautiful eyes and long eyelashes was being led away. The beauty swung her udder enticingly. The owner of the mechanical organ danced to the tune of the deafening music of his contraption. A swing in the shape of a boat attached to a green metallic rigging made a complete circle. When those who were swinging were high in the sky, their heads down, the pure-hearted and hysterical feminine scream that broke forth carried us at once from the state of Connecticut to the state of Moscow, to the Park of Culture and Rest. The vendors of salted nuts and cheese-cracker sandwiches yelled at the top of their voices.

An automobile race is an empty spectacle, dreary and morbid. Red, white, and yellow racing machines with straddling wheels and numbers painted on the sides, shooting out like rocket volleys, flew past us. One round was succeeded by the next. Five, six, sometimes ten, machines competed at the same time. The audience roared. It was frightfully boring. The only thing that could possibly amuse the public would be an automobile accident. As a matter of fact, that is what people came here for. At last it occurred. Suddenly, alarm signals were heard. Everyone jumped from his seat. One of the automobiles flew off the track while going full-speed. We were still pushing our way through the crowd which surrounded the stadium when we heard the frightful baying of the ambulance. Through its window-panes we managed to see the injured driver. He no longer wore his leather helmet. He sat there, holding on to his blue skull with both hands. He had an angry look. He had lost the prize for which he had risked his life.

In the intervals between heats, on a wooden platform inside the circle, circus comedians were playing a scene which portrayed four clumsy fellows building a house. Naturally, bricks fell on the four fools. They smeared each other with the cement mixture. They beat each other with hammers by mistake, and in sheer self-forgetfulness sawed off their own legs. All this concoction of tricks, which had its origin in the distant antiquity of Greece and Rome and is still brilliantly carried on by such great master clowns as Fratellini, was excellently done by the clowns of the Danbury fair. It is always pleasant to watch good circus work, and its ways, polished through ages, are never boresome.

The fair came to an end. The visitors in the wooden pavilions were few in number. On long tables in the pavilions lay large lacquered vegetables that seemed inedible. The orchestras performed farewell marches, and all the visitors *en masse*, raising clouds of dust over the clean dark yellow sand, made their way to their automobiles. Here were demonstrated (and sold, of course) trailers for automobiles.

Pairs of Americans, in most cases composed of man and wife, would go inside and exclaim for a long time, impressed by the trailers. They examined the enticing inside of the trailer, the comfortable beds, the lace curtains on the windows, the couch, the convenient and simple metal stove. What could be better? You attach a trailer like that to an automobile, drive out of the thundering city, and drive and drive to wherever your eyes may lead you. That is, you know where you are driving. The eyes "look into the forest," and they see the Great Lakes, the beaches of the Pacific Ocean, the canyons, and the broad rivers.

Groaning, man and wife would crawl out of a trailer. It was too expensive. Here in Danbury were trailers at $350 and some at $700. But where can you get $700? Where can you get the time for a long trip?

The long columns of machines flew soundlessly back to New York, and after an hour and a half at a good clip we saw the flaming sky. Skyscrapers shone from top to bottom. Over the earth gleamed the flowing lights of the cinemas and the theatres.

Carried away by the storm of life, we decided to devote the evening to acquaintanceship with entertainment for common people.

A "nickel" is what Americans call a small nickel coin of five cents. With all its appearance nocturnal New York tells the pleasure-seeker:

"Give me your nickel! Drop your nickel! Part with your nickel and you will be happy!"

The clicking noise comes out of the large amusement stores. Here stand scores of pinball tables of all kinds. You drop a nickel in the proper slot; automatically a cue is liberated by a spring, and the pleasure-seeker, having decided to spend the evening in revelry, can shoot a steel ball five times. For a certain number of points won he receives a cardboard certificate from the master of the establishment. A half-year spent at regular play and, in consequence of the regular dropping of nickels, the reveller has the necessary number of points to receive his prize—one of those beautiful prizes that stand on the shelf. That may be a glass vase or an aluminium cocktail-shaker, or a table clock, or a cheap fountain pen or safety razor. In brief, here are all the treasures at the mere sight of which the heart of a housewife, a child, or a gangster contracts with sweetness. Americans spend hours in such lonely entertainment, in a concentrated, indifferent manner, without anger and without exultation.

Having finished with the pinball, one may go to an automatic soothsayer. She sits in a glass case, yellow-faced and thin. Before her in semicircle lies cards. It is taken for granted that you must drop a nickel. Then the soothsayer comes to life. Her head begins to bob, her chest to heave, and a wax arm glides over the cards. This is no spectacle for impressionable people. It is all so stupid and so horrible that one is in danger of losing one's mind. A half-minute later the fortune-teller freezes into her previous position. Now you must pull a handle. From the crack falls the prophecy of your fate. It is in most cases a portrait of your future wife and a short description of her attributes.

The stores of these idiotic wonders are disgusting even when they are located in the centre of a city full of tinsel and noise. But somewhere on the East Side, in the dark alleys, where the sidewalks and pavements are littered with the refuse of the daytime trade, among signboards which testify to the extreme poverty (here you can get a shave for five cents, lodging for fifteen), such a store, dimly lighted, dirty, where two or three figures silently and joylessly click at pinball, where by comparison an ordinary game of billiards becomes a genuine triumph of culture and intellect—there it is mortal boredom.

The head can ache from work. But it can also ache from amusement.

After the amusement stores we found ourselves in another strange amusement establishment.

The clatter of jazz imitates so far as possible the clatter of the elevated railway. People crowd around a glass booth in which sits a live cashier girl with a set, waxy smile on her face. This is a theatre called "Burlesque." This is a variety show for thirty-five cents.

The hall was full, and the young, determined ushers placed people anywhere at all. Some did not find seats. They stood in the aisles without taking their eyes off the stage.

On the stage a woman sang. She did not know how to sing. She had the kind of voice that did not entitle her to hold forth even at birthday parties for the most indulgent relatives. She also danced. One did not have to be a balletomane to realize that this person would never become a ballerina. Yet the public smiled approvingly. Apparently in this audience there were no fanatics of singing and no balletomanes. The audience had come here for something else.

The "something else" was explained when this singer of songs and dancer of dances suddenly began to tittup across the stage, casting off her clothes as she cut her capers. She cast them off quite slowly so that the audience might examine this artistic *mise en scène* in all its detail. Suddenly the jazz cackled, the music stopped, and with a bedroom scream the girl ran into the wings. The young men who filled the hall applauded enthusiastically. A master of ceremonies, a man of athletic appearance dressed in a dinner jacket, came out on the stage and made a businesslike proposition:

"If you applaud harder she will take off something else."

Such an explosion of applause broke loose then as even Mattia Battistini or Anna Pavlova or Keane himself, the greatest of the great, could never expect in a lifetime from any audience. No! Mere talent cannot win such a public!

The performer again passed across the stage, sacrificing what little was left of her garments. To satisfy the theatre censorship, she held a bit of clothing before her with one hand.

After the first dancer and singer another came out and repeated exactly what her predecessor had done. The third one did what the second had done. The fourth, fifth, and sixth did not make any new contributions. They sang without voice and without ear, and they danced with the grace of a kangaroo. But they disrobed. The other ten girls took their turns in faithfully repeating the same performance.

The only difference between them was that some were brunettes (these were fewer in number), while others were light-haired lambs (there were more of these).

This Zulu solemnity continued for several hours. It is pornography mechanized to such an extent that it acquires a kind of industrial and factory character. There is as little eroticism in this spectacle as in a serial production of vacuum cleaners or adding machines.

A small soundless rain fell on the street. But had there been a storm with thunder and lightning it would not have been heard.

New York itself thunders and gleams much more thoroughly than any storm. It is an excruciating city. It constantly rivets all attention to itself. It makes your eyes ache.

Yet it is impossible not to look upon it.

6

Papa and Mamma

BEFORE DEPARTING from Moscow we had collected numerous letters of introduction. It was explained to us that America was the land of letters of introduction. Without them you could not turn around.

Americans of our acquaintance whom we visited before departure at once and in silence sat down at their typewriters and began to pound out:

"Dear Sir: My friends, whom I commend to your attention . . ."

And so on and so forth. "Regards to your wife"—and in brief all that is proper to write on such occasions. They knew beforehand what we had come for.

The correspondent of the New York *Times*, Walter Duranty, wrote with incredible speed, taking the cigarette out of his mouth only in order to swallow some Crimean Madeira. We carried away from him a dozen letters. In farewell he told us:

"Go, go to America! It is much more interesting there now than here in your Russia. With you everything goes up." He indicated with his hand the rising steps of a stairway. "With you here everything is clear. But with us everything is not yet clear. And no one knows what may happen."

A colossal catch awaited us at Louis Fischer's, a journalist well known in American left-wing circles. He spent at least half of his working day on us.

"You are threatened in America," he said, "with the danger of finding yourself at once in radical and intellectual circles, getting lost there, seeing nothing, and returning home with the conviction that all Americans are very progressive and intellectual people. Yet it is far from the truth. You must see as many different kinds of people as possible. Try to see rich people, the unemployed, officials, farmers. Look for average people, because it is they who make up America."

He regarded us with his black and kindly eyes and wished us a happy and fruitful journey.

We were in the throes of greed. Although our suitcases were bulging with letters, it seemed to us that we did not have enough of them. We recalled that Eisenstein had at one time been in America, so we went to see him at Potylikha. .

This famous cinema village is laid out on the picturesque shores of the Moskva River.

Eisenstein lived in a small apartment in the midst of chandeliers and huge Mexican hats. In his workroom was a good grand piano and the skeleton of a child under a bell glass. In the reception-rooms of famous physicians bronze clocks usually stand under such bell glasses. Eisenstein greeted us in his green-striped pyjamas. He spent the whole evening writing letters, told us about America, regarded us with his childlike, crystal-clear eyes, and treated us to jam.

After a week of hard labour we were the possessors of hundreds of letters addressed to governors, actors, editors, senators, a woman photographer, and simply kind people, including a Negro minister and a dentist from Proskurov.

When we showed all this harvest, garnered after arduous labour, to Jean Lvovich Arens, our consul-general in New York, he turned pale.

"In order to see every one of these people separately . . . you will need two years."

"What shall we do, then?"

"The best thing you could do would be to put all these letters back into the suitcase and go back to Moscow. But since you are already here, we'll have to think up something for you."

Subsequently we convinced ourselves more than once that the consul could always think up something whenever it was necessary. On this occasion he thought up something grandiose: to send all these letters to their proper addresses and to arrange a reception for all at once.

Three days later, on the corner of Sixty-first Street and Fifth Avenue, in the salons of the consulate, a reception was held. We stood on the landing of the stairway at the second floor. Its walls were hung with immense photographs of the Dnieper Hydro-electric Station, the harvesting of grain with combines, and children's crèches. We stood beside the consul and with undisguised fear looked at the ladies and gentlemen who were walking up from below. They moved in an uninterrupted flow for two hours. These were the spirits called forth by the united efforts of Duranty, Fischer, Eisenstein, and a score of other of our benefactors. The spirits came with their wives—and were in excellent spirits. They were full of eagerness to do everything they had been asked to do in the letters, and to help us learn what the United States was like.

The guests greeted us, exchanged a few remarks, and passed into the salons, where there were bowls of claret cup and small diplomatic sandwiches.

In the simplicity of our souls we thought that when all would come together we, the reason for the occasion, if one may so, would follow into the salon and also raise cups and eat small diplomatic sandwiches. But that is not what happened. We learned that we were supposed to stand on the landing until the last guest departed.

From the salons came gay laughter and noisy exclamations, while we stood endlessly, greeting the late-comers, seeing off those who were departing, and in every other way fulfilling the function of hosts. More than a hundred and fifty guests had gathered, and in the end we did not even manage to find out which of them was a governor and which the native of Proskurov. It was a notable company of grey-haired ladies in spectacles, pink-cheeked gentlemen, broad-shouldered young men, and tall thin young ladies. Since every one of the spirits conjured out of our envelopes represented an indubitable point of interest, we deeply regretted the impossibility of talking at length with each and every one of them.

Three hours later the stream of guests was directed down the stairway.

A fat little man with a clean-shaven head on which glistened large beads of icy sweat came up to us. He regarded us through the magnifying lenses of his spectacles, shook his head, and with much feeling said in fairly good Russian:

"Oh, yes, yes! That's all right! Mr. Ilf and Mr. Petrov, I have received a letter from Fischer. No, no, don't tell me anything. You don't understand. I know what you need. We'll meet again."

He disappeared, small, compact, with a remarkably strong, almost an iron body. In the confusion of bidding farewell to guests we could not talk with him and puzzle out the meaning of his words.

Several days later, when we were still lounging in our beds, thinking about where at least we would find the ideal creature so indispensable to us, the telephone rang and the voice of a stranger told us that Mr. Adams was speaking and that he wanted to come right up to see us. We dressed quickly, wondering who Mr. Adams was and what he wanted of us.

Into our hotel room entered the same fat little man with the iron body whom we had seen at the reception in our consulate.

"Gentlemen," he said, without any preliminaries, "I want to help you. No, no, no! You don't understand. I regard it as my duty to help every Soviet person who comes to America."

We asked him to sit down, but he refused. He ran through our small hotel rooms, pushing us now and then with his hard, protruding stomach. The three lower buttons of his vest were unbuttoned and the tail of his necktie stuck out.

Suddenly he cried:

"I am beholden for much to the Soviet Union. Yes, yes, very much! No, don't talk; you don't even understand what you are doing there in your country!"

He became so excited that by mistake he jumped out through the open door and found himself in the hall. We had quite a time of it, dragging him back into our room.

"Were you ever in the Soviet Union?"

"Surely!" cried Mr. Adams. "Of course! No, no, no! Don't say, 'Were you ever in the Soviet Union!' I lived there a long time. Yes, yes, yes! I worked in your country for seven years. You spoiled me in Russia. No, no, no! You cannot understand that!"

Several minutes of association with Mr. Adams made it clear to us that we do not understand America at all, that we do not understand the Soviet Union at all, and that in general we understand nothing of anything at all, like newborn calves.

But it was quite impossible to be annoyed with Mr. Adams. When informed of our intention to undertake an automobile journey through the States, he cried: "Surely!" and attained such a state of excitement that he suddenly opened the umbrella which he carried under his arm and for some time stood under it, as if protecting himself from rain.

"Surely!" he repeated. "Of course! It would be foolish to think that you could find out anything about America by sitting in New York. Isn't it true, Mr. Ilf and Mr. Petrov?"

Much later, when our friendship had deepened considerably, we noticed that Mr. Adams, after expressing any thought, always demanded confirmation of its correctness and would not rest until he received that confirmation.

"No, no, gentlemen! You don't understand anything! We need a plan! A plan for the journey! That's the main thing! And I will make that plan for you. No, no, don't talk! You cannot possibly know anything about it!"

He suddenly took off his coat, pulled off his spectacles, flung them on the couch (later he looked for them in his pockets for about ten minutes), spread an automobile road map of America on his lap, and began to trace curious lines on it.

Right there before our eyes he was transformed from a wild eccentric into a businesslike American. We exchanged glances. Was this not perchance the ideal creature of whom we had dreamed? Was this not the luxuriant hybrid which even Michurin and Burbank together could not have brought forth?

In the course of two hours we travelled over the map of America. What an exhilarating occupation that was!

For some time we discussed the advisability of driving into Milwaukee, in the state of Wisconsin. There you find at once two La Follettes, one a governor and one a senator, and it was possible to get letters of introduction to both of them. An enviable situation! Two Muscovites sit in New York and decide the question of a journey to Milwaukee. If they like, they'll go there; if not, they won't!

Old man Adams sat there, calm, clean, self-contained. No, he did not recommend that we go to the Pacific Ocean by the northern route through Salt Lake City, the city of the salt lake. By the time we arrived there, the mountain passes might be in snow.

"Gentlemen!" exclaimed Mr. Adams. "This is very, very dangerous. It would be foolish to risk your lives. No, no, no! You cannot imagine what an automobile journey is."

"But the Mormons?" we moaned.

"No, no! Mormons—that is very interesting. Yes, yes, Mormons are the same Americans as others. But snow—that is very dangerous!"

How delightful it was to talk of dangers, of mountain passes, of prairies! But even more delightful was it to calculate, pencil in hand, the extent to which an automobile was cheaper than going by railway, the number of gallons of petrol needed for a thousand miles, the cost of dinners, of a modest dinner for a tourist. For the first time we heard the words "camp" and "tourist-room." Although we had not yet begun the journey we were already concerned about keeping expenses down, and although we had no automobile we were already concerned about greasing it. We began to regard New York as a dark hole from which we must forthwith escape.

When our elated discussion passed into the stage of incomprehensible shouts, Mr. Adams suddenly jumped off the couch, caught his head in his hands, squinted in dumb desperation, and stood like that for a full minute.

We were frightened.

Without opening his eyes, Mr. Adams began to knead his head in his hands and to mutter:

"Gentlemen, everything is lost! You don't understand anything!"

And then what we did not understand became clear. Mr. Adams had come here with his wife and, having left her in their automobile, had run up to see us for just a second in order to ask us to his house for lunch. He had run in for just a second!

We raced down the corridor, frightening the old ladies who always populate American hotels. In the elevator Mr. Adams jumped with impatience, so eager was he to reach the protective wing of his wife.

Around the corner from Lexington Avenue, on Forty-eighth Street, in a neat but no longer new Chrysler sat a young lady who wore the same kind of protruding spectacles as did Mr. Adams.

"Becky!" groaned our new friend, stretching forth his fat little arms toward the Chrysler.

In the confusion his hat flew off and his round head glistened in the reflected light of New York's autumn sun.

"And where is the umbrella?" asked the lady, smiling wanly.

The sun went out on the head of Mr. Adams. He forgot the umbrella in our room, he forgot his wife in the street, the umbrella was upstairs. Under such circumstances occurred our meeting with Mrs. Rebecca Adams.

With bitterness we noticed that it was not Mr. Adams, but his wife, who took the wheel. We again exchanged glances.

"No, evidently this is not the hybrid we need. Our hybrid must know how to drive an automobile."

Mr. Adams regained his calm and normal state and talked about things as if nothing untoward had happened. On the entire trip to Central Park West, where his apartment was located, old man Adams assured us that the most important thing for us is our future travelling companion.

"No, no, no, you don't understand! This is very, very important!" We became sad. We ourselves knew how important that was.

The door of the Adams's apartment was opened to us by a Negress to whose skirts clung a two-year-old girl. The little girl had a firmly moulded little body. She was a little Adams without spectacles.

She looked at her parents, and said in her thin little voice:

"Papa and Mamma."

Papa and Mamma groaned from sheer satisfaction and happiness.

We exchanged glances for the third time.

"Besides, he has a child! No, this is most decidedly not the hybrid!"

7
The Electric Chair

THE AMERICAN writer, Ernest Hemingway, author of the recently published *Fiesta*, which evoked much discussion in Soviet literary circles, happened to be in New York while we were there.

And another American writer, John Dos Passos, who is even better known among us and who provoked even more discussions in connection with the polemics on formalism in art, came in to see us and introduced us to Hemingway.

Incidentally, whenever mention was made some years ago of a soulless formalist, he was always understood to be some house manager by the name of Nezabudkin who had insulted an old lady for no good reason or who did not provide needed information on time. Nowadays no one thinks of house managers, and the words "a soulless formalist" do not fail to call forth in memory the figure of some writer or composer or of some other hairy votary of the Muses.

The round-headed, broad-nosed Dos Passos stutters a little. He begins every sentence with a laugh, but he ends it seriously. He looked at us benevolently and said:

"I am writing a new book. It is called *Big Money*. I wonder how it will fare. Every one of my succeeding books has had a smaller circulation than its predecessor: *42nd Parallel* had a circulation of twenty thousand copies; *1919*, fifteen thousand; this one will probably have ten thousand."

When we told Dos Passos that ten thousand copies of his *1919* disappeared from Soviet book counters in several hours, he replied:

"In your country people have been taught to read books, but with us here . . . Listen, we'll have to get together some time and have dinner

in the Hollywood Restaurant on Broadway. There you will see what
occupies the average American while in your country people read books.
You will see the happiness of a New York counter-jumper."

Hemingway came to New York for a week. His permanent home is
at Key West, a small town at the extreme southern tip of Florida. He
proved to be a large man with moustaches and a peeling sunburnt nose.
He wore flannel trousers, a woollen vest which did not come together
on his mighty chest, and his bare feet were in house slippers.

We stood together, in the middle of one of the hotel rooms in which
Hemingway lived, engaged in the usual American occupation. In our
hands were high and wide glasses of highballs—whisky mixed with
water. So far as we have been able to observe, everything in America
begins with a drink. Even when we came on literary business to our
publishers, Farrar and Rinehart, the gay, red-headed Mr. Farrar, publisher
and poet, at once led us into their library. He had many books there,
but also a large icebox. From that box the publisher took various bottles
and cubes of ice, asked us whether we preferred Manhattan, Bacardi or
Martini cocktails, and at once began to mix with such skill, as if he had
never in his life published books, had never written verse, but had always
worked as a barman. Americans enjoy mixing cocktails.

We happened to talk of Florida, when Hemingway at once passed to
what seemed to be his favourite theme:

"During your automobile journey, don't fail to visit me at Key West.
We'll go fishing there."

And with his arms he showed us the size of fish one can catch at Key
West. That is, like every fisherman he spread his arms as far apart as
he could. The fish must have been about the size of a sperm whale.

We looked at each other in alarm and promised, come what might, to
drop in on him at Key West so that we might go fishing and have a
really serious talk on literature. But we were unreasoning optimists.
If we were to carry out everything we had promised during our meetings
and interviews, we could not have returned to Moscow before 1940.
We wanted very much to go fishing with Hemingway. We were not
even embarrassed by the problem of managing spinning and other
involved tackle, especially since Dos Passos declared that by the time we
arrived in Florida he would also be living in Key West.

Then we talked of what we had seen in New York and what else
we wanted to see before going west. We happened to mention Sing
Sing. Sing Sing is the prison of the state of New York. We had heard
of it since childhood, having been then ardently interested in the adventures of two famous detectives, Nat Pinkerton and Nick Carter.
Suddenly Hemingway said:

"Do you know, my father-in-law happens to be here with me. He is
acquainted with the warden of Sing Sing. Maybe he can arrange it for
you to visit the prison."

He went to the adjoining room and returned with a neat little old man whose thin neck was encased in a very high and old-fashioned starched collar. Our wish was explained to the old man while he impatiently chewed his lips and at last said vaguely that he would see what he could do. Then we returned to our previous conversation about fishing, journeys, and other excellent things. Hemingway and Dos Passos wanted to go to the Soviet Union, to the Altai. While we tried to find out why they had chosen the Altai and praised also other parts of the Union, we quite forgot the promise about Sing Sing. People are likely to say anything in the course of a pleasant conversation, highballs in hand.

But a day later we learned that Americans are no idle talkers. We received two letters. One of them was addressed to us. Hemingway's father-in-law informed us respectfully that he had discussed the matter with the warden of the prison, Mr. Lewis E. Lawes, and that we might examine Sing Sing any day we chose. In the second letter the old man recommended us to Mr. Lewis E. Lawes.

We noted this American characteristic and more than once had convincing confirmation that Americans never say anything they do not mean. Not even once did we run across what we know as "idle chatter" or more crudely as "talking through your hat."

One of our New York friends once suggested to us that we might go on a fruit company ship to Cuba, Jamaica, and Colombia. He said that the trip would be free of charge, and besides, we would be seated at the captain's table. There is no greater honour at sea. Of course, we consented.

"Very well," said our friend. "You go on your automobile journey, and when you return, telephone me. Everything will be arranged."

On our return trip from California to New York we recalled this promise almost every day. After all, even this promise was made during cocktails. On that occasion it was not a highball, but some complex mixture with large green leaves, sugar, and a cherry at the bottom of the glass. Finally, from the city of San Antonio, Texas, we sent a telegram of reminder and quickly received a reply. Its tone was even a little bit hurt:

Your tropical journey arranged long ago.

We did not take that tropical journey because we did not have the time for it. But the mere recollection of American sincerity and the American ability to keep a word comfort us to this day whenever we begin to torment ourselves with the thought that we lost an opportunity to visit South America.

We asked Mr. Adams to go with us to Sing Sing. After repeatedly calling us "Gentlemen," he consented.

The next day we took our places in the Adams Chrysler; after a wretched hour with New York traffic signals we finally escaped from the city. That which is called street movement in New York might just as well be called street standing. At any rate, there is much more standing than moving.

After travelling thirty miles we discovered that Mr. Adams had for-

B*

gotten the name of the city where Sing Sing is located. We were obliged to stop. At the edge of the road a workman was unloading some neat little boxes from an automobile. We asked him the road to Sing Sing.

At once he stopped his work and walked up to us. Here is another excellent characteristic. The most preoccupied American will always find the time to explain to a traveller, briefly, to the point, and patiently, what road he should take, and while doing so he will not get things mixed up and will tell no lies. If he tells you something, he knows whereof he speaks.

Having finished his explanation, the workman smiled and said:

"Hurrying to the electric chair? Wish you luck!"

Twice again after that, more in order to clear our conscience, we verified the road, and both times Mr. Adams did not fail to add that we were hurrying to the electric chair. And in reply we heard laughter.

The prison is located on the edge of the little town of Ossining. Two rows of automobiles stood at the prison gate. Our heart contracted at once when we saw that out of the machine which had driven up simultaneously with us came a stooped, pleasant old man with two large paper bags in his hand. In those bags lay packages of food and oranges. The old man went to the entrance carrying the "outside bundle." What kinsman of his could be sitting there? Probably a son, whom most likely the old man had thought a well-behaved, splendid boy, yet he was a bandit, or maybe even a murderer. Old men have a hard time of it.

The tremendous entrance fenced off by a grille was as large as a lion's cage. On either side of it wrought-iron lanterns were welded into the walls. In the doorway stood three policemen. Each one of them weighed no less than two hundred pounds, and these were pounds not of fat but of muscle, pounds used for suppression, for subjugation.

We did not find Mr. Lewis E. Lawes in the prison. This happened to be the day for electing representatives to the legislature of the state of New York, so the warden was away. But that made no difference we were told. They knew where he was, and would telephone him in New York. Five minutes later they received a reply from Mr. Lawes. He was very sorry that circumstances did not permit his showing us Sing Sing personally, but he gave instructions to his assistant to do everything possible for us.

After that we were led into the anteroom, a white room with spittoons, polished and shining like samovars, and a grate was closed behind us. We had never been in prison as inmates, yet even here, in the midst of the shining cleanliness of a bank, the clang of a closing cage made us shudder.

The assistant warden of Sing Sing was a spare, strongly built man. We turned at once to the inspection.

This was visitors' day. Three visitors could call on every prisoner—provided he had no infraction of discipline charged against him. Polished barriers divide the large room into squares. In each square, facing each other, are two short benches—the kind you find in a street-car, let us say. On these benches sit the prisoner and his guests. The visit lasts an hour. At the exit door stands a warden. The prisoners are supposed to wear the grey prison uniform. They don't have to wear all of it, but some part of it must be government issue, either the trousers or the grey sweater.

The hubbub of conversation in the room was reminiscent of a similar hubbub in the foyer of a motion-picture theatre. Children who had come to visit their fathers ran to taps to drink water. The old man we had previously seen did not take his eyes off his beloved son. A woman was weeping softly, and her husband, the prisoner, was looking sadly at his own hands.

The conditions of the visits were such that most certainly visitors could transmit forbidden objects to the prisoners. But that would be useless. Every prisoner, when returning to his cell, is searched immediately the door of the visiting hall is closed.

Because of the election, this was a prison holiday. Passing through the yards we saw small groups of prisoners who were taking a sun-bath in the autumn sun or playing a game of ball which was unfamiliar to us (our guide said that it was an Italian game, that there are many Italians in Sing Sing). However, here were few people. Most of the prisoners were at the time in the prison motion-picture theatre.

"At present there are 2,299 people in prison," said Mr. Lawes's assistant. "Of these, eighty-five have life sentences and sixteen are to be electrocuted. And all these sixteen will undoubtedly be electrocuted, although they hope for a pardon."

The new buildings of Sing Sing are very interesting. Undoubtedly, the high general standard of American technique in building dwellings had affected its construction, especially the level of American life—what in America is called "the standard of living."

A photograph would give the best idea of an American prison, but to our regret we were not allowed to take photographs inside Sing Sing.

A prison building consists of six stories of narrow cabins, like those aboard ship, standing side by side and provided with vertical lion-cage grates. Through the length of every story stretch these metal galleries, connected with each other by metal stairways. It resembles least of all a place to live in, even a prison. The utilitarianism of the construction invests it with the appearance of a factory. The resemblance to some kind of mechanism is reinforced by the fact that all this is enclosed in a brick box, the walls of which are almost entirely occupied with windows. It is through these that daylight (and to a small extent sunlight) enters the cells, because the cells themselves have no windows.

In every such cell there is a bed, a table, and a waste can topped with a lacquered cover. On a nail hang radio earphones. There are two or three books on the table. Several photographs are on the walls—beautiful girls or baseball players or God's angels, depending upon the inclinations of the prisoner.

In the three new buildings each prisoner is lodged in a separate cell.

This is an improved prison, Americanized to the limit, and comfortable, if one may apply such an honest, good word to a prison. It is light, and the air is comparatively good.

"In the new buildings," said our escort, "are lodged eighteen hundred men. The remaining five hundred are in the old building, constructed a hundred years ago. Let's go there."

That was indeed a real Constantinople prison of the era of the sultans.

It was impossible to stand to one's full height in these cells. When you sat down on the bed your knees touched the wall opposite. The two cots were one above the other. It was dark, damp, and frightful. Here were no shining waste cans, no soothing pictures of angels.

Something of our reaction was evidently reflected in our faces, for the assistant warden hastened to distract us.

"When they send you to me," he said, "I'll place you in the new buildings. I'll even find you a cell with a view of the Hudson. We have such cells for especially deserving prisoners."

He added quite seriously:

"I hear that in your country the penitentiary system has as its object the correction of the criminal and his return to the ranks of society. Alas, we are occupied only with the punishment of criminals."

We began to talk about life terms.

"I have a prisoner here," said our guide, "who has been here for twenty-two years. Every year he files a petition of clemency and each time his case is considered his petition is decisively turned down, so beastly was the crime which he committed. I would let him out. He is now quite a different man. As a matter of fact I would liberate about half the prisoners, for they no longer present any danger to society. But I am only a jailer, and I can't do anything about it."

We were shown the hospital, the library, the dental office, in fact, all the establishments of piety, culture, and enlightenment. We went up in elevators, we walked down beautiful corridors. Punitive cells and similar things we were not shown, of course, and out of quite comprehensible politeness we did not inquire about them.

In one of the yards we went to a one-story brick building, and the assistant warden himself opened the doors with a large key. In this house executions in the electric chair are carried out by order of the courts of the state of New York.

We noticed the chair at once.

It stands in a roomy chamber without windows, so the light comes through a glass lantern in the ceiling. We took two steps on the white marble floor and stopped. Behind the chair on the door opposite the one we entered is traced in large black letters the word:

"Silence!"

The condemned are admitted through that door.

The condemned is informed early in the morning that his petition for clemency has been rejected and that the execution will take place that day. Then he is prepared for the execution. A small circle is shaved on his head to enable the electric current to pass without impediment.

Throughout the day the condemned sits in his cell. Now that the circle had been shaved on his head, he has nothing to hope for.

The execution occurs at about eleven or twelve o'clock at night.

"The fact that throughout the entire day a man experiences the torments of expectant death is very sad indeed," declared our guide, "but we can do nothing about it. Such is the demand of the law. The law regards this circumstance as an additional punishment. On this chair two hundred men and three women have been executed."

Nevertheless, the chair looks quite new.

This is a yellow wooden chair with a high back and arm rests. At first glance it seems innocuous, and if it were not for the leather bracelets with which the hands and feet of the condemned are tied, it could very well stand in some highly moral family home. A deafish grandfather might well be sitting in it to read his newspapers there.

But an instant later the chair was very repellent to us, and especially depressing were its polished arm rests. Better not to think about those who had polished them with their elbows.

A few yards from the chair stand four substantial railway station benches. These are for the witnesses. Here is a small table. A washstand is built into the wall. That is all there is to the furnishings in the midst of which is accomplished the transition from a worse into a better world. No doubt, young Thomas Alva Edison never dreamed that his electricity would perform such depressing duties.

The door in the left corner leads to a compartment larger than a telephone booth. On its wall is a marble switchboard, the most ordinary kind of switchboard with a heavy old-fashioned knife switch, the kind available at any mechanical shop or in the operating booth of a provincial motion-picture theatre. The knife switch is pushed in, and the current beats with great force through the helmet into the head of the condemned. That is all. That is the entire technique.

"The man who turns on the current," said our guide, "receives a hundred and fifty dollars for each such performance. There are any number of applicants for this job."

Of course, all the talk we had heard about three men switching on the current and that not one of them knows which of them actually is responsible for the execution proved to be an invention. No, it is all much simpler. The man switches on the current himself and knows all that happens, and fears only one thing—that competitors may take this profitable work away from him.

From the room where the execution is carried out a door leads to the morgue, and beyond that is a very quiet room filled to the ceiling with simple wooden coffins.

"The coffins are made right here in prison by the prisoners themselves," our guide informed us.

Well, we thought we had seen enough! It was time to go!

Suddenly Mr. Adams asked to be allowed to sit in the electric chair, so that he might experience the sensation of a man condemned to death.

"No, no, gentlemen!" he muttered. "It will not take very long."

He settled himself firmly on the spacious seat and looked at us triumphantly. The usual procedure was being carried out on him. He was strapped to the back of the chair with a wide leather belt, his legs were pressed with bracelets against the oaken chair legs, his hands were tied to the arm rests. Again these accursed arm rests! They did not put the helmet on Mr. Adams, but he begged them so that they finally attached the end of the electric connection to his shining pate. It all became very frightful for a minute. Mr. Adams's eyes shone with incredible curiosity. It was evident at once that he was one of those people who want to do everything, who want to touch everything with their hands, to see and hear everything themselves.

Before departing from Sing Sing we went into the church where at the time a motion-picture performance was going on. Fifteen hundred prisoners were looking at a picture entitled *Doctor Socrates*. Here we saw the laudable effort of the administration to provide the imprisoned men with the very latest motion picture. As a matter of fact, outside the prison *Doctor Socrates* was being exhibited that very day in the city of Ossining. What utterly amazed us, however, was the fact that the picture portrayed the life of bandits, and to show it to the prisoners was tantamount to teasing an alcoholic with a vision of a bottle of vodka.

But it was already late. We thanked the administration for a pleasant visit, the lion's cage opened, and we went away. After sitting in the electric chair, Mr. Adams suddenly became melancholy; he was silent all the way back.

Returning, we saw a truck that had run off the road. Its rear part was entirely off. A crowd was discussing the accident. Another crowd, much larger, was listening to an orator who was talking about that day's election. Here all the automobiles were carrying election stickers on their rear windows. Farther on, in the groves and forests flared the mad autumn.

In the evening we went with Dos Passos to look at the happiness of a New York counter-jumper. It was seven o'clock. A marquee the size of half a house was alight over the entrance of the Hollywood Restaurant. Young men in semi-military uniform, customary among hotel, restaurant, and theatre servants, were skilfully pushing people in. In the lobby hung photographs of naked girls pining with love for the populace.

As in all restaurants where it is customary to dance, the centre of the Hollywood was occupied by a longish platform, the floor of which was no more polished than the arm rests of the electric chair. On the sides of this platform and rising somewhat above it were the tables. Over all rose the tumultuous jazz.

Jazz may be disliked, especially in America, where it is impossible to hide from it. But, generally speaking, American jazz is well played.

The jazz of the Hollywood Restaurant presented an amazingly well-composed eccentric musical intricacy altogether pleasant to the ear.

When plates of rather uninteresting and in no way inspiring American soup stood before us, from behind the orchestra suddenly ran out girls half naked, three-quarters naked, and nine-tenths naked. They began to dance zealously on their floor space, their feathers dipping occasionally into plates of soup or jars of mustard.

It must have been thus, no doubt, that the ruthless fighters of Mohammed imagined their paradise—food on the table, a warm place, and houris performing their ancient tasks.

Later the girls ran out again a number of times: in the interval between the first and the second course, before coffee, and during coffee. The proprietor of the Hollywood would not let them be idle.

This joining of primitive American cooking with the passion of service somewhat upset us.

The restaurant was full of people. The dinner cost about two dollars per person. That means that the average New Yorker can come here about once a month or less frequently. But then his pleasure is complete. He listens to jazz, he eats a cutlet, he looks at the houris, and he himself dances.

The faces of some of the dancers were stupid, others were pathetic, still others were cruel, but all were equally weary.

Three blocks away from the restaurant a black poodle with gay eyes was watching Dos Passos' old machine.

We parted. We had become saddened by New York's happiness.

"Good-bye, until Moscow," said the nice Dos.

"Good-bye, until Moscow," we replied.

8

A New York Arena

THE MEMBERS of the Dutch Treat Club meet every Tuesday in a white salon of the New York Hotel Ambassador.

The very name of the club gives a precise conception of the rights and duties of its members. Everyone pays for himself. On this powerful economic basis quite a number of journalists and writers joined together. Yet there is an exception. Guests of honour do not pay. But they are obliged to deliver an amusing speech. It does not matter what the subject is, so long as the speech is amusing and brief. If it turns out not to be funny, then at any rate it must be short, because the meeting is at lunch-time and the entire celebration lasts only one hour.

In reward for his speech the guest receives a light lunch and a large plaster-of-Paris medal of the club on which is portrayed a reveller, in a crushed top-hat, who has fallen asleep under the club's initials.

While all applaud, the medal is hung around the neck of the guest, and all quickly depart. Tuesday is a business day. All the members of the Dutch Treat Club are business people. At the stroke of two they are already sitting in their offices and doing business. They advance culture or simply make money.

At such a gathering we met the manager of Madison Square Garden, the largest New York arena, where boxing matches of importance are held, where the very biggest meetings and the very biggest of everything take place.

On this particular Tuesday the guests were ourselves, the newly arrived Soviet authors, a famous American motion-picture actor, and the manager of Madison Square Garden whom we have just mentioned.

We prepared a speech, emphasizing chiefly not its humour but its brevity, and we attained the latter completely. The speech was translated into English and one of us, in no way embarrassed by the fact that he found himself in such a large gathering of experts of the English language, read it from a sheet of paper.

Here it is:

"Mr. Chairman, Gentlemen:

"We have come on a great journey from Moscow to see America. Besides New York we have had time to be in Washington and in Hartford. After living a month in New York we felt the pangs of love for your great and purely American city.

"Suddenly we were doused with cold water.

"'New York is not America,' we were told by our New York friends. 'New York is only the bridge between Europe and America. You are still on the bridge.'

"Then we went to Washington, District of Columbia, the capital of the United States, assuming thoughtlessly that surely this city was America. By the evening of the second day we felt with satisfaction that we were beginning to discriminate a little in matters American.

"'Washington is not America,' we were told. 'It is a city of government officials. If you really want to see America, you are wasting your time here.'

"We dutifully put our scratched suitcases into an automobile and went to Hartford, in the state of Connecticut, where the great American writer, Mark Twain, spent his mature years.

"Here we were again honestly warned:

"'Bear in mind that Hartford is not yet America.'

"When we began to ask about the location of America, the Hartfordites pointed vaguely to the side.

"Now we have come to you, Mr. Chairman and Gentlemen, and ask you to show where America really is located, because we have come here in order to learn as much as we can about it."

The speech was a great success. The members of the Dutch Treat Club applauded it a long time. Only much later we learned that most of the members of the club did not understand a single word of this speech, because the strange Russo-English accent of the orator drowned out completely the profound thoughts concealed in it.

Mr. Chairman, however, who sat near us, had evidently caught the sense of the speech. Turning his thin and clever face to us, he struck his little gavel and, stopping thus the storm of applause, said in the ensuing silence:

"I regret very much that I myself cannot tell you at the moment where America is located. Come here again on the sixth of November, 1936, for it will be clear then what is America and where it is located."

This was a witty and the only correct answer to our question. On November 6th was to be held the presidential election, and Americans felt that it would determine the path along which America was to proceed.

Then the tall man whom the chairman called "Colonel" was given the floor. The colonel began to bark at once, looking ironically at those forgathered here.

"My business," he said, "consists of renting Madison Square Garden to all-comers, and anything in the world that may happen there suits me. The Communists want it for a meeting against Hitler, so I rent the hall to the Communists. The Hitlerites want a meeting against the Communists, I rent the hall to the Hitlerites. In my building the Democrats may be cursing the Republicans today, but tomorrow the Republicans contend from the same platform that Mr. Roosevelt is a Bolshevik and leads America to anarchy. My hall is for everybody. I do my business. I nevertheless do have my convictions. Not long ago the defenders of Bruno Hauptmann, who killed the Lindbergh baby, wanted to rent my hall for agitation in favour of Hauptmann. I refused to rent my hall to those people. But anybody else is welcome to come. Pay your money and take your places, no matter who you are, Bolsheviks, anarchists, reactionaries, Baptists, it's all the same to me."

Having roared this out, the manly colonel sat down and took to finishing his coffee.

In Madison Square Garden, in this "hall for all," to use the colonel's expression, we saw a feature boxing match between the former world champion, the Italian Carnera, and a German boxer, not the best but a first-rate one.

The arena of Madison Square Garden is not a circle like the usual circus arenas, but an elongated rectangle. At a very sharp incline around the rectangle rise rows of chairs. Even before the match begins the eyes of the onlooker are presented with an inspiring spectacle—he sees twenty-five thousand chairs at once, he sees twenty-five thousand seats in one theatre. In the event of a boxing match, chairs are placed also in the arena, surrounding the entire ring.

A strong white light fell on the platform of the ring. The rest of the place was in twilight. Raucous cries of vendors in white two-horned caps resounded throughout the huge building. The vendors, making their way between the rows of chairs, offered salted nuts, salted biscuits, chewing gum, and small bottles of whisky. Americans are by their nature a chewing people: they chew gum, candy, the ends of cigars; their jaws are always moving, clicking, and snapping.

Carnera appeared in the next to the last match. Amid deafening greetings he walked into the ring and looked around with that sullen and apprehensive glance which is the attribute of all extremely tall and exceedingly strong men. It is the look of a man who is constantly fearful of crushing something or of mangling it.

Carnera is not known in his native Italy by his surname. There he has a nickname: "Il Gigante." "Il Gigante" is an exceedingly rangy and long-armed person. If he were a conductor of a Moscow street-car, he would very easily collect fares from people all over the car while standing on the front platform. "Il Gigante" threw off a bright-coloured robe and displayed himself in all his beauty—long, bony, looking like an unfinished Gothic cathedral.

His opponent was a sturdy blond German of middle height.

The signal sounded, the managers ran out of the ring, and Carnera quietly began to beat up the German. And he did not so much beat him as thrash him. The peasant Carnera seemed to be performing the agricultural work customary to him. His two-metre-long arms rose and fell with the regularity of flails. Most frequently they struck the air, but on those rare occasions when they fell on the German the New York public shouted: "Carnera, boo!" The inequality of strength between the opponents was altogether too evident. Carnera was much taller and heavier than the German.

The audience was excited, nevertheless, and yelled as if the issue of this fight had not been predetermined. Americans make a very noisy audience. At times it seems that they come to boxing and football matches not to look on, but to yell. The roar was constant throughout the match. Whenever the fans did not like something or thought that one of the boxers was not fighting fairly, was being cowardly or dishonest, they yelled in chorus: "Boo, boo!" and the auditorium was transformed into a drove of nice bisons in soft hats. The onlookers helped the fighters with their outcries. For the three and a half rounds of the fight between Carnera and the German the fans expended so much energy, made so many motions, that had this potential been properly utilized, it would have sufficed to build a six-story house with a flat sun roof and a cafeteria on the first floor.

In the third round the German finished almost blind. His eye had been badly hurt. In the middle of the fourth round he suddenly swung out his arms like a card player who was losing and walked out of the ring, refusing to continue the fight.

A frightful "Boo! boo!" filled the vast spaces of the Garden. It was not considered sporting to walk out of the ring. Boxers must be carried out of the ring; which is exactly what the audience expects for its money.

But the German was evidently so nauseated by the prospect of being knocked out in another minute or two that he decided to stop fighting.

The onlookers booed all the time that the unfortunate boxer was making his way back-stage. They were so indignant at the behaviour of the German that they did not even bother to cheer the victor. "Il Gigante" clasped his hands overhead, then put on his beautiful silken robe, befitting a courtesan, dived under the ropes of the ring, and in a dignified manner returned to the dressing-room, walking like an old work horse returning to the stable to shove its long muzzle into a bag of oats.

The last pair presented no special interest, and soon with others we were walking out. At the exit the newsvendors were selling the night editions of *Daily News* and *Daily Mirror*, on the first pages of which in large letters was printed the news that Carnera won over his opponent in the fourth round. Between the minute this event occurred and the moment we bought the newspaper containing the news about the match no more than half an hour had elapsed.

In the nocturnal sky flamed the electric sign "Jack Dempsey." Having finished his career in the ring, the great boxing champion opened near Madison Square Garden a bar and restaurant where sport fans gather. It would never occur to any American to blame Dempsey for turning from a sportsman into a barman. The man is making money, he is doing business. Does it make any difference how he earns his money? That money is best of which there is most!

Boxing may be liked or disliked. That is the private affair of every man. Boxing is a sport, perhaps a rough and even an unnecessary sport, but still a sport. As for the American wrestling match, that is a spectacle which is in no way sporting, however astounding it may be.

We saw such a wrestling match in the same Madison Square Garden.

According to the rules of American wrestling . . . As a matter of fact, why speak of rules, when the peculiarity of this combat consists precisely in that it has no rules whatever? You may do anything you like: break your opponent's arm; shove fingers into his mouth in an effort to tear it, while at the same time the opponent tries to bite off the fingers; pull the hair; simply beat him up; tear the face with finger-nails, pull off ears; choke his throat—everything is permitted. This form of combat is called wrestling, and there are actually people who evince a genuine interest in it.

The fighters roll in the ring, pressing against each other, and lie like that for ten minutes at a stretch. They weep in anguish and anger, they snort, spit, scream, and in general carry on in a disgusting and shameless manner—like sinners in hell.

The disgust is increased when a half-hour later you begin to understand that all this is the silliest kind of sham, that it is not even a street fight between two drunken hooligans. When one strong man really wants to break the arm of another he can do it at any time with a certain twist. In wrestling, however, despite all the frightful gestures, there is never any harm done to the parts of the body. But Americans, like children, believe this naïve deception and are frantic with delight.

Even if wrestling were carried on seriously it would merit nothing but contempt.

Certainly, this vulgar spectacle cannot compare with the competition of the cowboys! In this same rectangular arena, sullied by wrestling, we once saw a rodeo, a competition of Western cowherds.

This time there was no ring and there were no chairs. Clean sand lay from one end to the other of the huge arena. On a stand sat musicians in cowboy hats and blew for all they were worth into their horns and fifes. The gates opened into the wooden enclosure, and out came the parade of the participants.

On fine little horses rode the representatives of the romantic states of America, cowboys and cowgirls from Texas, Arizona, Nevada. The brims of the heroic hats swayed. The girls greeted the public by raising their arms in a mannish salute. There were already several hundred riders in the arena, yet more cowboys continued to ride in.

When the gala part of the performance was over, the artistic part began.

The cowboys took their turns in riding out of the gates atop short, but wildly jumping, steers. In all probability these steers had been hurt before and were brought into the arena because they bucked with incredible persistence. The task of the rider was to stay on the back of the animal as long as possible, without catching on with his hands and while holding his hat in his right hand. From the ceiling hung a huge stop clock which the entire hall could watch. One cowboy held on to an infuriated bull for seventeen seconds, another for twenty-five. Some riders were thrown to the ground after two or three seconds. The winner managed to hang on for something like forty seconds. The cowboys had the intent, bashful faces of country lads who did not want to disgrace themselves before their guests.

Later, one after the other, the cowboys rode out on their horses, swinging a lasso wound in a circle. In front of the horse, its little tail up, a calf hopped around in an exhilarating gallop. Again the stop clock went into action. Unexpectedly the rope flew out from the hands of the cowboys. The loop hung in the air like something alive. For a second the calf lay on the ground, and the cowboy hurried to it in order as quickly as possible to bind it according to all the rules of the Texas science and to transform it into a well-tied, although a desperately bellowing, bundle.

The rodeo fans yelled and put down in their little books the seconds and fractions of seconds.

The most difficult feat was left to the end. Here the cowboys had something to work on. An angry, bucking cow was led out of the gates. She dashed over the arena with a speed one would never expect of any domesticated animal. The mounted cowboy pursued the cow, jumped on her neck at full gallop, and, seizing her by the horns, forced her to the ground. The most important and the most difficult part was to throw the cow to the ground. Many did not succeed in that. Having felled the cow, it was necessary to bind all her four legs and to milk a little milk into a little bottle, which the cowboy hurriedly pulled out of his pocket. He was allowed only one minute for all this. Having milked the cow, the cowboy triumphantly lifted the little bottle over his head and cheerily ran behind the barrier.

The brilliant exercises of the cowboys, their songs sung in a minor key, and their black guitars, made us forget the heavy thuds of boxing gloves, the dripping maws, and the tear-smeared faces of the wrestlers.

The colonel was right. In his arena one could see both the good and the bad.

9
We Purchase an Automobile and Depart

ON THE way to Sing Sing and even before that, during lunch with Mr. Adams, we began urging him to join us in a great trip across America. Since we had no real arguments to offer, we repeated monotonously one and the same refrain:

"Come, come with us! It will be very interesting."

We coaxed him just as a young man coaxes a young girl to love him. There is no reason for it, but he wants someone to fall in love with him, so he presses his suit.

Mr. Adams did not say anything to it. He looked as coy as a young girl and tried to change the subject.

Then we increased the pressure. We even thought up a torture to which we subjected this good-natured elderly gentleman throughout an entire week.

"Remember, Mr. Adams, that you will be responsible if we come to a bad end. We are likely to get lost in that country filled with gangsters, petrol pumps, and ham and eggs. We shall get lousy right before your eyes in this New York, and that will be the end of us."

"No, no, gentlemen!" said Mr. Adams. "No! You mustn't press me so hard. It is most inconsiderate of you. You don't understand that, Mr. Ilf and Mr. Petrov!"

But we persisted, pitilessly egging our new friend on to the point of wavering, and then as soon as possible we would strike this fat iron, encased in a neat grey suit, while it was hot.

Mr. Adams and his wife belonged to that sort of loving couples who understand each other from the first glance.

In Mrs. Adams's glance could be read:

"I know that you want very much to go. You are scarcely able to contain yourself from starting on a journey with the first people you meet. Such is your nature. It means nothing to you to abandon Baby and me. You are as curious as a little piccaninny, although you are already sixty-three years old. Just think of the number of times you have crossed America by automobile and by train! You know the country as well as you know your own apartment. But if you want to take another look at it, go ahead; I am ready to do anything for you. But one thing I cannot understand: which one of you will drive the car? However, do the best you can and don't bother about me at all!"

"No, no, Becky!" One could read the response in Mr. Adams's glance. "It would be unfair and presumptuous to think of me so harshly. I don't want to go anywhere at all. I merely want to help these people. Besides, I would be lost without you. You had better go with us—that would be best. You are ever so much more curious than I. Everybody knows that. Come along. Incidentally, you will drive the car."

"And the baby?" replied Mrs. Adams's glance.

"Yes, yes! The baby! That's terrible! I quite forgot!"

Whenever the wordless conversation reached that point, Mr. Adams turned toward us and exclaimed:

"No, no! It is quite impossible!"

"Why impossible?" we asked plaintively. "Everything is possible. It will be so nice, so very nice. We'll travel, stop to see places, stay in hotels."

"Whoever heard of anybody stopping in hotels?" Mr. Adams suddenly cried out. "We will stop in tourist houses or in camps."

"There! You see!" we caught him up. "You know everything! Come along with us! Please come with us! We beg you! Mrs. Adams, you come with us! Come with the whole family!"

"And the baby?" cried both parents.

We answered cavalierly:

"You can put the baby in a public nursery."

"No, no, gentlemen! Oh, no! You forgot; there are no nurseries here. You are not in Moscow!"

That was right. We were not in Moscow. From the windows of the Adams apartment could be seen the denuded trees of Central Park, and from the Zoological Garden came the hoarse cries of parrots in imitation of automobile horns.

"Then leave her with your friends," we continued.

Husband and wife became thoughtful. At this point everything was spoiled by the baby herself entering the room in a night-suit with a Mickey Mouse embroidered on the chest. She came to say good-night before going to bed. With groans the parents ran to their little daughter. They embraced her, kissed her, and each time turned to us. Now you could read the same thing in the glances of both of them:

"What? To exchange this beautiful little daughter of ours for these two foreigners? Never!"

The appearance of the baby threw us back to where we had started. We had to begin all over again. So we launched new attacks.

"What a fine baby! How old is she? Is she really only two years old? Why, she looks as if she were eight! What an amazingly independent child! You should really give her more freedom! Don't you think that the constant care of parents retards the development of a child?"

"Yes, yes, gentlemen!" said the happy father, pressing the child to his stomach. "You are only joking!"

When the child was put to bed we talked for about five minutes of this and that, for the sake of appearances, and then we again began to press our suit.

We proposed a number of things about the baby, but not one of them was suitable. In utter despair we suddenly said, as if remarking, idly:

"Don't you know some respectable lady who could live with the baby during our absence?"

There was, it seemed, such a lady. We began to develop the idea, when Mr. Adams rose suddenly. The lenses of his spectacles began to gleam. He grew serious.

"Gentlemen, we need two days to decide this question."

For two days we wandered around New York, annoying each other with questions as to what might happen in case the Adamses refused to go on the journey with us. Where will we then find our ideal creature? And we spent a long time in front of stores that sold things for the road. Scotch cloth bags with zippers, rucksacks of sailcloth, soft leather suitcases, plaids, and thermos bottles—everything reminded one of a journey and lured one to start on it.

Exactly at the appointed hour, Mr. Adams appeared in our hotel room. He was unrecognizable. He was solemn and deliberate. All the buttons of his vest were buttoned. Thus the ambassador of a neighbouring friendly power comes to call on the minister of foreign affairs and declares that the government of his excellency considers itself now in a state of war with the power the representative of which is the above-mentioned minister of foreign affairs.

"Mr. Ilf and Mr. Petrov," said the little fat man, puffing and wiping icy sweat off his bald head, "we have decided to accept your proposal."

We wanted to embrace him, but he wouldn't let us, saying:

"This is too serious an occasion, gentlemen. We cannot lose any more time. You must understand it."

In the course of those two days Mr. Adams not only made up his mind and reached a decision, but he worked out our itinerary in detail. The itinerary made our heads go around.

At first we were to cross the long and narrow state of New York throughout its length, stopping in Schenectady, the city of the electric industry. The next important stop was to be Buffalo.

"It may seem too trivial to take a look at Niagara Falls, gentlemen, but it must be seen."

Then, along the shore of Lake Erie, we were to proceed to Detroit. There we were to examine the Ford plants. Then on to Chicago. After that the road was to take us into Kansas City. Through Oklahoma we would drive into Texas. From Texas to Santa Fé in the state of New Mexico. Here we visit the Indian territory. Beyond Albuquerque we cross the Rocky Mountains and drive into the Grand Canyon. Then Las Vegas and the famous dam on the Colorado River, Boulder Dam. Then on to California after crossing the Sierra Nevada range. Coming back from the shores of the Pacific Ocean we return along the Mexican border through El Paso, San Antonio, and Houston. Here we go along the Gulf of Mexico. We are now in the Black Belt: Louisiana, Mississippi, Alabama. We stop in New Orleans, and across the northern corner of Florida, through Tallahassee, Savannah, and Charleston, we move toward Washington, the capital of the United States.

Now it is easy to write about it. But then . . . how many shouts, arguments, attempts to persuade one another! We wanted to go everywhere, but we were limited by time. The entire automobile journey had to be made in two months, not a day longer. The Adamses declared firmly that they could part from their baby for sixty days and no more.

The difficulty now was an automobile: what kind of an automobile to buy?

Although we knew beforehand that we would buy the cheapest automobile that we could find anywhere in the United States, we nevertheless decided to visit the automobile show of 1936. It was the month of November, 1935, and the show had just opened.

On the two stories of the exhibition building, as if by sleight-of-hand, were gathered all the fairy-tale constellations of the American automobile world. There were no orchestras, no palms, no refreshment stands—in a word, there were no additional attractions. The automobiles themselves were so beautiful that nothing else was needed. The chastity of the American technical style consists in this: that the essence of the thing is not spoiled with anything extraneous. An automobile is the object for which people came here, so only that was here. One was free to touch it, one could sit in it, turn its wheel, light its lamps, examine its motor.

The long bodies of expensive Packards, Cadillacs, and Rolls-Royces stood on mirrored stands. On special platforms were specially polished chassis and motors. Nickelled wheels, displaying the elasticity of the springs, were spun around, and gears were shifted to demonstrate their smooth meshing.

Each firm demonstrated its own technical trick, its one improvement, designed to clinch the enticement of the purchaser—upset his, but chiefly his wife's, equanimity. All the automobiles displayed by the Chrysler firm were gold coloured—there are such bugs, coffee-gold in colour. These automobiles were surrounded by one huge moan. Thin pretty little American women with the blue eyes of vestal virgins were ready to commit murder for the sake of owning such a machine. Their husbands turned pale at the thought that that night they would have to remain alone with their wives, with nowhere to run to. Many, many are the conversations in New York at night after the opening of an automobile show! It goes ill with a man on the opening day of such an exhibit. He will wander for a long time around the marital couch where, cuddling like a kitten, the beloved creature sobs while he pleads:

"But, Mabel, our Plymouth has gone only twenty thousand miles. It's an ideal car."

But the lovely creature does not even listen to her husband. She will repeat one thing over and over:

"I want a golden Chrysler!"

And that night the marital couch will be transformed for the husband into an Indian fakir's couch covered with spikes.

But the low powerful Cords with crystal lights, which during the day are hidden in the fenders for better streamlining, compel one to forget the golden bugs. American women walk into these machines and sit in them by the hour. But they have not the strength to walk out. Their emotions are completely disturbed. They press a button, and the lamps triumphantly creep out of the fenders. They again touch the button, and the lamps hide in their nests, and again nothing is seen on the outside, except the chaste, shining fender.

But everything dims—even the gold and the crystal—before the rare and apparently old-fashioned forms of the huge Rolls-Royces. At first you want to go past these machines. At first you are even surprised that, in the midst of these slick models, hidden lights and golden colours, stand these black simple machines. But on looking closely you discover that therein precisely lies their distinctiveness. Here is a machine for the rest of your life, the machine for exceedingly wealthy old ladies, the machine for princes. Here Mabel discovers that she will never attain complete happiness, that she will never be a princess. Her Frank earns altogether too little money in his office.

Never will this automobile be out of fashion. Never will it grow old, just as diamonds and sables never grow old. Ah, it is terrible even to sit in it! You feel like the lord protector of the seal who has lost the seal and will be instantly dismissed.

We sat a while in a Rolls-Royce, but decided not to buy it. It was too luxurious for us. It would have been of hardly any use on that trying journey which was before us. Besides, it cost many thousands of dollars.

Then we moved from automobile to automobile. We sat in a blue Buick and in a small and cheap Chevrolet. We called forth Cord lights out of their hiding places by pressing a button, we passed our hands over Plymouths, Oldsmobiles, Studebakers, Hudsons, Nashes. We even pressed the horn of a Cadillac, assuming the air that on that alone depended our decision to buy or not to buy. But after evoking a truly

marvellous and mighty roar of the steppes from the nether regions of
the machine, we walked away. No! We would not buy it! It was
not within our means!

We visited other automobile showrooms. They were located for the
most part under the open sky on vacant city lots, but all their grandeur
was spoiled by a huge sign reading, "Used Automobiles."

Here also were Studebakers, Oldsmobiles, Hudsons, and Plymouths.
But what time had done to them! No repair work could hide their
respectable old age.

"These machines are for very wealthy people," Mr. Adams said
suddenly. "I advise you to buy a new Ford. A used car costs little,
but you never can tell how many times you will have to repair it on the
road nor how much petrol and oil it consumes. No, no, gentlemen!
It would be a foolish thing to buy second-hand stuff."

Although in every one of these markets under a special shed stood an
automobile decorated with the attractive placard "Today's Bargain," and
although we were insanely intent on acquiring this bargain (the price
was incredibly low and it looked simply remarkable), Mr. Adams was
implacable and restrained us from a dangerous purchase.

We bought a new Ford.

At first we wanted to buy a Ford with a radio set, but we were dis-
suaded by a terrible story. Not long ago an accident occurred. In the
mountains an automobile was smashed. The wounded people lay in it
for several hours under the sound of fox-trots broadcast by the surviving
radio set. After hearing that we refused to buy a radio. Incidentally, it
cost only forty-two dollars.

We also declined to purchase a heater. What's the use of a heater
when you have to keep a window open anyway? Otherwise the windshield will sweat. Besides, the heater cost a lot—twelve dollars.

An ash-tray was inexpensive, but we didn't have the time to buy one.

In a word, we bought the most ordinary Ford, without a radio,
without a heater, without an ash-tray, without a rear trunk, but with an
electric lighter.

It was sold to us by a dealer in the lower part of town, somewhere on
Second Avenue, corner First Street—not the most aristocratic part of
the city. Our new automobile, or, as they say in America, the "car,"
stood in an empty garage. The garage was dark and dirty, and the
dealer looked like a gangster and didn't even express any special desire to
sell us the machine. If we buy it, all right! If we don't, don't! Nevertheless, we saw at once that this was just what we had sought. The
automobile was quite new, of a sedate mouse colour, looked expensive,
yet cost little. What else can one ask in an automobile? Free cakes?—
as Mayakovsky used to say. There are no such wonders in the world!
We bought it at once.

We fell in love with our new car, and when all the arrangements were
over, when we received the documents entitling us to the possession of

the machine, when it already had its yellow number 30-99-74, and the inscription "New York," and was insured against the possibility of our running into anyone, and also against the possibility of someone running into us, when for the first time we drove with our own machine through New York and Mrs. Adams sat at the wheel, while Mr. Adams himself sat beside her—we were very proud and did not understand why the great city did not say anything about it. To make us feel good, old man Adams said that in all his life he had never, never seen a better, more comfortable, and easier riding, and more economical, automobile than ours.

"Yes, it is remarkably comfortable, and it is easy to drive. You were very fortunate that you bought this and no other automobile," Mrs. Adams confirmed.

We, too, were puffed up with satisfaction at having managed to pick out the very best automobile out of the twenty-five million automobiles in America.

We spent the last night with the Adamses.

We decided to rise as early as possible and drive off while poor Baby was still asleep. But we failed in that. The little girl discovered us in the act of moving suitcases. It was pitiful to look at the Adamses. With lying voices they assured Baby that they would return in an hour. The Negress wept. We felt that we were utter scoundrels.

The machine glided over the damp asphalt of Central Park West. The speedometer began to register miles. We started on our long trek.

PART II
THROUGH THE EASTERN STATES

10

On the Automobile Highway

THE PROUD towers of New York were behind us. Framed in stainless steel, the facets of the Empire State Building shone in the morning murkiness hovering over the gigantic city. A thin mist enveloped the summits of Radio City, Chrysler, Woolworth, and other skyscrapers, named and unnamed. Now we were driving through a lively and unpretentious suburb.

Muddy water ran over the pavement, which was lined with parallel strips. The green iron trestle of the elevated railway slit the street lengthwise at the height of the fifth story. The high-strung people of New York raced in their automobiles on their sundry errands. A striped barber pole flashed by; it was a revolving glass cylinder with green, red, and blue stripes. In a red-brick house toasted sandwiches were sold. As a matter of fact, all the houses here were brick and all were red. What can one like here, what can one learn to love here?

Like all the large cities of the world, New York is an appalling city. Here millions of people bravely struggle for mere existence. There is too much money in this city. Some people have too much while others have too little. And it is this that casts a tragic light on all that happens in New York.

We parted from the city for two months.

The route of the first day was clear. We were going to Schenectady along U.S. Highway No. 9, through Poughkeepsie (it actually takes twelve letters to write that word in English), the Hudson, and the capital of the state of New York, Albany.

The regimen of the journey was also clear. We had at our disposal sixty days, and we had approximately ten thousand miles to cover in that time. Even if we were to drive at the rate of two hundred and fifty miles a day, we would cover that distance in forty days. We set aside fifteen days for surveys, sightseeing, and so forth. All told, fifty-five days. That left us with five days in reserve for unforeseen developments. To this it should be added that a mile consists of one and six-tenth kilometres.

The suitcase with our belongings was placed in the baggage rack located under our back seat. In it were our shirts, handkerchiefs, and, most important of all, letters of introduction—new letters of introduction to cover the entire route. Again, the addressees were professors, people of the theatre, poets, engineers, politicians, governors, and senators.

To the numerous letters received from Dos Passos was attached a long list with the characteristics of each addressee, who he was, what was his occupation, and in what way he could be useful to us.

In brief, we had a lot of recommendational merchandise.

It is high time to keep our promise and write a separate chapter about American roads. They deserve it. Maybe they deserve even more— a whole inspired book.

This was not our first time on an automobile road. Yet, although since then we have become used to munificent highway arrangements, our first impression remains ineradicable. We drove over a white iron and concrete plate, eleven inches thick. This ideally even surface, being slightly rough, had a large coefficient of traction. Rain did not make it slippery. We drove over it with the ease and noiselessness with which a drop of rain runs down glass. Along its length the road was marked with white, thick stripes. Four automobiles could travel down this road at once in both directions. These roads, like the roads of ancient Rome, are built practically for eternity.

Mrs. Adams looked at us appealingly from time to time, but we pretended we did not understand her glances, although we really did. Mrs. Adams wanted to drive faster. But at the time he sold us the machine, the dealer recommended that the first few days it be driven no faster than forty miles an hour. This is necessary so as not to damage the motor before it has time to get under way. Mr. Adams glanced at the speedometer and, seeing the beautiful thin arrow wavering close to the figure 50, became anxious at once:

"No, no, Becky, it's impossible! It's impossible! The car is too stiff. You must be very, very careful with it. Isn't it so, gentlemen?"

Not understanding anything yet about the treatment of automobiles, we merely nodded, without taking our eyes off the white stripes of the road.

Oh, that road! For two months it ran to meet us—concrete, asphalt, or grained, made of gravel and permeated with heavy oil.

It is madness to think that it is possible to drive slowly down an American federal highway. It is not enough to have the desire to be careful. Side by side with your machine pass hundreds of other machines, and thousands push from behind. You meet with tens of thousands passing by, and all of them drive for all they are worth, sweeping you along with them in their satanic flight. All of America speeds somewhere, and evidently never will stop. Steel dogs and birds gleam on the noses of its machines.

Among the millions of automobiles flying from ocean to ocean, we, too, were a grain of dust chased by a petrol storm which has been raging for ever so many years over America.

Our machine raced past rows of petrol stations, each of which had six, eight, or even ten red or yellow pumps. We stopped at one of these to fill our tank.

From a small neat building, in the large glass show window of which could be seen all kinds of automobile greases and cleaning powders, came a man in a cap with a striped top and in striped overalls, the unbuttoned upper part of which revealed a striped collar with a black leather bow tie. Such is the style of mechanics—to wear leather ties. He placed a rubber spigot into the opening of the tank, and the columnlike pump began to count off automatically the number of gallons swallowed by our automobile. Simultaneously, figures jumped out on the counting machine of the little column, indicating the cost of the petrol. With each new gallon the apparatus gave off a melodic ring. This ringing is mere mechanical smartness. One can get along without it.

The tank was filled and we were ready to drive on, but the gentleman in the striped cap and leather necktie did not consider his task completed, although he had done everything that he was supposed to do. He had sold us eleven gallons of petrol, exactly as much as we had asked for. But only then did the great American service begin.

The man from the petrol station lifts the hood of the machine and tests the level of oil in the motor with a calibrated metallic ruler. If it is necessary to add oil, he brings it at once in a handsome tin can or a tall wide-necked bottle.

Then he tests the air pressure in the tires. We carried a pressure of thirty-five pounds in the front tyres and thirty in the rear. He will let out extra air or add as much as is needed.

Then the striped gentleman turns his attention to the windshield. He wipes it with a clean soft rag. If the pane is very dirty, he rubs it with a special powder.

All of this is done quickly but without any fuss. While this work is going on, which does not cost the traveller a single cent, the man at the petrol station will tell you about the road and about the weather you may expect to encounter on your route.

After everything is in order and it seems that nothing else could be added in the way of service rendered to the automobile, the traveller, spoiled by service, begins to imagine that the right front door of his machine does not close tightly enough. Smiling his good wishes, the striped gentleman pulls instruments from his rear pockets—and in two minutes the door is in order.

Besides that, the traveller receives an excellent map of the state printed by the oil companies that sell petrol on the roads. There are road maps published by Standard Oil, Shell, Socony, Conoco, and Esso. All these are beautifully printed on excellent paper. They are easy to read and they give absolutely accurate and the very latest information. It is impossible to receive a map which would tell about the condition of the road the year before. All the maps are up to date, and if there is any serious repair work going on on any of the roads it is indicated on the map. On the reverse side are listed the hotels and tourist homes in which one may spend the night. Even the sights along the road are enumerated.

All this service is given free of charge with the petrol you purchase. The same service is rendered even when you buy only two gallons of it. Difference in treatment is unknown here. A dilapidated Chevrolet or a shining Deusenberg that costs thousands of dollars, the wonder of the automobile show of 1936, will find here the same impartial, rapid, and unruffled service.

In farewell, the attendant of the petrol station told us that he personally would drive the new machine not at the rate of forty miles an hour but at thirty, and not only the first five hundred miles but the first thousand. That would make the motor work ideally in the future. Mrs. Adams was completely overwhelmed by this, and, smiling wryly, held her speed at 28-29 miles.

We men, however, were occupied with calculations. How pleasant it is to be busy when one really has no business to attend to! Our sedate, mouse-coloured Ford showed that it used one gallon of petrol (three and a half litres) every sixteen miles. In the state of New York petrol costs sixteen cents a gallon. That meant that a full tank of fourteen gallons, costing two dollars and twenty-four cents, presented us with the possibility of driving two hundred and twenty-four miles. After converting the miles into kilometres, we discovered that an automobile journey is much less expensive in the United States than in Europe.

This comforting arithmetic helped us endure the insults of the automobiles that passed us. There is something insulting in being passed. In America the passion to pass each other is strongly developed and leads to a greater number of collisions and all the other kinds of road mishaps which in America bear the name of "accident." Americans travel fast. Every year they travel faster and faster. Every year the roads become better and better, and the automobile motors more and more powerful. They drive fast, daringly, and, on the whole, not too carefully. At any rate, dogs in America have a better understanding of what an automobile highway is than do the automobilists themselves. Wise American dogs never run out on the highway and never race after an automobile with an optimistic bark. They know what that leads to. They will be crushed— and that's all there is to it.

We stopped for lunch at a roadway restaurant with the sign "Dine and Dance." We were the only ones in a large, dim room which had a square in the middle for dancing.

Out of small bowls we ate a brownish soup, accompanied by crackers, small salty rusks which justified their name by their incredible crackling when bitten. When we were attacking the large T-bone steaks—beefsteaks of frozen meat with a T-shaped bone in the middle—the owner of the restaurant and entertainment aggregate "Dine and Dance" drove up in an old Ford. He began to drag out of his machine and into the hall bundles of dried cornstalks to decorate the room with them. That

evening the youth of the district was to assemble and dance. It was all
very pleasant and peaceful—even patriarchal—yet we had driven only a
hundred miles away from New York. Only a hundred miles behind us
was the noisiest population in the world, while here was quiet, peace,
heart-throbbing bucolic flirtation during dances, cornstalks, even flowers.

At the very doors of the quiet restaurant lay the dun concrete of a first-
class highway. Again the wound in Mrs. Adams's heart opened the
moment she took the wheel. Thirty miles an hour—and not another mile!

A foreigner, even one who has no command of English, can drive out
on an American road without any apprehension. He will never get lost,
no matter how strange the country is to him. Even a child, even a deaf-
and-dumb person can freely make his way along these roads. They are
carefully numbered, and the numbers are met so frequently that it is
impossible to make a mistake of direction.

Occasionally, two roads become one for a time. Then the roadway
post contains two numbers—the number of the federal road above that
of the state road. At times, five, seven, even ten roads come together.
Then the quantity of numbers grows, and with it the post on which
they are inscribed, so that the indicator begins to look like an ancient
Indian totem pole.

There is a great variety of different signposts on the road, but—
remarkable distinction!—not one among them is superfluous, not one
might distract the attention of the driver. The signs are placed sufficiently
low above-ground so that the driver may see them on his right without
taking his eyes off the road. They are never conditional and never require
any decoding. In America you will never find a mysterious blue triangle
in a red square, a sign over which you may wrack your brain for hours.

Most of the road indicators are on round mirrored glasses which at
night reflect the glare of automobile lights. Thus, the sign shines of
itself. Black inscriptions against a yellow background (these are the
most noticeable colours) warn: "Slow," "School Zone," "Stop Danger,"
"Narrow Bridge," "Speed Limit 30 Miles," "Railroad Crossing," or
"Dip 30 Feet Away"—and precisely thirty feet away there will be a rut.
However, such an inscription is met with as rarely as the dip itself. At
each road crossing stand poles with thick wooden arrows. On the
arrows are the names of cities and the mileage to them.

Noisily, and making a baying sound, heavy silver autotanks with milk
fled past us. They carry milk for New York's seven million population.
They frighten you to death—these huge milk machines which suddenly
appear, approaching with the rapidity of a squall. The tanks are especially
grandiose at night when, surrounded by a chain of green and red lanterns,
they fly without a stop toward New York. Seven million people want
to drink milk, so it must be delivered on time.

Even more imposing are the trucks with special attachments which
transport at once three or four new automobiles. At a distance of
approximately a thousand miles, delivery by truck costs less than by

railroad—so, again a storm descends upon us, this time gleaming with lacquer and nickel. We close our eyes for a second against its unendurable glare, and drive on.

Roads are one of the most remarkable phenomena of American life—of its life and not only of its technique. The United States has hundreds of thousands of miles of so-called highways, roads of high quality, along which regular automobile communication passes. Autobuses race on schedule at the rate of sixty miles per hour, and transportation on them is twice as cheap as by rail.

At any time of day, at any time of year, in the worst possible weather, passenger autobuses race across America. When at night you see a heavy and threatening machine flying across the waste spaces and the deserts, you involuntarily remember the post diligences of Bret Harte run by desperate drivers.

An autobus travels down a gravel highway. It turns large stones over and sucks the small ones after itself. It cannot be late. Where are we? In the state of New Mexico? Faster, faster! The young chauffeur steps on the throttle, Carlsbad, Lordsburg, Las Cruces! The machine fills with noisy wind, and in it the passengers, slumbering in their easy-chairs, suddenly hear the great melody of the American continent.

America is located on a large automobile highway.

When we shut our eyes and try to resurrect in memory the country in which we spent four months, we see before us not Washington with its gardens, columns, and a full collection of monuments, not New York with its skyscrapers, its poverty and its wealth, not San Francisco, with its steep streets and suspension bridges, not hills, not factories, not canyons, but the crossing of two roads and a petrol station against the background of telegraph wires and advertising bill-boards.

I I

The Small Town

WE STOPPED in a small town and dined in a drug-store.

It is necessary to explain here the nature of a small American town, and what sort of drug-store it is in which one may dine. That story might be entitled "Pharmacist Without Mysticism, or The Secret of the American Drug-store."

When America's big business men, in search of profit, directed their attention to the drug business, they were first of all curious to find out what pharmacists were really doing behind their partitions.

What were they grinding there with their pestles in those thick china mortars, while frowning importantly? Was it medicines? Well, now, how many medicines are there in the world? Let's say fifty—a hundred

c

—well, a hundred and twenty at the most! A hundred and twenty febrifugal, stimulant, or sedative medicines! Why then prepare them in an amateurish way in drug-stores? They should be produced in mass quantity in factories.

The fact that medicines began to be prepared in factories didn't make it any easier for the sick man—the medicines were no cheaper. But the pharmacists lost their income. That was taken over by drug manufacturers.

To recoup their lost incomes the outsmarted pharmacists began to sell ice-cream, thirst-quenching waters, small notions, toys, cigarettes, kitchen utensils—in a word, they went in for anything at all.

And so the present-day American drug-store is a large bar with a high counter and revolving grand piano stools before it. Behind the counter, back and forth, run red-headed young men with white sailor caps cocked on the sides of their heads, and coquettish young women, with permanent waves that will last for years, who look like the latest and at the moment the most fashionable movie star. At times they resemble Kay Francis, at other times Greta Garbo; before that they all looked like Gloria Swanson. The girls whip cream, open highly polished nickel taps out of which emerge noisy streams of seltzer water, roast chickens, and throw pieces of ice into a glass with a resounding tinkle.

Although the drug-store has been long ago converted into an eating establishment, its proprietor is nevertheless obliged to be a pharmacist and have a certain baggage of learning, which is insistently indispensable while serving coffee, ice-cream, toasted bread, and other drug-store merchandise.

In the most distant corner of this lively establishment is a small glass closet with little jars, boxes, and bottles. One has to spend at least a half-hour in a drug-store before one notices this little closet. In it are stored the drugs.

There is not one drug-store left in New York where the pharmacist himself prepares medicines. Oh, this remarkable establishment is wrapped in the aureole of medical mysteries! To prove that here medicines are actually prepared by hand, the proprietor of the drug-store displays in the window a pile of old yellowed prescriptions. It all looks like the den of a medieval alchemist. This is no ordinary drug-store. In the latter you can eat, buy a pocket watch or an alarm clock, a pot or a toy; you can even buy or rent a book.

We looked sadly at the menu. Dinner #1, Dinner #2, Dinner #3, Dinner #4—Dinner Number One, Dinner Number Two, Dinner Number Three, Dinner Number Four! Dinner #4 costs twice as much as Dinner #2, but that doesn't mean that it is twice as good. No! There is simply twice as much of it. If in Dinner #2 a course called "country sausage" consists of three chopped off sausages, then in Dinner #4 there will be six chopped off sausages, but the taste will be exactly the same.

After dinner we become interested in the spiritual fare in which the drug-store traded. Here were wildly decorated picture postcards with views of local sights—very cheap, two for five cents. Black ones cost five cents apiece. The difference in price was right. The black postcards were excellent, while the coloured ones were a lot of trash. We examined the shelf of books. They were all novels: *Sinning is Man's Game, The Flame of Burnt-Out Love, First Night, Affairs of the Married.*

"You must not be shocked, gentlemen," said Mr. Adams. "You are in a small American town."

Many people think that America is a land of skyscrapers, that day and night one hears the clatter of elevated and underground railways, the hellish roar of automobiles and the overwhelming desperate cries of stock exchange dealers who rush among the skyscrapers, constantly waving their constantly falling stocks and bonds. This conception is firm, ancient, and customary.

Of course, it's all there—the skyscrapers, the elevated railways, and the falling stocks. But those are the attributes only of New York and Chicago. And even there the stockbrokers don't rush around sidewalks, throwing American citizens off their feet, but, entirely unnoticed by the population of America, they abide in their stock exchanges, performing all their machinations inside those monumental buildings.

New York has many skyscrapers; Chicago has a few less; but in the other large cities they are few in number—maybe two or three per city. They tower there in a lonely fashion, in the manner of a waterworks or a firehouse tower. In small towns there are no skyscrapers.

America is preponderantly a country of one-story and two-story houses. The majority of the American population lives in small cities where the population is three, five, ten, fifteen thousand.

What traveller has not experienced that first and unrepeatable feeling of excited expectation that possesses the soul upon entering a city where he has never been before? Every street and every lane open new and newer mysteries to the thirsty eyes of the traveller. Toward evening it begins to seem to him that he has fallen in love with that city. The sight of the street mob, the architecture of the buildings, the smell of the market, and finally the colour peculiar only to that city, compose the traveller's first and truest impressions. He can live in the city a year, explore its nooks and corners, make friends, then forget the names of all those friends, forget all that he had so conscientiously learned, yet he will never forget his first impressions.

Nothing of the kind can be said about American cities. Of course, even in America there are a few cities that have their inimitable personalities—San Francisco, New York, New Orleans, Santa Fé. One can be enthusiastic about them, one can be amazed by them, love them or detest them—at any rate, they evoke some definite feeling—but almost all other American cities resemble each other like the Canadian quintuplets, whom even their tender mother mistakes for each other. This colourless and depersonalized gathering of brick, asphalt, automobiles, and bill-boards evokes in the traveller only a sense of annoyance and disappointment.

And if the traveller drives into the first small town with a feeling of excited expectation, then in the next town this feeling cools considerably, in the third it is exceeded by astonishment, in the fourth by an ironic smile, in the fifth, seventeenth, eighty-sixth, and hundred and fiftieth it is transformed into indifference—as if the speeding automobile were being met not by the new and unknown cities of an unexplored country, but rather by ordinary railroad sidings with the inevitable bell, hot-water boiler, and the watchman in the red cap.

The city's principal street passes right through the city. It is called Main Street (which means the principal street) or State Street (the street of the state) or Broadway.

Every small town wants to be like New York. There are New Yorks of two thousand population, there are New Yorks of eighteen hundred. We even found one New York consisting of nine hundred inhabitants, and it was a real city. Its inhabitants walked on their Broadway, their noses high in the air. They weren't quite sure which Broadway was generally regarded as the more important, theirs or New York's.

The architecture of the buildings in the principal street cannot present the eye with artistic delights. It consists of brick, the frankest kind of brick, laid in two-story cubes. Here people make money, so there is no room for abstract embellishments.

The lower part of the city (downtown) is called the business centre. Here are the trading establishments, business offices, the motion-picture theatres. There are no people on the sidewalks, but the streets are full of automobiles. They occupy all the free places at the side. They are forbidden to stop only before fire hydrants or driveways, which is indicated by the sign "No Parking."

It becomes at times a task of torment to find a place where you may leave your machine or, as the Russians in America say, where you can "park" it. One evening we were in San Diego, a city on the shores of the Pacific Ocean. We had to park our machine in order to have our dinner, so we drove a full hour through the city, consumed with the desire to park. The city was so full of machines that there wasn't room for just one additional machine.

An American small town acquires its character not from its buildings, but from its automobiles and everything that is connected with them—petrol stations, repair stations, Ford stores, or General Motors stores. These attributes apply to all American cities. You may drive a thousand miles, two thousand, three thousand, natural phenomena will change and the climate, the watch will have to be moved ahead, but the little town in which you stop for the night will be exactly the same as the one which you had seen somewhere two weeks before. Like the previous one, it will have no pedestrians, there will be as many if not more automobiles parking at the sidewalk, the signs of drug-stores and garages will shine with the same neons or argons, the principal street will be called, as before, Broadway, Main Street, or State Street, the only possible difference being that some of the houses may be built of different materials.

The residential part, or the uptown, is always utterly deserted. The silence there is broken only by the rustle of the hoods of passing automobiles. While the men work in the business centre, the housewives are busy house-cleaning. In the one- or two-storied houses vacuum cleaners hiss, furniture is moved, and the gold frames of photographic portraits are dusted. There is much work, for there are six or seven rooms in each house. It is enough to be in one of them in order to know what furniture will be found in millions of other such houses, to know even how it would be arranged. In the disposition of the rooms, of the placing of the furniture, in all those respects, there is amazing similarity.

The houses and the yards—in which there is the inevitable light garage made of boards, which is never locked—are never separated by fences. A cement strip leads from the door of the house to the sidewalk. A thick layer of fallen leaves lies on the squares of the lawns. The neat little houses shine under the light of the autumn sun.

At times that section of the residential part where well-to-do people live produces an astonishing impression. Here is such an idyllic haven of wealth that it seems as if it were possible only in a fairy-tale. Black nurses in white aprons and caps walk with little gentlemen. Red-haired girls with blue eyes roll light yellow hoops. Splendid sedans stand beside wealthy houses.

But beside this higher world, quite close, is located the severe iron and brick business centre, the ever-frightful American centre of business, where all the houses look like fire stations, where money is made in order to provide for the idyllic haven just described. There is such a cruel difference between these two parts that at first one does not believe they actually are located in the same city. Alas, they are always together! This is precisely why the business centre is so frightful—because all its strength goes to the creation of an idyllic haven for people of wealth. One can come to understand quite a lot after a sojourn in a small town. It does not matter where you see it, whether in the East, the West, or the South. It will be the same.

The machine flies down the road. Little cities flash by. What pretentious names! Syracuse, Pompeii, Batavia, Warsaw, Caledonia, Waterloo, Geneva, Moscow—a lovely little Moscow, where you can get lunch #2 in a drug-store, griddle cakes covered with maple syrup, and where for dinner you are entitled to sweet-salty pickles, where in the motion-picture theatre a film of bandit life is unreeled—a purely American Moscow.

There are several Parises, Londons, there is a Shanghai, a Harbin, and a score of Petersburgs. There is a Moscow in the state of Ohio, and there are eighteen other Moscows, in other states. One of the Petersburgs has a hundred thousand population. There are Odessas. It doesn't matter that near the Odessas there is not only no Black Sea but not any sea at all. One is located in the state of Texas. Who was the Odessaite who had wandered so far? Did he find his happiness there? No one, of course, will ever know that. There are Naples and Florence. Near Naples, instead of Vesuvius, is the smokestack of a canning factory, while in Florence it is undoubtedly quite useless to venture a conversation about frescoes and similar subjects of little interest and devoid of all possibility of producing a definite income.

But then, in all these cities you can buy the latest model automobile and electric refrigerator (the dream of the newly-weds), there is hot and cold water in all the taps of all the houses, and, if the little town is of slightly better grade, it has a decent hotel, where in your room you will have *three* kinds of water: hot, cold, and iced.

Each city has several churches—Methodist, Congregational, Baptist. There will inevitably be a many-columned building of the Christian Science Church. But if you are not a Baptist or a Methodist and do not believe in Christian Science, then there is nothing for you to do but to go to a "movie pitcher," to look at a beautifully photographed, beautifully sounding motion picture, the contents of which befog your senses with their foolishness.

In every small town are the excellent buildings of elementary and middle schools. It may even be regarded as a rule that the best building in a small town will inevitably be a school building. But after school the boys go to the motion-picture theatre, where they watch the adventures of gangsters, play gangsters in the streets, and tirelessly wield revolvers and machine-guns manufactured in incredible quantities by toy factories.

Everlasting is the automobile and petrol tedium of small cities.

Many of the rebellious writers of America have come from the small towns of the Middle West. Theirs is a revolt against sameness, against the deadly and futile quest of the dollar.

Some of the towns make heroic efforts to distinguish themselves from their brethren of the same type. Signs are hung at the entrance to the town, quite, let us say, like signs over the entrance to a store, so that the customer may know what is being sold there.

"Redwood City!"

And under it in verse is written: "Climate best by government test!" Here they trade in climate.

The climate may be the best, but the life is the same as in the cities that have no splendid climate.

Main Street. In large show windows stand automobiles wrapped, for the occasion of the approaching New Year, in cellophane and tied with coloured ribbons. Behind somewhat smaller windows learned druggists squeeze the juice out of oranges, or fry eggs with bacon, and through the heart of the city, not on a mound or over a bridge, but right through the main street, a long freight train passes at full-speed. The engine bell swings and rings out sonorously.

Such is the small town, be it Paris or Moscow or Cairo or one of the innumerable American Springfields.

12

A Big Little Town

AN AUTOMOBILE journey across America is like a journey across an ocean, monotonous and magnificent. Whenever you go out on deck, in the morning or in the evening, in a storm or a calm, on Monday or on Thursday, you will always find water, of which there is no end. Whenever you look out the window of an automobile there will always be an excellent smooth road, with petrol stations, tourist houses, and billboards on the sides. You saw all this yesterday and the day before, and you know that you will see the very same thing tomorrow and the day after. And the dinner in the state of Ohio will be the same as yesterday's when you passed through the state of New York—quite as on a steamer, where the change of latitude and longitude introduces no changes in the menu of your dinner, or in the disposition of the passengers' day. It is in this consistent sameness that the colossal dimensions and the incalculable wealth of the United States are expressed. Before saying about Eastern America that this is a mountainous or a desert or a forest land, one wants to say the main thing, the most important thing, about it—it is the land of automobiles and electricity.

The journey was scarcely begun when we managed to violate the principal point of our daily itinerary as worked out by Mr. Adams.

"Gentlemen!" he had said before our departure. "Travel on American roads is a serious and dangerous thing."

"But American roads are the best in the world," we countered.

"That is precisely why they are the most dangerous. No, no, don't contradict me! You simply do not want to understand! The better the roads, the greater the speed with which the automobiles travel over them. No, no, no, gentlemen! This is very, very dangerous! We must agree definitely that with the approach of evening we retire for the night, and that's the end of it! Finished!"

That is exactly how we agreed to behave.

But now an evening found us on the road, and we not only did not stop as Mr. Adams demanded, but put on the lights and continued to fly across the long state of New York.

We were approaching the world centre of the electrical industry, the town of Schenectady.

It is frightful to race at night over an American highway. Darkness to the right and to the left. But the face is struck by the lightning flashes of automobile headlights coming at you. They fly past, one after the other, like small hurricanes of light, with a curt and irate feline spit. The speed is the same as in the daytime, but it seems to have doubled. In front, on a long incline, stretches the mobile prospect of display lights, which seem to put out of sight the red lights of the automobiles immediately in front of us. Through the rear window of the machine constantly penetrates the impatient light of the vehicles that are catching up with us. It is impossible to stop or to decrease speed. You must race ahead, ever ahead. The measured, blinding spurts of light cause a man to begin yawning. The indifference of sleep possesses him. It is no longer comprehensible whither you are riding or what for, and only somewhere in the nethermost depth of the brain persists the frightful thought: any minute now some gay and drunken idiot with an optimistic grin will cut into our machine, and there will be an accident, a catastrophe.

Mr. Adams was restless in his seat beside his wife, who with true American self-assurance entered into the mad tempo of this nocturnal race.

"Why, Becky, Becky!" he muttered in desperation. "What are you doing? It's impossible!"

He turned to us. His spectacles flared with alarm.

"Gentlemen!" he pronounced in the voice of a prophet. "You do not understand the meaning of an automobile catastrophe in America!"

Finally he managed to persuade Mrs. Adams to decrease her speed considerably and to deny herself the pleasure of outracing trucks. He accustomed us to the monastic routine of genuine automobile travellers, whose aim is to study the country and not to lay down their bones in a neatly dug trench beside the road.

Only a good deal later, toward the end of the journey, did we begin to appreciate the value of his advice. During its one and a half year's participation in the World War America lost fifty thousand killed, while during the past year and a half fifty-six thousand of America's peaceful inhabitants perished as a consequence of automobile catastrophes. And there is no power in America that can prevent this mass murder.

We were still about twenty miles from Schenectady, but the city was already demonstrating its electrical might. Street lamps appeared on the highway. Elongated, like melons, they gave off a strong, yet at the same time not a blinding, yellow light. One could see it gathering in those lamps—that which was not a light but an amazing luminous thing.

The city came upon us unnoticeably. That is a peculiarity of American cities when you approach them by automobile. The road is the same, only there are presently more bill-boards and petrol stations.

One American town hung before the entrance to its main street the placard:

THE BIGGEST SMALL TOWN IN THE UNITED STATES

This description—the biggest small town—splendidly suits Schenectady, and, as a matter of fact, also the majority of American towns that have risen around large factories, grain elevators, or oil wells. It is the same as the other small towns, with its business centre and residential part, with its Broadway or Main Street, but only bigger in length and width. As a matter of fact, it is a large city. It has much asphalt, brick, and many electric lights, probably more than Rome, and certainly it is bound to have more electric refrigerators than Rome, and more washing machines, vacuum cleaners, baths, and automobiles. But this city is exceedingly small spiritually, and in that regard it could very well dispose of itself in one of our little lanes.

In this city where, with amazing skill, are manufactured the smallest and the largest electrical machines that have ever existed in the world, from an egg-beater to electric generators for the Boulder Dam Hydroelectric Station on the Colorado River, the following incident happened:

A certain engineer fell in love with the wife of another engineer. It ended with her divorcing her husband and marrying the man she loved. The entire big small town knew that this was an ideally pure romance, that the wife had not been unfaithful to her husband, that she patiently waited for the divorce. The American god himself, as demanding as a new district attorney, could not have found any fault. The newly-weds began to lead a new life, happy in the thought that their tribulations were over. As a matter of fact, their tribulations were only beginning. People stopped going to their home, people ceased to invite them out. Everybody turned away from them. It was a real boycott, the more devastating because it happened in a big small town, where the principal recreation consists of calling and receiving callers for a game of bridge or poker. Essentially, all these people who drove the young couple out of their midst were in their heart of hearts quite indifferent to the problem of who lives with whom, but—a decent American must not get divorced. That is indecent. All this led to the driving out of town of the man who permitted himself to fall in love with a woman and to marry her. It was a good thing that at that time there was no depression and he could easily find another job.

The society of a town which grew up around a large industrial enterprise and is entirely connected with its interests, or rather with the interests of the bosses of the enterprise, is invested with a terrible power. Officially a man is never dismissed because of his convictions. In America one is free to profess any views, any beliefs. He is a free citizen. However, let him try not to go to church or let him try to praise communism, and something will happen whereby he will stop working in the big little town. He himself will not even notice how it happened. The people who will get rid of him themselves do not believe in God, but they go to church. It is indecent to refrain from going to church. As for communism, that is something for dirty Mexicans, Slavs, and Negroes. It is no business for Americans.

In Schenectady we stopped at a hotel that provided three kinds of water—hot, cold, and iced—and went for a walk through the city. It was only about ten o'clock in the evening, yet there were almost no pedestrians. Against the kerbs stood dark automobiles. At the left of the hotel was a deserted field overgrown with grass. It was quite dark

c*

there. Beyond the field, on the roof of a six-story building, a sign lit up and went out slowly—G.E.—General Electric Company. It was like the monogram of an emperor. But never did emperors have such might at their disposal as these electrical gentlemen who have conquered Asia, Africa, who have firmly implanted their trade-mark over the Old and the New World, for everything in the world which is in any way connected with electricity is in the end connected with General Electric.

Beyond the hotel on the principal thoroughfare wavered strips of light. There a feverish automobile life was on. But here was an excellent concrete road running around the field, which was dark and deserted. There was not even a sidewalk here. It seemed that the builders of the road thought it improbable that there could be found people in the world who would approach the office of the General Electric on foot instead of driving up in an automobile.

Opposite the office was a glass booth on wheels attached to an ancient trucklike automobile. In it sat an elderly, moustached man. He was selling popcorn, a roasted corn which bursts open in the form of white boutonnières. On the counter glowed a gasoline flare with three bright wicks. We tried to guess what popcorn was made of.

"This is corn," the vendor said unexpectedly in Ukrainian Russian. "Can't you see? It's ordinary corn. But where are you from that you speak Russian?"

"From Moscow."

"No fooling?"

"No."

The popcorn vendor became quite excited and walked out of his booth.

"Well, now, let's see—are you here as delegates from the Soviet government," he asked, "or did you come here to work, to perfect yourselves?"

We explained that we were merely travelling.

"I see, I see. Just taking a look at how things are going in our United States?"

We stood a long time at the glass booth, eating popcorn and listening to the vendor's story, which was full of English words.

This man had come to the United States some thirty years ago from a small village in the government of Volhynia. Now this little village is in Polish territory. At first he worked in mines, digging coal. Then he was a labourer on a farm. Then workers were being hired for the loco-motive works in Schenectady, so he went to work in the locomotive works.

"That's how my life passed, like one day," he said sadly.

But now for six years he had been without work. He sold everything he had. He was evicted from his home.

"I have a Pole as my manager. We sell popcorn together."

"Do you earn much?"

"Why, no, hardly enough for dinner. I'm starving. My clothes—you

can see for yourself what they're like. I haven't anything to wear for
going out into the street."

"Why don't you go back to Volhynia?"

"It is even worse there. People write it's very bad. But tell me how
is it with you, in Russia? People say different things about you. I
simply don't know whom to believe and whom to disbelieve."

We found out that this man who had left Russia in the dim past
attentively follows everything that is said and written in Schenectady
about his former homeland.

"Various lecturers come here," he said, "and speak at the high school.
Some are for the Soviet government, others are against it. And whoever
speaks for the Soviet government, they write bad things about him, very bad.

"For example, Colonel Cooper spoke well about the Soviet government, so they wrote about him that he sold out. Got two million for it.
A millionaire farmer returned and praised the Soviet state farms. It was
said that they built a special Soviet state farm for him. Not long ago a
woman school teacher from Schenectady went to Leningrad, lived there,
and then came back and praised Russia. Even about her they said that
she left a boy friend there, that she loves him, and that is why she doesn't
want to say anything against the Soviet government."

"But what do you think yourself?"

"What difference does it make what I think—would anybody ask me?
I only know one thing—I'm going to the dogs here in Schenectady."

He looked at the slowly glowing initials of the electric rulers of the
world and added:

"They have built machines. Everything is made with machines.
The working man hasn't a chance to live."

"What do you think—what should be done so that the working man
may live an easier life?"

"Break up and destroy all machines!" replied the vendor of popcorn
firmly and with conviction.

More than once in America we heard talk of destroying machines.
This may seem incredible, but in a land where the building of machines
has reached the point of virtuosity, where the national genius has
expressed itself in the invention and production of machines which replace
completely and improve many times the labour of man—it is precisely in
this country that you hear talk that would seem insane even in a madhouse.

Looking at this vendor, we involuntarily remembered a New York
cafeteria on Lexington Avenue where we used to go for lunch every
day. There at the entrance used to stand a pleasant girl in an orange
calico apron, marcelled and rouged (she undoubtedly had to be up at
six in the morning in order to have time to arrange her hair), who
distributed punch tickets. Six days later, in the very same place, we saw
a metal machine doing the work of the girl automatically—and at the
same time it gave off pleasant chimes, which, of course, one could not
very well expect from the girl. We remembered also the story we heard

in New York of a certain Negro who worked on a wharf as a controller, counting bales of cotton. The work suggested to him the idea of inventing a machine that would count 'the bales. He invented such a machine. His boss took advantage of this invention gladly, but dismissed the Negro, who henceforth was jobless.

The next day we visited the factories of the General Electric. We are not specialists; therefore, we cannot describe the factories as they deserve to be described. We don't want to give the reader an artistic ornament instead of the real thing. We ourselves would read with pleasure a description of these factories made by a Soviet engineer. We did, however, carry away from there an impression of high technical wisdom and organization.

In the laboratories we saw several of the best physicists in the world, who sat at their work with their coats off. They are working for the General Electric Company. The company doesn't give them very much money—not more than twenty thousand dollars a year. Such salaries are received only by the most prominent scientists. There are few of these people. But there are no limits to the means necessary for experiment and investigation. If a million is needed, they'll give a million. That is why the company has managed to get the best physicists in the world. No university can give them such opportunities for research as they receive here in a factory laboratory.

But then, everything that these idealists invent remains the property of the firm. The scientists advance science. The firm makes money.

At a luncheon in a cosy and beautiful engineers' club, several of the engineers, to our great surprise, expressed thoughts that reminded us very much of what the unemployed vendor of popcorn had been saying. Naturally they were not expressed in such primitive form, but the essence remained the same.

"Too many machines! Too much technique! The machines are responsible for the difficulties that confront the country."

This was said by people who themselves produce all kinds of remarkable machines. Perhaps they were already foreseeing the moment when the machine will deprive of work not only workers but even themselves, the engineers.

Toward the end of the luncheon we were introduced to a thin and tall grey-haired gentleman on whose cheeks played a healthy tomato-coloured flush. He proved to be an old friend of Mr. Adams's. Little fat Adams and his friend whacked each other's shoulders for a long time, as if they wanted to beat the dust out of each other's coats.

"Gentlemen," the beaming Mr. Adams told us, "I present to you Mr. Ripley. You can get a lot of good out of this man if you want to understand the meaning of American electrical industry. But, but! You must ask Mr. Ripley to show you his electric house."

We asked.

"Very well," said Mr. Ripley. "I will show you my electric house." And Mr. Ripley asked us to follow him.

13
Mr. Ripley's Electric House

MR. RIPLEY led us to the entrance of his little house and asked us to press the button of an electric bell.

Instead of the usual bell we heard melodic sounds as if issuing from a music-box. The door opened by itself, and we found ourselves in the anteroom.

Mr. Ripley walked up to a box hanging on the wall, opened a small door with an accustomed gesture, and showed us an electric machine.

"Five types of electric bells," he said, with a smile. "If a guest rings at the door, you hear the melody that you have just heard. If you press the button in order to call for a servant from the room, you hear an aria from *Carmen*."

Mr. Ripley pressed a button and the apparatus actually played "Love like a bird, but unearthly . . ."

"The bell for breakfast is the Yale University March, and the bell for dinner is an English Christmas carol. There is also an alarm signal. Altogether there are five types of electric bells. It's a pity that our firm has not yet invented a signal which could tell what kind of guest was ringing—pleasant or unpleasant," said the master of the house.

Having made this joke, Mr. Ripley laughed.

"But this is nothing—merely an electrical curiosity. Now I will ask you to come into my office."

Mr. Ripley represented a widely scattered type in America, the pink-cheeked and grey-haired business man. This type is made up of Americans between forty and fifty years old, prospering on good incomes, a good appetite, and a tremendous reserve of optimism. Having at the age of forty become pink-cheeked and grey-haired, the gentleman remains so to the end of his days, and after that it is no longer possible to say how old he is, whether fifty or sixty-eight. Arriving in his office, Mr. Ripley sat down at once in an easy-chair between his writing-table and a shelf of books, and, placing his feet on a chair, lit a cigarette.

"This is how I rest after work," he remarked, exhaling the smoke through his mouth.

He puffed hastily, without inhaling, intent on blowing out as much smoke as possible.

"It is not so harmful to smoke," he informed us, "as it is to breathe in the smoke which has gathered in a room, isn't that so? Most harmful of all is bad air."

Here we noticed that the smoke did not spread through the room and did not gather as usual, but before our eyes it drifted in the direction of the bookshelf and disappeared among the books. Having noted the effect produced by his actions, Mr. Ripley began to smoke harder than ever. In the most miraculous way the smoke crept to the bookshelf, momentarily surrounded the edges of the books, and immediately disappeared. Not even the smell of tobacco remained in the room.

"Behind the books is hidden an electrical ventilation system," Mr. Ripley explained.

He walked to a round glass mechanism containing several arrows and said:

"The electrical instrument for regulating the temperature of the room. You like to have it cool at night—let's say, about fifty-three degrees. And from seven o'clock in the morning you want it to be about sixty-five, or anything else you may desire. You turn the arrow like that, and this arrow like this, and you may calmly go to sleep. The instrument will carry out your desire. It will be warm here when it is cold in the street, and cool here when it is hot in the street. It will be done automatically. Everything else in this office is a trifle. This lamp shade throws a comfortable light at the writing-desk. If you turn it, the lamp will illuminate the ceiling, which will reflect the light and spread it over the entire room. Now the room is softly lighted, while the source of light is hidden and does not cut the eyes."

Then Mr. Ripley went into the dining-room. Here were various electrical instruments which were well made, although they did not astound us with their novelty: a coffee-pot, a toaster, a tea-kettle with a whistle, and a frying-pan for cooking America's national dish, bacon or ham and eggs. All these were the latest models. On the buffet, apparently for contrast, was an old spirit lamp. Americans like to demonstrate graphically the history of technique. Ford, side by side with his modern factory, has a museum where are exhibited old automobiles and engines. In the yard of the factory of General Electric stands one of the first electrical machines as a kind of monument; and in the cable shop, beside a lathe from which uninterruptedly crawls the latest model of cable that is automatically covered with a silvery lead casing, is exhibited Edison's first cable encased in a clumsy cast-iron pipe.

But Mr. Ripley delivered the main blow to his visitors in the kitchen. Here stood an electric stove of amazingly clear creamy whiteness.

"In the lower part of the stove is a drawer for dishes," said Mr. Ripley. "Here the plates are always warm and it is not necessary to heat them specially before dinner. You want to cook dinner, soup, and roast. You prepare the soup meat and the vegetables, put them in the pot, add water, and put it on top of the stove. Then you prepare the meat for the roast and put it in the oven. Then you go up to a special apparatus on the right side of the stove and move one arrow to 'soup' and the other to 'roast.' After that you can calmly go to work. The dinner will not be spoiled, even if you do not return until evening. As soon as it is ready, the heating automatically decreases. Only a low temperature will be kept up, so that the dinner should not be cold by the time of your arrival.

There is never any soot in my kitchen, because there is an electric draught right over the stove."

Mr. Ripley quickly took a piece of paper out of his pocket and lit it. The smoke and the soot disappeared immediately.

"But one thing is bad! After all the cooking there are many bones, potato peelings, and other garbage."

Mr. Ripley's face expressed suffering, but a second later it was lighted up with an optimistic smile. He walked up to a square metallic drum placed beside the stove and raised its lid.

"Here you throw all the refuse and garbage and, after closing the lid, turn on the electricity. In a few minutes the drum will be empty and clean. The refuse is ground and carried away through the drains."

Mr. Ripley quickly seized a Sunday newspaper, which weighed five pounds, crumpled it with difficulty, threw it into the drum. We heard a brief clatter, and the pink-cheeked gentleman lifted the lid with triumph. The drum was empty.

In the course of ten minutes Mr. Ripley, as deftly as a juggler, solved with the aid of electricity two more great kitchen problems—the preservation of supplies and the washing of dishes.

He showed us an electric refrigerator, which not only needed no ice but, on the contrary, prepared it in a special little white bath-tub, which looked like a photographer's, in the shape of neat transparent little cubes. In this refrigerator were compartments for meat, milk, fish, eggs, and fruit.

Then the lid of another drum was taken off. It had a number of various shelves, shelvelets, and hooks.

"Here you place the soiled dishes, spoons, plates, pots. Then you close the lid and turn on the electric current. From all sides streams of hot water beat against the dishes, and a few minutes later they are clean. Now it is necessary to dry them. Oh, what a job that is and how unpleasant to wipe dishes! Isn't that true? But no! After washing, the supply of water automatically stops and in its place dry air pours out of special jets. A few more minutes—and your dishes, gentlemen, are clean and dry."

Mr. Ripley quickly showed us an electric machine for beating eggs, and then asked us to go upstairs to the bedroom. There he quickly took off his coat and lay down on the bed.

"Imagine that I am asleep."

Without any effort we painted in our imagination the restful picture entitled, "Papa Sleeps."

"But now it is morning. It is time to rise. Oh, oh, oh!"

He rose and yawned quite naturally.

"Pay attention to this lamp. I turn on the electricity, and while I, stretching and yawning, take off my pyjamas, the lamp shines on my body. But this is no ordinary lamp. It is an artificial sun, which gives a normal tan. There are ten minutes at my disposal. I rise from my bed and walk up to this gymnastic apparatus. Here I turn on another quartz lamp and, continuing to be tanned while lying in the sun, I begin my gymnastics.

People don't like to do gymnastics in the morning. Our firm took that into consideration. Therefore, you don't have to make any movements. You only put these belts around you and turn on the electricity. The apparatus massages you in the most conscientious manner. However, according to the physicians, it is harmful to do this for more than five minutes. But man, gentlemen, is far from being a perfect instrument. He might forget to look at his watch and to turn off the electricity. The apparatus will not let him forget. It will stop its activity of its own volition, and it will do so precisely in five minutes."

We had more than once met with this type of phenomenon in American technique. It is called "foolproof"—protection from the fool. High technique distrusts man, has no faith in his resourcefulness. Wherever possible it tries to protect itself from errors native to a living creature. The term which was invented to describe it is cruel, ruthless—foolproof —protection from the fool! At the construction of the largest hydro-electric station in the world, Boulder Dam, we saw a crane which lowered wagon-loads of materials into a deep ravine. It is easy to imagine all the complexity and danger of such an operation. It is sufficient merely to confuse the electric buttons that regulate this apparatus to cause a catastrophe. But there can be no mistake. In the steering booth where the mechanic sits there is only one button. The machine does everything on its own. It will never come to work in a state of inebriety. It is always composed, and its resourcefulness is beyond all praise.

Mr. Ripley continued to show us more and more new electric wonders of his little house. Here were an electric razor and the latest model vacuum cleaner and a washing machine and a special ironing press, which has taken the place of the electric iron, that anachronism of the twentieth century. When from under a smoothly polished table he pulled an electric sewing machine, we were already worn out. If at that moment Mr. Ripley would have led us into the yard and, turning to the house, had said: "Stand, little house, with your back to New York, with your front facing me," and the little house, like the little hut on hen's legs, would have fulfilled this request with the aid of electricity, we would not have been much surprised.

It is time to tell who this Mr. Ripley is. He is in charge of the publicity department of the General Electric Company. Translated into Russian, publicity means advertising, yet this is too simple an explanation. Publicity is a much broader concept. In American life it plays a role perhaps no less important than that of technique itself.

We have come to associate with American publicity the vociferousness of barkers, countless placards, premiums, gleaming electric signs, and so forth. There is, of course, that kind of advertising in America. However, this method of uninterruptedly stunning the consumer is used only by manufacturers of cigarettes, chewing gum, alcohol, or that cooling drink, Coca-Cola.

Mr. Ripley's little house is not an advertising house. It is a scientific

house. Here the grey-haired gentleman, day in and day out, month in
and month out, calculates the cost of exploiting this or that electric
appliance. By the side of each one of them hangs a meter. Mr. Ripley
carries on experiments and tests the new machines from the point of view
of economy. Then he writes a book. He is an author. And in that book
there are no chauvinistic cries to the effect that the products of General
Electric are better than the products of Westinghouse. On the contrary,
when we asked Mr. Ripley whether Westinghouse refrigerators are good,
he told us that they are very good. In his book he explains how convenient it is to use electricity in everyday life, and proves with the aid
of authentic figures that electricity is cheaper than gas, oil, and coal. In
his book there is precise information about the cost of an electric stove
per hour, per day, per week, and per month. In conclusion he informs
you that the exploitation of the entire electric house costs seven dollars
a week. He knows well that this is the best method of persuading the
consumer.

Contemporary American technique is incomparably higher than
American social conditions—that of a capitalist society. While that
technique produces ideal things which make life easier, social conditions
do not let the American earn enough money to buy these things.

Deferred payment is the foundation of American trade. All things in
the home of an American are bought on the instalment system: the stove
on which he cooks, the furniture on which he sits, the vacuum cleaner with
which he cleans his rooms, the house itself in which he lives—everything is
acquired on the instalment system. For all this he must pay money over a
score of years. Essentially, neither the house nor the furniture nor the
wonderful gadgets of an almost ideal life belong to him. The law is very
strict. If out of a hundred payments he makes ninety-nine and does not
have enough money to make the hundredth payment, the thing he is paying for will be taken away. For the vast majority, property is a fiction.
Everything, even the bed on which this desperate optimist and enthusiastic defender of property sleeps, belongs not to him but to the
industrial company or to the bank. It is enough for a man to lose his
job, and the very next day he begins to understand clearly that he is no
kind of proprietor at all, but the most ordinary slave, like a Negro, only
white in colour.

Yet it is impossible to refrain from buying.

A polite ringing of the door-bell and in the room appears an utter
stranger. Without wasting time on any introductory speeches, the
visitor says:

"I have come here to place a new electric stove in your kitchen."

"But I already have a gas stove," replies the astonished proprietor of
the little house, the washing machine, and the standardized furniture,
which he must still pay for over many years.

"The electric stove is much better and more economical. However
I'm not going to argue with you. I will install it and I shall return in a

month. If you don't like it, I will take it away. But if you like it, the
terms are very easy: twenty-five dollars the first month, and then . . ."

He installs the stove. In a month the master of the house has had
time to assure himself that the stove is really remarkable. He is already
accustomed to it and cannot part with it. He signs a new agreement and
begins to feel as rich as Rockefeller.

You will agree that this is much more convincing than an electric sign.

It would seem that in the life of the average American—or, in other
words, of the American who has a job—there must come the moment
when he will pay up all his debts and really become a proprietor. But
that is not so easy. His automobile has become old. The firm offers him
a new excellent model. The firm takes the old machine back for a hundred
dollars, and for the remaining five hundred it gives him wonderfully easy
terms: the first month so many dollars, and then . . .

Then the happy owner somehow loses his job, and his new automobile,
with its two signals, electric lighter and radio set, is returned to its real
owner, the finance company which gave him the easy terms.

That's the trouble! They don't sell him trash, but really fine things.
In recent years the production of objects of mass consumption has
reached perfection in America. Well, now, how can you restrain yourself
and refrain from buying a *new* vacuum cleaner in spite of the fact that the
old one is good enough to use for another ten years?

Not long ago in New York a new method of advertising was begun.

Into the apartment of a New Yorker who has been through the mill
and knows all the ropes enters a man and says:

"Hello. I am a chef. I want to cook a good nourishing dinner for
you and your guests—with my groceries."

Noticing a sardonic smile on the face of the New Yorker, the newcomer adds hastily:

"It will not cost you a single cent. I make only two conditions. In
the first place, the dinner must be cooked in my pots, which I will bring
with me, and, in the second place, you must invite no fewer than seven
ladies to the dinner."

On the appointed day the chef comes with his pots and prepares a
palatable dinner. Toward the end of the banquet he solemnly appears
in the dining-room, asks whether the guests are satisfied with the dinner,
and writes down the addresses of the women present. Everybody is
delighted with the dinner. The chef modestly tells them that a dinner
like that can be cooked by any housewife, if she will only use his special
pots. The entire company goes into the kitchen and examines the pots.
Every one of them is divided into three sections. They have some kind
of special bottom which presumably aids the preservation of vitamins.
However, there is very little untruth here. The pots are really good,
and the conditions of purchase are easy. The next day the chef goes to
the various addresses and closes his deals. The enchanted housewives
purchase full sets of pots. Again—deferred payments. The pots are

actually better than the old. But it is no easier to live. On the contrary, it is harder, because there are additional debts.

No! Electric signs and newspaper advertisements are merely the preparatory work.

Every year in America an interesting event occurs. A building company, having united with the society of architects and electric firms, builds a house. It is something like Mr. Ripley's house. But there, in addition to the electric novelties, everything is a novelty—the architecture, the building materials, the furniture, even the yard. Having built this house, the entrepreneurs, consolidating on a commercial basis, announce a national competition for the description of this house. Any citizen of the United States is free to describe this house, in verse or in prose. The author of the best description receives the best-described house as his premium. This event does not fail to arouse tremendous interest. The last time the house was received by a poor sixteen-year-old girl. The newspapers were glad to print her biography and portrait. She was offered a job in the advertising department of a large enterprise—but the girl is, of course, beside the point. The point is that, carried away by her startling happiness, the readers were carried away at the same time with projects for perfecting their own lives. In the evenings fathers of families put on their spectacles and, pencil in hand, calculated that the purchase of such a house on very easy terms was not such a terrible thing at all: the first payment would come to so many dollars, and then . . .

Leaving the hospitable Mr. Ripley, we thanked him and in farewell we asked:

"Now you have lost several hours because of us. You knew very well that we would not buy a refrigerator or a stove, didn't you?"

"But maybe some day you will write about my little house," replied the grey-haired, pink-cheeked gentleman. "Good publicity is never wasted."

14
America Cannot Be Caught Napping

WHEN WE had driven thirty miles away from Schenectady, Mrs. Adams said to her husband:

"It's getting cold; put on your hat."

Mr. Adams fidgeted for some time, rose a little and searched his seat with his hands. Then, groaning, he bent over and began to look under his feet. Finally he turned to us.

"Gentlemen," he said, in a tearful voice, "will you look and see whether my hat is back there?"

There was no hat.

Mrs. Adams drew up to the side. We got out of the machine and began to search systematically. We examined the baggage rack, we opened all the suitcases. Mr. Adams even slapped his pockets. The hat had disappeared.

"And yet," remarked Mr. Adams, "I remember quite distinctly that I had a hat."

"Do you really remember it?" asked his wife with a smile that made Mr. Adams quake. "What an excellent memory!"

"It is quite incomprehensible!" muttered Mr. Adams. "An excellent hat . . ."

"You forgot your hat in Schenectady!" exclaimed his wife.

"But, Becky, Becky, don't talk like that—forgot in Schenectady! Oh, no! It hurts me to hear you say that I forgot my hat in Schenectady."

"Well, then, where is it?"

"No. Becky, seriously, how can I tell you where it is?"

He pulled a handkerchief out of his pocket and began to mop his head with it.

"What is this?" asked Mrs. Adams.

"This is a handkerchief, Becky!"

"This is not a handkerchief. This is a napkin. Let me have it. That's just what it is—a napkin with the initials of the hotel. How did it get into your pocket?"

Mr. Adams squirmed. He stood beside the machine, the collar of his coat turned up, and impatiently stood first on one foot, then on the other. Drops of rain fell on his bald head.

We began to consider the newly arisen situation with some heat. We decided that we had seen the hat for the last time in the hotel restaurant. It lay on a chair beside Mr. Adams. During luncheon there was a great argument about the Italo-Abyssinian War.

"Evidently it was then that you shoved the napkin into your pocket instead of your handkerchief!" Mrs. Adams conjectured.

"Ach, Becky, you must not talk like that—put a napkin in my pocket! No, no, no! It is cruel of you to talk like that!"

"What shall we do, then? Go back to Schenectady to get your hat?"

"No, gentlemen," said Mr. Adams, who by this time had managed to recover from the shock, "that would be a silly thing to do—to return to Schenectady. Would it be a wise thing to do? My hat cost four dollars in 1930, plus cleaning in 1933, fifty cents: altogether, four dollars and fifty cents."

Mr. Adams took a pencil and a notebook out of his pocket and began to calculate.

"In its present condition my hat is worth no more than a dollar-fifty. It is sixty miles to Schenectady and back. Our car makes on an average of sixteen—well, let us say, fifteen—miles per gallon of petrol. Altogether we would have to spend four gallons at sixteen cents per gallon; total, sixty-four cents. Now we must take into consideration the amortization of the automobile, expenses for oil and grease. Seriously, it would be silly to return to Schenectady for my hat."

Mrs. Adams suggested that we return the napkin by mail, asking the management of the hotel to send the hat to General Delivery, say in Detroit, where we would be two days later.

While we were lunching at a small café in the next little town, which was either Springfield or Geneva, Mr. Adams went to the post office. He soon returned with the proud and independent air of a man who had fulfilled his duty.

This was the third day of our journey. The month in New York had brought many impressions, but the more we saw of people and things the less we understood America. We tried to generalize. Scores of times we exclaimed:

"Americans are as naïve as children!"

"Americans are excellent workers!"

"Americans are sanctimonious!"

"Americans are a great nation!"

"Americans are stingy!"

"Americans are senselessly generous!"

"Americans are radical!"

"Americans are stupid, conservative, hopeless!"

"There will never be a revolution in America!"

"There will be a revolution in America within a few days!"

It was an awful muddle from which we wanted to extricate ourselves as soon as possible. And then gradually this deliverance began. One after the other various phases of American life, which had hitherto been hidden in the clatter and tinsel of New York, began to disclose themselves to us.

We knew. There was no need to hurry. It was too soon to generalize. First of all, we must see as much as possible.

We glided over the country, as over the chapters of a long, entertaining novel, repressing in ourselves the legitimate desire of the impatient reader to take a look at the last page. And it became clear to us: the main thing was order and system.

In the electric house of Mr. Ripley we understood the meaning of publicity. Let us call it advertising. It did not desert us for a single minute. It dogged our footsteps.

It so happened that for about five minutes we did not run across a single advertisement on either side of the road. This was so surprising that one of us exclaimed over it:

"Bill-boards have disappeared. Look: here are fields, trees, but no bill-boards!"

But the rash speaker was punished for his lack of faith in the power of American publicity. He had scarcely pronounced the last word of his sentence when from around the curve droves of large and small advertisements flew to greet our machine.

No! Americans cannot be caught napping!

Advertisements have penetrated American life to such an extent that, if upon waking some amazing morning Americans were to find all advertisements gone, the majority of them would be in the most desperate of plights. They would not know:

What cigarettes to smoke?

In what store to buy ready-made clothes?

Which cooling drink best quenches thirst—Coca-Cola or ginger ale?

Which whisky to drink—White Horse or Johnny Walker?

Which petrol to buy—Shell or Standard Oil?

Which god to worship—the Baptist or the Presbyterian?

It would be utterly impossible to decide whether it was worth while to chew gum!

Or which film was remarkable and which simply a work of genius!

Whether one should enlist in the Navy!

Whether the climate of California is beneficial or harmful?

In short, without advertisements, the devil alone knows what might happen!

Life would become incredibly complex. One would have to think for oneself at every step.

No, it is much easier with advertisements. Americans don't have to think about anything. The large business houses do the thinking for them.

There's no use bothering your head when selecting a cooling drink.

Drink "Coca-Cola!" Drink "Coca-Cola!"

"Coca-Cola" refreshes the dry throat!

"Coca-Cola" stimulates the nervous system!

"Coca-Cola" benefits the organism and the fatherland!

In brief, he who drinks "Coca-Cola" will be well off!

The average American, despite his outward show of activity, is really a passive person by nature. He must have everything presented to him in finished form, like a spoiled husband. Tell him which drink is the best, and he will drink it. Tell him which political party suits him best, and he will vote for it. Tell him which god is the true god, and he will worship him. But one thing you must not make him do. You must not make him think after working hours. He doesn't like it, and he is not used to it. And if you want him to believe your words you must repeat them as often as possible. This is the foundation on which is built a considerable portion of American advertising, political as well as commercial and every other kind.

And everywhere you go an advertisement lies in wait for you: at home and while calling, on the street and on the highway, in the taxi, in the subway, on the train, in the airplane, in the ambulance, everywhere!

We were still aboard the *Normandie* in the harbour of New York, when two objects attracted our attention. One of them was small, greenish—the Statue of Liberty. But the other was huge and impudent—an advertising shield propagandizing Wrigley's Chewing Gum—a chewing gum! From that moment on the flat green little mug with its huge megaphone, drawn on the advertisement, pursued us all through America, arguing, pleading, persuading, begging, demanding that we chew Wrigley's—the aromatic, inimitable, first-class gum.

The first month we resisted it. We drank no "Coca-Cola." We held out almost to the end of our journey. A few more days and we would be on the ocean, out of danger. Yet the advertisement won out. We could not hold out, but succumbed to that drink. We can testify truthfully: Yes, Coca-Cola really does refresh the throat, stimulates the nerves, soothes health disturbances, softens the torments of the soul, and makes a man a genius like Leo Tolstoy. We defy ourselves not to say that, after it has been driven into our heads for three months, every day, every hour, and every minute.

Even more frightful, more insistent, and more screaming is the advertisement of cigarettes. "Chesterfield," "Camel," "Lucky Strike," and other tobacco products are advertised with a hysteria which can be equalled only in the dances of the dervishes or at the celebration of "Shakhsei-Vakhsei," which no longer exists, and the participants of which were wont to stab each other with daggers in sheer abandon and drench themselves in blood for the glory of their divinity. All through the night over America flame the electric inscriptions and all through the day the eyes are stabbed with the coloured bill-boards: "The best in the world! Toasted cigarettes! They bring luck! The best in the solar system!"

As a matter of fact, the more widespread the advertising the more trivial the object designated in it. Only the sale of utter trifles can pay for this mad advertising. The houses of America, the roads, fields, and trees are mutilated by the boresome bill-boards. It is the purchaser who pays for these bill-boards. We were told that the five-cent bottle of "Coca-Cola" costs the manufacturer one cent, but that three cents are spent on advertising it. Where the fifth cent goes there is no need to say. That is quite clear.

The manufacturers of the remarkable and useful objects of technique and comfort with which America abounds cannot advertise their merchandise with the abandon indulged in by some trashy chewing gum or some brown whisky with a strong drug-store odour and utterly repellent taste.

Once, passing through a little town, we saw behind a wire grating a white plaster-of-Paris horse standing on green grass among the trees. At first we thought this was a monument to the unknown horse which heroically fell in a war between the North and the South for the liberation of the Negroes. Alas, no! This horse with the inspired eyes silently reminds those who drive by of the existence of that inimitable whisky, White Horse, which fortifies the soul, refreshes the brain, feeds learning to youths and brings delights to the old. More detailed information about this truly miraculous drink the consumer can find in the "White Tavern," located right there in the garden. Here he can learn that one can get drunk on this whisky in five minutes, that the wife of him who

drinks it will never deceive him, and that his children will grow up
without any mishaps and will even find good jobs.

The peculiarity of this type of advertising consists of grotesque
exaggerations calculated to bring out a smile in the purchaser. It is
important that he should read the advertisement. That is sufficient. In
due time it will act upon him like a slow Oriental poison.

On the road we happened to notice a wandering circus wagon with
gilt trimmings. Beside it, right on the highway, danced two large
penguins and distributed Christmas candy to children. Seeing our
machine, the penguins raced after it on roller coasters. They gave each
of us a long stick of candy, although we had long since outgrown our
childhood. Deeply moved, we drove on, but when we began to examine
the gift, we saw that it had nothing to do with Christmas or with love
of children. On the candy was printed the advertisement of the Shell
Company, which sells petrol.

The advertisement spoiled the journey somewhat. No matter where
the traveller's glance is directed, he will inevitably stumble on some
invitation, demand, insistent reminder.

"If you want your words to be believed, repeat them as often as
possible." In the East, in a small town we passed, all the telegraph poles
of the main street were pasted over with exactly the same placards—
a portrait of a minor Republican candidate for Congress.

Not only clothes, candidates, drinks, and petrol are advertised, but
entire cities. On the road you will pass a colossal bill-board twenty times
the size of an automobile. The city of Carlsbad, state of New Mexico,
says of itself:

"Twenty-three miles to Carlsbad. Good roads. Famous mineral
springs [the American might really think that this was the real Karlsbad],
good churches, theatres [evidently they are thinking of two motion-
picture theatres showing gangster pictures]. Free beach. Fine hotels.
Drive to Carlsbad!"

The city is interested in having the traveller drive into it. Even if he
is not enticed by the famous springs, he will undoubtedly buy a little
petrol on the way or will dine in the city. Thus, a few dollars will be
shown to the benefit of Carlsbad tradesmen. It is at least some small
benefit. Moreover, the traveller might even look into one of Carlsbad's
good churches. Then God, too, will be pleased.

Church people are not far behind laymen. Neon signs are alight all
night in America, informing the parishioners about entertainments of
spiritual and unspiritual character awaiting them in the temples of worship.
One church attracts with a school choir, another with an hour devoted to
social service work. To that is added a sentence right out of the vocabulary
of a grocery store: "Come in! You will be satisfied with our service!"

We have already remarked that the word "publicity" has a broad
meaning. It is not only direct advertising, but also every kind of
mention of the advertised object. When, let us say, publicity is arranged

for some actor, then even the notice in the newspapers that he recently had a successful operation and that he is now convalescing is regarded as advertising. One American told us with a good deal of envy in his voice that the Lord God has excellent publicity in the United States. Fifty thousand priests talk about him every day.

There is still another form of advertising. In a certain sense it is scientific and educational. Suddenly along the road appears a series of advertising placards stretched out for several miles. It is something in the nature of a "Victorine." The same kind of yellow boards with black letters ask questions of the travellers. Some hundred feet later they themselves answer these questions. Bible texts, anecdotes, and various information of a geographical nature are cited. Finally, on exactly the same kind of yellow board from which the bored traveller hopes to derive a few more bits of useful information, he finds the name of the warmly recommended shaving soap, and realizes with disgust that that name is now lodged in his memory for the rest of his life.

No matter where the American looks—forward, backward, to the right, or to the left—he sees announcements. Even when he raises his eyes to the sky he notices an advertisement. Airplanes deftly inscribe on the blue heavens words which are publicity for someone or for something.

Our grey car rolled farther and farther across the state of New York.

"Stop!" Mr. Adams suddenly shouted. "You must see it and write it down in your notebooks."

The machine stopped.

We saw quite a large yellow bill-board inspired by no mere commercial idea. Some American philosopher, with the aid of a press agency, had placed on the road the following declaration: "Revolution is a form of government possible only abroad."

Mr. Adams gloated.

"No, gentlemen," he said, in his joy forgetting about his hat, "you simply don't understand what is advertising in America. The American is accustomed to believe in advertisements. You must understand that. Revolution is simply impossible in our country. You are told that on a highway as infallible truth by this press agency. Yes, yes! No use arguing! The agency knows exactly what it says!"

Here was the very original and daring affirmation that revolution is "a form of government." On the other hand, the very fact of the appearance of such a bill-board would indicate that there are people in America whom it is necessary to persuade that there can be no revolution in America.

"When you see twenty-five out of every thirty-five columns of a Sunday newspaper occupied with advertisements, don't think that no one reads them. It would be foolish to think that. There is no advertisement that does not have its reader!"

Toward evening we arrived at Niagara Falls.

Drenched with spray, we gazed for a long time at the Falls, which from the height of a skyscraper dropped thousands of tons of water that had not yet been poured into little bottles to be sold as the most refreshing, the most healthful drink, of benefit to the thyroid gland, which aids in the study of mathematics and helps to consummate successful deals on the stock exchange.

Mr. Adams was shouting, but the noise of the waterfall drowned out his voice.

In the evening, departing from the city of Niagara, Mrs. Adams stopped the automobile at the kerb in order to find out about the road to Cleveland, which was on our way to Detroit. The street was deserted, not counting two elderly men, workmen in appearance, who stood by a street lamp. Mr. Adams was still lowering the window on his side, when they ran up to the machine, pushing each other aside, in order to find out as soon as possible what we wanted. Mr. Adams asked about the road to Cleveland. They began to talk together. For a while we could not understand anything, but one of them finally took the initiative, pushed his companion aside and began to explain to us:

"My God! The road to Cleveland!" He spoke with ardour. "Why, I was born in Cleveland! I should certainly know the road to Cleveland! Why, of course! You may rely on me! The road to Cleveland! You certainly are lucky that you ran into me!"

He was so happy to help us, explained with such enthusiasm where we were supposed to turn to the right and where to the left and where we could buy supper cheaply, that his companion nearly wept with envy. All along he tried to enter into the conversation, but the native of Cleveland would not let him make a peep. He would not even let Mr. Adams say a word. He was sorry to see us go. He was ready to go with us to Cleveland itself, just to make sure that we would not get off the road. They finally saw us off with mighty "good nights," as if we were their kinsmen departing for the wars.

15

Dearborn

OUR CAR drove triumphantly into the very place where it had been manufactured only a few months before, into the city of Dearborn, the centre of Ford's automobile industry. Good God! How many mouse-coloured cars we saw here! They stood aside, waiting for their masters, or rolled along the wide concrete alleys of Dearborn Park, or quite new, just off the assembly line, they rested on passing trucks. Yet we had thought we bought an automobile unique and inimitable in colour! True, on the road we had already met a number of little automobiles of the same mouse colour, but we had comforted ourselves with the thought that those were shades of the same colour, different shades, or they did not have the same flowing lines as ours, and did not really resemble it as two drops of water are alike. We were determined in our belief that our automobile was unique. Then suddenly this blow!

If cities could select their weather as man selects his necktie to match his socks, Dearborn would have undoubtedly selected, to match its two-storied brick houses, an inclement day with a greyish-yellow stripe of rain. The day was awful. A cold mist was in the air, covering with its repulsive sheen the roofs and sides of automobiles and the low buildings on Michigan Avenue, which connects Dearborn with Detroit. Through the rain could be seen drug-store signs lighted since early morning.

"On just such a day," said Mr. Adams, turning to us, "a certain gentleman, as Dickens tells us, put on his top-hat as usual and departed for his office. I must tell you that the business affairs of this gentleman were in excellent order. He had a beautiful wife, blue-eyed children, and he was making a lot of money. That was evident at least from the fact that he wore a top-hat. Not every man in England goes to work in a silk hat. Yet suddenly, one day, while passing the bridge across the Thames, the gentleman silently jumped into the water and drowned. Gentlemen, you must understand this: A happy man on the way to his office throws himself into the water! A gentleman in a top-hat flings himself into the Thames! Don't you think that in Dearborn one is also inclined to put on his top-hat?"

The street came to an end. From the height of the embankment could be seen a sombre industrial vista. The signal bells of engines coursing between shops rang out. A large steamship glided down the canal, whistling, going toward the middle of the creek. In brief, here we saw everything that distinguishes an industrial district from a kindergarten—a lot of smoke, steam, clatter, few smiles and little happy chatter. Here one sensed a special kind of seriousness, as in a theatre of military action in the region of the front-line trenches. Somewhere near by people participate in something significant—the manufacture of automobiles.

While Mr. Adams and Mr. Grozny, who was not at all a mister, but was Comrade Grozny, representative of our *Avtostroi* in Dearborn, were getting permission for us to visit the factory we stood in a hall of the information bureau and examined the new model Ford on the hardwood floor. In the hall it seemed larger than on the street. It seemed incredible that Ford's factories produce each day seven thousand such complicated and beautiful machines.

Although it was the end of 1935, all of Dearborn and Detroit were full of the advertising samples of the 1936 models. They stood in hotel vestibules, in the stores of the dealers, even in the show windows of drug-stores and confectionery shops, among cakes, syringes, and cigar-boxes. Automobile wheels turned on thick Firestone tires. Mr. Henry Ford made no mystery of his production. He displayed it wherever he could. In his laboratory, however, stood the one sacred object—Model 1938, concerning which the most contradictory rumours were afloat.

In that model the motor was presumably located at the rear, there was presumably no radiator, the coupé presumably was twice as large, and, in brief, all of it was a thousand and one automobile nights. For the time being no one was to see it, certainly not the General Motors people who, a few miles from Ford, manufacture Chevrolets, machines of the Ford class.

Our permit was granted very quickly. The management placed at our disposal a Lincoln for guests, in which there was even a bear rug, evidently because of the desire to provide the guests from the distant North with surroundings as close and native to them as possible. With the Lincoln were a chauffeur and a guide. We drove into the factory yard.

Along a glass-covered gallery which connected two buildings, in the yellowish light of day, slowly floated automobile parts hung on conveyor chains. This slow, stubborn, irrevocable movement could be seen everywhere. Everywhere, overhead, on the level of the shoulder or almost at the level of the floor rode automobile parts—stamped sides of hoods, radiators, wheels, motor blocks; sand forms in which the liquid metal still shone; brass horns, lights, fenders, steering wheels, gears. They either went up or came down or turned the corner. At times they came out into the fresh air and moved under a little wall, swaying on their hooks like the bodies of sheep. Millions of objects floated simultaneously. It took one's breath away to behold this spectacle.

This was no factory; this was a river, sure of itself, a trifle deliberate, which increases the rate of its flow as it reaches its mouth. It flowed day and night, in inclement weather and on sunny days. Millions of parts were carried by this river to one point, where the miracle happened—the hatching of an automobile.

On the chief Ford conveyor the work proceeds with feverish speed. We were amazed by the gloomy and worried appearance of people busy at a conveyor. Their work absorbed them completely. There was not even time enough to raise their heads. But it was not only a matter of physical fatigue. These people seemed to be depressed in spirit, seemed to be overcome at the conveyor with a state of daily madness that lasts for six hours, after which, upon returning home, they must rest for a long time, get well, recuperate, in order on the next day again to grow mad for a while.

The work is so divided here that the men on the conveyors don't know how to do anything, have no professions, no trades. Workers here do not manage the machines; they merely tend them. Therefore, one does not see here that sense of self-esteem which is found among trained American workers with a trade. The Ford employee receives a good wage. He himself represents no technical value. Any minute he can be dismissed, replaced by somebody else. In twenty-two minutes his successor will learn to manufacture automobiles. Working for Ford gives a man a livelihood, but does not raise his qualifications and does not assure his future. That is why Americans try not to work for Ford; and when they do, they go as mechanics or as clerks. The men who work for Ford are Mexicans, Poles, Czechs, Italians, Negroes.

The conveyor moves. One after the other excellent cheap machines roll off. They drive through the wide gates into the world, into the prairie, into freedom. The people who have made them remain behind, in confinement. Here is an astounding picture of the triumph of technique and the misfortune of man.

Down the conveyor came automobiles of all colours—black, Washington blue, green, gun-metal (so they are officially designated), even, oh, oh, of a sedate mouse colour. There was one bright orange hood, apparently a future taxi.

Through the commotion of assembly and the clatter of automatic bolt wrenches, only one man maintained a grandiose calm. He was the painter whose duty it was to draw with his thin brush a coloured line around the hood. He had no accessories, not even a maulstick, to hold up his arm. On his left arm hung little jars with various pigments. He was in no hurry. He even had the time to regard his work with an appraising glance. Around the mouse-coloured automobiles he passed a green stripe. Around the orange taxi he passed a blue stripe. He was a free artist, the only man in a Ford factory who has no relation to technique, a kind of Nuremberg Meistersinger, a freedom-loving master of the paint shop. The Ford laboratory must have discovered that it paid best to have these stripes drawn in this medieval way.

A bell rang out. The conveyor stopped. Little automobile trains with lunch for the workers drove into the building. Without washing their hands, the workers walked up to the little wagons, bought their sandwiches, tomato juice, oranges, and sat down on the floor.

Mr. Adams suddenly came to life. "Gentlemen, do you know why in Mr. Ford's plant the workers have their lunch on the cement floor? This is very, very interesting! It is of no moment to Mr. Ford how his workers lunch. He knows that the conveyor will compel them to do their work irrespective of where they eat, on the floor, at a table, or don't eat at all. Take, for example, General Electric. It would be foolish to think, gentlemen, that the management of General Electric loves its workers more than Mr. Ford does; maybe, even less. Nevertheless, it has excellent dining-rooms for its workers. The point is that at General Electric are employed qualified and trained workers, and one must take their wishes into consideration. They might go away to another factory. It is a purely American characteristic not to do any more than necessary. Don't doubt for a moment that Mr. Ford regards himself as a friend of the workers; but he will not spend one extra penny on them."

We were invited to sit down in a machine that had just come off the line. Each machine drives around a special factory road two or three times as a test. This is in a sense a model bad road. One could drive all over the United States and not find such a road. As a matter of fact, the road was not so very bad. A few regular dips, a small, rather attractive puddle—that was all there was to it—nothing frightful.

The automobile made before our eyes by people who have no trade exhibited remarkable qualities. It made sharp turns at a speed of fifty-five miles an hour, was very steady, in third gear went no faster than five miles an hour, and took the dip as gently as if there were no dip at all.

"Yes, yes!" Mr. Adams said exultantly. "Mr. Ford knows how to make automobiles. You do not even begin to appreciate progress made in this business. A 1935 Ford is better than a 1928 Cadillac. In seven years the machine of the cheap class has become better than the machine of the best class. Write that down in your little book, Mr. Ilf and Mr. Petrov, if you want to know what America is."

Here not only flowed parts combining into automobiles, and not only automobiles flowed out of the factory gates in an uninterrupted line, but the factory itself changed constantly, improved upon itself, and augmented its equipment.

In the foundry, Comrade Grozny suddenly began to cackle enthusiastically. He had been here less than two weeks, and in that time serious and important changes had occurred in this department. He stood in the middle of the shop, and on his face, lighted by flares of fire, was reflected such elation that none but another engineer, a real engineer, not an engineer of human souls, could appreciate fully and understand him.

The yellowish-grey day soon passed into a yellowish-black twilight. When we were leaving the factory a tremendous number of completed automobiles were already standing in the yard, and among them somewhere in the centre we noticed the bright orange taxi which a little while ago had been moving along the conveyor.

In a barber shop on Michigan Avenue, where we had our hair cut, one barber was a Serbian, another was a Spaniard, a third was a Slovak, while a fourth was a Jew born in Jerusalem, which might be deemed a joke of nature. We dined in a Polish restaurant, where we were waited upon by a German girl. The man whom we asked for directions in the street did not speak English. He was a Greek who had arrived here recently, right into the devil's own hell, from the Peloponnesus. He had the sad black eyes of a philosopher in exile. At the cinema we suddenly heard in the darkness this sentence spoken out loud: "Manya, I told you that we should not have come to this picture."

"Here, gentlemen," said Mr. Adams, "now you are in the real America."

In the morning we called on Mr. Sorensen, manager of all the Ford plants scattered throughout the world.

We passed through a hall, on the clean hardwood floor of which were spread out the parts of a standard automobile. Just as we were, in our hats and coats, we were led into the glass-enclosed office of the manager. Here stood a large desk. There was not a single piece of paper on it—only one telephone and a calendar. We wanted to find out as soon as possible what occupies the time of a manager who does not sign any papers, who does not ply the telephone morning, noon, and night, a manager in whose anteroom, instead of even a single visitor, lie oiled machine parts.

A tall thin man in a grey suit entered the office. His head was grey, his face was ruddy, and his walk was that of an athlete. In his hand was a small black object made of some plastic. This was Mr. Sorensen, a Dane by descent, the son of a stove-setter, himself at one time a stove-setter but later a patternmaker.

Before we left America we read in a Washington newspaper a list of the ten people who received the highest salaries in the country that year. Mr. Sorensen was in the last place. The first place was occupied by Mae West, the motion-picture star. In 1935 she was paid $450,000. Sorensen received $112,000. Needless to say, the head and hands of this man are infinitely more valuable than the pornographic bosom of any film star.

He at once began to talk about the machine part he held in his hand. At one time it used to be made of steel; now it is made out of plastic and tested at once.

"We are constantly on the move," said Mr. Sorensen. "Therein lies the essence of the automobile industry. We cannot stop for a minute. Otherwise we shall be left behind. We must think now of what we shall be doing in 1940."

He stepped out of the room and at once returned with a mould in his hands. That was the block of a motor he had himself cast in mould out of steel—with his own managerial hands.

"We will be testing this for a long time. But it looks as if this might be a part of our automobile."

We touched the block cast that would be part of a machine a few years hence, and began to talk about Ford.

"I met Mr. Ford thirty-five years ago," said Sorensen.

"What are your relations today?"

"Oh," said Mr. Sorensen, "thirty-five years ago Mr. Ford built his automobile in some barn and came to me in the small foundry where I was working. At that time he was an ordinary mechanic, while I was a patternmaker. He brought me his blueprint and asked me to make a model. And nothing has changed since that day. To this day Mr. Ford brings me his ideas and I put them into practice."

He said that nothing had changed. Yet even the most cursory glance could see the progress that had been caused by a little Dearborn mechanic and his young friend, the patternmaker.

Mr. Sorensen led us to a photograph showing him together with the manager of the Gorky factory, Dyakonov, and with Grozny. Smiling artlessly, the three men were looking straight into the camera.

"There is only one permanent thing in this world," Mr. Sorensen told us in parting—"incessant change."

We managed to squeeze into our conversation the notion that we should like to see Mr. Ford, and Mr. Sorensen said that he would find out whether that was possible. However, we were not certain that the interview would actually occur. Everyone had warned us that this was very difficult, that Mr. Ford is old, busy, and unwilling to meet people.

16

Henry Ford

IN THE morning Mr. Sorensen telephoned to say that Mr. Ford would receive us. Again we had proof that Americans are meticulous and businesslike. As a matter of fact, Mr. Sorensen did not promise anything and had every moral right never to refer to the matter again. He regarded the most casual remark as important business as any contract signed by him.

We were asked to drop in on Mr. Cameron, Mr. Ford's private secretary. Mr. Cameron was located in the construction bureau building.

"Mr. Ford is not here now," he informed us, "and I cannot tell you exactly when you will be able to see him. But you are looking over the factory anyway and are likely to drive past our office at least ten times in the course of the day. Whenever you drive by, drop in to find out whether Mr. Ford happens to be in at that time."

We already knew that Mr. Ford has no office of his own, did not lock himself in, but is constantly on the go through the plant. We were, therefore, not at all surprised to hear this, and, covering ourselves with the bear rug, we drove off through the wonders of Dearborn.

We began that day with the machine museum.

One of the halls of the museum building covers twenty acres. The floor is of teakwood, which rings underfoot like steel. The hall is supported by metal columns. They are at the same time the heating apparatus.

The museum was not yet finished, but remarkable exhibits are brought here from all over the world. Here are scores of steam-engines and machines, beginning almost with Watt's boiler. All the machines are set in foundations, so that after the opening of the museum they will be able to perform, actually demonstrating ancient technique. Among them are extraordinarily elaborate models—clumsy, heavy, on cast-iron Corinthian columns, painted with green oil paint. The automobile department is tremendous. Here evidently have been assembled all the types and models of automobiles that have ever existed anywhere in the world. And it cannot be said that a conception of beauty was foreign to the builders of automobiles of thirty years ago. Of course, almost all these machines seem strange to our eye today. Yet among them are some beautiful examples. Here is a lot of red copper, shining green brass, plate glass, and morocco leather. On the other hand, these automobiles underline the greatness of contemporary automobile technique: they show how much better automobiles are made now, how much cheaper, simpler, stronger, and more elegant.

Perhaps Henry Ford himself does not yet know what his museum will look like. One does not feel here any leading idea in the layout of the departments and in the disposition of the exhibits. But evidently Henry Ford was moved by one aim—to gather together all examples of ancient technique scattered all over the world and uncared for, before it all rusts away and falls apart on dump heaps. He is in a hurry. Newer and newer exhibits are constantly being brought to this museum. Here are wooden ploughs, harrows, wooden spinning wheels, the first sewing machines, the first typewriters, ancient gramophones, engines, locomotives, trains.

On rails embedded in the polished hardwood floor stands an antique train with carved cast-iron bars on tambours. The outside walls of the cars are painted in rosettes and leaves, while under the windows, inside of medallions, are painted country scenes. The carriages are attached to a small engine with bronze headlights, handle bars and emblems. On just such a train some seventy-five years ago a little boy by the name of Edison was selling newspapers to the passengers. On just such a train he received the historic box on the ear from a conductor, after which he lost his sense of hearing. In 1927, during the celebration of Edison's eightieth birthday, Mr. Ford, who is no longer a youngster himself, arranged for a very touching celebration. The old railway branch line between Detroit and Dearborn was restored, and this very same train, with its flowers and country scenes, carried the great inventor. Just as he had done seventy-five years ago, Edison sold newspapers to the guests who sat in this train. The only thing lacking was the rough-neck conductor who had thrown the boy off the train. Yet, when Edison was asked whether his deafness had had any effect on his work, he replied:

"Not the slightest. I was even spared the necessity of listening to all the foolishness with which people are so generous."

The amusing train, jingling, rolled into Dearborn. All around it, on the entire globe, electricity burned, telephones rang, phonograph disks resounded, electric waves belted the world. All that had been called forth into life by this deaf old man with the face of a captain of armies, who slowly, supported by his guides and kept from falling, was passing from carriage to carriage and selling his newspapers.

Ford maintains the Edison cult in America. To a certain extent, this cult has reference to Ford himself. He is a man of the same generation as Edison. He, too, brought the machine into life and gave it to the masses.

When we were leaving the museum we saw in a vestibule a concrete plate laid in the floor. In it were the prints of Edison's feet and his signature in his own hand.

We went to another of Ford's museums, into the so-called "village"— "Greenfield village." The village covers a large territory, and to examine it visitors are given antique carriages, traps, and buggies. On the coach boxes sit coachmen in top-hats and fur coats with the fur on the outside. They crack their whips. It is as strange to see the coachmen as the horses they are driving here. No automobile is allowed to drive into Greenfield Village. We sat down in a carriage and rolled along the kind of road we had not seen in ages. It was a genuine old road, a wonder of the fifties of

D

the nineteenth century—dirt, slightly sprinkled with gravel. We rolled along it with the measured jog-trot of the landed gentry epoch.

The village is a recent undertaking of Ford's. It is difficult to say what it really is. Even Ford himself could scarcely explain the need for it. Maybe he wanted to resurrect the old, for which he pines. Or, on the contrary, maybe he wanted to emphasize the poverty of those old days by comparison with the technical wonders of today. Yet, in this undertaking there is none of the traditional and absurd eccentricity of American billionaires. Although it is not yet clear what Ford is trying to attain in his museum, it is undoubtedly wise to gather and preserve for posterity exhibits of the old technique.

Edison's old laboratory was brought in its entirety from Menlo Park into this museum village—the same laboratory where innumerable experiments had been carried on to find the thread of the first electric lamp, where this lamp was first lighted, where the phonograph first played, where a number of things happened for the first time.

In that poor wooden house with creaking floors and sooty walls was born the technique of our days. The traces of Edison's genius and his titanic application may be seen there even now. There were so many glass and metal instruments, so many jars and retorts in that laboratory that it would take a whole week only to dust them.

When we entered the laboratory we were met by a shaggy old man with ardent black eyes. On his head was a little silk skull-cap, the kind usually worn by academicians. He began to attend to us with enthusiasm. He was one of Edison's collaborators, perhaps the only one still alive today.

He threw up both his arms and cried out with all his might:

"Everything that the world received here was made by the youth and strength of Edison! Edison in his old age was nothing compared with the young Edison! He was a lion of science!"

And the old man showed us a gallery of Edison's photographic portraits. In one of these the young inventor resembles Bonaparte, a proud bang falling across his pale forehead. On another he looks like Chekhov in his student days. The old man continued to wave his hands with great animation. It occurred to us to wonder how an American could muster such powers of exultation. But we soon discovered that the old man was a Frenchman.

Speaking about his great friend, the scientist became more and more wound up. We proved to be attentive listeners, and were amply rewarded for that. The old man showed us the first electric lamp that ever burned in the world. He even showed us, by means of impersonations, how it occurred, how they all sat around the little lamp, awaiting the results. All the little threads lighted for an instant and at once went out. But finally they found the one thread that would not go out. They sat for an hour, and the lamp glowed. They sat for two hours, without stirring. The lamp still glowed. They sat through the night. That was victory.

"Science can go nowhere away from Edison!" cried the old man.

"Even the radio tubes of our day were born with the light of this incandescent lamp."

With trembling yet deft hands the old man attached the first Edison lamp to a radio set and caught several stations. The amplification was not great, but it was sufficiently audible.

Then the old scientist seized a piece of zinc paper and placed it in the phonograph, that first machine which began to speak with a human voice. Until then machines could only roar, rumble, or whistle. The phonograph was started, and into the horn the old man spoke the very same words which once in his presence had been spoken into the same horn by Edison. These were the words of the old children's song about Mary and Her Little Lamb, which ends up with laughter.

"Ha, ha, ha!" the phonograph said clearly.

We had the feeling that this instrument had been born in our presence.

"That night Edison became immortal!" the old man cried.

Tears appeared in his eyes.

And he repeated:

"Youth was Edison's strength!"

Having learned that we were writers, the old man suddenly became serious. He looked at us solemnly and said:

"Write only what you think, not for England, not for France, but write for the whole world!"

The old man did not want to let us go. He talked to us about Ford, again about Edison, about the Abyssinian War, cursing Italy, cursing war, and praising science. In vain did Mr. Adams try in the course of an hour to inject one word into this storm of thoughts, conceptions, and exclamations. He could not manage to do it. The Frenchman did not give him a chance to open his mouth. Finally, it was time to bid farewell, and here both old men showed us how it should be done. They slapped each other's arms, shoulders, and backs.

"Good-bye, sir!" cried Adams.

"Good-bye, good-bye!" the old man shouted.

"Thank you very, very much!" cried Adams, going down the stairs. "Thank you very much indeed!"

"Very! Very!" we heard from above.

"No, gentlemen," said Mr. Adams, "you don't understand anything. There are some very good people in America."

And he took out of his pocket a large red-checked family-sized handkerchief and, without taking off his spectacles, wiped his eyes with it.

When we drove past the laboratory we were informed that Mr. Ford had not yet arrived. We went on to the Ford headlight factory located fifteen miles from Dearborn. Our young guide proved quite unexpectedly to be a conversationalist, so he entertained us all the way down the road. We learned that the Ford factories have their own police force. It is composed of five hundred men; among them is the former chief of the Detroit police, and Joe Louis, the world's boxing champion. With the aid of these capable gentlemen complete peace reigns in Dearborn. There were no trade-union organizations there yet. They had been driven underground.

The factory for which we were bound presented a special interest. This was no mere factory, but the epitome of a definite new technical and political idea. We heard a lot about it, because it is very much the theme of the day in connection with all the talk one hears in America about the dictatorship of the machine and about how to make life happy while preserving at the same time the capitalist system.

In conversation with us, Mr. Sorensen and Mr. Cameron, who together represent the right and left hands of Henry Ford, told us that if they had to build the Ford enterprises all over again, they would never have constructed a gigantic factory. Instead of one factory they would have constructed a hundred midget factories located a certain distance from each other.

We heard a new slogan in Dearborn: "Country life with city earnings."

"Imagine," we were told, "a little forest, a field, a quiet river, even a very small one. Here is a small factory. Around it live farmers. They cultivate their plots and they also work in our little factory. Excellent air, good houses, cows, geese. When a depression begins and we cut down production, the worker will not die of hunger, because he has land, bread, milk. You know we are no benefactors; we are concerned with other things. We build good cheap automobiles. If these midget factories did not produce considerable technical results, Mr. Henry Ford would never have turned to that idea. But we have already determined with precision that in a midget factory, where there is no great congregation of machines and workers, the productivity of labour is much higher than in a big factory. Thus, the worker leads a healthy and inexpensive country life while he has a city income. Moreover, we free him from the tyranny of the merchants. We noticed that as soon as we raise wages even a little, all the prices in Dearborn rise in proportion. That will stop with the disappearance of concentration in one place of hundreds of thousands of workers."

This idea occurred to Ford, as he later told us, some twenty years ago. Like all American undertakings, it had first been tested over a long period of time before being applied on a wide scale. Now there are about twenty of these midget factories, and Ford expects to increase their number every year. Distances between factories of ten, twenty, or even fifty miles is no problem to Ford. Considering the ideal condition of American highways, that is no problem at all.

And so everything in this idea tends in the direction of general welfare. Country life, city earnings, the depression is not terrible, technical perfection is attained. There was one thing we were not told, that there was important politics in this idea—to rid themselves of the dangerous concentration of workers in large industrial centres. Incidentally, the special Ford police would then have nothing to do. Even they could be given a cow apiece for good measure. Let the great Negro, Joe Louis, milk himself some milk bucolically and let the former chief of the Detroit police wander over the fields with a wreath on his brow, like Ophelia, and mutter:

"I have nothing to do. I am bored, bored, gentlemen!"

With Americans, words lead to action. Having reached the top of a hillock, we saw the picture which had been so graphically described to us. The headlight factory was located on a small river, where the dam created only a seven-foot fall of water. But this was sufficient for bringing two small turbines into activity. Around the factory there were actually a small wood and a meadow. One could see farms, hear the crowing of cocks, the clucking of hens, the barking of dogs—in a word, all the country sounds.

The factory itself is one small building made almost entirely of glass. The most remarkable thing about it all is that this factory in which only five hundred men work was making headlights, tail-lights, and ceiling lights for all the other Ford factories. In the midst of feudal cock-crowing and pig-squealing, the factory in one hour makes a thousand headlights, six hundred tail-lights, and five hundred ceiling lights. Ninety-seven per cent. of the workers are farmers, and each one of them tills from five to fifty acres of land. The factory works in two shifts. But if it worked full strength, its production would be one and a half times its present one. What workers who have no acres will do is not mentioned in the new idea, although those are the people who make up the entire working class of the United States.

In spite of the village landscapes spread around the factory, the workers who crowded around the small conveyors had the same sombrely intent expression as the Dearborn people. When the bell sounded for lunch, the workers, just as in Dearborn, sat down on the floor and quickly consumed their sandwiches.

"Listen," we said to the manager—that is, to the director of the factory, who walked with us along the conveyor. "Do you know how many headlights you have produced today?"

The manager walked up to the wall, where long narrow papers hung on a nail, took off the top one, and read:

"Up to twelve o'clock we made 4,023 headlights, 2,438 tail-lights, and 1,192 ceiling lights."

We looked at our watches.

It was a quarter-past twelve.

"I receive information about the production every hour," the manager added, and hung the paper on the nail.

We again drove to the Ford office. This time we were met by Mr. Cameron, who came out hurriedly to greet us and asked us to come in. In his office, Mr. Cameron counted us with his eyes and asked that another chair be brought in. We sat in our overcoats. We were not comfortable in them, but when we finally decided to take them off Henry Ford appeared in the doorway. He looked quizzically at his guests and bowed. There was a bit of commotion accompanied by handshaking, and, as a

result of this transmigration, Ford found himself in that corner of the room
where there was no chair. Mr. Cameron soon rectified matters. Ford sat
down in a chair, crossed his legs, and lightly began swinging one leg over
the other. He was a thin, almost flat, slightly stooping old man with a
clever wrinkled face and silver hair. He wore a new grey suit, black shoes,
red necktie. Ford looked younger than his seventy-three years, and only
his old brown hands with their swollen knuckles betrayed his age. We
were told that occasionally in the evenings he goes out dancing.

We began at once to talk about the midget factories.

"Yes," said Mr. Ford, "I see the possibility of creating small factories,
even steel foundries. But so far I am not yet opposed to large factories."

He said that he sees the future country covered with small factories,
sees the workers liberated from the oppression of traders and financiers.

"The farmer," continued Ford, "makes bread. We make automobiles.
But between us stands Wall Street, the banks, which want to have a
share of our work without doing anything themselves."

At this point he quickly waved his hand before his face, as if he were
chasing away a mosquito, and said:

"They know how to do only one thing—to scheme tricks, to juggle
money."

Ford detests Wall Street. He knows full well that if Morgan is given
even one share of stock, all the other shares will soon likewise be his.
The Ford enterprise is the only one in the United States not dependent
on the banks.

In the course of the conversation, Ford was constantly moving his
feet. He either pressed them against the desk or crossed his legs, holding
them up with his hands, or again placed both his feet on the floor and
began to sway. His eyes are set close together, the prickly eyes of a
peasant. As a matter of fact, he looks very much like a sharp-nosed
Russian peasant, a self-made inventor, who suddenly had his beard shaved
off and put on an English suit of clothes.

Ford goes to work when all the others go and spends his entire day
at the factory. To this very day not a single blueprint goes out without
his signature. We have already said that Ford has no office of his own.
Cameron had this to say about him:

"Mr. Ford circulates."

How much strength and will a man must have in order to circulate
with such ease at the age of seventy-three!

The Ford method of work long ago exceeded the limits of mere manufacture of automobiles or other objects. Yet, although all his activities
and the activities of other industrialists have transformed America into
a country where no one knows any longer what will happen tomorrow,
he continues to tell himself and the people around him:

"That is no concern of mine. I have my task. I make automobiles."

In farewell, Henry Ford, who is interested in the Soviet Union and is
quite sympathetic to it, asked us:

"What is the financial situation of your country now?"

The day previous we happened to have read in *Pravda* the famous article by Grinko, and were, therefore, able to give him the very latest information.

"That's very good," said the amazing mechanic, smiling suddenly the wrinkled smile of a grandfather. "Don't ever get into debt, and help one another."

We said that that is how we usually do things, but nevertheless promised to transmit his words verbatim to Michael Ivanovich Kalinin.

Again there was a little commotion accompanied by handshaking in farewell, and the inspection of one of the greatest sights in America—Henry Ford—came to an end.

17

That Horrible Town, Chicago

A WEEK had passed since our departure from New York. We gradually developed a system of travel. We spent the nights in camps or tourist homes, that is, ordinary little houses where the owners rent to travellers cheap, clean rooms with wide comfortable beds, on which you will inevitably find several thick and thin woollen, cotton, and quilted blankets, commodes with mirrors, a rocking-chair, a wall closet, a spool of thread with a needle stuck into it, which touches your heart, and a Bible on the bedtable. The masters of these houses are workers, small merchants, and widows, who successfully compete with hotels, driving the owners of the latter to commercial philosophy. Frequently along the road we met advertising signs of hotels which quite nervously pleaded with travellers to come to their senses and return their goodwill to the hotels.

LET YOUR HEART FILL WITH PRIDE WHEN YOU UTTER
THE NAME OF THE HOTEL IN WHICH YOU STOPPED

These were veiled slurs against the unknown tourist homes and camps.

"No, no, gentlemen," said Mr. Adams when dusk was falling and it was necessary to consider a lodging for the night. "I ask you seriously, do you want your heart to fill with pride? It is very interesting when a heart fills with pride while the purse is emptied in proportion."

No, we didn't want our hearts to fill with pride! So, as soon as it grew dark and our mouse-coloured car drove along the residential part of the next small town, be it Syracuse or Vienna, we stopped near a house which was distinguished from the other houses of the city only with the placard: "Rooms for Tourists." We entered and said in an uneven chorus: "How do you do?" to which we forthwith heard in response another "How do you do?" and from the kitchen emerged an elderly person in an

apron and with knitting in hand. Here Mr. Adams took the stage. A
child or a court investigator could very well envy his curiosity. Small,
fat, impatiently moving from one foot to the other and wiping his head
with a handkerchief, delighted with an opportunity to converse, he
methodically squeezed out of the hostess all the local news.

"Surely!" he exclaimed, upon learning that the town had two thousand
population, that there had been a lottery the day before, that the local
doctor was about to get married, and that not long ago there was a case
of infantile paralysis. "Surely! Of course!"

He asked the hostess how long she had been a widow, where her
children were studying, what was the price of meat, and how many
more years she had to make payments on her house at the bank.

We were already in our beds on the second floor, when from below
we still heard:

"Surely! Surely!"

Then our ears would hear the creaking of the wooden stairway.
Mr. Adams was walking upstairs and stopped for a minute at the door
of our room. He was overcome with the desire to talk.

"Gentlemen," he asked, "are you asleep?"

Receiving no reply, he proceeded to his room.

But in the morning, at seven o'clock sharp, he would take advantage
of his uncontested right as captain and chief of the expedition, would
noisily enter our room, fresh, shaven, in suspenders, with drops of water
on his eyebrows, and shout:

"Get up, get up, get up! Good morning!"

And the new day of travel would begin.

We drank tomato juice and coffee in thick cups, ate ham and eggs in
a little café on Main Street, which at that hour was sleepy and depopu-
lated, and took our places in the machine. Mr. Adams was waiting for
that moment. He would turn to us and begin to talk. And he talked
almost without interruption all through the day. He evidently consented
to go with us principally because he sensed in us good listeners and
conversationalists.

But most remarkable of all was that in no sense could he have been
called an idle chatterer. Everything he said was interesting and wise.
Throughout the two months of the journey he never once repeated
himself. He possessed accurate information on almost all phases of life.
An engineer by profession, he had recently retired and was living on a
small capital which, in addition to modest means, gave him independence,
something he treasured very much and without which he evidently could
not live a minute.

"Only by sheer accident I did not become a capitalist," Mr. Adams
told us on one occasion. "This is quite serious. It will be interesting for
you to hear this. There was a time when I dreamed of becoming a rich
man. I made a lot of money and decided to insure myself, so that by
the age of fifty I would receive large sums from insurance companies.

There is such a form of insurance. I had to pay colossal premiums. But I agreed to that in order to be a rich man in my old age. I selected two of the most respectable insurance companies in the world. The Petersburg Rossiya Company and another very honest German company in Munich. Gentlemen! I felt that even if the rest of the world goes to the devil, nothing could ever happen in Germany and Russia. Their stability was beyond all doubt. But in 1917 you had a revolution, and the insurance company Rossiya went out of existence. Then I transferred all of my hopes to Germany. In 1923 I was exactly fifty years old. I had four hundred thousand marks coming to me. That's very big money, that's colossal money! And in 1923 I received from the Munich Insurance Company a letter like this: 'Most respected Herr Adams: Our company congratulates you on your fiftieth birthday and attaches herewith a cheque for four hundred thousand marks.' This was the most honest insurance company in the world. But, gentlemen, listen! This is very interesting. For all of that money I could buy only one box of matches, because at that time in Germany there was inflation and bills in denominations of billions circulated through the country. I assure you, capitalism is the most elusive thing in the world. But I am happy. I received the greatest prize of all. I did not become a capitalist."

Mr. Adams had an easy-going attitude toward money—a little humour, and very little respect. In that sense he did not at all resemble an American. A real American is ready to be humorous about everything in the world but not about money. Mr. Adams knew many languages. He had lived in Japan, Russia, Germany, India, knew the Soviet Union well —better than many Soviet people know it. He had worked at Dnieprostroi, in Stalingrad, Cheliabinsk. A knowledge of old Russia made it possible for him to understand the Soviet land as it is rarely understood by foreigners. He had travelled across the U.S.S.R. in hard cars, entered into conversation with workers and collective farmers. He saw the country not only as it opened to his gaze, but he saw it as it had been yesterday and as it would become tomorrow. He saw it in motion, and for that purpose he studied Marx and Lenin, read the speeches of Stalin, and subscribed to *Pravda*.

Mr. Adams was very absent-minded. Yet his was not the traditional meek absent-mindedness of a scientist, but rather the stormy, aggressive absent-mindedness of a healthy person full of curiosity carried away by a conversation or a thought and for the time being forgetting the rest of the world.

In everything concerned with the journey Mr. Adams was unusually careful and conservative.

"This evening we shall arrive in Chicago," said Mrs. Adams.

"But, Becky, don't talk like that! Maybe we'll arrive and maybe we won't," he replied.

"Look here," we intervened. "It is only a hundred miles to Chicago, and if we figure that we make an average of thirty miles an hour . . ."

D*

"Yes, yes, gentlemen!" muttered Mr. Adams. "Oh, but! You don't know anything yet."

"What do you mean, we don't know? It is now four o'clock. We are averaging thirty miles an hour. Thus, we shall be in Chicago at about eight o'clock."

"Maybe we will and maybe we won't. Seriously, gentlemen, seriously, nothing is certain. Oh, no!"

"But what will keep us from reaching Chicago by eight o'clock?"

"You mustn't talk like that! It would be simply foolish to think like that. You don't understand that."

Yet he talked with assurance about world politics and did not want to hear any contradiction. For example, he declared that there would be war in five years.

"But why in exactly five? Why not in seven?"

"No, no, gentlemen! Exactly in five years!"

"But why?"

"Don't ask me why! I know. I tell you there will be war in five years!"

He became very annoyed when contradicted.

"No, no, we won't talk about it!" he exclaimed. "It is downright foolish and ridiculous to think that there will be no war in five years!"

"All right. When we get to Chicago this evening we'll talk about it seriously."

"Gentlemen, you mustn't talk like that—we will be in Chicago this evening. Maybe we'll get there and maybe we won't!"

Not far from Chicago our speedometer indicated the first thousand miles. We shouted hurrah!

"Hooray! Hooray!" cried Mr. Adams, jumping up excitedly on his little cushion. "Hear, hear, gentlemen! Now I can tell you quite definitely: we have covered a thousand miles. Yes, yes! Not 'maybe we have covered'; but we have surely covered it! Now we know!"

Every thousand miles it was necessary to change the oil in the machine and to grease it.

We stopped near a service station, which in the moment of need was always at hand. Our machine was lifted on a special electrical frame and, while the mechanic in a striped cap drained out the dark, polluted oil, poured in the new, tested the brakes and greased the parts, Mr. Adams learned how much the man earned, where he was from, and how the people in this town lived. Every, even a passing, acquaintance-ship gave Mr. Adams a lot of pleasure. This man was born to mingle with people, to be friends with them. He derived the same pleasure from conversations with a waiter, a druggist, a passer-by from whom he found out about the roads, a six-year-old Negro boy, whom he called "sir," the mistress of a tourist home, or the director of a large bank.

He stood, his hands deep in the pockets of his top-coat, his collar up, without a hat (the parcel, for some reason, did not arrive in Detroit), and greedily yessed the man with whom he was talking:

"Surely! I hear you, sir! Yes, yes, yes! Oh, but, this is very, very interesting! Surely!"

Chicago at night—we were approaching along the broad shore drive that separates the city from Lake Michigan—proved to be astoundingly splendid. To the right was blackness filled with the measured roar of a sea as its waves broke against the shore. Along the shore drive, almost touching each other, several rows of automobiles moved at inordinate speed, casting on the asphalt pavement the dazzling reflection of their headlights. On the left rows of skyscrapers stretched for several miles. Their lighted windows faced the lake. The lights of the upper stories of the skyscrapers mingled with the stars. The electric advertisements seemed possessed. Here, as in New York, electricity was trained. It extolled the same gods: Coca-Cola, Johnny Walker Whisky, Camel Cigarettes. Here, too, were the infants that had annoyed us all through the week: the thin infant who did not drink orange juice, and his prospering antipode—the fat, good infant who, appreciating the efforts of the juice manufacturer, consumed it in horse-sized doses.

We drove up to a skyscraper with the white electric sign "Stevens Hotel." Judging by the advertising prospectus, this was the biggest hotel in the world, with three thousand rooms, huge halls, stores, restaurants, cafeterias, concert and ball-rooms. In brief, the hotel was quite like a transoceanic steamer, the comforts of which are adapted to the needs of people who for a certain time are entirely cut off from the world. Only, the hotel was much larger. One could undoubtedly live a whole lifetime there without once going out into the streets, since there is really no need for it. Perhaps only to take a walk? But one could take a walk on the flat roof of the hotel, and it is even better there than in the street. There is no risk of being run over by an automobile.

Several times we went out on the esplanade, which is called Michigan Avenue, surveyed with pleasure that remarkable avenue and the elaborate façades of skyscrapers that look out upon it, turned into the first cross street off the shore, and suddenly stopped.

"No, no, gentlemen!" cried Mr. Adams, delighted with our amazement. "You must not be amazed. Oh, but! This is America! Seriously! It would be foolish to think that the Chicago meat kings would build you a sanatorium here."

The street was narrow, not too well lighted, depressingly dull. It was crossed by quite narrow, dark, dirty lanes paved with cobblestones, real dives with the blackened brick walls of shoddy houses, fire-escapes, and garbage-cans.

We knew that Chicago has its dives, that there must be dives there. But that these were located in the centre of the city—that was a complete surprise. It looked as if Michigan Avenue were only the tinsel, and that it was only necessary to lift it in order to see the real city.

This first impression proved in the main to be correct. We wandered over the city for several days, wondering more and more at the helter-skelter accumulation of its various parts. Even from the point of view of capitalism, which has raised the simultaneous coexistence on earth of both wealth and poverty into a law, Chicago must perforce appear a heavy, clumsy, uncomfortable city. Scarcely anywhere else in the world have heaven and hell intertwined so intimately as in Chicago. Side by side with the marble and granite facing of skyscrapers on Michigan Avenue are the disgusting alleys, dirty and stinking. In the centre of the city factory chimneys jut out and trains pass, enveloping the houses in steam and smoke. Some of the poor streets look as they would after an earthquake: broken fences, twisted roofs of boarded kennels, wires askew, piles of rusty metal trash, broken chamber-pots, and half-rotted soles, filthy children in rags. Yet only a few blocks away—fine broad streets lined with trees, filled with beautiful private residences with mirror-like walls, red-brick roofs, with Packards or Cadillacs at their entrances. Ultimately this close proximity of hell makes life in paradise not too pleasant. All this in one of the richest cities, if not the very richest city, in the world!

Down the street ran newsvendors, shouting:

"Policeman murdered!"

"Bank Robbery!"

"Detective Thomas Killed!"

"Gangster Filios, Alias 'Little Angel,' Killed Instead of Detective Patterson!"

"Racketeer Arrested!"

"Kidnapping on Michigan Avenue!"

In this city shooting goes on. It would be surprising if people did not shoot here, if they did not steal millionaires' children (that is what they call kidnapping), if they did not maintain houses of ill-fame, if they did not occupy themselves with rackets. A racket is the surest and most profitable profession, if it may be called a profession. There is hardly a single form of human activity that is beyond the reach of a racket. Broad-shouldered young men in light hats walk into a store and ask the merchant to pay them—these young men in light hats—a salary, regularly, every month. For that they will try to reduce the taxes which the merchant pays the state. If the merchant does not agree, the young men take out machine-guns and begin to shoot at his counter. Then the merchant agrees. That constitutes a racket. Later other young men come in and politely ask the merchant to pay them a salary for ridding him of the first group of young men. They, too, shoot up his place. That is another racket. Trade-union officials receive money from manufacturers for calling off strikes. From the workers they likewise receive money for getting them jobs. That, too, is a racket. Artists pay ten per cent. of their earnings to employment agents even when they find the jobs themselves. That also is a racket. A doctor of internal medicine sends a man whose liver is out of order to a dentist for consultation and receives from the latter forty per cent. of his fee. That is likewise a racket.

And other things happen. Here is one told us by a Chicago doctor:

"Just before elections to the Congress of the state of Illinois," said the doctor, "a man whom I had never seen before in my life came into my house. He was a politician of the Republican party. A politician is a business man whose profession is only politics. Politics is his means of earning a livelihood. I detest people of that type: they are brazen, crude, impudent. They always have a wet cigar in their mouth, their hat is always askew, they have stupid eyes, and an imitation ring on a fat finger. 'Good mawnin', doc,' the man said to me (meaning 'Hello, doctor!'), 'who are you going to vote for?' I wanted to hit him in the mug and throw him out into the street. But having appraised the width of his shoulders, I realized that if anyone were thrown out into the street, it would most likely be I. Therefore, I said modestly that I would vote for my favourite candidate. 'All right,' said the politician. 'I believe you have a daughter who has been waiting for four years to get a job as a school-teacher.' I told him that that was so. 'All right, then,' said my uninvited guest, 'if you will vote for our candidate, we will try to get a job for your daughter. We don't promise you anything definite, but if you vote for our opponent, then I can tell you quite definitely, your daughter will never get a job, she will never be a school-teacher.' That was the end of our conversation. 'Good-bye, doctor,' he said in farewell. 'I'll come in to see you on election day.' Well, of course, I was very much ashamed. I was indignant at this outrage. But on election day he actually drove up in his automobile to call for me. Again his fat cigar came in at the door of my home. 'Good mawnin', doc,' he said, 'can I give you a lift to the voting booth?' And, do you know, I actually went with him. I thought to myself, in the end does it make any difference who is elected —a Democrat or a Republican—and maybe my daughter might get a job. I haven't told this story to anyone except you—I was so ashamed. But I am not the only one who leads such a political existence. Everywhere there is compulsion in one form or another. And if you want to be really honest, you must become a Communist. But to do that I must at once sacrifice everything, and that's too hard!"

The Chicago racket is the most famous in America. Chicago had a mayor whose name was Čermak. He came from the workers, was a trade-union leader for a while, and was popular. He was even a friend of the present President, Roosevelt. The newspapers wrote about the touching friendship of the President and the simple workman. (You see, children, what a man can attain with his own horny hands in America?) Three years or so ago Čermak was killed. He left three million dollars, fifty houses of ill-fame, which, it developed, had been kept by the busy Čermak. And so—for a certain time a racketeer was mayor of Chicago.

It does not follow from this fact that all the mayors of American cities are racketeers. The incident with Čermak, however, does give some insight into Chicago, a city in the state of Illinois.

On our first evening in New York we were disturbed by its poverty and wealth. Here in Chicago one is overcome with anger at people who, in their chase for the almighty dollar, have reared on a fertile prairie on the shores of the full-watered Michigan, this horrible town. It is impossible to accept the thought that this city arose, not as a result of poverty, but as a result of wealth, of extraordinary development in technique, of agriculture, and of cattle raising. The earth gave man all that he could take from it. Man applied himself with admirable skill. So much grain was grown, so much oil was drilled, and so many machines were built that there was enough of all to satisfy nearly half the globe. Yet, on this amply fertilized soil, instead of gleaming palaces of joy, there sprang up, in defiance of all reason, a huge, ugly, poisonous fungus, the city of Chicago in the state of Illinois. It is a kind of triumph of absurdity. Here one begins to think quite seriously that technique in the hands of capitalism is a knife in the hands of a madman.

One might say that we were too impressionable, that we are over-stating our case, that Chicago has an excellent university, a Philharmonic orchestra, presumably the best water system in the world, a wise radical intelligentsia, that here was a grandiose world's fair, that Michigan Avenue is the most beautiful street on earth. That is true! There are these things in Chicago. But all of it emphasizes more than ever the depth of the poverty, the ugliness of the buildings, and the lawlessness of the racketeers. The fine university does not teach youths how to fight poverty, the water system does not give people soup, the radical intelligentsia is powerless, the police shoot not so much at bandits as at strikers reduced to despair, the world's fair brought happiness only to the proprietors of hotels, and the most-beautiful-in-the-world Michigan Avenue loses a lot by being the neighbour of slums.

Kind people in Chicago decided to entertain us and took us to a student club in Chicago University, where a ball was held to celebrate the granting of independence to the Philippines. After seeing pictures of Chicago life, we wanted a little diversity.

The student ball was sober, gay, and pleasant in every respect. In a large hall danced broad-nosed, black-eyed, beautiful Filipino girls; across the hardwood floor also glided Japanese boys and Chinese girls; and above the crowd towered the white silk turban of a young Hindu. The Hindu was in a swallow-tail with a white shirt front—a lean seducer with ardent eyes.

"Excellent ball, gentlemen!" said Mr. Adams, tittering mysteriously.

"Don't you like it?"

"No, gentlemen! I told you: very good ball."

And he suddenly attacked the Hindu, took him aside and began to cross-examine him about his life in his dormitory, how many rupees a month his mother sends him, and to what line of work he intends to dedicate himself after graduating from the university. The Hindu politely answered all the questions, and with inexpressible boredom looked in the direction of the crowd of dancers from which he had been so suddenly dragged away.

From the ceiling were suspended Philippine and American flags. The orchestra on the stage was flooded with violet light. Musicians raised their saxophones. There it was—a harmless, quiet family ball, without drunkards, without anyone being hurt, without scandal. It was pleasant to be aware of the fact that we were present at a historic occasion. After all, the Filipinos were being liberated; independence was being given to the Philippines. It need not have been given, yet it was granted! And granted willingly! That was honourable!

All the way back to the hotel, Mr. Adams muttered something.

"Seriously, gentlemen!"

"What, seriously?"

"I want to ask you: why did we suddenly give independence to the Philippines? Seriously, gentlemen, we are good people. Just think of it, we gave them independence of our own free will! Yes, we are good people, but we don't like to have anybody stretch out his hand for our purses. These devilish Filipinos produce very cheap sugar, and, of course, they ship it here to our country without any duty. They were part of the United States until today. Their sugar was so cheap that our sugar manufacturers could not compete with them. Now that they have received from us the independence they have been hoping for so long, they will have to pay duty for sugar, like other foreign merchants. At the same time, we really don't lose the Philippines, because the good Filipinos consented to take their independence from us only on condition that we leave with them our army and our administration. Now, tell me, gentlemen, could we deny them this request? No! Truly, I want you to appreciate our honourableness! I demand it!"

18

The Best Musicians in the World

IN THE evening, having carelessly left our automobile in front of the hotel entrance, we went to a concert by Kreisler.

Rich America has taken possession of the best musicians in the world. In New York, in Carnegie Hall, we heard Rachmaninoff and Stokowski.

Rachmaninoff, according to what a composer told us, before coming out on the stage sits in his dressing-room and tells anecdotes. But as soon as the bell rings, he rises from his seat and, assuming the expression of a Russian exile's great sorrow, goes forth to the stage.

The night we went to hear him he appeared, tall, bent, and thin, with a long, sad face, his hair closely clipped; he sat down at the piano, separated the folds of his old-fashioned black swallow-tail, adjusted one of his cuffs with his large hand, and turned to the public. His expression seemed to say: "Yes, I am an unfortunate exile and am obliged to play before you for your contemptible dollars, and for all this humiliation I ask very little—silence."

There was such dead silence, as if the thousand auditors in the gallery lay dead, poisoned by some new, hitherto unknown, musical gas. Rachmaninoff finished. We expected an explosion. But in the orchestra only normal applause resounded. We did not trust our ears. We sensed cold indifference—as if the public had come, not to hear remarkable music remarkably played, but rather to discharge a dull duty. Only from the gallery did we hear several enthusiastic exclamations.

All the concerts we attended in America produced the same impression. All of fashionable New York was at the concert of the famous Philadelphia Orchestra, conducted by Stokowski. It is incomprehensible what guides fashionable New York. The fact is that it does not go to all the concerts. Meat and copper kings and princes of chewing gum in swallowtails, railroad queens, and simply dollar princesses in décolleté and diamonds, took their places in the dress circle. Stokowski evidently knew that music alone was not enough for this public, that it needed also the outer trimmings. So the talented director devised for himself an effective entrance, almost a circus entrance. He no longer abided by the traditional striking of the baton against the music rack. Prior to his appearance the orchestra tuned its instruments, and then there was utter silence. He came out from behind the curtains, slightly bent, looking like Meyerhold. Without so much as glancing at anyone, he walked to his place in front of the stage, flung up his arms suddenly, and just as suddenly began the overture to *Die Meistersinger*. It was a tempo purely American. Not a second of hesitation. Time is money! The performance was faultless. It stirred no emotions in the hall.

Meat and copper kings and railroad queens, princes of chewing gum and dollar princesses were interested at the time in Bach, Brahms, and Shostakovich. Why they were drawn at the same time to the profound and abstruse Bach, to the cold Brahms, and to the stormy, ironical Shostakovich, they did not know, of course, did not wish to know, and would never know. A year hence, just as madly ("Oh, what a strong, all-embracing feeling!"), they will be carried away at the same time by Mozart, Tchaikovsky, and Prokofiev.

The bourgeoisie had stolen art from the people, but it did not even wish to support that stolen art. Performers are bought in America, and big money is paid for them. The bored rich men have had their fill of the Chaliapins, Heifetzes, Horowitzes, Rachmaninoffs, Stravinskys, Giglis, and Totti del Montes. It is not at all difficult for a millionaire to pay ten dollars for a ticket. But as for opera or a symphonic orchestra— that, you see, is too expensive. Those forms of art in all the world demand donations. The state does not give money for it. Well-known American charity remains. The benefactors keep up in America only three opera houses, and of those only the New York Metropolitan Opera works regularly a whole three months a year. When we remarked that in

Moscow there are four opera houses which work the year around, except for an interval of three months, Americans wondered politely, but in the depths of their hearts they did not believe us.

A few years ago the Maecenases got a public slap in the face from the great director Toscanini, who at that time conducted the New York Philharmonic. The affairs of the Philharmonic were in a bad way. There was no money. The Maecenases were preoccupied with their businesses and gave no thought to the fate of clarinets, cellos, and bass viols. Finally came the moment when the Philharmonic had to close its doors. That coincided with the seventieth birthday of Arturo Toscanini. That great musician found a way out. He did not turn to the meat and copper kings for money. He turned to the people. After a radio concert he asked every radio listener to send a dollar in exchange for a photograph which Toscanini would autograph. And Toscanini was rewarded for his long and difficult life. The Philharmonic received the necessary means, received it from people who did not have the money to buy tickets to a theatre and to see the living Toscanini. It is said that the majority of these people were poor Italian immigrants.

In the life of Toscanini was a small, but interesting, occurrence:

When he was a director of La Scala, in Milan, a competition was announced for the best opera. Toscanini was a member of the jury. A certain quite untalented composer, before presenting his manuscript, spent a long time flattering the famous musician and paying court to him in every way. He asked that his opera be submitted separately to Toscanini for the latter's opinion. That opinion was unfavourable. The opera was rejected. Ten years passed, and the talentless composer again met Toscanini, this time in New York.

"Well, maestro, it is a matter of the past," the composer said to him, "but I should like to know why you then rejected my opera."

"I didn't like it," replied Toscanini.

"But I am sure, maestro, that you never even read it. If you had read it, you could not have failed liking it."

"Don't talk nonsense," replied Toscanini, "I remember your manuscript perfectly. It's no good. Listen to this!" He sat down at the grand piano and played from memory several passages from the dead opera which he had rejected ten years before. "No, it's no good," he kept saying as he played. "It's beneath all criticism!"

And then came the evening when we went to a Kreisler concert after carelessly leaving our automobile in front of the hotel. A cold wind blew from the lake. We were quite chilled, although we had to go only a short distance. We were glad that we had bought our tickets ahead of time.

The foyer was quite empty. In fact, at first we thought that we were late, and that the concert had already begun. In the hall itself there were few people, not more than half the hall being occupied.

"The Chicagoans certainly like to come late," we decided.

But it was unfair of us and premature to accuse Chicagoans of unpunctuality, for they really are a punctual people. They did not come late. They simply did not come at all. The concert began and ended in a half-empty hall.

On the stage stood an elderly man in a broad cutaway, a man with quite a large stomach on which dangled a watch chain with fobs. There he stood, his legs apart, holding on to his violin with an irate chin. That was Kreisler, the greatest violinist in the world. The violin is a precarious instrument. One cannot play on it passably well or merely well, as on a piano. Mediocre violin playing is frightful, while good violin playing is mediocre and scarcely tolerable. The violin must be played remarkably well. Only then can the performance afford any pleasure. Kreisler played with the utmost perfection. He played subtly, poetically, and wisely. In Moscow he would have received an ovation of half an hour after such a concert. It would have been necessary to take away the piano and to put out all the lights in order to stop the ovation. But here, as in New York, his playing called forth no rapture from the public. They applauded Kreisler, but one did not feel gratitude in their applause. The public seemed to be saying to the violinist: "Yes, you know how to play the violin. You have brought your art to perfection. But, after all, art is not such a very important thing. Is it worth while to get excited about it?" Kreisler evidently wanted to stir the public up a bit. It would have been better if he had not done it. He turned to pieces which were increasingly banal—pretty little waltzes and other light pieces—the productions of low taste. He finally attained his objective, for the public came to life and demanded encores. It was the great humiliation of a great artist who had begged for charity.

We came out on Michigan Avenue with a heavy heart.

"There, there, gentlemen," Mr. Adams told us. "You demand too much from America. A score of years ago something very interesting happened to me. You will find it interesting to hear this. The first time Wagner's *Parsifal* was presented in New York I went, of course. I love Wagner very much. I took my place in the seventh row and prepared to listen. Beside me sat a large red-haired gentleman. Five minutes after the beginning of the performance I noticed that the red-haired gentleman was asleep. That would not have been so terrible if in his sleep he had not leaned on my shoulder and emitted a quite unpleasant snore. I wakened him. But a minute later he was again asleep, all the time leaning his head on my shoulder, as if it were a pillow. Gentlemen, I am not a mean man, but I could not endure this. With all my strength I shoved my elbow into the red-headed gentleman's side. He awakened and stared at me for a long time with an uncomprehending look. Then I saw suffering on his face. 'I beg your pardon, sir,' he said, 'but I am a very unhappy man. I came from San Francisco to New York for two days only, and I have many things to attend to. But in San Francisco I have a wife, who is a German. You know, sir, the Germans are crazy people; they are mad about music. My wife is no exception. When I was leaving, she said,

"James, give me your word that you will go to the first performance of *Parsifal*. What a treat to be at the first performance of *Parsifal*! Since I cannot go, at least you must go. You must do it for me. Give me your word of honour." I gave her my word, and we business people know how to keep our word. And so, I am here, sir!' I advised him to go back to the hotel, since he had already kept his word and there was no danger that he would become a dishonest person, and he immediately ran away after warmly pressing my hand. You know, I liked that red-headed gentleman. You must not judge Americans too harshly. They are an honest people. They deserve the utmost respect."

While listening to Mr. Adams's tale we walked up to the hotel, and here to our great horror we did not find our automobile. Our sedately mouse-coloured car had disappeared. Mrs. Adams looked in her bag and did not find the key. The most terrible thing that could have happened to anyone on the road had happened to us. The automobile had disappeared, key, licence, and all.

"Oh, Becky, Becky," Mr. Adams wailed in despair. "I told you, I told you . . ."

"What did you tell me?" asked Mrs. Adams.

"Oh, but! Becky! What did you do? Everything is lost! I told you, you must be careful!"

We recalled that in the machine were the suitcases we had packed away for the road, since we had decided to leave Chicago immediately after the concert and to spend the night in some little town. We walked along Michigan Avenue, literally tottering from grief. We no longer felt the icy wind that blew our overcoats apart.

Then suddenly we saw our car. There it was—on the opposite side of the street. The left front wheel was on the sidewalk, the doors were open. Inside, the light was on, and even the headlights of our sedate mouse-coloured treasure shone in confusion.

We ran to it, yelping with joy. What luck! Everything was in its place, including the key, the licence, and the baggage. Preoccupied with the examination of the automobile, we did not notice the approach of a huge policeman.

"Is that your automobile?" he asked in a thunderous voice.

"Yes, sir!" Mr. Adams piped in fright.

"A-a-a!" roared the giant, looking down upon fat little Adams. "Do you know—the devil take you!—where to park a machine in the city of Chicago?"

"No, Mr. Officer," Adams replied meekly.

"I am not an officer!" cried the policeman. "I am only a policeman! Don't you know that you must not leave your automobile in front of a hotel on a thoroughfare like Michigan Avenue? This is not New York. I'll teach you to drive in Chicago!"

Mr. Adams evidently thought that Mr. Officer would beat him up, so he shielded his head with his arms.

"This is not New York," shouted the policeman, "where you can throw your trough in the middle of the main street!" He was evidently settling some ancient account with New York. "Do you know that I had to squeeze myself into your lousy little car, move it to this place, and then watch it for two hours, so that no one should steal it?"

"Yes, Mr. Officer!" chimed in Adams.

"I am not an officer!"

"Oh, no! Mr. Policeman! I am very, very sorry! I apologize most humbly!"

"Well," said the policeman, softening, "this is Chicago and not New York!"

We thought that he would give us a ticket (whoever gets a ticket must appear in court), that we would be fined mercilessly, and maybe even placed in the electric chair (who can tell about the customs of Chicago?). But the giant suddenly laughed aloud in a terrifying basso and said:

"Well, run along. But next time remember, this is Chicago, not New York!"

We hastily got into the machine.

"Good-bye!" cried Mr. Adams, who became lively again after the machine started. "Good-bye, Mr. Officer!"

In reply we heard only an indistinct roar.

PART III

TOWARD THE PACIFIC OCEAN

19

In Mark Twain's Country

AT THE beginning of our journey we passed through the states of New York, Pennsylvania, Ohio, Michigan, Indiana, and Illinois. The names of countless little cities where we had lunch or dinner, where we went to the motion-picture theatre, or where we spent the night, remained in our memories. Poughkeepsie, Hudson, Albany, Troy, Auburn, Waterloo, Avon, Fredonia, Erie, Sandusky, Toledo, Peoria, Springfield.

In all these towns, and in hundreds of others unmentioned here, on the main square stand monuments to the soldier of the Civil War, the war between the North and the South. These are very nice monuments, small in stature, and not at all militant. Somewhere in old Europe a bronze or stone warrior inevitably waves his sword or gallops on a rearing horse, or, at any rate, he shouts something in the nature of, "Forward, wonderful heroes!" But the monuments of American cities are entirely devoid of exuberance. The little soldier stands, idly leaning on a rifle, the haversack on his back is buttoned in accordance with the rules and regulations, his head droops on his arm, and at almost any moment this fighter for the liberation of the Negroes may doze off, lulled to slumber by the peaceful autumn atmosphere.

These momuments were imported from Germany. They are quite alike. They do not differ from one another any more than a standard model of one Ford differs from the next, which may differ by an ash-tray and therefore may cost half a dollar more. Some of the cheap little soldiers are so small that you could keep them in your room. Others, more expensive, were somewhat like the one we have just described. There is, if one may put it that way, a de luxe model of a soldier at whose feet lies a cannon-ball. To make a long story short, this German merchandise was available in all prices, so that each little town chose its monument according to its means. It is only comparatively recently that Americans freed themselves from such dependence on foreign countries and at last began to make cast-iron and stone soldiers with their own hands and out of their own materials.

Besides that, each American town, the denizens of which are not devoid of a legitimate feeling of patriotism, has likewise at its disposal a cannon of the times of the same war between the North and the South, and a small pile of cannon-balls. The cannon and the cannon-balls are usually placed not too far from the soldier, and together make up the military and historical division of the town. Its contemporary part is already known to us. It is composed of automobile establishments, drug-stores, restaurants, five-and-ten-cent stores, and grocery stores belonging to the firm "Atlantic and Pacific." The stores of that company are built according to one model, and no matter in what corner of the land a customer may find himself, he always knows that in an Atlantic and Pacific store pepper stands on a certain shelf, vanilla on such and such a shelf, and coconut on such and such a shelf. This magnificent sameness even invests the Atlantic and Pacific company with certain attributes of immortality. One imagines that in case of the destruction of our planet, the last lights to go out would be in the stores of this Atlantic and Pacific company which so zealously and devotedly serves the consumer, offering him always a wide and fresh assortment of grocery goods, from bananas to cigarettes and cigars of domestic as well as imported tobacco.

The same inclement weather pursued us throughout the journey. Only on the first day of our trip did the frozen sun light the way. In Buffalo it was already raining, while in Cleveland the rain increased. In Detroit it became real punishment, while in Chicago it was succeeded by a ferociously cold wind that tore off hats and almost put out electric signs.

Shortly before we reached Chicago in rain and fog we saw the murky phantom of the metallurgical plant at Gary. Metallurgy and inclemency conspired to create a depressing ensemble that gave us goose-pimples. Only the day after our mad dash out of Chicago did we first see the blue sky across which the wind quickly and unceremoniously chased the clouds.

The roads changed—not the road itself but rather everything that surrounded it. We had passed at last through the industrial East and found ourselves in the Middle West.

There are three true indications whereby Americans infalliby determine whether the real West has actually begun. From the show windows of small restaurants and drug-stores announcements advertising "hot dogs" disappear. A "hot dog" is not really far removed from an ordinary dog —it is a hot sausage. Throughout the world there are witticisms concerning sausages and dogdom, but only in Eastern America has this witticism become current to the extent of making dog the official name for sausage.

Instead of "hot dogs" the restaurants and drug-stores display in their show windows placards advertising a purely Western edible: "barbecue," sandwiches of grilled pork.

Then, instead of the optimistic "all right" and "O.K." in the conversation of Westerners one hears the no less optimistic but purely local "you bet!" which means "I wager" but is used for all occasions. For example, if you should ask just as a matter of form whether the steak you order on Dinner # 3 is likely to taste good, the girl will answer with a pleasant smile:

"You bet!"

But the last and most important indication is—old automobiles, and not merely used ones, but real antiques. Machines of the year 1910 carry on their small wheels the respectable denizens of the West in droves of entire families. Perched in high old Ford coupés farmers in blue overalls with the white threads of all the seams showing, move on their way. The hefty hands of the farmers lie firmly on their steering wheels. Somewhere a family of Negroes is wandering off. In front sits a young Negro; beside him is his wife. In the back seat slumbers the grey-haired mother-in-law, while young piccaninnies examine our yellow New York licence-plate with popping eyes. The family is evidently travelling from afar, because a bucket and a wooden step-ladder are fastened to the machine. Spindle-shanked mules with long ears are pulling village wagons and drays down the road. The drivers, also in overalls, drive standing. Not once throughout the journey did we see a mule driver sitting in his wagon. That seems to be the style—to stand in his vehicle. Then more and more old Fords. Their lines are old-fashioned, a little funny, but at the same time touching. One senses respectability in them. In a curious way they suggest old Henry Ford himself. They are old and thin, but at the same time durable. They inspire confidence and respect.

Ford need have no compunction about being proud of these machines. They are twenty or twenty-five years old, yet they still run, pull, work— these honest, cheap, black horseless carriages. And always, whenever we met or overtook an ancient model, we exclaimed with candid joy:

"There goes another Old Henry!"

The Old Henry can scarcely breathe, everything in it shakes, only tatters are left of the canvas top and nothing but a rusty rim of the spare wheel, yet the old fellow moves on, does his duty, an appealing and somewhat comical automobile veteran.

We are in the West. We have been driving away from winter and toward summer. Thus we gained not only as to the season of the year, but also in time itself. From the Atlantic we moved into the Central Belt, and gained an extra hour on that. It was now ten o'clock in New York, but only nine here. On the road to San Francisco we would move our watches back twice again. From the Midwestern on to the Mountain and then to the Pacific Belt.

At the intersection of three roads, opposite a small café made of boards, which advertised as something new that it sold beer not in bottles but in tin-cans, stood a post to which were attached broad arrows with the names of towns. Besides directions and distances, the arrows pointed out that in the West Americans do the same as in the East—they choose for their cities beautiful, dignified, and famous names. It was pleasant to learn in this little town that it was only forty-two miles from there to Eden, sixty-six to Memphis, forty-four to Mexico, and a mere seventeen miles to Paris. But we chose neither Paris nor Memphis. We were looking for the city of Hannibal. The arrow indicated that we should drive to the right, and that it was thirty-nine miles to Hannibal.

"Gentlemen," said Mr. Adams, "remind me to tell you this evening about beer in tin-cans. It is a very, very interesting business."

Exactly thirty-nine miles later Hannibal appeared. A cast-iron plaque placed by "The Historical Society of the State of Missouri" before the entrance to the town, announced that here the great humourist, Mark Twain, had spent his childhood, that somewhere in this town were Mark Twain's house, a park with a view of the Mississippi River, monuments, caves, and so forth.

While we were looking for a night's lodging and Mr. Adams was finding out from the lady of the house how business was in the city, how the depression had affected it, and what our landlady, who was a neat old American lady, thought of Roosevelt, it had grown dark. We had to postpone the examination of the sights of the city recommended by the Historical Society of the State of Missouri until the next morning. While the old landlady told us at great length that business in Hannibal was so-so and that a fairly large portion of the city's income was derived from tourists who came to see the Mark Twain relics, that the depression at one time was quite bad but that they managed to get along better than in the East, and that President Roosevelt was a very good man and looked out for the interests of the poor folks, it had grown still darker. That evening we managed to visit only the Mark Twain museum, which was located on the main street.

That was a temporary museum constructed for the celebration of the one hundredth anniversary of Mark Twain's birth. It was located in the building of a bank called the Hannibal Trust Company, which had gone bankrupt shortly before the anniversary. That is why the photographs and the various relics were strangely mixed here with office partitions and the steel locks of safety deposit boxes. Over the huge (alas, for ever empty!) safe hung the steering wheel of the river-boat. A wheel just like that had been turned by Mark Twain when in his youth he was a sailor on the Mississippi. Besides us there was one other visitor, but even he had such a sad face that we had no doubt he must have been at one time a depositor of the Hannibal Trust Company and had come here only in order to take one more look at the magnificent and quite empty bank vault where at one time his modest savings had lain.

Photographs hung on the walls. In a special little room stood a bed brought here especially for the anniversary, the bed on which the author died. Everywhere lay manuscripts, first editions of his books, shoes, scarves, and black lacy fans of the little girl who was the model for Mark Twain's "Becky Thatcher." On the whole, the museum had been assembled helter-skelter, and did not present any special interest.

There was likewise in the museum a plaster model of the monument, for the construction of which a national subscription had already been announced. Here the great writer was surrounded by his heroes. Here were fifty figures, if not more. The monument would cost about a million dollars, and at such a comparatively low price would be, judging by the model, one of the most hideous monuments in the world.

We dined, or rather supped, in a lunch-room across from the museum. Mr. Adams, who never drank anything, suddenly ordered beer. The young waiter brought two tin-cans, the kind in which we sell green peas.

"This is a tremendous business," said Mr. Adams, watching the waiter open the tin-cans of beer, "and until now no one could make a go of it. The trouble was with the odour of the tin. Beer demands an oaken barrel and glassware, but you must understand, gentlemen, that it is not convenient to transport beer in bottles, besides being too costly. Bottles take up too much room. They add to the excessive expense of transportation. Recently a lacquer has been perfected which corresponds perfectly to the odour of a beer barrel, if one may say so. By the way, they looked for this lacquer to fill the needs of a certain electric production, and not for the sake of beer. Now they cover with it the inside of tin-cans, and the beer has no foreign taste at all. This is a big business!"

He drank two glasses of beer, which he really didn't like at all. He drank it out of respect for technique. The beer was quite good.

While we were leaving the tourist home in the morning we saw a small, old and not at all a well-to-do little town. It lay beautifully on hills going down to the Mississippi. The ascents and the slopes were quite as in a small town along the Volga, standing on a precipitous shore. We didn't learn the names of the little streets, but it seemed to us that they must be like the names of the streets along the Volga—Obvalnaya or Osypnaya.

So this was the city of Hannibal, the city of Tom Sawyer and Huck Finn!

A remarkable thing! This city is famous not for its production of automobiles, like Detroit, nor for slaughter-houses and bandits, like Chicago! It was made famous by the literary heroes of *The Adventures of Tom Sawyer*, the most appealing and the happiest adventures that ever existed in world literature.

As everywhere else, there were almost no people on the streets. But those whom we did meet were real Twain types. Timorous and good-natured Negroes, an honourable judge who early in the morning attached himself to a cheap cigar that dangled between his teeth, and boys without end, in velvet-belted corduroy trousers that cannot be worn out, gathered in groups and huddles. The boys were playing some game. Judging by the way they were stealthily looking to the sides, they were playing for money.

The street where Mark Twain had passed his childhood as the barefooted, bare-legged Sam Clemens has been preserved in complete faithfulness. Over the entrance to the writer's house hangs a round white lantern with the inscription "Mark Twain House." By the way, Americans do not say *Tven* but *Twain*, and they don't say *Tohm* Sawyer but *Tom* Sawyer, and even the most serious, the most businesslike American, whenever he speaks of this world-renowned boy, begins to smile and his eyes become gentle.

In the house live two poor, almost impoverished, old women, distant kin of the Clemens family. They are so old and thin that they sway like blades of grass. It is dangerous to take a deep breath in this little house, because you might blow the old ladies out the window.

The two little rooms of the first floor were dusty and crowded. No, Mr. Clemens the Elder, Mark Twain's father, although he was the editor of the local Hannibal newspaper, must have lived very modestly. The easy-chairs with their springs sticking out and the shaky tables for photographs indicated that.

"In this chair," said one of the old ladies, "Aunt Polly always sat, and it was through this window that the cat Peter jumped out after Tom Sawyer gave him castor oil. It was at this table that the entire family sat when they thought that Tom had been drowned, while he was standing right there at the time and eavesdropping."

The old lady spoke as if everything that Twain had related in *Tom Sawyer* had actually occurred. She ended up by offering photographs for sale. The old ladies exist on the income from that. Each of us bought a half-dollar photograph.

"People come in here so rarely," said the old lady with a sigh.

In the room nearest to the exit hung a memorial tablet with the image of the writer and an ideologically correct inscription composed by the local banker, a disinterested admirer of Mark Twain:

"The life of Mark Twain teaches us that poverty is a stimulus rather than a deterrent."

However, the appearance of the impoverished and forgotten old ladies eloquently refuted this stout philosophic concept.

Side by side with the house stood a low ordinary fence. But the enterprising Historical Society of the State of Missouri had already managed to attach to it a plaque which declared that this was the successor of the fence which Tom Sawyer had allowed his friends to paint in exchange for an apple, a blue glass ball, and other fine articles.

In brief the Historical Society of the State of Missouri was acting in a purely American manner. Everything was short and to the point. It did not write: "Here is the house where lived the girl who was the model for Becky Thatcher from *Tom Sawyer*." No, that would have been true, of course, but it would have been too wordy for the American tourist. He had to be told exactly whether that was or was not that particular girl. So, he was assured: "Yes, yes, don't worry! It's the very one. You did not use your petrol and time on this trip for nothing. This is she!"

And so at the house standing opposite the dwelling of old Clemens hangs another cast-iron board: "The house of Becky Thatcher, Tom Sawyer's first sweetheart."

The old ladies sold us several photographs. On one of these Becky Thatcher herself was represented in her old age. It seems that she had married an attorney. Some time before his death, Mark Twain came to Hannibal and was photographed with her. A large photograph of these two old people hangs in the museum with the touching inscription: "Tom Sawyer and Becky Thatcher."

On another photograph is represented an Indian portrayed by Twain under the name of "Indian Joe." This photograph was made in 1921. The Indian was then a hundred years old. So, at any rate, affirms the city of Hannibal.

Finally, we went to Cardiff Hill, where stands one of the rarest monuments in the world, a monument to literary heroes. Tom Sawyer and Huck Finn are on their way to some of their gay adventures. Not far from the monument fairly big boys were playing. They were in no way different from their cast-iron models. There was gay noise at the foot of the monument.

It was still quite early when we departed from Hannibal. Along the road sleepy travelling salesmen drove full-speed ahead. They work in the daytime, sleep in the evening, while at night they travel from place to place. At night the road is clear, and these demons of commerce take advantage of the possibility of racing.

We rode past cornfields and wheatfields recently harvested, past red barns and yards where metal windmills pump the water out of the wells, and toward the middle of the day we reached Kansas City. Roughly speaking, Kansas City is in the centre of America. It is approximately the same distance from there to New York, to San Francisco, to New Orleans and to the Canadian border.

And so, we were in the centre of the United States, in the centre of the prairies, in Kansas City, on the Missouri River. What could be more American than such a place? Nevertheless, the owner of the lunch-room into which we ran for a minute to warm up on a cup of coffee was a Bessarabian Jew from the city of Bendery. A microscopic Masonic star gleamed on the lapel of his coat. Bendery, Missouri, Bessarabia, Masonry —here was enough to make anyone's head whirl!

From his pocket he drew small brown photographs and showed them to us. These were his relatives who had remained in Bendery—two provincial young men whose delicate curly heads were supported by upstanding collars. At the same time the owner of the restaurant showed us his Masonic card, and told us that he had come to America thirty years ago.

"Yes," he said, "I came to America to better myself, to get rich."

"Where is your fifty thousand dollars, then?" asked Mr. Adams gaily.

"What fifty thousand dollars?" asked the proprietor.

"No, no, sir, don't say 'what'! Yours! Your fifty thousand dollars! You came to America to make money. Where is that money?"

"In the bank!" replied the lunch-room proprietor with dark humour. "There all of it lies, to the last kopeck. But not in my name."

In his figure, buffeted by years and by struggle, in his desperate humour, we seemed to recognize something familiar. Afterward, while racing down the road to Amarillo, Texas, we remembered whom our Bendery Mason resembled.

In 1933 we were in Athens. There is no need to tell how we hastened to look at the Acropolis and other ancient things. It's a long story. But one incident we must tell.

Tantalized by reminiscences of schooldays, we decided to go from Athens to Marathon. We were told how to do it. We had to go to the square from which autobuses depart for Marathon, there buy tickets and ride—that was all. We boldly started on our journey, but somewhere quite close to the square we lost our way. The barber from whom we asked the way stopped shaving his client and came out into the street to explain to us how best to go. The client also came out of the establishment and, not at all embarrassed because he was covered with lather, took an active part in working out the itinerary for us. Little by little, quite a crowd gathered, in the centre of which we stood, rather embarrassed, shy, and sorry that we had caused this commotion. Finally, to make absolutely sure, we were given a five-year-old boy as a guide.

The Greek for boy is *mikro*. The mikro led us, beckoning with his finger from time to time and parting his thick Algerian lips good-humouredly.

In the square we saw old autobuses, to the backs of which worn suitcases were tied with ropes. These were the Marathon autobuses. The silliness and dullness of our enterprise was at once clear to us. Without saying a word to each other, we decided not to take the trip. The mikro received five drachmas for his trouble, while we went to a coffee-house across the way from the bus stop, to rest and drink some of the fine Greek coffee.

Four handsome and poorly dressed young idlers played cards on a woollen carpet which covered a marble table. Behind the counter was the proprietor, a man obviously down at the heel. He wore a vest, but no collar. He was shaved, but his hair was not combed. In a word, here was a man who no longer cared for anything at all and merely continued to drag out his existence. If customers come in, very well. If not, it is also of no consequence. Anyway, he did not expect anything unusual to happen in his life. He accepted our order with indifference, and went behind the stand to make the coffee.

And then we saw on the wall a photographic portrait of the proprietor in his youth: a round, energetic head, a conquering look, moustaches pointing to the very sky, a marble collar, an eternal necktie, the strength and brilliance of youth. Oh, how many years were needed, how many failures in life, to drag down this moustached Athenian to the pathetic creature we had found! It was simply frightful to compare the portrait with its original! There was no need for any explanation. The entire life of this Greek who had failed stood before us.

This is what our lunch-room host had reminded us of—this Bessarabian Jew and Mason of Kansas City.

20

A Marine

IN AN Oklahoma newspaper we saw the photograph of a girl lying in a white hospital bed, and the inscription: "She smiles even on her couch of suffering." There was no time to try to divine the reason for the girl's smiling on her couch of suffering, and the newspaper was put aside. Mr. Adams, however, happened to read the notice under the photograph while he was taking his coffee. He wrinkled his face, and stared with displeasure into the gas fireplace in the lunch-room. We were hastily filling up on eggs and bacon before departing from Oklahoma.

In many places of the Middle West there are natural gas openings. This gas is brought in through special piping into the city and costs comparatively little. Mr. Adams looked at the pink and blue streams of flame which played in the nickel-plated fireplace and wheezed angrily.

"Gentlemen," he said, "I am myself a great optimist, yet at times I am in the throes of despair because of American optimism."

And he repeated with disgust:

"She smiles even on her couch of suffering!"

We had to hurry; hence, conversation on this theme, which so disturbed Mr. Adams, did not catch on. Along the way he seemed to have forgotten about it, carried away by the amazing view before us. We were driving through a bright aluminium oil forest.

Yesterday, racing toward Oklahoma through a steppe overgrown only with unattractive dusty bouquets, we had seen our first oil derricks. The extensive fields were tightly packed with iron masts and cages. Thick wooden shafts rocked up and down, emitting a slight creaking noise. No people were in sight. Here, in the quiet of the steppe, in profound silence, oil was being pumped. We drove a long time. The forest of derricks became thicker. The rocking shafts creaked and only occasionally one saw the figure of a workman in overalls (working clothes made out of bright blue denim). He plodded from one derrick to another.

The forest of derricks was bright, because they were all covered with aluminium paint. It was the colour of Christmas-tree tinsel. It lends to technical America an extraordinarily attractive appearance. Oil tanks, automobile tanks for milk or petrol, railroad bridges, lamp-posts in cities, and even wooden posts along the roads are covered with this aluminium paint.

In Oklahoma, too, we were greeted by derricks and by the measured rocking of their shafts. Oil was discovered in the capital itself. The derricks came closer and closer to Oklahoma City and finally, breaking down weak resistance, invaded its streets. The city was pillaged and plundered. In private yards, on sidewalks, on streets, opposite school buildings, opposite banks and hotels—everywhere oil was being pumped. Everybody who believed in God pumped. Oil tanks stood beside large ten-story buildings. The bacon and eggs reeked of oil. On a vacant lot that somehow managed to survive children were playing with pieces of iron and with rusty wrenches. Houses were demolished, their places taken by derricks and rockshafts. And where yesterday somebody's grandmother sat at a round table knitting a woollen scarf, today a rock-shaft creaked and a new master in a businesslike suède vest was joyfully counting the gallons he had extracted.

Everywhere we saw the screed-in masts and heard the optimistic creaking.

Besides oil derricks Oklahoma City astonished us with its multitude of funeral parlours. While looking for night's lodging, we usually drove in the direction of the residential part on our quest for rooms. Without looking around we drove up to a little house on which was a lighted sign, and to our horror we discovered that it was a funeral parlour. On three other occasions we blindly drove to attractively lighted buildings and each time jumped back: they were all funeral parlours. We did not find a single tourist sign; no one was renting lodgings to travellers. Here was offered only eternal rest, eternal quietude. Evidently the inhabitants of Oklahoma City had so successfully filled up on oil that they had no need of such trivial income as may be derived from the rental of rooms.

We were finally obliged to fill our hearts with pride and take rooms in a hotel. The second-rate hotel we selected after much captious choosing bore the resplendent name " Cadillac." But surely it must have been erected before the oil boom, for from the hot-water tap cold water poured, while from the cold-water tap nothing poured. Mr. Adams was genuinely worried. Instead of the talkative landlady of a little house who knew all the city news, he was confronted by a porter about fifty years old who countered all eager queries with the composed indifference of " Yes, sir " or " No, sir." Moreover, he smoked such a vile cigar that after he left us Mr. Adams coughed and blew his nose intermittently, like a drowning man recently pulled up on shore but still on the verge of collapsing. An hour later Mr. Adams came to the door of our room and knocked hopefully. Since it was quite impossible to open our eyelids, we did not reply. Mr. Adams again rapped gently on the door. There was no answer.

"Gentlemen," he said in a voice that could have broken any heart, "are you asleep?"

But we were frantic for sleep. We did not answer. Mr. Adams waited another minute at our door. He wanted so very much to talk, yet he had to go back to his room with an unburdened soul. The damned Oklahomans has spoiled his evening for him.

In the morning Mr. Adams was full of strength and gay, as usual. The concrete road went up in sweeping undulations and could be seen for several miles ahead. At the edge of the road, the thumb of his right hand up, stood a young marine, his coat unbuttoned. Beside him stood exactly the same type of soldier. The thumb of his right hand was also up. The machine travelling ahead of us passed these young men without stopping. It was apparently full. We stopped.

Thumb up means in America a request for a ride. A man who goes out on the road is certain that someone will give him a lift. If not the first machine, the fifth, the seventh, the tenth, but someone is sure to take him. Thus one may effect quite a journey—travel a hundred miles with one, another hundred with another, or maybe five hundred with the third.

We could not take two men, because there were four of us in the machine. The young men made an appointment to meet at the post office of the city of Amarillo, and one of them, stooping down, entered our automobile. He neatly placed his little suitcase at his feet, took out a cigarette and asked permission to smoke. Mr. Adams immediately turned his body around as far as possible and began to overwhelm our fellow-traveller with questions. Oh, Mr. Adams took a terrible revenge for the Oklahoma devastation! He laid the young marine out before our eyes like a laboratory specimen.

He was a mere boy, with a handsome, somewhat over-confident, even somewhat impudent face. Nevertheless, he was a rather likeable youngster. He answered all questions willingly.

There was no use worrying about his comrade. He would catch up with him in some other machine. They had done that before. They were making a long "trip," a journey. They had been given transfers in their services from New York to San Francisco. They had asked for this transfer. But they were told that they would have to make their own way. They took a month's leave and had already been on the road three weeks, moving from one automobile to another. They had expected to spend three hours in Chicago but they spent nine days there.

"We met some nice girls."

At Des Moines they had also got stuck. They were given a lift by a lady who appeared to be quite proud. Then they took out a bottle of whisky and had a drink. The lady took a drink with them, and all her pride disappeared. Then she treated them to beer; then they drove to her sister's house, whose husband was away. There they had a good time for four days until the husband returned. Then they had to run away.

The uniform cap sat jauntily on the marine's handsome head. The large buttons of his uniform shone as per regulations. On the collar gleamed the brass globe with crossed anchors. The marine was not at all given to boasting. Americans are very rarely braggarts. We asked him to tell about himself and he simply told us.

We heard a friendly roar behind us and we were overtaken by a black Buick that flashed by. Beside the driver of that car sat our fellow-traveller's comrade. They exchanged gay, incoherent yells. Our conversation continued.

The marine told us about his sojourn in France. There also he had an interesting experience. Once when their ship came to Havre, seven of them were given leave for a trip to Paris. Well, they looked over the city, then found themselves on Grand Boulevard and decided to dine. They went into a restaurant and began modestly by ordering ham and eggs. Then they got started, drank champagne, and so forth. They had, of course, no money to pay for it. How could a marine buy champagne? The garçon called the maître d'hôtel, so they told the latter:

"You know what? Deduct the price of our dinner from the war debt, the debt France still owes to America."

So there was an enormous scandal. The newspapers even took it up. But their commanding officer didn't punish them for it, and only reprimanded them.

What did he think of war?

"War? You know yourself. Not long ago we fought in Nicaragua. Don't I know that we fought not in the interests of the United States but in the interests of United Fruit, the banana company? That's just what we call this war in the fleet, the banana war. But when I'll be told to go to war, I'll go. I am a soldier, so I must submit to discipline."

His wages were twenty-five dollars a month. He expected to get better advancement in San Francisco than in New York, and that is why he had asked for a transfer. In New York he had a wife and child. He gives his wife ten dollars a month. In addition, the wife has a job. Of course, he should not have got married. He was only twenty-one years old. But since it had already happened, what could you do about it?

In Amarillo the marine left us. He gratefully saluted us for the last time, sent us his winning smile and went to the post office. He was so refreshingly young that even his misbehaviour did not seem offensive to us.

We spent the night in the plywood cabins of Amarillo Camp. We put out the stove and the gas ovens and fell asleep. The camp stood at the very edge of the road. Automobiles passed like the noise of the wind. The demonized travelling salesmen whizzed by and huge motor trucks rattled by heavily. The light of their headlights was constantly passing over the walls of our cabin.

Amarillo is a new and clean city. It grew up on wheat. And although it is not yet fifty years old, it is already a real American city. Here is a complete set of city accessories—lamp-posts covered with aluminium, dwelling-houses of polished lilac brick, a huge ten-story hotel, and several drug-stores. As the saying goes, everything the heart desires; or, rather, everything for the body. For the soul, there is exactly nothing here.

In the drug-store we saw many girls. They were having their breakfast before going to work. If at eight o'clock in the morning, or at half-past eight, a neatly dressed girl with plucked eyebrows, rouged as girls rouge only in the United States (that is, heavily and coarsely), with manicured finger-nails—briefly, ready for parade—is having her breakfast, then you know that she is about to go off to work. A girl like that dresses in accordance with her taste and means, but always neatly. Otherwise, she may not hold her job, may not work. And these girls are excellent workers. Every last one of them knows stenography, knows how to operate a comptometer, knows how to conduct correspondence and how to type. Without this knowledge she cannot secure employment. However, these days it is hard to get a job even with all this knowledge.

The majority of such girls live with their parents. Their earnings go to help their parents pay for the little house or for the refrigerator bought on the instalment plan. The future of the girl is that she, too, will some day marry. Then she herself will buy a house on instalment, and her husband will work for ten years without interruption in order to pay the three, five, or seven thousand dollars, whichever happens to be the price of the little house. And throughout the ten years the happy husband and wife will quake with fear lest they lose their jobs and have not the wherewithal for paying on the house. For then the house will be taken away. Oh, what a fearful life these millions of American people lead in the struggle for their tiny electrical happiness!

The girls wore short deerskin or muskrat jackets. They smiled as they broke off the toasted bread with their heavenly little fingers. Kind, hard-working girls, fooled by insane American happiness!

On one of the drug-store counters we saw a case of German drawing instruments.

"Mr. Adams, is it possible that America does not make its own drawing instruments?"

"Of course not!" Mr. Adams replied with ardour. "We cannot make drawing instruments. Gentlemen, don't laugh! Not that we do not want to; no, we cannot. America with all of its grandiose technique does not know how to manufacture drawing instruments. The same America which makes millions of automobiles a year! And do you know wherein the trouble lies? If the drawing instruments were needed by the entire population, we would organize mass production and would produce tens of millions of drawing instruments at an amazingly low price. But the population of the United States does not need tens of millions of drawing instruments. It needs only tens of thousands. That means that it is impossible to establish mass production, and drawing instruments would have to be made by hand. And everything which in America is made not by machinery, but by the hand of man, costs incredibly much. So our drawing instruments would cost ten times more than the German ones. Mr. Ilf and Mr. Petrov, write this down in your little books, that this great America finds itself at times helpless before pathetic old Europe. That is very, very important to know!"

E

2 1

Rogers and His Wife

A MIDDLING wide promontory of the northern part of Texas separates
the states of Oklahoma and New Mexico. On the way from Amarillo,
which is in Texas, to Santa Fé we occasionally met some of the colourful
local people.

Two cowboys were driving a herd of small steppe cows, shaggy, like
dogs. Large felt hats protected the cowboys from the hot sun of the
desert. Large spurs adorned their boots, which had elegant ladies' heels
ornamented with figures. The cowboys hooted, their horses cavorted at
full gallop. It all seemed a little more elaborate and ostentatious than it
should have been for the modest purposes of directing a herd of cows.
But there it was! You may be sure that here they know how to graze
cows! It was not for us city folk to give them advice!

In an old glass-enclosed Ford rode other cowboys. These healthy
fellows were crowded in the little machine, and they sat quite immobile,
occasionally touching each other with the rigid edges of their incredible
hats. Catching up with them, we saw through the window their rustic
profiles and their manly sideburns. Five cowboys, five hats, and five pairs of
sideburns—that was quite a load for the thin-legged Ford of the year 1917.
But Old Henry, creaking with might and main, moved ahead little by little.

Trucks with high sides were transporting horses and mules. It is, after
all, an amazing country—this America! Here even horses ride in automobiles. Surely, it is not possible to think up a greater degradation for
that animal! Over the high enclosures there mournfully emerged the
long ears of mules and occasionally the noble muzzle of a horse, the
inexpressible boredom of travel reflected in its eyes.

We had scarcely left Amarillo when we saw a new hitchhiker with
thumb up. In America hitchhikers are people who ask for a ride. Our
marine of yesterday belonged to that category. We stopped. The
hitchhiker dropped his hand. He was in overalls that revealed the
open collars of two shirts. Over his overalls he wore a light-coloured
and clean corduroy coat. He told us that he was bound for the city
of Phoenix in the state of Arizona. We were not driving in that direction,
but we were driving as far as Santa Fé, which was on the hitchhiker's
way, so we asked him to get into the machine.

Mr. Adams lost no time in beginning his interrogation.

Our fellow traveller was called Rogers. He placed his black hat on his
knees, and gladly began to tell us about himself. Another good trait of
the Americans—they are sociable.

One of Rogers's friends had written to him that he had found work
for him in Phoenix, packing fruit at eighteen dollars a week. So he had

to travel seven hundred miles and, of course, he did not have the money for such a long journey. He had not slept all night, having travelled in a freight car, where it was very cold. He met several tramps in the car. Rogers's conscience hurt him to travel without paying his fare, and so at each station he got off to help the conductors load the baggage. But the tramps slept, regardless of the cold, and their consciences did not bother them at all. Rogers was travelling from Oklahoma City. There his wife was in a hospital.

He pulled out of his pocket a newspaper clipping, and we recognized the photograph of the young woman lying in a white hospital bed and the inscription:

"She smiles even on her couch of suffering."

Mr. Adams waved his hands excitedly.

"Why, sir!" he cried. "I read about your wife in a newspaper!"

For several hours on end Rogers talked, telling us the story of his life. He spoke unhurriedly, without getting excited, without appealing to pity or to compassion. He was asked to tell about himself, so he talked.

He was originally from Texas. His father and stepfather were carpenters. He graduated from high school but did not have the means to pursue his education further. He worked in a small village cannery, where he became foreman. Work in such a factory lasts only about three months of the year. Those seasonal workers are hired who usually move with their families over the country. At first they work in the South, then gradually they go up North, where harvesting begins later. These are very real nomads. It makes no difference that they are white and that they live in America. They are settled people whom contemporary technique forced to assume a nomad form of life. Men were paid twenty cents an hour and women seventeen cents. They received their indispensable merchandise from the factory store, and the cost of it was later deducted from their salary. They also had special relations with the farmers. To farmers, the boss of such a factory gives seeds ahead of time on credit and buys their crops of vegetables on the root before harvest. And not even on the root, but rather before that. The crop is bought before anything has been planted. It does not pay the farmers to deal that way, but the boss selects springtime for the consummation of deals, when the farmers are especially badly off. In a word, the boss of such a factory knows how to make money.

Concerning the making of money, Rogers expressed himself not with indignation but with approval.

As it happens, his boss has no easy life. He is tormented by the local banks. His future is uncertain. Undoubtedly the banks will swallow him up. That is how everything ends in America.

So, he was a foreman for a small manufacturer, and married the latter's daughter. It was a very happy marriage. The young married folks did everything together—went to the motion-picture theatre, to see their friends, even danced only with each other. She was a teacher, a good and a bright girl. She did not want any children, because she feared that they might take her away from her husband. Their affairs were shipshape. During four years of living together they saved two thousand dollars. They had eighteen pedigreed cows and their own automobile. Everything went so well they could not wish for anything better. And then in February of 1934 a mishap occurred. His wife fell off a ladder and her spine was broken in a very complicated way. Operations began, , treatments, and in the course of a year and a half everything that they owned went to the doctors. When you come right down to it, it looked more like a bandit raid than humane medical help. The doctors took everything, including their savings as well as the money obtained from the sale of the eighteen pedigreed cows and the automobile. The couple was left penniless. The first hospital charged at the rate of twenty-five dollars a week and the Oklahoma City hospital had to be paid now at the rate of fifty dollars. His wife must have a metal corset; that will cost another hundred and twenty dollars.

Speaking of the doctors, Rogers did not in the least complain about them. No, he spoke of them very calmly.

"It can't be helped. Tough luck!"

When some misfortune strikes an American he seldom tries to fathom the roots of the trouble that overwhelmed him. That is not in the American character. When things go well with him he will not say that anyone had been his benefactor. He himself earned the money with his own hands. When things go badly, however, he will not blame anyone either. He will say just as Rogers told us: "Tough luck!" or "Didn't turn out right with me. That means I didn't know how to do it." The doctors robbed Rogers. Yet, instead of contemplating whether that was just or unjust, he comforted himself with the thought that it was bad luck and with the hope that a year from now he would have good luck. At times, even a note left by a man who has committed suicide contains only the one primitive thought: "I had bad luck in life."

Rogers did not complain. Yet, within one year he had lost everything. His wife had become a cripple for life, his possessions and savings had been raided by medical robbers. He himself was standing at the side of the road begging strangers for a ride. The only thing he still had left was the uplifted thumb of his right hand.

In Phoenix he expected to receive eighteen dollars a week. He planned to live on six or seven dollars. The balance he proposed to spend on his wife's treatments. The poor woman still wants to work. She was thinking of teaching Latin at home. But who in Oklahoma City will want to take Latin lessons at home? It was unlikely.

Smiling gloomily, Rogers again showed us the newspaper clipping. Under the photograph was the optimistic inscription:

"She knows that she is paralysed for life, yet she looks at the future with a smile. 'But my husband is with me,' said the poor woman when interviewed by our correspondent."

Mr. Adams suddenly seized Rogers's hand and shook it.

"Good boy!" he muttered, and turned away. "Good boy!"

Rogers put away the clipping and became silent. He seemed to be about twenty-eight years old, a self-possessed young man with a handsome, manly face and black eyes. His slight aquiline nose made him look a little Indian. Rogers soon explained to us that he was actually one-quarter Indian.

The devil take those Texans! They know how to herd cows and how to endure the blows of fate. Was it perchance the admixture of Indian blood that made our fellow traveller so stoically calm! A Frenchman or an Italian in his place would probably have fallen into religious madness, would have probably cursed God, while the American was calm. He was asked to tell about himself, so he told us.

And so we talked with him for several hours. We asked him a hundred questions, and we found out from him everything that one could possibly find out. We naturally expected that he might want to find out something from us, too. That was the more to be expected since we talked among ourselves in Russian, a language which he had hardly heard in Texas. Would not the sound of this speech which he had never heard before arouse his interest in his interlocutors? But he did not ask us anything, was not interested to know who we were, where we were going, what language we were speaking.

Surprised by such lack of curiosity, we asked him whether he knew anything about the Soviet Union, whether he had ever heard of it.

"Yes," said Rogers, "I heard about the Russians, but I don't know anything about them. Now, my wife reads newspapers, so she must know."

We understood then that he failed to question us not because he was unusually considerate. On the contrary, he was simply not interested, just as he was undoubtedly not interested in Mexico, which lay near by, or even in New York.

We stopped for lunch not far from Santa Rosa in a hamlet near a railway station baked by the sun. The proprietor of the establishment where we ate cheese sandwiches and canned ham sandwiches was a Mexican with a large bony nose. The sandwiches were made by him, by his wife, who did not know a word of English, and by his son, a thin boy with crooked cavalry legs and in a cowboy belt decorated with brass. The Mexican family was preparing sandwiches with much shouting and noise, as if they were dividing an estate. The sensible calm American service disappeared as if it had never existed. Besides, the charges for the sandwiches were twice their usual price. On the main street of the hamlet was a store of Indian goods. In its show window were hand-made blankets, ornamented pots, and Indian gods with tremendous cylindrical noses. All this railroad wealth was illuminated by a hot November sun. This was not, however, the real heat of summer but a weakened, quite like a canned, kind of heat.

Some miles away from the hamlet through which we had but recently walked with the haughty manner of foreigners occurred our first automobile mishap. We very nearly landed in a ditch.

We will not say how it happened. At any rate, it was not any too elegant. Nor will we tell whose fault it was. We are, however, willing to guarantee that it was neither Mrs. Adams's fault nor her husband's. We can plead only one thing in our own defence: when the machine began to swerve into the ditch, neither of us raised his hands to heaven nor bade farewell to his near ones and his friends. Each behaved as he should have. We maintained a profound silence, curious to see where the machine would land.

The automobile did not turn over, however. Bent badly, it stopped on the very edge. We crept out gingerly, scarcely able to maintain our balance (including our spiritual balance).

We scarcely had the time to exchange one word about what happened to us when the first machine that passed by (it happened to be a truck) stopped, and a man with a fine new rope in his hand jumped out of it.

Without saying a word, he tied one end of the rope to the truck, the other to our machine, and in no time he pulled us back to the road. All passing automobilists stopped and asked if we needed their help. In a word, the rescuers flung themselves upon us like birds of prey. Every second new brakes screeched and a new passer-by offered his services.

It was a touching spectacle. The automobiles assembled around us without any prearrangement, just as ants do, when they see a fellow in trouble. Word of honour, we were even glad that we had this small accident, otherwise we would never have discovered this amazing American trait. Only after learning that their help was not needed did the automobilists proceed.

Our rescuer wished us a happy journey and drove off. Before going, in farewell, he glanced at Mrs. Adams and barked out something to the effect that a man should drive a car rather than a woman. Mrs. Adams behaved like a perfect lady. She did not even venture to say that on that occasion she had not been driving the car.

The American who had pulled us back to the road did not even care to listen to our thanks. Help on the road is not regarded in America as any special virtue. If our rescuer himself had got into trouble, he would have been helped just as quickly and silently as he had helped us. You cannot even mention an offer of money for such help, or you would be rebuked for it.

Two days later we ourselves appeared in the role of rescuers.

We were returning along the mountain road into Santa Fé from an Indian village near the town of Taos. A wet snow fell. The road was icy. Now and then our automobile took precarious turns of its own free will, bringing us to the very edge of the road. We drove slowly. We did not feel any too easy in our hearts.

Suddenly from around a bend we saw across the road a small truck lying on its side. Near it in complete bewilderment wandered a young

Mexican. We could see from afar that he was a Mexican. He wore a pink shirt, a blue necktie, a grey vest, raspberry shoes, green socks, and a dark violet hat. Two paces from him, on a slope, his back in a pool of blood, lay another Mexican in delicately green velvet trousers. He appeared to be dead.

The accident had evidently just occurred, and the survivor had lost his senses to such an extent that he could not tell us coherently what had happened. He walked around the truck and muttered something senselessly. He seemed insane.

The man who was lying on his back opened his eyes and groaned. That horrible sound brought the multi-coloured Mexican back to consciousness, and he turned to us with a plea to take the wounded man to his home in the village of Willard. We offered to take him to the nearest hospital, but the Mexican insisted that we must take him to the village. To do that we had to make a detour of thirty miles off our road. Altogether we got the wounded man with difficulty into our automobile.

In the meantime an American drove up behind us. He asked whether any help was needed. We thanked him and said that we were taking the wounded man. The multi-coloured Mexican stayed with his broken truck.

The road was very difficult, and three hours passed before we reached Willard. The entire village immediately ran to our machine. God only knows with what the local residents are occupied. In spite of the fact that it was an ordinary day, they were all dressed in new jackets made of leather and fur. We surrendered the wounded Mexican to his relatives. For a minute he regained consciousness and told them what had happened. He was carried to his home. Just then from behind, bobbing over the ruts, up drove the machine with the American who had offered his help. He had driven behind us all the way.

"You see," he said, "you are very careless. This Mexican might have died in your machine. You did not know how badly he had been injured. Maybe he was already dying. Can you imagine what could have happened? You arrive in a Mexican village, where nobody knows you, and bring to them the corpse of one of their fellow residents. The Mexicans would think right away that you had run over him. How could you prove that he had injured himself in his own machine? The Mexicans are hot-tempered people, and you might have found yourself in a bad mess. So I thought I had better follow behind you and, in case of anything, be your witness."

Such an act tells a lot about the nature of Americans.

Before we parted and drove away in divergent directions, the American gave us his calling card. Suppose, after all, his testimony of this case might be of use to us. Then his address would come in handy. From his calling card we learned that our witness was the principal of a grammar school—an elementary school. In order to do us this favour, he had had to make a considerable detour.

In the character of the American people there are many splendid and appealing traits.

They are excellent workers; they have golden hands. Our engineers say that it is a genuine pleasure to work with Americans. Americans are precise, yet far from pedantic. They are neat, they are accurate, they know how to keep their word, and they trust the word of others. They are always ready to come to your aid. They are excellent comrades and easy to get along with.

But one fine trait—curiosity—is almost non-existent with Americans. That is especially true of the youth. We covered sixteen thousand kilometres of American roads in our automobile, and we saw a multitude of people. Almost every day we took hitchhikers into our car. All of them were very willing to talk, but not one of them was curious enough to ask us who we were.

On the road we were met by a wooden arch:

"Welcome to New Mexico."

Near the arch we were charged twenty-four cents for a gallon of petrol. Petrol in New Mexico costs more than in Texas. The greeting of welcome was somewhat poisoned by the commercial spirit. Various prices are charged for petrol in various states, ranging from fourteen to thirty cents per gallon. It is most expensive, of course, in deserts, where it has to be delivered from afar. Hence, frequently at the borders of states one meets with placards like this one:

"Stock up on petrol here. In Arizona it costs four cents more."

Naturally, under the circumstances you can't hold out. You stock up!

The clay at the side of the road was red, the desert was yellow, the sky was blue. At times we ran across stunted cedars. For two hundred miles we drove over a fairly well-beaten gravel road, but beside it was being built a highway from Los Angeles to New York.

We stopped at an old well over which hung the large announcement:

"Your grandfather drank water here on his way to California for gold."

In another announcement this well called itself the first in America. Beside the historical well a man sat in his little booth and sold coloured postcards with views of the same well. Around the post which was driven into the ground walked two chained young bears. The man told us that they were very vicious. But the bears did not know English, it would seem, because they stood up on their rear paws in a most toadying manner and begged the travellers for gifts. Behind the booth could be seen an old fortress with its wooden belfry of the Wayne Reid type. In a word, it smelled of scalping and similar childish joys. The only thing lacking was an Indian arrow striking the belfry and still quivering from its flight.

A battered old machine stopped at the well just as we pulled up. In it, among pillows and cotton blankets, sat the most ordinary mamma with a tow-headed howling boy on her knee. On the footboard in a special rack stood an obedient dog, its thick and kindly tail twisted up. The husband squeezed his way out from behind the wheel and stretched his legs, while talking with the keeper of the historical well.

Wiping her son's nose, Mamma quickly told us about her family affairs.

They were going from Kansas City to California. Her husband had found work there. All their possessions were right here in the automobile.

The dog was fidgeting restlessly in its rack. Beside it on the footboard was attached an additional little tank of petrol, and the odour stifled the dog. It looked piteously at its mistress. It was evidently eager to arrive in California as soon as possible.

In the evening we drove into Santa Fé, one of the oldest cities of America.

22

Santa Fé

AS A matter of fact, we still do not know what guided us in selecting a hotel in a new city. Usually, we drove slowly down the street, passed several hotels in silence, as if we knew something bad about them, and then, just as silently, without any previous agreement, we would stop at the next hotel, as if we knew something good about it.

We don't know what played a greater role here: whether it was our writers' intuition or the experience of that veteran traveller, Mr. Adams, but the hotel always satisfied our needs. No doubt, those we had rejected would have been no worse. A four-dollar room for two had beds with good springs, several blankets and pillows as flat as a dollar, a bathroom with a white mosaic floor, and an eternally hissing steam radiator.

But then, we did know definitely that modest travellers should not stop in hotels called "Mayflower." "Mayflower," or "Flower of the May," was the name of the ship on which the first settlers from England came to America, so that is the name usually given now to the most expensive hotel in the city.

In Santa Fé we stopped at the Hotel Montezuma.

When we entered the halls of the Montezuma several Americans lolling in rocking-chairs with newspapers in their hands, regarded us avidly. In their eyes glowed the unquenchable desire to talk to someone, to chatter, to while the time away. Strange as it may seem, in busy super-business America there are such people. For the most part they are gentlemen who are no longer young, in decorous suits of a colour peculiar to doctors. Either because they have already earned enough dollars or because they have lost all hope of earning any more, the fact remains that they always seem to have a lot of free time; hence, see-sawing in their hotel rockers, they eagerly lie in wait for their prey. God forbid that you hook such a man with a careless question! He will not let his interlocutor go for several hours. In the loud voice of the American optimist he will tell you everything he knows, and in every phrase there will be "Sure," which means "Of course," and "Surely," which means "Of course," and "Of

E*

course," which also means "Of course." Besides that, in almost every phrase there will not fail to be the word "Nice!"

We quickly slipped past the people in the rockers, washed, and went out into the street to find a place where we could have supper.

In activities of this kind we showed a greater system than in the search for a hotel. During the month and a half that we had lived in the States we had become so sick of American cooking that we were agreeable to any other kinds of edibles—Italian, Chinese, Jewish—anything but Breakfast No. 2 or Dinner No. 1, anything but this numbered, standardized, and centralized food. In fact, if it is possible to speak of bad taste in food, then Anglo-American cooking undoubtedly is the expression of a bad, silly, and eccentric taste that has brought forth such hybrids as sweet and sour pickles, bacon fried to the consistency of plywood, or blindingly white and utterly tasteless (no, having the taste of cotton!) bread.

We therefore looked with tenderness at the luminous sign "Original Mexican Restaurant." The sign promised bliss, so we quickly walked in.

On the walls of the restaurant hung coarse and beautiful Mexican rugs, while the waiters wore orange silk blouses and satin neckties the colour of a drunkard's liver. Enchanted, as they say, by this orgy of colours, we twittered light-heartedly while selecting the dishes. We ordered a soup, the name of which we have now forgotten, and something else called "enchilada."

The name of the soup was forgotten because the very first spoon knocked everything out of our heads except the desire to seize a fire extinguisher and to put out the bonfire that broke out in the mouth. As for the enchilada, they proved to be long, appetizing blintzes filled with red pepper and gunpowder, thinly cut, and covered with nitroglycerine. It is simply impossible to sit down to such a dinner without wearing a fireman's helmet. We ran out of the Original Mexican Restaurant, hungry, angry, dying of thirst. Five minutes later we sat in a drug-store, the most ordinary American drug-store, and ate (oh, humiliation!) centralized, standardized, and numbered food, which we had cursed only half an hour before, drinking beforehand ten bottles of Coca-Cola apiece to quiet our disturbed nervous system.

Scarcely able to drag our legs after these horrible adventures, we went out for a walk through Santa Fé. American brick and wood had disappeared. Here stood Spanish houses of clay supported by heavy buttresses. From under the roofs emerged ends of square or round ceiling beams. Cowboys walked down the streets, their high heels clicking. An automobile drove up to a motion-picture theatre, and from it stepped down an Indian and his wife. On the forehead of the Indian was a broad bright-red bandage. On the ankles of the Indian woman could be seen thick white puttees. The Indians locked their automobile and went to see the picture. On the high stools of a shoe-shining shop sat four American boys with brilliantined hair. They were about thirteen or fourteen years old and looked exceptionally independent.

Mr. Adams eyed these boys for a long time, and finally, after calling the "gentlemen," found out what they proposed to do that evening.

"We are having our shoes shined," said one of the boys, "because we are going to a dance."

Failing to draw anything else out of these young gentlemen, we returned to our hotel, where the hissing radiator had heated the air in our rooms to seventy-seven degrees.

In the matter of temperatures Americans are inclined to extremes. They work in overheated dwellings and drink overcooled drinks. Everything not offered piping hot is offered ice-cold. There is no middle ground.

The heat of the room and the smouldering flame of the enchilada reduced us by morning to a dried-out and well-tempered consistency, ready for further adventure.

Santa Fé is the capital of the state of New Mexico, the youngest state in America. The capital of the youngest state of America is one of the oldest of American cities. However, besides a few really ancient ones, all the buildings in the town are clean, new, built in the style of the old Spanish missions. The city as a whole seems somehow artificial, as if it were made for American tourists.

In the long building of the old governor's palace is now located the state museum. Its exhibits offer a fairly good notion of Indian, Spanish, and Mexican material culture. Americans have few antique things. They are devoted to them, carefully preserve them, and do not treat tourists interested in antiquities as a source of profit. Oh, they will show you things without end, explain, provide you with printed, excellently published materials, all of it free, even without charging an admission fee to the museum.

Among forbidding red hills beyond the city stands the fine building of the Rockefeller Institute of Anthropology. The institute is supported by one of Rockefeller's sons. But what would happen if Rockefeller's son had not been interested in anthropology? That, we dare say, could not be answered even by the assistant director, Mr. Chapman himself, who was acquainting us with the work of the institute.

Having shown us the excellently organized closets where on thin metallic shelves the rich collections of decorated Indian dishes were neatly displayed; storerooms where Indian rugs and textiles lay in a constantly maintained special temperature which guarantees their preservation; laboratories in which young scientists sat thoughtfully over apparently ordinary stones—having shown us all of this, Mr. Chapman, a man with an excellent, energetic, and spare American face, said:

"The Indians are doomed to disappear. We study them well, but we do little to preserve them as a people."

We entered the cathedral toward one o'clock, but the priest was so kind that he postponed his dinner a little. He opened the cathedral, quickly and dexterously genuflected, and, rising, led us to look at a wall with remarkable Spanish sculptures. We stood in a dusty storeroom, where in disorder, helter-skelter, on the shelves, on the floor, and in closets, stood Jesuses, Mothers of God, and saints. The figures were primitive and inimitable. Catholic splendour astounded one in these painted and gilded little statues.

Having learned that we had come from the Soviet Union, the father became more courteous than ever.

"I am also a communist," he said, "but not, of course, the kind you are. Christ was more than a man. That is why he did not act the way people do. But, of course, we cannot discuss that."

The abbot of the old Church of St. Miguel, built in 1541, proved to be a Frenchman and a Franciscan monk. His enterprise was on a commercial footing. In the first place, he took seventy-five cents from us for looking around. The building of the church itself was old, but all the sculptures were new German factory work. But the greedy abbot liked them and assiduously urged us to admire. This led us to conclude that the venerable Franciscan did not know anything at all about art.

He, too, asked us where we had come from, but said nothing about his own convictions. He merely remarked that the Franciscan Order was no longer doing any work in Russia, and suggested that we buy postcards with the coloured representation of the Church of St. Miguel.

When we returned to the hotel we began to look over the piles of letters of introduction we had accumulated, and began to free ourselves from those we had not used and would not have occasion to use. Out of the package of letters we had received from Dos Passos, one, addressed to the famous American poet, Witter Bynner, was needed by us today. About twenty letters were addressed to places which we would still visit, while three letters were no longer needed.

Since letters of introduction are not sealed, we looked at them casually before destroying them. The letters were very hearty, we were described from our best side, but for some strange reason we were recommended in all of them as passionate admirers of Mark Twain. We could not understand for a long time what had driven the benevolent Dos Passos to single out this particular in our biographies. Finally, we remembered that once we had told Dos Passos about our visit to the city of Hartford in the state of Connecticut, where Mark Twain lived during the years when he was already famous and well off. We described to Dos Passos Twain's wonderful, restful home, which stood beside the home of Harriet Beecher Stowe, who had written *Uncle Tom's Cabin*, a novel famous in its time, told him that in that house there was now a library, and that on the walls of the library we saw the original illustrations for *The Prince and the Pauper*, which we had known since our childhood.

Our English being far from remarkable, our conversation must have been accompanied by energetic gestures which probably led Dos Passos to the impression that we were fanatical devotees of Mark Twain.

Taking along our letter, we went to call on Witter Bynner. On the streets of Santa Fé one is likely to see Indians of the Pueblo tribe who had come from their village to sell a rug or a bowl. Indians come also to the museum, where their bows and thin aquarelle drawings, which portray war dances with remarkable faithfulness, are bought. Costumes, decorations, and the arms are reproduced with scientific conscientiousness, and these aquarelles can serve as texts in studying Indian culture.

Mr. Witter Bynner lives in a house filled from its foundation to its roof with Indian rugs, Indian ware, and silver decoration. It is a real museum.

When the American poet read Dos Passos' letter, his face became transfigured with a joyous smile.

"Dos writes me," he said, "that you are crazy about Mark Twain."

We exchanged glances.

"That's wonderful," said the poet. "I myself was very friendly with Twain. I have a pleasant surprise for you. Twain at one time gave me his photograph with a dedication written in verse. It is a very rare thing —verses by Mark Twain. You as his passionate devotees will find them interesting reading."

He dragged us up a stairway the walls of which were hung with photographs of American and non-American writers. We conscientiously looked at a portrait of Twain and listened to the versified dedication.

We spent an interesting evening with Mr. Bynner and learned from him precisely where we should go on the morrow to look for Indians.

Mr. Bynner told us that in Santa Fé, located in the centre of three ancient civilizations—Indian, Spanish, and Mexican—live many writers, artists, and poets. They fled there from contemporary America. But America fled after them. Following the poets and the artists, millionaires rushed into Santa Fé. They built villas and likewise breathed the atmosphere of ancient civilizations, having previously stocked up on contemporary dollars.

Here also lived McCormick, the famous industrialist, who had many enterprises in old Russia. He had, of course, lost all those enterprises. Not long ago he journeyed to the Soviet Union as a tourist, spent eleven days there and upon returning lectured in Santa Fé about his journey, talking mostly about "Intourist," because in such a short period of time he did not learn anything else.

"So many millionaires have already gathered here," said Witter Bynner, "that it is time to migrate to some other place. But then they will follow there too. There is no escaping them."

23
Meeting the Indians

WITTER BYNNER advised us to go to the city of Taos, two miles from which is a large Indian village of the Pueblo tribe.

We left Santa Fé and the Hotel Montezuma with its hissing radiator. By morning it had hissed the temperature of our room up to eighty-six degrees above zero, so we greedily inhaled the fresh air as we raced over the mountain road.

We drove along the Rio Grande, which was a small green river here, and after a few score miles we found ourselves in an Indian village of San Ildefonso. This splendid Spanish name hid no Catholic missions, no important prelates, no young people of pure Castilian blood. A small square was surrounded by adobe houses. Protruding from the ground at each house were small cupola-shaped structures. These were ovens, hearths. In the middle of the square stood a tremendous woman. Two thick braids, which fell over her fat bosom, were intertwined with red and green woollen threads. In her fleshy ears were holes for ear-rings.

When we asked her about the Indian, Agapito Pina, with whom Mr. Bynner advised us to get acquainted, we discovered that this woman was Agapito Pina, and that he was not at all a woman but a fat Indian with a woman's figure.

Agapito Pina proved to be a gay fellow and very sociable. He asked us into his home, which was clean and looked like a Ukrainian hut.

It was a grey winter day. Suddenly it began to snow, and soon everything was white, including the remarkable cupola-shaped ovens, the few barren trees that looked like smoke turned to stone, and all of this poor peasant's square. In a small hearth of Agapito's home blazed one log of wood, which stood on a slant. An old dried-out Indian woman sat on her haunches before the fire. She was Agapito Pina's mother. She was eighty-three years old, but she was only half-grey. Agapito himself was sixty years old, but there was not a single grey hair in his head. The old woman accepted the cigarette we offered her and smoked with pleasure. Agapito also took a cigarette, but he put it away in his pocket, evidently for his beloved mamma.

Presently Agapito began to sing an Indian song, beating time with his foot. The room was small. Agapito danced quite close to us. He looked into our eyes and, having finished one song, immediately began another. On the clay step lay photographs of Indians performing military dances. It began to smell of extortion, as in Naples or Pompeii.

However, having finished his song and dance, Agapito Pina did not at all ask for money, did not attempt to press any photographs on us. It appeared that he simply wanted to please his guests. We were happy to be reassured that, after all, this was not Naples, but an Indian reservation, and that our redskin brothers regarded tourists without that commercial passion with which their white-faced brothers invest this business.

On the clean walls of the room hung bunches of multi-coloured cornstalks. In the corners stood the beautifully embroidered ceremonial moccasins of our host.

The occupation of the village was agriculture. Every person was entitled to an acre of land. Agapito did not know about the existence of

Europe and of oceans. True, one Indian of his acquaintance had told him not long ago that there was a city called New York somewhere in the world.

He came out into the square to see us off. Thick snowflakes fell on his dark straight hair.

The road lay between red pumice mountains with flat decapitated tops. Their colour was remarkably like the colour of Agapito Pina's skin, a subdued red, a darkened, ancient red. The redness of Indian skin is unique. It is the colour of their porous cliffs, the colour of their autumnal nature. Their very nature is redskin.

The day was raw, tearful, autumn and winter at the same time. At first the snow fell, then rain drizzled, and finally, toward the end of the day, a fog moved in. The headlights gleamed dimly. We met almost no automobiles. We were alone in the midst of the threatening Indian nature. Far below, interminably but rather quietly, the Rio Grande roared.

Having reached Taos, we stopped in the grey and blue camp of Captain O'Hay. The tall captain took the keys and led the way to our cabin.

He was really a captain and had served in the American army. He had forsaken the service because he was sick of it. Here in Taos he liked it. Business was good. Eight months out of the year his camp was full. The captain and his wife were never bored. Every day new people stop at the camp, people from all parts of the country, and in the evening, when there is time to talk, an interesting person can be found to talk to.

"It is better to be the owner of a camp than a captain in the army," said Captain O'Hay, opening the door, "and life along the highway is more interesting than in a large city."

The captain maintained his establishment in an exemplary fashion. The walls of the neat rooms were decorated in red and blue Indian ornaments. Here stood low soft beds. At the fat little stove were neatly piled pieces of firewood and a little pail of coal. From the pail stuck fire-tongs so that the traveller would not have to take the coal with his hands and soil himself. In the small kitchen stood a gas stove with two ovens.

Beside each cabin was a small garage for one machine. As almost everywhere in America, the garage was never closed. The garages of Captain O'Hay did not even have an outside door. Theoretically, your machine may be stolen, but actually it seldom happens. Who will take the trouble at night to roll out a locked machine, change the licence number and hide from the police? It was too complicated, did not pay. It was no occupation for a respectable thief. It simply did not pay. If there was money lying around . . .

Mr. Adams spoke more than once on that subject.

"In our small towns," he said, "people leave their doors open when they go away. Gentlemen, it may seem to you that you are now in a land where there are none but honest people. But, as a matter of fact, we are just as much thieves as anyone else—as the French or the Greeks or the Italians. The point is that we begin to steal at a higher level. We are

much wealthier than Europe, so no one here will steal a coat, shoes, or
bread. I am not speaking of hungry people. A hungry man might take
these things. That happens, although rarely. I am referring to thieves.
It doesn't pay for them to bother with second-hand coats. It's too complicated. The same is true of automobiles. But I wouldn't advise you to
leave a hundred-dollar bill lying around. I'm sorry to disappoint you,
gentlemen, but I am quite sure it would be stolen at once. Write that
down in your little notebooks. Beginning with a hundred dollars—no,
even with fifty dollars—Americans are as much addicted to stealing as
the rest of humankind. And they make up for it by securing sums of
which poor Europe has never even dreamed."

We again took our places in the machine and drove to the Indians. In
the advancing twilight our mouse-coloured car almost merged with the
barren, ashen landscape. After two miles we were at the entrance to a
village of the Pueblo Indians, the only Indian tribe which still lives
where it had lived before the appearance of the white man in America.
All the other tribes have been driven off their territories and driven about
repeatedly into sundry places, each worse than its predecessor. The
Pueblos have preserved their ancient land only because nothing of
interest to the white man could be found there. Here is neither oil nor
gold nor coal nor good pasture.

The inscription on a wooden sign announced that it is necessary to
secure the permission of the governor of the tribe before investigating the
village. The governor's small hut was near by. The air resounding with
our cheerful good-evenings and our hats rising in greeting, we went in
to see the governor, and stopped in astonishment. Before the hearth,
where two logs burned brightly, squatted an old Indian. The reflection
of the flame glided over the smooth red skin of his face. Sitting thus,
with his eyes shut, he looked like a hawk dropping off to sleep in a
zoological garden, occasionally raising his eyelids in order to regard the
people around his cage with detestation and boredom or in order to
lunge with his beak at the little sign with the Latin inscription which
testified that he was actually a hawk, the ruler of mountain-tops and of
mountain ranges.

Before us sat one of those who at one time smoked the pipe of peace or
"went out on the warpath," a bloodthirsty and honourable Indian. As a
matter of fact, neither Captain Mayne Reid nor Gustav Emarre had
deceived us. In our childhood we had imagined Indians to be just like that.

He did not respond to our greeting, his face remaining to the fire.
When we said that we wanted to look over the village, he scarcely
nodded his head in indifference, without uttering a word. A young Indian
approached us and said that the governor was very old and weak and
that he was dying.

When we came out of the house of the chief, boys had already
surrounded our automobile. These were Indian children, dark-eyed, with
straight black hair, small aquiline noses, and skin the colour of a copper

coin. They regarded us from a safe distance, but there was no fear in their scrutiny. They behaved like young lions. One cub, by the way, ended up by coming closer to us and demanding proudly that we give him five cents. When we refused, he did not deign to beg, but turned away contemptuously.

Around us stood remarkable houses. Nearly a thousand people live in the village, and all of them have managed to lodge in two or three houses. These are huge clay buildings of several stories, made up of individual rooms adjoining each other. The houses rise in terraces, and each floor has a flat roof. The stories communicate with each other by means of attached wooden ladders, ordinary, easily slapped together ladders of the kind used by janitors and house painters. Previously, when the Pueblos were independent, the entire tribe lived in one colossal clay house. When the stepladders were taken into the house, the house became a fortress, with only its bare walls on the outside. Thus they live even today, although conditions are radically different now.

There was an odour of smoke and manure in the square. Lively rust-coloured shoats ran underfoot. Several Indians stood on the roofs of a house. They were wrapped from head to foot in their blankets and looked at us silently. Kindly Indian dogs ran up and down the step-ladders with the dexterity of boatswains. It was quickly turning dark.

A grey Indian with an imperious face approached us. He was the village policeman. He was wrapped up to his head in a baize blanket which was white with blue. In spite of his high calling, his duties were quite peaceable and not at all onerous. He told us that his business was to chase the children to school every morning. He invited us to come in and see him tomorrow morning at this school, and he would show us the village. It was too late now and people were already going to bed. This conversation was carried on while we were standing beside a stream that meandered between the houses. A wide log thrown across the stream served as a bridge. Nothing here was reminiscent of the year 1935, and our automobile, outlined dimly in the darkness, seemed a Wellsian time machine that had just arrived. We returned to Taos.

In five minutes we passed through the several centuries that separate the village from Taos. In the town were well-lighted stores, automobiles standing at kerbs, genuine American popcorn was being roasted in a little store, orange juice was being served in the drug-store, everything went on its way as if there never had been any Indians in the world.

We drove into the quadrangular square. Its principal ornament was a combination of antiquary and restaurant establishment entitled "Don Fernando." For a town which was far from the railroad and had only two thousand inhabitants, the little restaurant was very good. We were served by small, silent Indian women, who were supervised by a man with the sad face of a Vilna Jew. He came and took our order. He was Don Fernando himself. Our guess proved only half right. Don Fernando was actually a Jew. But he was not a Vilna Jew. He was a

Swiss Jew. He told us that himself. As to the circumstances under which he acquired the title of don, he kept quiet; but it may be supposed that if commercial interests demanded it, he would not have hesitated to call himself even a grandee.

He told us that out of the two thousand population of Taos nearly two hundred are people devoted to art. They paint pictures, compose verses, create symphonies and sculptures, chisel or carve one thing or another. They have been drawn here by the environment. The wildness of nature, the juncture point of three cultures—Indian, Mexican, and pioneer American—as well as by the low cost of living.

Not far from us sat a little lady in a black suit who kept constantly looking at us. The more she stared at us, the more excited she became.

When we were in the curio section of the restaurant and were examining there the Indian dolls made of suede and the brightly coloured gods with green and red noses, Don Fernando again approached us. He said that a Mrs. Feshina, a Russian lady who had been living in Taos for a long time, would like to speak with us. It was very interesting, indeed, to meet a Russian living in Indian territory. A minute later the lady who had been sitting in the restaurant came over, smiling nervously.

"You will excuse me," she said in Russian, "but when I heard your conversation I could not restrain myself. You are Russians, aren't you?"

We confirmed it.

"Have you been long in America?" continued Mrs. Feshina.

"Two months."

"Where did you come from, then?"

"From Moscow."

"Directly from Moscow?"

She was astounded.

"You know, this is simply a miracle! I have been living here so many years among these Americans, and suddenly—Russians!"

We saw that she wanted very much to talk, that this was really a great event for her, and so we asked her to call on us at our camp. A few minutes later she drove up alone in her little old automobile. She sat with us a long time, talking without end.

She had left Kazan in 1923. Her husband was the painter Feshin who was quite well known in Russia in his day. He was friendly with Americans from the American Relief Administration, who had been on the Volga, and they arranged for him to be invited to America. He decided to remain here for ever, not to return to the Soviet Union. This was determined in the main by his business success. His pictures sold and he accumulated a lot of money. Being a genuine Russian, Feshin could not live in a large American city, and therefore moved here to Taos. They built themselves a house, a remarkable house. It took them three summers to build, and it cost them about twenty thousand dollars. They built and built, and when the house was finished they parted. They decided that it had been wrong for them to have lived together at all, that they were not at all suited to each other. Feshin left Taos and went to Mexico City. Their daughter is now studying in a Hollywood ballet school. Mrs. Feshina remained alone in Taos. She has no money, she has not even enough to heat her splendid house in the winter. That is why for the winter she rented a little house for three dollars a month in the village of Rio Chiquito, where there are only Mexicans who do not even know English but who are very good people. There is no electricity in Rio Chiquito. She is obliged to earn her own living. She decided to write for the cinema, but so far she has not earned anything. It is a pity to sell the house. It cost twenty thousand, but now during the depression it could not bring more than five thousand.

Our guest spoke eagerly, wanted to have her fill in talking, constantly applied her hands to her nervous face and kept repeating:

"It is strange to speak Russian in Taos, with new people. Tell me, do I make mistakes in Russian?"

She spoke very well, but occasionally she hesitated, trying to remember the necessary word.

We said to her:

"Listen, why do you stay here? Why don't you ask for permission to return to the Soviet Union?"

"I would go with pleasure, but where shall I go? They are all new people there. I don't know anybody. It's too late for me to begin a new life."

She made us promise to come and see how she lived at Rio Chiquito, explained to us how to drive there, and disappeared in her lumbering old car.

A strange fate! Where was this Russian woman living? In Rio Chiquito, in the state of New Mexico, in the United States of America, among Indians, Mexicans and Americans.

In the morning we at once departed for the school in the Pueblo village to look for our policeman. There was a fog in Pueblo. In it were dimly outlined grey trees, distant and near-by hills, melancholy Indians in blankets standing as ever on the roofs and looking like the shut-in inmates of a harem. Dogs ran over their houses, without touching us, ran quickly up the ladders and disappeared in doorways.

The school was large and excellently managed, like all schools in the States. We saw large splendid class-rooms, hardwood floors, shining porcelain washbasins, nickel-plated taps.

The policeman could not go with us. His duties detained him at the school. Right now he was preoccupied with settling a conflict. One Indian boy had struck another Indian boy on the head. The policeman was calmly reprimanding the guilty one. Around him stood the boys, silent and important, like chieftains at a large conclave. The usual childish hubbub was not there. Everyone listened solemnly to the policeman, lifting now and then their handsome eagle-beak noses or scratching their straight, gleaming black hair. But as soon as the policeman, shuffling away in his slippers, went off, the boys began to jump and run like all the little mischiefs in the world.

The director of the school, a historian by specialty, abandoned the cultured East and came here because he wanted to learn to know the Indians better.

"Very talented children, a very talented people, and of course especially inclined toward art," said the director. "A talented and an enigmatic people. I have lived many years among them, but this people is still incomprehensible to me. Indians are obliged to send their children to school because education is compulsory. Otherwise they would not send a single child. All the instructors are white people, and instruction is in English. For the most part, the children study very well. But suddenly some of the boys in a certain year who pass their tenth or eleventh birthday stop going to school. They do not go for the entire year. That year they get their own native training somewhere, but we have never been able to find out where. And when such a boy again appears in school, he is already a real Indian and he will never again be white in culture. When the children finish school the old men tell them: 'Choose! If you want to be a white man, then go to them and never come back to us. But if you want to remain an Indian, then forget everything that you have been taught.' And almost always the children remain at home. Two or three years after graduation from school, they return occasionally and ask to be allowed to look through old American newspapers, but soon after that they stop coming altogether. These are Indians, the real Indians, without electricity, automobiles, and other nonsense. They live among the whites, full of silent contempt for them. To this day they do not recognize them as masters of their country. And this is not at all surprising when one recalls that in the history of the Indian people there was not even one occasion when one tribe enslaved another. An Indian tribe cannot be enslaved. It can only be exterminated (there were such cases), and only then may one consider that an Indian tribe has been conquered."

We were guided through the village by a fifteen-year-old Indian girl. Suddenly she said:

"Do you know an Indian woman that lives in Chicago? She's my sister."

That was a rare case. Her sister had married a white man, an artist. He was undoubtedly one of the visionaries of Taos, who had come here to inhale the atmosphere of an ancient civilization.

In the middle of the village stood an old Spanish church. The Pueblos are Catholics, but very strange Catholics. For Christmas and Easter they bring down the statue of the Madonna and perform a war dance around her. Then they go away to some praying hole and there pray—but hardly in accordance with Catholic rites.

Looking at the silent and stately redskins, as proud as ancient Romans, we repeated to ourselves, recalling the words of the school director:

"Yes, yes, they are Catholics, and they speak English and they have seen automobiles and the like; but they are nevertheless Indians, real Indians, and above all Indians—and nothing else."

Frightened by the accident on the frozen highway, of which we have already told, the first thing we did in Santa Fé was to buy wonderful gold-coloured chains and drove out in the direction of Albuquerque.

24
A Day of Mishaps

WE LEFT Santa Fé for Albuquerque on tiptoe, if one may apply such an expression to an automobile.

Prior to our departure, Mr. and Mrs. Adams were occupied with their favourite activity; hand in hand, they went off "to get information." They visited the "A.A.A." (the automobile club), several petrol stations, tourist bureaux, and returned loaded with maps. Mr. Adams's face expressed despair. Mrs. Adams's, on the contrary, was full of determination. Waiting in the machine, we could hear their excited voices even from afar.

"Gentlemen!" Mr. Adams said to us solemnly. "We have got the information. It is a hundred miles to Albuquerque. Ahead of us is rain. In one part of the journey the road drops a thousand feet within a mile. No, gentlemen, do not speak. It's terrible!"

"But what of it?" asked Mrs. Adams calmly.

"Becky! Becky! Don't say 'what of it'! You don't know what you're talking about!"

"Well, now, you're always right! Still, I'd like to know what you're driving at."

"Becky, you must not talk like that. You must be reasonable! I warn you, gentlemen, that danger threatens us!"

"But still, what is it that you want?" asked Mrs. Adams, without raising her voice. "Do you want us to turn back?"

"Oh, Becky, don't say 'turn back'! How can you say such things!"

"Then, let's go!"

"Seriously! There is a drop of one thousand feet in one mile! You must not say 'let's go'! Becky, you are no longer a little girl!"

"Very well, in that case we shall stop at Santa Fé!"

"You're always like that," moaned Mr. Adams. "It hurts me to hear your words. How can you say 'let's stop at Santa Fé'? Don't talk like that! Gentlemen, it is terrible!"

Mrs. Adams silently started the motor and we drove off.

But before we left the city Mrs. Adams several times again "got information." This was the only weakness of our stalwart driver and guide. She would drive up to a pump and blow her signal. From the booth a brisk young man in a striped cap would run out. Mrs. Adams would ask the way to the nearest town.

"The third street to the right, ma'am," replied the youth, wiping his hands in waste, "and then to the right, ma'am."

"Keep to the right?" asked Mrs. Adams.

"Yes, ma'am."

"And first we must go through that street for three blocks?"

"Yes, ma'am."

"And then to the right?"

"Yes, ma'am."

Mrs. Adams was silent for a while, looking intently out of her little window.

"So it's the second street to the right?"

"No, ma'am, the third street."

The youth attempted to run away.

"And is the road good?" asked Mrs. Adams, reaching for the gears.

"Yes, ma'am."

"Thank you very, very much!" Mr. Adams cried helpfully.

"Very, very," his wife would add.

"Very much," we supported them.

Our machine left its place, but only to stop again at the next pump.

"We must check up," Mrs. Adams would say anxiously.

"It never hurts to check up," Mr. Adams would confirm, rubbing his hands.

Then would begin "Yes, ma'am" and "No, ma'am" all over again.

Information was being gathered that day until about five o'clock in the afternoon, so that we did not leave Santa Fé until dusk, which increased Mr. Adams's apprehensions. He was silent until we reached Albuquerque itself. Evidently his restless soul was oppressed by heavy foreboding.

It was utterly dark. Our pale headlights, manufactured with exemplary efficiency at one of Ford's midget plants, scarcely managed to pierce the fog-laden darkness.

Only once did Mr. Adams break his tragic silence.

"Becky!" he exclaimed. "We forgot to go to the post office in Santa Fé for my hat, which they surely must have had time to send from Kansas City. Gentlemen, that hat will drive me mad!"

"It's all right. We'll send a postcard from Albuquerque and ask them to forward the hat to San Francisco," Mrs. Adams replied.

The journey to Albuquerque ended auspiciously. We could not even tell where exactly we had passed the thousand-foot descent, despite our apprehensive peering into the darkness for several hours on end.

It was in the city itself, while seeking a camp for the night, that we drove off the road and landed in a deep mudhole. For the first time in the course of our journey we, who had been spoiled by macadam roads and service, had to wade right into the mud and, cursing our luck, push our beloved car, which had sunk right down to its rear end.

The machine did not budge.

"Gentlemen!" exclaimed Mr. Adams, wringing his short fat little hands, "you simply do not understand. You do not want to understand the significance of an automobile journey! No, seriously, you don't understand!"

Then appeared the gentleman in a vest, his hat pulled down to his nose. He approached Mrs. Adams, called her "ma'am," took her place at the wheel, and plied the throttle so vigorously that our car was enveloped in stinking fumes. Then a hysterical buzzing resounded, Mr. Adams beat a frightened retreat, and the machine, scattering tons of soupy mud, drove back on to the road.

That was the first link in the chain of mishaps that befell us the following day.

We drove out of Albuquerque on a frightful morning. The beautiful adobe houses with the ends of their ceiling beams emerging, the Coca-Cola signs, the monasteries, the drug-stores, the ancient Spanish missions, the same kind of petrol stations as in the East—all of it was covered with grey rain. At the entrances to the houses hung wooden yokes of bullock harness (in memory of the pioneer gold-miners); on the roofs of the Mexican huts soaked bunches of red pepper. Likewise soaking were advertisements of excursions to neighbouring Indian villages and Spanish missions (to the very nearest it was one hundred and eighty miles).

That morning we were supposed to cross the Rocky Mountains.

Suddenly, out of the muggy darkness emerged a beautiful clearing of green sky. The road went up. We saw no mountains. The only things visible were low hills and fissures of earth. The rain stopped. The sun looked out. We began to admire the landscape, and were as happy as the three famous little pigs, suspecting no danger.

Rising higher and higher, the automobile drove out finally on a vast plateau. Melting snow and ice were piled high on the road. The day was bright and crisp, like a day in early spring. We were at twelve thousand feet elevation, a little higher than the top of Mont Blanc.

"Look, look!" cried Mrs. Adams. "What cliffs on the horizon! What beauty! A shadow, a shadow! The green shadow of a cliff!"

"This is magnificent!" Mr. Adams shouted at the top of his voice, turning excitedly in his seat. "This vision ennobles the soul, uplifts . . ."

He was suddenly silent. Craning his neck, he stared at the road.

The machine began to swerve from side to side and to slip on the frosty slush. It foundered, and then the rear wheels skidded to one side. Mrs. Adams pulled the emergency brake. The machine landed across the road and stopped dead in its tracks.

Oh, how we hated to step out of our cosy machine and sink our feet in thin city shoes into this icy water. We decided to put on the chains. Although Mr. Adams took no direct part in that, he nevertheless deemed it his duty to follow us out of the machine and get his feet wet with the rest of us.

"I ask you only one thing," Mrs. Adams said to him, directing the work. "Don't bother us!"

"But, Becky," muttered her grief-stricken husband, "I'm obliged to work along with everybody."

And thus the Rocky Mountains remained in our memory: a bright and cold springlike day of late November, small, compact clouds racing across a greenish and translucent sky, and over the edges of the plateau grey and blue cliffs as even as a fence. Back of us, below, were Texas, Chicago, New York, the Atlantic Ocean, Europe. Ahead of us, below, were California, the Pacific Ocean, Japan, Siberia, Moscow. There we were ankle-deep in icy slush, clumsily tugging the chains over the hard tyres washed clean by the water.

An hour later the chains were on and Mrs. Adams was starting the motor. On the very highest peak of the mountain pass we found a dilapidated wooden hut with the sign "Café-Bar." In charge of it was a girl in breeches, boots, and a thin blouse with short sleeves. Although there was no dwelling for many miles around, the girl did not seem at all bucolic. She was a typical New York, Chicago, or Amarillo girl from a café, with neat marcel, rouged cheeks, plucked eyebrows, polished finger-nails, and a faultless professional knack of working.

We each drank a small glass of gin, warmed up, and went on our way, all our sorrows forgotten.

But the moment we began to admire the landscape, we heard a horrible racket, and Mrs. Adams, stopping the machine, looked first at us and then at Mr. Adams.

"Oh, Becky! You see, you see, I told you . . ."

"What did you tell me?"

"Becky! Don't ask me about anything. This is terrible!"

However, nothing especially terrible had actually occurred. All that happened was that one of the chains which was not firmly attached had broken and damaged the support of the left fender.

We took off the chains and carefully drove ahead. The sun warmed us more and more. The ice disappeared entirely, and like the little pigs we came to life again. We exclaimed over the stern beauty of the plateau and the cool brightness of the day.

"We're well off, gentlemen!" said Mr. Adams. "Just think of how the pioneers fared when they crossed this road for weeks, for months, without food and without water. Yes, gentlemen, without water. With wives and little children . . ."

But Mr. Adams suddenly dropped into silence, so we never found out how the pioneers had fared. Craning his neck, he stared ahead, blank horror in his eyes.

The road was blocked by a board. On it was this sign:

"Road under repair. Detour eleven miles."

"Detour" meant that we had to drive around and about. Here really was the rare occasion when one actually needs chains in America. But we were already short of one set of chains. In the middle of the detour, which was mostly swashy red clay, a blue, double-deck autobus of the Greyhound Company stood to one side. It was bound for Los Angeles. If this mighty machine got stuck, what would happen to us? The autobus leaned like a ship grounded on a reef. A bright yellow caterpillar tractor and a road plough were coming to its aid.

Ahead of us for several hours travelled a strange creature which only out of sheer pity could be called an automobile. It was not really an automobile; rather was it an auto wigwam with a rusty iron stovepipe and torn cotton comforters that flapped in the wind, albeit they were intended for the walls of this imaginary cabin. Inside could be seen a metal vat and large dirty children.

To our amazement the auto wigwam boldly plunged into the deep thin mud. We followed suit. From the windows of the Greyhound bored passengers looked out. Those eleven miles were evidently the very worst in America, and one simply had to be blessed with extraordinary automobile luck to strike those particular eleven miles. At any rate, throughout our entire journey in America we never again struck such a bad piece of road.

Several times we landed in immense puddles of thin mud and put our shoulders to the automobile. Our shoes, our trousers, the skirts of our overcoats, our shoulders, and even our faces—all were covered with pink clay.

Having come out on a hard road, the auto wigwam stopped. Out of it emerged a numerous family, which began to gather kindling for a fire. The family had evidently decided to dine. We drove past, regarding the family with a certain amount of envy. After all the suffering we had endured we wanted to eat.

The sun baking quite vigorously now, we quickly became dry and our spirits rose.

"Look! Look!" Mrs. Adams shouted, waving her arms. "What cliffs!"

"Becky! Don't let go the steering wheel! Keep your eyes on the road!" said Mr. Adams. "We will describe all the views to you later on!"

"No, but just look! That cliff looks like a castle!"

"And that one looks like a tower!"

"Gentlemen! Look quick. This is simply remarkable. The cliff looks like a huge piece of cheese."

"No, rather like a pie."

"A meat pie."

"Like a very long, long sausage. You know the kind. There is a certain Milan sausage that is very tasty."

We waxed hungrier and hungrier. While driving by some beautiful cliffs which, according to Mr. Adams, looked like a plate of hot soup, we realized that we were famished.

However, a new event distracted our troubled reveries. Mr. Adams accidentally opened the door on the traffic side, and a gust of wind almost threw him out of the machine.

While we were driving along the main street of Gallup, looking for a restaurant, we heard a crack which, by comparison with the already familiar sound of a snapping chain, seemed to us the melodic chirping of a cricket. Our car shuddered and stopped. The first second we realized that we were alive, and were overjoyed at the thought. The next second we realized that we were the victims of an accident. An old green, clean little semi-truck had bumped into the side of our new grey dirty car.

At once a crowd gathered around our automobiles. We looked sadly at the dented side and the slightly bent step. The man responsible for this mishap climbed off his semi-truck and muttered apologies.

"Sir," said Mr. Adams defiantly, "you cut into our car."

He was spoiling for a fight.

But there was no fight. Our opponent did not even think of denying his guilt and laid the blame mostly on his own "damned brakes." He was so embarrassed by the occurrence, and the damage he had done to us was so small, that we decided not to drag the matter into the courts, and parted.

Gallup gave us a good insight into America. As a matter of fact, this town did not at all differ from other small towns, thus considerably facilitating the writer's task by making a physical description of the town entirely superfluous. Any old Gallupian who had stayed away for two or three years would have scarcely recognized his native town— because there is not a single distinctive attribute by which he could distinguish it from any other American town.

"What city is that?" he might ask, poking his head out of his automobile, and only after learning that this actually was Gallup, and not Springfield or Geneva, could he begin to kiss his native soil (pavement). And it is precisely because of this absence of originality that the town of Gallup is remarkable. If Americans should ever fly to the moon, they would not fail to build there towns identically like Gallup. After all, it lies right in the heart of New Mexico's moonlit deserts—this petrol oasis with its "Main Street"; its "Manhattan Café," where you may drink tomato juice, eat apple pie, and upon depositing five cents in a slot machine may hear a phonograph record or a mechanical violin; with its department store, where you may buy corduroy trousers the colour of rust, socks, neckties, and a cowboy shirt; with its Ford automobiles; with its motion-picture theatres, where you may see unroll before your eyes the life of the rich or of bandits; with its drug-stores, where neat girls, as dandified as Polish lieutenants, eat ham and eggs before going to work. Good old Gallup! It is not interested in what is happening in Europe, Asia and Africa. Gallup is not even any too interested in general American affairs. It is proud, because, although it numbers only six thousand inhabitants, it has hot and cold water, bathrooms, showers,

refrigerators, toilet paper in lavatories—in short, it has the same comforts
and conveniences as Kansas City and Chicago.

Although it was not yet three o'clock, Mr. Adams persuaded us not
to go any farther.

"This is a fateful day, gentlemen," he said. "It is a day of bad luck. It
would be foolish not to understand that. Gentlemen, we shall outwit
fate. Tomorrow it will be powerless to interfere with our journey."

And he went off to a Ford dealer to find out how much we would have
to pay to repair the damages. He asked us to wait in the automobile,
around the corner. For about twenty minutes we sat there, discussing
with Mrs. Adams the unfortunate occurrences of that fateful day.

"Well, we have nothing more to fear today," said Mrs. Adams. "All
our bad luck is behind us."

Ten more minutes passed, but Mr. Adams still did not appear.

"I knew it!" exclaimed Mrs. Adams. "You must never let him go
anywhere alone. I am certain that right now he is sitting with the dealer
and discussing with him the League of Nations, having utterly forgotten
that we are waiting for him."

Another ten minutes passed, and a boy messenger came running with
the message that Mr. Adams asked us immediately to go to him at the
store. Mrs. Adams turned pale.

"Has anything happened to him?" she asked quickly.

"No, ma'am," replied the boy, looking askance.

We ran full speed into the store.

A strange spectacle met our eye. It seemed to us that not only we but
not a single inhabitant of Gallup throughout the entire existence of this
little town had ever seen the like. It looked as if a heavy Caproni bombing
plane had suddenly dropped here its entire reserve of bombs assigned
exclusively for Haile Selassie. The large plate-glass window of the store
lay shattered on the sidewalk. In the empty frame of the window, against
a background of two new Fords, stood Mr. Adams, holding in his hands
the frame of his glasses. A finger on his right hand was cut, but he did
not pay any attention to that and was explaining something about the
League of Nations to the bewildered owner of the store.

"No, no, sir!" he was saying. "You don't understand the League
of Nations!"

"What have you done?" exclaimed Mrs. Adams, gasping.

"But, Becky, I didn't do anything. I walked through the show
window. I was talking to this gentleman, and did not notice that instead
of going through the door I went through the window. What can I do,
if this window is so large that it looks like the door? And besides, it
goes right down to the ground!"

Mrs. Adams began to inspect her beloved husband. It was simply incredible. Mr. Adams was quite uninjured; only his glasses were broken.

"And it didn't hurt you?" asked Mrs. Adams. "This is, after all,
very thick plate-glass."

"But, Becky, I was so surprised that I didn't feel anything!"

Mr. Adams compensated the bewildered dealer for the damage and said joyously:

"You must not think, gentlemen, that I wasted my time here. I found out everything about the repair of our car. It does not pay to repair it now. This is not the last accident. Others will run into us. When we return to New York we shall repair everything and paint it all up at once. Let us not hurry, gentlemen! You will always have the opportunity and the time to spend your dollars."

We were so afraid that the misfortunes of that day had not yet come to an end that we walked down the street, moving our feet carefully and looking around like hunted deer. Only when we were already in bed did we quiet down somewhat, realizing that at last the day of mishaps was over.

25
The Desert

AMERICA WAS preparing for Christmas. Before the stores of the small towns electric lamps of various colours were already lighted on the cardboard Christmas trees that decorated all the street lamps. The traditional Santa Claus, the kindly Christmas grandfather with a long white beard, was driving through the streets in his gilded chariot. Electric fans scattered artificial snow from the chariot. Choruses of radio angels chanted old English carols. Santa Claus held in both his hands a department store sign which proclaimed: "Christmas Presents on Credit." Newspapers wrote that the holiday trade was better this year than the year before.

The closer we moved in the direction of California, the warmer the sun became, while the sky turned purer and bluer, the more there was of artificial snow, of cardboard fir trees and grey beards, and the more liberal became the credit for Christmas presents.

We crossed the border into Arizona. The keen, strong light of the desert lay on the excellent highway that led to Flagstaff. The obtrusive bill-boards almost disappeared, and only occasionally from behind a cactus or a yellowed tumbleweed emerged an impudent little Coca-Cola placard on a stick. The petrol stations became less and less frequent. But to make up for that, the hats of the rare residents here became broader and broader. Never before had we seen, and probably never again shall we see, such large hats as in Arizona, the land of deserts and canyons.

One can scarcely find anything more grandiose and more beautiful in the world than an American desert. We drove over it for an entire week and never tired of admiring it. We were fortunate. Winter in the desert is like a bright and clean summer, only without the oppressive heat and the dust.

The region into which we drove was utterly wild and desolate. Yet we did not feel that we were cut off from the world. The road and the automobile have brought the desert nearer, have torn off its shroud of mystery, without making it any less attractive. On the contrary, the beauty created by nature was supplemented by the beauty created by the deft hands of men. Admiring the pure colours of the desert, its complex and mighty architecture, we never ceased to admire the broad even highway with its silvery bridges, its neatly placed water-mains, its mounds and dips. Even the petrol stations which had become boresome in the East and in the Middle West, here in the desert looked like proud monuments to man's might. And the automobile in the desert seemed twice as beautiful as in the city. Its fluent, polished surface reflected the sun; and its shadow, deep and sharply lined, fell proudly on the virgin sands.

Desert roads are indubitably one of the most remarkable achievements of American technique. They are as good as in populated places. The same neat and clear black and yellow signs reminding you of curves, of narrow places, and of zigzags. The same white signs in a black border showing the number of the road, while the wooden arrows with the names of cities show the distance to them. In the desert there are, in addition, those wooden constructions which are met quite frequently and are called "cattle guards." Vast parcels of land belonging to cattlemen were separated from each other by barbed wire, so that the cattle should not cross from one parcel of land to the other, thereby avoiding quarrels and keeping the picturesque cowboys from bringing their Colts into action. But what to do to keep the cattle from passing from parcel to parcel across the highway? Surely, the highway cannot be crossed with barbed wire! So, an anonymous inventor thought of the solution. The wire stretched on either side of the highway. A ditch was dug across the road and over the ditch a metal grate was placed. There is no interference whatever with automobiles, while cows, afraid that their hooves may go through the grating, refrain from undesirable excursions into other people's land. It's all very simple in America.

In America travellers are never oppressed by the usual doubts of the journey: "Where are we now? Shall we find a night's lodging? Is the speedometer lying? Didn't we go too far to the west and is it not necessary, therefore, to reset our watches?" No! The traveller is not disturbed by the problem of a night's lodging. He is accustomed to find waiting for him camps consisting of several small houses (in each little house is a room, a shower, and a gas range, and beside the little house is a garage). Daily on the road you will find a bill-board reading: "Half a mile ahead—check speedometers." And actually a half-mile farther along stands a new petrol pump, and from that to the next one will be five miles, and you can check the correctness of your speedometer by it, as it marks off the distance covered. Later on, you may find the touchingly solicitous announcement: "Time to reset your watch." While to the question: "Where are we now?" there is the precise and somewhat solemn answer:

"You are leaving New Mexico. You are entering Arizona."

It sounds as if you were leaving the earth and entering heaven.

We rolled cheerily across the desert, having completely forgotten yesterday's horrors. It seemed incredible that there were such things as slush, snow, and frost in the world. Mr. Adams, who had a good night's sleep in Gallup and who had eaten well on the road, was in excellent spirits. He was full of ideas—and dying to talk. We discussed ten different subjects. We listened to Mr. Adams's ideas on the situation in Germany after the fascist coup, on the state of schools in America, on Roosevelt's chances in the next elections, and about the latest session of the Pacific Institute.

But all this seemed not enough for Mr. Adams. He kept looking impatiently at the road in the hope of finding a man with an uplifted thumb. But only red sand greeted the machine. There were no people in the desert. Fortunately, Mr. Adams was rescued at that point by nature itself, to whom indeed he yielded the reserve of emotions that was tearing him apart.

We were passing through the painted desert.

Smooth sandhills stretched to the very horizon like a stormy ocean whose waves have suddenly turned to stone. They crept upon each other, formed crests and thick round folds. They were magnificent, beautifully painted by nature in blue, pink, reddish-brown, and pastel colours. The tones were blindingly pure.

The word "desert" is frequently used as a symbol of monotony. The American desert is unprecedently varied. The face of the desert changed every two or three hours. Hills and cliffs in the form of pyramids, towers, recumbent elephants and antediluvian reptiles passed by.

But ahead of us was something even more remarkable.

We entered a reservation of petrified forest, fenced off by barbed wire. At first we did not notice anything special, but upon looking closely we saw emerging from the sand and the gravel, stumps and trunks of trees lying everywhere. Coming closer, we discerned that the gravel itself was composed of small particles of a petrified forest.

In this spot several scores of million years ago a forest grew. Not long ago this forest was discovered in the shape of broken petrified trunks. It is an astounding spectacle to find in the midst of the great silence of the desert prone trunks of petrified trees which have preserved the outward appearance of the most ordinary reddish-brown wooden trunks. The process of altering the wood of the trees into salt, lime, and iron had gone on for millions of years. These trees have acquired the hardness of marble.

On the reservation is a small museum where the bits of petrified wood are prepared. They are sawed and polished. The surface of the segment, while preserving all the lines of the wood, begins to gleam with its red, blue, and yellow veins. There is no marble or malachite that can rival the beauty of a polished bit of petrified wood.

At the museum we were told that these trees are a hundred and fifty million years old. The museum itself was probably no more than a year old. It was a small but quite modern building, with metal frames for doors and windows, with a water main, with hot and cold water. Emerging from such a little building, you would expect to find a subway, an airport, and a department store; instead, you find at once, without the slightest transition, a desert extending for hundreds of miles.

The reservation of the petrified forest is carefully guarded, so that one cannot take along a single grain of sand. But as soon as we emerged beyond the borders of the reservation, we saw a petrol station surrounded by a fence made up helter-skelter out of the petrified trees. Here was carried on a lively trade in pieces of wood at fifteen cents and up. A handicraft man with a motor that roared throughout the desert feverishly manufactured souvenirs in the form of brooches and bracelets. He sawed, sharpened, polished. Was it worth while to lie for so many millions of years in order to be transformed into an unprepossessing brooch with the inscription "Souvenir of . . ."?

We put several pieces of wood away into our automobile and, imagining how in due time they would travel inside of our valises across the ocean, set out again on our journey.

Not far from the little factory, on the edge of the road, thumb uplifted, stood a man with a suitcase.

We have already said that Americans are very gregarious, good-natured, and ever obliging. When you are being helped, let us say, by having your automobile pulled out of a rut or a ditch, it is done simply, modestly, quickly, without any calculation as to thanks, even verbal gratitude. The American helps you, cracks a joke, and goes on.

The uplifted thumb, as everyone knows, indicates a request for transportation. This signal has become as inseparable a part of American automobile travel as road signs which indicate curves, speed limit, and railroad crossing.

For a writer, a fisher of souls and subjects, such a custom presents great conveniences. The heroes come into your automobile of their own free will and at once willingly tell you the story of their lives.

We stopped. The man with the suitcase had to go to San Diego, California. We were going in the same direction as far as Flagstaff. Our new fellow traveller got into the machine, placed his baggage on his lap and, having waited for the question as to who he was and where he came from, began to tell us his story.

He hailed from the state of Massachusetts. There he had worked all his life as a locksmith. Five years ago he had moved to another city, lost his job right away, and with that his old life came to an end. A new life began for him, one to which he could not accustom himself. He was constantly travelling in search of employment. He had many times crossed the country from ocean to ocean, yet he had found no job. Occasionally he would get a lift in an automobile; most of the time, however, he travelled with tramps in railway freight cars. That was faster. But he himself was not a tramp. That he reiterated several times stubbornly and emphatically. Evidently he had been taken for a tramp more than once.

He received no relief because he had no permanent residence.

"I often meet people like myself," he said, "and among them there are even men with college education—doctors, lawyers. I became friendly with one such doctor, and we travelled together. Then we decided to write a book. We wanted the whole world to know how we live. We began to record every day everything that we had seen. We wrote down quite a lot. I had heard that if you publish a book you get well paid for it. Once we came to the state of Nebraska. Here we were caught in the freight car. Our manuscript was found. It was torn in pieces. And we were beaten up and thrown out. That is how I live."

He did not complain. He merely told his tale, with the same simplicity with which the young marine had told us how he and his friend had met some girls in Chicago and unexpectedly stayed there a whole week. The marine did not brag. The unemployed did not seek sympathy.

A man had fallen out of society. Naturally, he felt that the social order should be changed. But what should be done about it?

"You must take the wealth from the rich."

We began to listen even more attentively. He angrily struck the back of his seat with his large dirty fist and repeated:

"Take away their money! Take away their money and leave them only five million apiece! Give the unemployed a piece of land, so they can raise their own food and eat it. And leave the others only five million apiece!"

We asked him whether five million was not perhaps too much.

But he was adamant.

"No, they must have at least five million apiece. You can't make it any less."

"But who will take the wealth away from them?"

"It'll be taken away! Roosevelt will take it away! If we only re-elect him president for the second time, he will do it!"

"But suppose Congress won't let him?"

"Never mind. Congress will agree to it! It's a fair thing to do. How can they fail to agree to it? It's perfectly obvious."

He was so carried away by this primitive idea, he was so desirous that injustice should disappear of its own accord and that everybody should be well off, that he did not even care to think how all of this should come about. He was a child who wanted everything to be made of chocolate. It seemed to him that all he had to do was to ask kindly, good-natured Santa Claus, and everything would be magically transformed. Santa Claus would come racing in on his cardboard, silvered deer, would arrange a warm snowstorm and everything would come about. Congress will agree. Roosevelt will politely take away the billions, and the rich men with meek smiles will give up those billions.

Millions of Americans are in the throes of such childish ideas.

How to be rid of the depression for ever and aye?

Oh, that's not hard at all! The government must give each old man, upon reaching the age of sixty, two hundred dollars a month on the condition that he obligate himself to spend this money. Then the buying power of the population will grow to unheard-of proportions and the depression will immediately end. At the same time the old folks will live remarkably well. It is all clear and simple. How all of this is to be arranged is not so important. The old people are so desirous of receiving two hundred dollars a month, and the young folks are so desirous to have the depression end and to secure a job at last, that it is sheer joy to all. Townsend, the inventor of this magic means, won millions of ardent disciples in a very short time.

Townsend clubs and committees sprang up throughout the country and, with the approach of presidential elections, the Townsendite idea was enriched by a new amendment. It proposed to give two hundred dollars to each person who attained the age of fifty.

The hypnosis of simple figures acts with a remarkable power. As a matter of fact, what child has not dreamed of how nice it would be if every adult should give him one penny? It doesn't cost the adult much, while the child can thus accumulate a pile of money.

We are not speaking here of advanced American workers nor about the radical intelligentsia. We are speaking about the so-called average American, the principal buyer and the principal voter. He is a simple and exceedingly democratic human being. He knows how to work, and he works hard. He loves his wife and his children, listens to the radio, frequently goes to the motion-picture theatre, and reads very little. Besides, he has a great respect for money. He does not feel for it the passion of a miser, but he respects it just as in one's family an uncle who is a famous professor is respected, and he wants everything in the world to be just as simple and understandable as it is in his home.

When someone sells him a refrigerator or an electric stove or a vacuum cleaner, the salesman never goes into abstract discussions. With precision and in a businesslike way he explains how many cents an hour the electric energy will cost, what cash payment he will have to make, and how much will be economized by this arrangement. The purchaser wants to know figures, advantages, expressed in dollars.

A political idea is sold to him in the same manner. Nothing abstract, no philosophy. He votes, and he is promised two hundred dollars a month or the equalization of wealth. These are figures. That is understandable. He will agree to that. Of course, he will be very much surprised to discover that these ideas do not work out as conscientiously as a refrigerator and a vacuum cleaner. But for the present he still believes in them.

In Flagstaff we parted with our fellow traveller.

When he left our automobile, we noticed the low level of poverty to which the man had sunk. His worn coat was in tatters. His greenish cheeks had not been shaved for a long time, and in his ears was gathered

F

the dust of Pennsylvania, Kansas, and Oklahoma. When he said good-
bye an optimistic smile lit up his sorrowing face.

"Soon everything will go well," he said. "But they get only five
millions, and not another cent!"

When we were driving out of Flagstaff, holding the course on the
Grand Canyon, Mr. Adams said:

"Well, what do you think? Why does this unfortunate man insist on
leaving five million apiece to the millionaires? Don't you know? Well,
then, I will tell you. In his heart of hearts he is still hoping that some
day he himself will become a millionaire. American upbringing is a
frightful thing, gentlemen!"

26
Grand Canyon

TOWARD EVENING of every day our old man, whom we learned to
like very much, would grow tired.

The three hundred miles we had driven, the impressions, the endless
conversations, finally his respectable age, took their toll: Mr. Adams
would grow tired, and some link or another would fall out of his actions.

If toward evening Mrs. Adams would ask her husband to ascertain
from somebody on the road whether we were travelling in the right
direction, the old man would begin to turn around restlessly in his seat.
From his movements, we could divine that he did not know how to
proceed. He simply forgot. He was supposed to open the window, put
his head out and, having said: "Pardon me, sir," which means "Excuse
me," find out about the road. All this he used to do very neatly, would
cry out: "Pardon me," and attempt to put his head out. But he would
forget the main thing—to drop the window. That link would fall out.
And each time, unable to understand why his head did not shove itself
out, he would attempt to break the glass with his elbow. Only the
unheard-of durability of American manufacturing processes saved the
head and arm of Mr. Adams from cuts. Toward evening we would take
care not to entrust him with commissions of that sort.

We moved very fast down the deserted road in order to reach Grand
Canyon the same day—Grand Canyon, one of the great geographical
wonders of the world!

We were tired and, therefore, forgot about the control over Mrs.
Adams. She noticed it at once, and advanced her speed from fifty miles
to sixty. Then she stealthily looked around and added another five miles.
Now we were going at a speed in excess of a hundred kilometres an hour.
That was a typical feminine trait. A woman always tries to drive faster
than circumstances warrant. The air roared, torn to shreds by our car.

Again we drove through the painted desert. Pure blue hills lay along the whole horizon. The sundown was likewise pure, naïve, as if it had been painted by some provincial young ladies long before the first horrifying thought of men entered their heads. The colours of the desert were so fresh and transparent that it is possible to transmit them only by means of an album of aquarelles. The few strands of wind that blew into our automobile through the lowered window pounced on each other like attic cats. In their fight they would strike us, tear off our hats and blow over Mr. Adams's head. Mr. Adams did not yet have his hat as a result of the complicated postal operations which we transacted throughout the journey. The evening, however, was quite cool and the skin of Mr. Adams's head turned blue and was now in no way distinguishable in colour from the hills.

In utter darkness, quiet, somewhat squelched by the beauties of nature we had seen, we arrived at the Grand Canyon and stopped in one of the camp houses. It was made of huge logs. It was supposed to give us some idea of primitive American pioneer life. But on the inside, to make up for its rusticity, it was furnished in a completely modern manner, and the beds, as always, were excellent (in America, a customer is sold not a bed, but good repose). So here they were, these rooms equipped with excellent repose, steam heat, hot and cold water, and New Yorkese portable lamps with large cardboard lampshades. These lamps are very tall, the height of a human being, and they do not stand on the table but on the floor.

After supper the tourists gathered in a small theatre hall of the hotel (also built of gigantic logs) and were shown a short advertising motion picture about the descent to the bottom of the canyon under the leadership of experienced guides. After the picture there was a concert.

Out on the stage came a fat boy with a banjo. He sat down on the platform and began to pluck the strings of his instrument, pounding away rhythmic taps with his feet in cowboy boots. He looked disdainfully at the public: anyone could see at once that to him only cowboys were human beings and all the others were just trash. After him appeared a tall thin long-nosed cowboy with a guitar. He looked at the public and said:

"Listen, three of us were supposed to sing, but the others aren't coming, I guess, so that I'm going to sing alone. But maybe I shouldn't sing at all. As a matter of fact, I'm no singer anyhow."

He had a handsome, ironic face. In his small black eyes was written:

"Well, now, why play the fool? Hadn't we better go out and have a drink? That would be much more fun. Don't you want to? Well, in that case, I'll sing for you. That's your hard luck!"

The fat boy continued to twang on the banjo. The guitar sounded rather low. The cowboy sang, or rather, talked his little songs, passing occasionally into a Tyrolean falsetto (yodelling). The songs were simple and funny. This is what one of them said:

"When as a boy I swam in the river. Somebody stole the clothes I left folded on the shore. I could not very well go home in the nude, so, while waiting for darkness to fall, I passed the time away cutting my initials on an old apple tree. Many years have passed since then. I found a beautiful girl and married her. Imagine my embarrassment when we went into the bedroom for the first time. My beautiful wife calmly took her artificial teeth out of her mouth and placed them in a glass of water. Then she took off her wig and disclosed her bald head. From her brassière she took huge wads of cotton. Right before my eyes my beauty was transformed into a scarecrow. But that wasn't all. She then took off her skirt and calmly unscrewed her wooden leg, and on that leg I suddenly saw initials. And the devil take me if they weren't the very same initials which I once cut on the old apple tree when in my childhood somebody stole my clothes."

Everybody laughed, and we joined in. It was very old-fashioned, naïve, and funny. The cowboy smiled satirically, as before. And as before, in his eyes gleamed an invitation to go with him somewhere around the corner and down a couple of large glasses of whisky. As to his saying that he couldn't sing, the cowboy lied. He sang well, and he amused us for a long while.

After him a Negro came out. There was no master of ceremonies here, and no one announced the names of the artistes. And they weren't even artistes. All of those who were appearing here were employees of the Grand Canyon. They were giving this concert as an accommodation.

The Negro was extremely young and lanky. His legs seemed to begin at his armpits. He tap-danced with genuine pleasure. His arms swung remarkably in time with his body. He wore trousers on suspenders and a work shirt. After finishing the dance, he gaily picked up a broom that stood in the corner and went away, baring his teeth.

In the morning we saw him near the log cabin in which we slept. He was sweeping up, and he swept with the same pleasure with which he had danced. It even seemed that he was continuing his dance and that the broom was only part of it. He opened his large grey lips and wished us good morning.

We went at once to see the canyon.

Imagine this: You take an immense mountain chain, cut it at the root, turn it upside down and push it into an even land covered with forests. Then you take it out. What remains is the mould of a mountain chain. Its mountains are upside down. That is the Grand Canyon.

Mountains must be looked at from below. The canyon—from the top down. The spectacle of the Grand Canyon does not have its equal anywhere on earth. It did not even resemble anything else on earth. The landscape upset all European concepts about the globe, if one may say so. It looked like some imaginary vision, which might occur to a boy while reading fantastic romances about the moon or Mars. We stood for a long time on the edge of this splendid abyss. We four gossipers did not speak a single word. Far below a bird floated by, slowly, like a fish. Even deeper, almost swallowed by shadows, flowed the Colorado River.

Grand Canyon is a grandiose national park which occupies hundreds of square miles. Like all American national parks (reservations), it is faultlessly organized. Hotels and roads, the distribution of printed and photographic publications, maps, prospectuses, guidebooks, and finally, oral explanations—all of it is here at a high standard of excellence. Here Americans come with their families to rest, and this rest is not expensive. A cabin in this camp costs no more than in any other, while food costs about the same as anywhere else. For visiting the park, the fee is only one dollar, after which a coloured label is pasted on the automobile windshield and one is free to live and wander throughout this park for a month, even for a year.

Of course, we should have gone down to the bottom of the canyon and lived there for half a year in a log cabin with steam heating, in the midst of the chaos of nature and ideal service, but we did not have the time for that. We did only what we could—drove around the canyon in an automobile.

Suddenly we saw a strange funeral. Down the excellent road of the park slowly moved an automobile bearing a casket. It moved with the speed of a pedestrian. Behind the casket walked people in white leather aprons pinned to ordinary dress-coats. One of them wore a silk top-hat and a morning coat. Some of those who walked behind the casket carried sticks on their shoulders. Behind the procession soundlessly moved more than a score of empty automobiles.

They were burying an old cowboy who had served in the park. The old cowboy had been a Mason, and all these people in white aprons were Masons. The sticks were the sticks of their banner. The funeral was going our way, so we attached ourselves to the end of the column. Out of the forest came a doe and looked in fright at the automobile flock. Hunting is, of course, forbidden in the park, so the doe was not afraid of being shot. But she wanted very much to cross the road. She attempted it several times and jumped back, puzzled by the petrol odour the Masons emitted. Finally, the doe made up her mind, gracefully jumped across the road in front of our car, all her four legs simultaneously leaving the earth, flashed once or twice among the trees, and was lost in the forest.

"Gentlemen," said Mr. Adams, "we must not tarry any longer. We must empty the water out of the radiator and pour into it an anti-freeze mixture. The nights are cold already and the water might freeze. Our radiator will go to the devil. Here in the park we left our machine in a warm garage. But I cannot guarantee that during the next night we shall find anything like that."

In the warm garage of the Grand Canyon we saw somebody's automobile after an accident. Thick branches of trees had broken in through the roof of the large Buick. The motor had pushed itself into the seat of the chauffeur. Inside the machine lay branches and green leaves. The man who had been driving that Buick had fallen asleep at the wheel. That happens in America. The even road, the lulling sway of the machine, the fatigue of the day—and the man, without noticing it himself, falls asleep while driving at a speed of fifty miles an hour. The awakening is almost always frightful. The Buick we saw hit a tree with such force that at the place of the accident one could not tell where the product of General Motors began and where the product of nature ended. Strange as it may seem, the sleeping driver not only remained alive, but was not even badly hurt. The boy from the garage told us in a respectful manner that he hoped the owner of the machine will henceforth sleep in more safe places than in a moving automobile—in bed, for example. We all looked at Mrs. Adams. Although she never fell asleep while driving, on all our faces was written: "You see?" as if we had already caught our driver snoring at the wheel. We did it anyway, for good measure.

Newer and newer colour schemes, each more imposing than the other, opened at every turn of the Grand Canyon. The bright blue and pink haze of early morning scattered. We stopped at some parapets and looked into the abyss. It was now apricot in colour. At a distance of a mile below us could be seen a river growing ever more luminous. We shouted for all we were worth, calling forth an echo, and for a long time our Moscow voices hopped over the cliffs, returned to us, and finally perished in space.

At last we passed the exit booth. There was no one there. Today was an important holiday—a day of thanks—Thanksgiving Day. And many of the employees did not work. However, on the glass of his booth there was a note which read: "Good-bye. Call again."

"Gentlemen," said Mr. Adams instructively, "put that down in your little books."

And he began to tell us long and interesting stories about American service. He talked like one inspired until we had driven some forty miles away from the canyon. Then he put his left hand over his eyes, and was petrified.

"Becky," he said, no longer inspired, "did you take my watch out from under my pillow?"

"No," said Becky, throwing a red-hot glance at her husband.

"But, but . . ." moaned Mr. Adams, "please don't look at me. You mustn't do that. Look only at the road."

"You left the watch in the camp," said Mrs. Adams, without taking her eyes off the road.

"No, no, Becky!" Mr. Adams spoke in excitement. "I did not leave it in the camp. I left it under the pillow."

We stopped. We learned that the watch cost a hundred and twenty-five dollars, but that wasn't the main thing. The real misfortune was that the watch had been given as a gift to her husband by Mrs. Adams herself.

We began to figure which was more to our advantage, to make an extra eighty miles to recover the watch or to forget about the watch and to go on. We decided that it paid to go back, especially since the object left behind was precious as a memento, which could in no way be said about the petrol.

Nevertheless, we did not turn back. We telephoned to the camp from the nearest petrol station. The camp replied that the worker who had cleaned our house had gone away at the moment, but there was no doubt that he would immediately turn over the watch to the management of the camp, provided the watch was under the pillow.

"Well," said Mrs. Adams, "in that case, we will not go back. You can send the watch to us in San Francisco, General Delivery."

The man from the camp replied that all that was very well, but at the same time asked that the key to the house, which Mr. Adams had taken along with him, be sent back. Mrs. Adams cast a withering glance at her husband and said that we would immediately return the key by mail.

In view of these circumstances, we drove for two whole hours in utter silence.

27
The Man in the Red Shirt

OUT OF Grand Canyon there was a new road, untravelled yet by tourists. The tall thick forests of the National Park became gradually thinner and finally disappeared altogether. They were succeeded by yellow cliffs which ended in a descent into the new desert. The road fell down in sharp curves. It was one of the most remarkable of American automobile roads, a scenic road, which meant a landscape road. The builders of it made it not only durable, broad, convenient, and safe during rain, but they even attained this: that every one of its turns compelled the traveller to admire ever newer and newer landscapes, scores of various facets of one and the same landscape.

"No, seriously," said Mr. Adams, sticking his head out of the machine every minute, "you want to understand what American service is. It is the highest degree of knowing how to serve. You don't have to climb over cliffs in order to find a convenient point for observation. You can see everything while sitting in your machine. Therefore, buy automobiles, buy petrol, buy oil!"

We had become accustomed to deserts, we had come to love them, and so we greeted the new desert, which opened before us from a considerable height, as an old friend. Here began the reservation of a nomad Indian tribe, the Navajo. This is one of the largest Indian tribes. It consists of sixty thousand people. Five years ago this region was altogether inaccessible, and only recently, with the advent of the new road, did tourists gradually begin to penetrate.

The Navajos loathe and detest their "white-faced brothers," who have been exterminating them for two centuries, driving them into worse and worse places, and finally into a fruitless desert. This hate is unmistakable in the Indian's every glance. He will attach his new-born baby to a little board and put it right down on the dirty earthen floor of the wigwam rather than take from the white man any part of his culture.

The Indians almost never mix with the whites. That is an age-long opposition of theirs, evidently, one of the most remarkable phenomena in the history of mankind.

The government, which formerly devoted itself to destroying the Indians, is now trying to preserve their small number of descendants. At the head of the Indian Department in Washington is a liberal gentleman. So-called Indian reservations have been built where the whites are permitted to trade with the Indians under state control. Having chased the Indians away from the fertile ground, they have reserved for them only a few pathetic parcels of desert, and this is regarded as a great act of beneficence. They have opened museums of Indian art. They buy from the Indians, for a pittance, their drawings, rugs, painted clay bowls, and silver bracelets. They have built several well-equipped schools for Indian children. Americans are rather proud of their Indians: even so does the director of a zoo take pride in a rare old lion. The proud beast is very old and is no longer dangerous: his claws are dull, his teeth have fallen out, but his skin is magnificent.

While arranging the reservations, schools, and museums they forgot that the foundation of a people's development is their native tongue. In Indian schools only white men teach, and they teach only in English. There is no Indian writing. True, every Indian tribe has its own peculiar language. But that is no obstacle. Where there is a will there is a way. And many American scientists, specialists of Indian culture, could create a written language for them in a short time, if only for a few of the more important tribes.

Toward noon we arrived in a habitation called Cameron. Here were a few houses—a post office, a trading post where merchandise is sold to Indians, a small but excellently equipped hotel with a little restaurant, a camp, and two adobe Indian wigwams.

We went into one of these. The father of the family was not at home. On the floor sat an Indian beauty who looked like a gypsy (Indian men are usually handsomer than the women). She was surrounded by a whole brood of children. The smallest, a suckling infant, was tied to a little board which lay on the floor. The oldest was about seven years old. The children were dirty but very handsome, like their mother.

"Becky, Becky!" Mr. Adams cried excitedly, "come here, quick! I found some children!"

The Adamses missed their baby and never let a youngster get by without taking him up in their arms, petting him and giving him a bit of candy. Children were very fond of Mr. Adams, went to his arms gladly, prattling something about lambs and ponies. Their mothers, flattered by this attention, regarded Mr. Adams with a grateful glance and in farewell would bid him a tender good-bye, as if he were not a casual traveller met on the road but a kind grandfather who had arrived from Kansas City for a visit with his dearly beloved grandchildren. In brief, the Adamses derived great pleasure from such meetings.

"Where are the children?" exclaimed Mrs. Adams, hastily taking out of her bag a piece of chocolate and stooping down in order to enter through the low door of the wigwam.

"Well, young gentlemen," said Mr. Adams cheerfully, "which one of you wants to be the first to get the chocolate?"

The youngsters began to bawl in fright. The beautiful mother distractedly tried to quiet them. Only the seven-year-old, who evidently also wanted to begin bawling, controlled himself, clenched his dirty little fists and looked at us with such ferocity that we immediately left.

"Here," said Mr. Adams in confusion, "Indians from the very earliest age teach their children hatred for the whites. Yes, yes, yes! The Navajo Indians are wise people. Why should they love the whites?"

When we were leaving the wigwam, a rusty old automobile (such an ancient specimen we had not seen even in Texas) drove up, and the father of the family walked out of it.

"How do you do, sir?" said Mr. Adams, trying to start a conversation.

The Indian did not reply. He pointed to his lips and made a negative gesture with his hand. He did not wish to converse with white people. Going to his wigwam with an armful of dry weeds, he did not even look in our direction. We interested him no more than the dust of the desert. Even an old English diplomat might envy the majesty of his gait and the inscrutability of his face.

How clearly we grasped at that moment the hypocrisy of all the Indian departments, schools, museums, reservations, all this busybody charity of an old sinner who clumsily tries to make up for the wrongs of the past!

When we were driving out of Cameron we were warned that from then on for a long time we would not find a place to stop.

A splendid road presented us with the opportunity to develop high speed. We raced across the desert for about five hours without meeting a soul, except that once a white horse appeared. It was going, in a sure manner, somewhere, alone, without a guide. A little farther on there was a detour for about ten miles. Here several workers in road machines were finishing up the final section of a road.

On both sides of the highway lay the painted desert. We were racing after the sun, which was slowly dropping into the Pacific Ocean, somewhere into Japan, which from the American point of view is the land of the setting sun. We crossed the territory of the Navajo; yet where were those sixty thousand poor but proud people? That we did not know. They must have been somewhere with their flocks, their fires, and their wigwams. Several times in the course of the day the figure of a rider would appear on the horizon, and with it a cloud of dust, and then both would quickly disappear.

If the desert had seemed varied to us, now it changed almost every

F*

minute. At first we saw level hills, which seemed to be covered over with cocoa, and in their forms reminiscent of wigwams (so this is where the Indians got the models for their architecture!). Then began a piling up of smooth and round dark-grey heights which looked as soft as pillows and were seamed at the edges like pillows. Then we found ourselves at the bottom of a small canyon. Here was such architecture—mausoleums, bastions, castles—that we gave up exclaiming over it, and, leaning out the windows, silently followed with our eyes the stone visions of the thousands of years that flew past us. The sun sank. The desert became pink. All of it culminated in a temple on a cliff surrounded by even terraces. The road turned toward this temple. Under it flowed the Little Colorado River. Across it was flung a new suspension bridge. Here was the end of the Navajo reservation.

It suddenly turned dark and cold. We ran out of petrol. We were hungry. But scarcely had Mr. Adams managed to express the thought that everything was over and we would have to sleep in the desert, when immediately from around the bridge a light gleamed, and we drove up to a house. Near the little house we noticed, with a sigh of relief, a petrol station. Nothing was there other than these two structures, which stood directly in the desert and were not even fenced in. The house represented what in Russian and in Spanish is called a "rancho" but in English a "ranch." So, here in the desert, where for two hundred miles around there is not a single settled habitation, we found: excellent beds, electric lights, steam heat, hot and cold water—we found all the conveniences of any house in New York, Chicago, or Gallup. In the dining-room we were served tomato juice in glasses and a steak with a bone in the shape of the letter T, just as handsome and as unappetizing as in Chicago, New York, or Gallup, and we were charged almost the same price as in Gallup, Chicago, or New York, although, if they wanted to take advantage of the helpless situation of the travellers, they could have got from us as much as they liked.

This spectacle of the American standard of living was no less grandiose than the painted desert. If we were asked to name the one distinguishing characteristic of America, we should say: this very little house in the desert. This little house contains all of American life: complete comfort in a desert side by side with the pauper wigwams of the Indians—quite as in Chicago, where side by side with Michigan Avenue is a rubbish heap of a slum. No matter where you might go as a traveller, to the North, to the South, or to the West, to New York, New Orleans, or New Jersey, you will see everywhere poverty and riches, which like two inseparable sisters stand hand in hand at all the roads and at all the bridges of this great country.

On the parapet of the entrance to the house lay an ox-yoke. At its sides were placed several chunks of petrified wood. On the porch we were met by a greyish cowboy, the master of the house and of the petrol station. He had come into the desert from Texas twenty years ago. In those days, without paying for it, any citizen of the United States could stake out in the desert sixty acres of land and take up cattle raising. All he had to invest in the land was two hundred dollars. In those days this cowboy was a young man. He brought his cattle, built a house, got married. Even five years ago it was two hundred miles from the house to the nearest road, and one could ride to it only on horseback. But recently the broader highway had been built, tourists began to appear, the cowboy built a petrol station, and converted his little house into a hotel. In the fireplace of his log hall a big fire blazes. On the walls hang deer heads, Indian rugs, and a leopard skin. Several rocking-chairs stand about and several portable lamps with cardboard shades (just exactly as they stood in our New York hotel room). There is a piano—and a radio which never stops playing or broadcasting news. His wife and daughter cook and serve. The cowboy himself, a typical American husband and father, with a kindly and somewhat wistful smile, helps them cook and serve, puts logs into the fireplace, and sells petrol. But there are already visible elements of the future large hotel. There is already a table with a special department for envelopes and writing paper. So far, the envelopes are just ordinary ones, but soon there will appear on them a vignette representing the façade of the hotel, an Indian profile, and the beautifully printed title: "Hotel Desert" or "Hotel Navajo Bridge." And already Indian rugs and trifles are offered for sale. Among those rugs were two which the owner did not want to sell, although he had been offered fifty dollars apiece.

"Now," said Mr. Adams, impatiently moving from foot to foot, "you must tell us what is remarkable about these rugs."

The old cowboy proved to be good company.

"Well," he began slowly, "these are Indian religious rugs, or, as the Indians call them, garments. I got them a long time ago from a certain Indian. You see, the Indians have a belief that should anyone become ill he must be wrapped in these garments. Therefore, they always come to me for them. I, of course, never refuse them. While the sick man lies wrapped in the rugs, the tribe dances a special dance dedicated to his convalescence. At times they dance several days on end. I love and respect the Navajos very much. It would be most unpleasant for me to sell these rugs and deprive them of such a means of healing."

The master rose, stamping resoundingly with the heels of his cowboy boots, walked toward the fireplace, and threw in a large log. Then he returned and continued:

"The Navajos are actually a remarkable people. They are faultlessly honest. There are never any crimes among them. It seems to me that they don't even know what a crime is. During the last twenty years I have learned to respect them as I have never respected any white man, and I am very sorry for them. Their children are dying at a great rate. You see, they don't want any help from the whites. They will not submit to white influence and will not allow white men in their wigwams.

I have friendly relations with the Navajos, but even after twenty years I am a stranger to them. Yet they are a remarkable people. It is hard to imagine how honest they are."

The old cowboy told us a story about a certain Indian of the Navajo tribe who suddenly decided to take up trade.

"Somehow the Indian managed to acquire an unusual amount of capital, two hundred dollars, either because he sold some cattle or found a little oil on his property; but anyhow, he got hold of a little money. So he decided to go into business. He went from the desert to the nearest town, bought two hundred dollars' worth of various merchandise, and brought it to his own native reservation. Just imagine an Indian engaged in commerce! It was the first occurrence of that kind in the entire history of the Navajo tribe. His trade went quite well. But I noticed that my Indian friend was carrying on his business in a rather peculiar way. I was so surprised that at first I thought he had lost his mind. You see, he was selling his merchandise for exactly the same price he had paid for it himself. So I began to explain to him that he can't carry on trade that way, that he would go bankrupt, that merchandise must be sold for more than the price paid for it.

"'Well, what do you mean by a higher price?' the Indian asked me.

"'Very simple,' I replied. 'Let's say you bought a thing for a dollar; so you must sell it for a dollar-twenty.'

"'How can I sell it for a dollar-twenty when it cost me only a dollar?' this merchant asked me.

"'But that is exactly what trade means,' I said. 'You buy cheaper and you sell for more.'

"But at this point my Indian became frightfully angry.

"'That's fraud!' he said. 'To buy for a dollar and to sell for a dollar-twenty! You're advising me to deceive people.'

"Then I said to him:

"'That's not fraud. You simply must earn money, must make a profit; don't you understand? Make a profit!'

"But something strange happened to my Indian friend. He suddenly stopped understanding the most ordinary things.

"'What do you mean, make a profit?' he asked.

"'Well,' I said, 'justify your expenses.'

"'I didn't have any expenses.'

"'But still, you went to the city; you bought; you brought it here; you worked.'

"'What kind of work is that?' the Indian told me. 'To buy, to bring it here—that's not work. No, you're giving me bad advice.'

"It was simply impossible to convince him. No matter how hard I tried, nothing came of it. He was as stubborn as a bull, and he kept repeating one and the same thing: 'You're advising me to do something dishonest.' I tell him, this is trade; and he tells me that in that case trade is a dishonest thing. And just imagine: he continued to trade that way, just as he began, though eventually he gave up this occupation. Thus, the only commercial enterprise with Indian capital in a Navajo tribe had to close up."

We remembered that Indian a month later when we were sitting in the Senate of the United States of America during the investigation ot John Pierpont Morgan, Jr., by a Senate Committee.

The Committee was concerned with the question of Morgan's role in so far as it helped to drag America into the World War.

"Tell me," asked Senator Nye, "didn't you know that by exporting money into Europe you were supporting war?"

"Yes, I knew it."

"Why did you do it, then?"

"What do you mean, why?" The huge old man was surprised, rising a little in his chair. "But that is business! Trade! They bought money and I sold it."

The wife called our host into the dining-room to help her set the table. Soon they called us too.

After we had finished our dinner, a tall man in boots, in a bright red shirt, held in by a cartridge belt, entered the room. His hair was reddish, with considerable grey in it. He wore horn-rimmed spectacles and a dazzling smile. He was accompanied by a woman. They greeted our host and sat down at the neighbouring table. The man in the red shirt heard us speaking among ourselves in some foreign tongue and said to the woman who had come there with him :

"Well, wife, these must be Frenchmen. Now you'll have a chance to talk French."

"I don't know French," replied his wife.

"What do you mean, you don't know it? Well, what do you know about that! We have been married for fifteen years and all that time every day you told me that you were born two hours' ride from Paris."

"So I was born two hours' ride from Paris."

"Well, why don't you talk French with these people?"

"But I tell you I don't know the French language. I was born in London, and London is actually two hours' ride from Paris if you go by airplane."

The man in the red shirt laughed noisily. It was evident that this family joke was repeated every time the couple met foreigners.

The ground was beautifully prepared for Mr. Adams to act, and he did not hesitate.

"I see, sir, that you are a cheerful person," said Mr. Adams, taking a polite little step forward.

"Sure!" exclaimed the man in the red shirt.

And he on his part took a step in the direction of Mr. Adams.

In the eyes of both men gleamed such an unquenchable and insane desire to talk that it was clear to us that they were bound to meet in the desert. They could not fail to meet. Only love at first sight flares up with such natural alacrity.

"How do you do, sir?" said Mr. Adams, taking one more step forward.

"How do you do?" said the man in the red shirt, and he also took an additional step. "Are you from New York?" he asked.

"Surely!" piped Mr. Adams. "And you live here?"

"Surely!" roared the stranger.

A second later they were already slapping each other on the shoulder with terrible gusto—though actually little Mr. Adams slapped his new friend across the waist, while his tall friend was whacking Mr. Adams almost on the back of his head.

Mr. Adams had an extraordinary nose for new acquaintances. The man in the red shirt proved to be one of the most interesting people we met in America.

"He is the only white man," our cowboy host said about him, "whom the Indians have accepted as one of their own. He lives with the Indians, but sometimes he comes to visit me."

The biography of this man is a real romance.

After graduating from college he became a missionary. Being a man with a purpose in life, he married and went to the post of his new field of duty—into the desert, to the Navajo Indians, in order to convert them to Christianity. However, it soon became evident to the fledgling missionary that the Indians did not want Christianity. All his efforts met the stubborn resistance of the Indians, who not only did not wish to accept the new faith, but more than that, refused to have anything at all to do with white people. Despite all rebuffs, he learned to like the Indians. A year later he went back to his superiors and declared that he refused to convert Indians to Christianity.

"I see my Christian duty in helping people," he said, "irrespective of what religion they profess. I have thought it all out thoroughly. If you have no objections, I shall remain in the desert with the Indians, but I warn you I will not make the slightest effort to convert them to Christianity. Otherwise, I could never be accepted by the Indians as one of them. I will simply help them the best I can. I will call doctors for them, explain to them how they must take care of their children. I will give them advice on how to live. So far there has never been a case of the Navajo accepting a white man. Only if I should succeed can we begin to consider the possibility of converting them to Christianity."

The church administration thought such talk too radical.

"You must act like all missionaries," they told him.

He refused.

Then they dismissed him. Yet, this odd fellow remained true to his dangerous ideas, although he had his wife to support and not a penny with which to do it.

He again went into the desert, this time with the firm determination never to return. That was eighteen years ago. He settled in a nomad camp of the Navajos and began to lead the life of an Indian. He had no money. Like the Indians, he took up hunting and cattle raising.

Years passed. The Indians became accustomed to the brave and cheerful man in eyeglasses. Little by little they began to show confidence in him, and he began to be one of them. Occasionally he would go into the city, arrange a public subscription for the Indian children, and persuade the Indians to go to doctors for medical aid and not to tie their infants to the little boards. He mastered the Navajo language. He came to love the Indians very much. He somehow could never begin his propaganda of Christianity. "I'll have time for that yet," he thought. But after a while he even stopped thinking about Christianity. Looking back, he understood that the greater and probably the better part of his life had already passed and that it had passed well. He was happy.

"I wanted to make Christians out of the Indians," the man in the red shirt, with a cartridge belt, told us, "but it didn't turn out as I expected: they made an Indian out of me. Yes! Now I am a real Indian. If you like I'll take your scalp off!"

And laughing loudly he pretended to scalp Mr. Adams.

Then he sat down and, still smiling, added thoughtfully:

"And to tell you the truth, I don't know more honest, noble, and clean-cut people than the Indians. They taught me to love the sun, the moon, the desert. They taught me to understand nature. I cannot imagine now how I could live away from the Indians."

"Sir," Mr. Adams said suddenly, "you are a good man."

He took out a handkerchief and wiped his eyes, without taking off his eyeglasses.

On the morrow we rose at six o'clock. Day was beginning to break, although the sun had not yet risen. It was as cold as it is in Moscow at that hour. We shivered under our topcoats. The little forest was covered with hoar frost. The desert seemed dark and not so beautiful as yesterday. We ran to the bridge for another look at the Little Colorado River. Above us was the cliff in the shape of a temple surrounded by terraces. Even that did not seem so magic to us as it had the day before. When in an effort to warm up we ran back to the little house, the sun appeared. The desert at once was alight and became beautiful. Half an hour later we took off our coats, and in another half-hour it was downright hot.

Before starting off on our long journey (we had to travel three hundred miles to Boulder Dam), we stopped at the petrol station. There we saw the missionary in the red shirt. He had taken the place of the cowboy, who was occupied with his household affairs. Again he and Adams began to whack each other's shoulder.

"I am a Bolshevik!" shouted the former missionary in farewell, pointing to his red shirt and roaring with laughter. "Good-bye!"

"Good-bye!" cried Mr. Adams in response.

The road went up into the hills. So, looking back on the desert of the Navajos, we could see for a long time the little house, and the bridge, and the petrol station beside which could be seen the red shirt of the missionary who had become an Indian. We were gazing for the last time at the Navajo desert, wondering how in the centre of the United States —between New York and Los Angeles, between Chicago and New Orleans, surrounded on all sides by electric stations, oil derricks, railways, millions, of automobiles, thousands of banks, stock exchanges and churches, deafened by the clamour of jazz bands, motion-picture films and gangster machine-guns—these people managed to preserve in its full untouchability their manner of living.

28
A Young Baptist

THE ASCENT among the yellow cliffs continued for an hour and a half. The little house of the cowboy, the petrol station, and the bridge across the Little Colorado River had long ago vanished from view, yet the desert of the Navajo Indians still lay in the valley behind us, the last barren refuge of pure-blooded, one-hundred-per-cent. Americans whose only misfortune was that their skin was red and that they had no aptitude for trade, but rather for drawing and for warlike but not dangerous dances.

Two or three more turns, and the desert disappeared. Suddenly we . found ourselves at a beautiful health resort in the Tyrol, in Switzerland, in the Caucasus. It was like the return of interplanetary travellers from Mars to earth, to one of its most beautiful corners, the virgin forest of Kanab. Pure flaky snow lay on the road. Large smooth pines rose on either side. And over all the sparkle of the December sun.

Such metamorphoses occur in America.

The beautiful vision soon came to an end. The road descended, and we entered the state of Utah, announced by a small bill-board. Here again was the desert, but this one was warmer. We passed a small settlement. Around the houses grew trees, and there were several petrol stations. Two white women passed. One of them wheeled a baby in a carriage, a civilized baby, whose parents knew about radio, pinball, and vitamins. This was no Indian baby strapped to a board!

"Did you know, gentlemen, that in the state of Utah live—Mormons?" asked Mr. Adams.

We were again sorry that we had not driven into Salt Lake City and that we would depart from America without having seen Mormons.

"Seriously, you must not talk like that," said Mr. Adams. "From Salt Lake City we could not have made our way to California, because at this time of the year the mountain passes are undoubtedly full of ice. Oh, no! I ask you to remember the Rocky Mountains!"

"Hitchhiker!" Mrs. Adams suddenly cried.

We saw a man standing at the side of the road, a suitcase between his legs.

"Shall we take him?" asked Mr. Adams.

For a little while we looked at the hitchhiker, appraising him. He wore a bright yellow gabardine duster. He appeared to be about twenty years old.

"Is it worth while? That duster he is wearing is altogether too optimistic and as dull as ditchwater."

"But suppose he is a Mormon!" said Mr. Adams.

That decided the matter.

"Let's take him!"

The hitchhiker, to our regret, proved to be not a Mormon, but a quite ordinary and devoutly professing Baptist.

He was a good boy. He took off his duster, disclosing a grey coat and rusty corduroy trousers. He had a swarthy, pimply face and small black sideburns. His story was the ordinary story of an American young man. The son of a poor farmer from Nebraska. Of course, he had graduated from high school. Of course, he had travelled to Arizona to find work and to save money for matriculation at some college. Of course, he did not find any work. Now he was ready to do anything at all. He had capable hands. And he was willing to work. He wanted to try his luck in California. If nothing happened there, he would have to return to his father and spend a dull country winter. Well, what of it? He would take to hunting wild cats and coyotes. And in the spring he would see. More truly he would see nothing. Business was bad. College was unattainable. And there was no hope that matters would improve. Like all young men of his age, our hitchhiker was completely devoid of any feeling of curiosity, and throughout the entire journey did not ask us about anything whatever. But to make up for that, he talked willingly about himself and answered all questions.

When he was asked what he knew about Moscow, he answered:

"Oh, they were putting through a five-year plan there."

"And what was that five-year plan?"

"Oh, that's when everybody works for the government, and they get three meals a day for it."

"Well! All right," said Mr. Adams, "let us suppose that that is so. What else have you heard?"

"I heard that the five-year plan was successful and that now they're putting through a second five-year plan."

"Well! And what is the second five-year plan like?"

"I don't know," answered the young man. "I heard that over there everybody works and people help each other. But what's the dfference? Soon there will be war, and right after war the second coming of Christ. And the Russians will perish, because they're atheists. Without faith in God no one can save himself from the tortures of hell. That's what the Bible says."

"But who told you that there will soon be the second coming?"

"Why, our pastor said it."

"Will it come soon?"

"Very soon," the young Baptist replied quite seriously. "In about two or three years."

"Very well!" exclaimed Mr. Adams. "Let us suppose that that is so. You just told us that the Russians help each other and that over there everybody has a job. Would you say they were good people?"

"Yes," replied the Baptist after a moment's thought.

"Excellent! They do not exploit each other and they love one another! From your point of view, they have organized God's Kingdom on Earth. But they do not believe in God. What shall we do about it? Answer me that question!"

"Since they do not believe in God, they will not go to heaven," the Baptist replied in a firm voice. "They will perish."

"But they are good people. You said so yourself!"

"That makes no difference. Yes, they do good things. Our pastor told us that himself, because, you understand, our pastor is a just man. But in the Bible it says that it is not enough to do good deeds. You must have faith. Therefore, they are doomed to perish."

"No, seriously," Mr. Adams insisted. "You are a smart young man— you graduated from high school. . . . Is it possible that Christ, coming to earth for the second time, will punish a hundred and seventy million excellent Russian fellows who have achieved the elimination of the hungry and the unemployed, so that everybody is well fed and happy? Just think of it! A hundred and seventy million people, people who toil, good, honest people. Is it possible that God will be so cruel that He would not admit them to heaven?"

Our hitchhiker sank into deep thought. It was evident that he was sorry for those good Russian fellows. He wavered for a long time before replying.

But even this remarkable, horrifying, and touching picture of the encounter between a hundred and seventy million Soviet atheists with the little Baptist God could not convince our fellow traveller.

"You see," he said, stammering, "it says so in the Bible, and you must either accept it as a whole, or . . ."

"Well, well, or . . . !" exclaimed Mr. Adams in complete exultation.

"Without faith in God no one can save himself," the boy muttered.

"Look! Look!" Mrs. Adams cried.

We were entering Zion Canyon, and the conversation with the young Baptist terminated.

No one was at the entrance booth. We stopped our machine and honked our horn several times, but no one came.

"I call your attention, gentlemen," said Mr. Adams, "to the fact that they don't want to take our dollars. We shall see Zion Canyon free of charge."

For some time we drove between crowded red cliffs from which pines and some strange roots stuck out in various directions.

The canyon widened. Some of the cliffs were cut through with long straight fissures. Others were scratched all over, like an arithmetic paper.

"If you like," said Mr. Adams, "I'll sell you an excellent literary simile. How much will you give me for it? You won't give me anything for it? You want it for nothing? Well, all right: The wind has written its history on these cliffs. Is it good? Write it down in your little books! I am sure I have enriched Russian literature with that."

We made several turns. The canyon broadened more and more. Yesterday it seemed to us that there could not be anything in the world more grandiose than Grand Canyon. But only one day had passed and we saw something which, while not so immense, was immeasurably more complex and fantastic. At Grand Canyon we looked from the bottom up. Through Zion Canyon we drove at the bottom or along those protuberances of its walls on which a road was laid. Grand Canyon appeared to us in the form of mountains, mountains turned inside out. Here we saw the walls of a canyon which looked to us like mountains in the ordinary sense of the word. The other landscape seemed to us the cold landscape of another planet. Here there were no comparisons and could not be any. We were in the magic kingdom of childish dreams and visions. On the road over which we drove lay a shadow, while the massive overhanging cliffs basked in the light of the sun. We passed through a brassy red hollow and found ourselves in a new vast canyon. Very high, against the background of the sky, could be seen red towers, carrousels, pyramids, the snouts of animals. Over the road and under it grew pines and firs, aslant. Dried-out beds of streams crept down. Far away, on a cliff lighted by the sun, gleamed a frozen stream like a neatly pasted-in bit of tin.

We drove into the tunnel. For some time we moved ahead in utter darkness. Then, ahead of us light appeared. In the wall of the tunnel had been hewed a broad arch which led to small terraces with stone ledges. We left the machine. The closing of the door sounded like a cannon shot. There were cliffs everywhere. We saw only a little of the sky. Below us lay a quiet pool of water. In such solemn surroundings man is either silent or he begins to do foolish things. For no reason whatever we suddenly began to emit piercing cries, in order to find out whether there was an echo here. We discovered that there was an echo.

Into the tunnel, which stretched for more than half a mile and was cut especially for viewing the canyon at a cost of over a million dollars, the builders built several windows. From each of these windows a new vista opened. Very far below shone the asphalt knot of the road on which tiny automobiles moved without a sound. Almost all the cliffs and their sharp shadows unfailingly reminded us of someone or of something—a cat's head, claws, the shadow of a railway locomotive. Crowning all was the colossal figure of an Indian, hewed out of the cliff by nature itself, an Indian with a calm, stern face and with a curious little box on top of his head which at the same time looked also like feathers.

We drove out of the tunnel. Five minutes later we were descending the very same knot of roads which we had looked upon through the window. On the highway were several fallen yellow leaves. We also came across several puddles covered with thin ice. The shadow of the opposite wall touched the feet of the Indian. The silence was without end. We drove at the very slowest speed, having turned off our motor. We moved down quietly and solemnly, like a floating bird.

A little tree with yellow chicklike leaves appeared. And after it another, with green leaves. We found ourselves in summer.

That day—in one day, or rather, in the course of a few hours—we had passed through all the four seasons of the year.

Before abandoning Zion Canyon we drove into the famous rift between the cliffs which the Indians worship and which was called the "Temple of the Sinonuava." In the middle of this rift on a tremendous socle sat a horrible bellied god. We stared at him for a long time before it dawned upon us that he had been shaped by man, not by nature. Around the monument a little river ran noisily, churning the pebbles.

We were no longer wondering at the fact that nature had excelled Indian architecture, Indian drawings and even the Indian himself. Such conclusions, inevitable after the Navajo desert, seemed at Zion Canyon too poor and inconclusive. It was clear here that all art—Egyptian and Greek and Chinese and Gothic and the Empire style and even formalism —had already existed before and had been invented by the genius of nature millions of years ago.

"Let's rejoice," said Mr. Adams, when we, having learned the road to Las Vegas, again picked up speed. "I ask you to bear in mind that we did not pay a single cent for all this beauty."

But he had scarcely said it, when we came to a booth from which a man in a uniformed cap looked out invitingly. He stopped us, took two dollars, and after licking his tongue over the round green paper, pasted it on the windshield of our car.

"Good-bye," said Mr. Adams sadly, and added immediately, "Seriously, gentlemen! Only two dollars for all this beauty! I figure that we get off very cheaply."

Our Baptist fellow traveller asked us to let him off at the nearest town. He shook our hands for a long time and kept repeating that we were good people. He placed his little paper suitcase on his shoulder, tucked his yellow duster under his arm, and went off. But after walking several steps away, he turned back and asked:

"If I came to Russia, could I have work too?"

"Of course," we replied, "just as all the other people in Russia."

"So . . ." said the young Baptist. "So I would have work? So . . ."

He wanted to say something else, but evidently he changed his mind and quickly, without looking back, went down the street.

29
On the Crest of the Dam

ALTHOUGH ON numerous occasions we had pledged our word of honour to Mr. Adams not to drive with the approach of twilight, our experienced car was entering the city of Las Vegas in complete darkness. The moon had not yet risen. Somewhere ahead, slowly, a white beacon gleamed. After some time it turned to the left and then appeared behind us. Its place was taken by another beam. At this point our path coincided with the route of the air line bound for Los Angeles. Occasionally out of the darkness broke a wavering light. It grew quickly. And there, high ahead of us, appeared two automobile eyes. For a minute they ran to meet us, then they disappeared again, and then quite close to us jumped out once more. The road went in waves from hill to hill. The great silence of the desert was broken only by the heavy sighs and mutterings of Mr. Adams.

"Becky! Becky! Not so fast. Forty miles an hour is too much!"

"Let me alone," Mrs. Adams replied, scarcely able to contain herself, "or I'll get out and let you all drive yourselves."

"Why, Becky, that's impossible!" groaned her husband.

"I don't want to talk to you!" exclaimed his wife.

And the couple had a verbal battle in English. The aerial beacons lighted their angry profiles and the glass of their spectacles.

Finally, ahead of us appeared the lights of Las Vegas.

What wouldn't a Muscovite imagine of a frosty December evening, hearing over the teacups talk about the bright shimmering lights of the city of Las Vegas? Las Vegas! He will quickly imagine passionate Mexican glances, lovelocks, curled like Carmen's, on saffron cheeks, the velvet breeches of toreadors, Navajos, guitars, banderillas, and tiger passions.

Although we had been certain for some time now that American cities never startle the traveller with the unexpected; nevertheless, we vaguely hoped for something even slightly out of the ordinary. Altogether too intriguing was the play of lights of the strange city in the warm black desert. Who could tell? Suppose, suddenly, upon awakening in our camp, we should go forth into the street and behold southern sidewalk cafés under tents, picturesque markets, where over mountains of vegetables would tower the arrogant snout of a camel, and would hear the chatter of bazaar crowds and the braying of donkeys! But—the United States with their united effort delivered a new blow to our imagination. Upon awakening in our camp and driving out into the street, we beheld the city of Gallup in all its glory of petrol pumps, drug-stores, empty sidewalks, and streets chockfull of automobiles. It even seemed to us that any moment now, just as in Gallup, a green little demi-truck would bob out from around the corner and swipe us sidewise, and Mr. Adams, that composed smile on his face, would walk through the show window of an automobile store. It was dull to look upon this standardized wealth. Passing through the desert we had stopped in a score of cities and, not counting Santa Fé, and perhaps also Albuquerque, they were all Gallups. It is scarcely possible to find anything more paradoxical in the world: standardized cities in a varied desert.

Las Vegas cured us completely. From then on we did not hope to run across anything unexpected in any new town. That helped a lot, because in the course of our journey remarkable surprises awaited us. The less we expected them, the more pleasing they were to us.

In Las Vegas we stopped just long enough at a drug-store to eat Breakfast No. 3 and, gathering momentum at a square overgrown with electric-light poles, we dashed out of town. We did it so hastily that we violated the traffic rules of the city of Las Vegas and faced a flood of automobiles: near the square each direction had its separate traffic lane. A police car immediately drove up to us. The policeman sitting in it ordered us to stop.

"I am very, very sorry," said Mrs. Adams meekly.

"Very, very, Mr. Officer." That old panicmonger, Mr. Adams, supported her.

But this time we did not get the dreaded ticket. The policeman was happy that the naïve New Yorker provincials promoted him to an officer, and limited himself to a short speech about the traffic rules of the city of Las Vegas, to which Mr. Adams listened in profound silence.

Finally the policeman told us what road to follow to Boulder City.

After going three blocks, we noticed that the police automobile was again chasing us. Was it possible that "Mr. Officer" had changed his mind and would, after all, give us a ticket? Mrs. Adams raced ahead, but the police Packard quickly caught up with us, and Mr. Officer, sticking his head out of the window, said:

"Lady! I drove after you because I was 'fraid you might miss the road. And that's just what happened. You went two extra blocks!"

"Thank you very, very much!" exclaimed Mr. Adams, breathing a sigh of relief.

"Very, very!" Mrs. Adams supported him.

"Very much!" we chimed in, like the echo in Zion Canyon.

It was only thirty miles to Boulder City. About fifty minutes later we were already driving up to the government booth, the same kind you find upon entering every American national park. Here the booth stood at the entrance to Boulder City, a town which sprang up during the construction of the biggest dam in the world, Boulder Dam, on the Colorado River. In the booth we were given tickets, on which were printed the rules for visiting the construction, and we drove into the little town.

Strange as it may seem, we heard little about Boulder Dam in America. The newspapers almost never mentioned its construction. Only when it was being completed, when Roosevelt participated in its solemn opening, did the newsreels devote a few flashes to it. We had seen that newsreel and we remembered the President's speech. He spoke about the significance of this government enterprise, praised some governors and senators who had something or other to do with the construction, but did not say one word about the men who designed the project and who built the dam—that great monument to man's triumph over nature.

Besides the possibility of seeing with our own eyes the technical wonder of it, visiting Boulder Dam was of special interest to us for another reason as well. We expected to meet there engineer Thompson, one of the few American engineers to have received from the Soviet Government the Order of the Red Banner.

The little white houses in Boulder City reflected the eternal sun of the desert so blindingly that it was impossible to look upon them. Although the city was built for temporary abode, was already half deserted, and after the end of the installation work at the powerhouse would be entirely deserted and most likely taken down, it made a much more pleasing impression upon us than the asphalto-petrol fraternity (of the Gallup type) which expects to exist for ever. It had many lawns, flower-beds, basketball and tennis courts.

We met Mr. Thompson at the hotel, and at once departed for the construction.

Thompson, the chief installation engineer of General Electric, a thin, black, forty-year-old man, with long coal-black eyelashes and very lively eyes, in spite of the fact that this was his day of rest (we arrived on a Sunday), was in his working trousers and a short leather jacket with a zip fastening. We were told that he is one of the best and perhaps the very best installation chief in the world, a kind of world champion at installing colossal electrical machines. The champion had sunburned calloused hands covered with fresh scratches. Thompson grew up in Scotland. In his faultless English one could easily detect the burring Scottish "r." During the war he was a British aviator. In his face lurked that shadow of sadness which is the attribute of all those who had given several years of their life to war. He smoked a pipe, and occasionally rolled his own cigarettes in yellow paper.

His profession had almost deprived him of a homeland, or so at least it seemed to us. Here is a British man who works for an American firm and travels all over the world. There is probably not a single part of the world in which Mr. Thompson had not installed several machines. He lived in the U.S.S.R. for several years, worked at Stalingrad and Dnieprostroi, was awarded the Order of the Red Banner, and now he was here in the desert, under this appalling sun, installing machinery for the Boulder Dam hydro-electric station. He would work here another year. What would he do then? He did not know. He might go to

South Africa. Or, maybe, General Electric would send him to some other place—India, Australia, China.

"I should like very much to go to the U.S.S.R.," said Thompson, "and see how things are there now. After all, I left a part of my heart in your country. You see, my wife and I have no children, so I call the machines that I install my children. I have several children in Russia, my most beloved children. I should like to see them again."

He began to recall some of the people with whom he had worked.

"I'll never forget the moment when the installation of the Dnieper electric station was finished and I transmitted the switch to Winter, so that he would turn on the electricity with his own hands. I said to him: 'Mr. Winter, the soup is ready.' There were tears in Winter's eyes. We kissed each other, Russian fashion. You have many good engineers, but Winter is an altogether exceptional figure. There are few people of his kind in the world. You can count them on the fingers of one hand. What is he doing now? Where is he?"

We told him that Winter was working in the State Planning Commission (Gosplan) and was in charge of the Central Energy Trust.

"That's a great pity," said Thompson. "A man like that should not work in an office."

We explained that the Gosplan is not an office, but something much more significant.

"I realize that," answered Thompson. "But anyway, that's no business for Mr. Winter. He is a captain of men. He must be on the battlefield. He must be the chief of some construction. I know, you are still building a lot. Now it's all in the past, so we can talk about it frankly. Most of our engineers did not believe that anything would come of the first five-year plan. It seemed incredible to them that your untrained workers and young engineers could ever master the complex and complicated production processes, and especially electrical technique. Well, look at it! You did it! Now it's a fact which no one can deny!"

Thompson asked Mrs. Adams to let him take the wheel of the automobile, since we had quite a dangerous part of our journey ahead of us, and he skilfully guided us down the dizzying descent to the bottom of the canyon.

Several times along the way we caught a view of the dam.

Imagine the rapidly flowing mountain river coursing on the bottom of a huge stone corridor, the walls of which represent the highest, almost overhanging, dark-red cliffs. The height of the cliffs is six hundred and fifty feet. And so, between two walls of the canyon fashioned by nature, the hands of man have reared a third wall of reinforced concrete, which bars the flow of the river. That wall runs in a semicircle, and it looks like a petrified waterfall.

Having admired Boulder Dam from below, we went up to walk across its top. Mr. Thompson asked us to keep to the right. From a tremendous height we saw the dried-out bottom of the canyon littered with remainders of the great construction—mill ends and pieces of building waste. A railway car hanging on a steel trestle was slowly being lowered to the bottom of the abyss.

We walked to the end of the dam, and turned back.

"Now you may pass to the left side," said Mr. Thompson.

This was a well-prepared effect.

On the other side of the dam lies a large, crystal-clear cool lake.

Going up to the centre of the dam Mr. Thompson suddenly stopped, spread his feet wide apart on either side of the white mark.·

"Now," he said, "I am standing with one foot in Arizona and with the other foot in Nevada."

Boulder Dam, located between those two states—and close to two more, Utah and California—gives the desert not only electricity, but also water. Besides the electric station, this will be the centre of the irrigation system of the All-American Canal.

"Tell me," we asked Mr. Thompson, "who is the author of the Boulder Dam project?"

To our surprise he did not answer that question. He could only tell us the name of the joint stock company which was doing the work under contract with the government.

"No doubt," he said, smiling, "if you were to ask some builder here who was installing the turbines, he would not be able to give you my name. He would simply tell you that the installation was being done by the General Electric Company. With us here in America, engineers don't enjoy fame. Only the firms are known."

"Excuse me, Mr. Thompson, but that is a great injustice. We know who built the Cathedral of St. Peter in Rome, although it was built several centuries ago. The authors of Boulder Dam, where such remarkable technique and such amazing construction art are united, are entitled to fame."

"No," said Mr. Thompson, "I don't see any injustice in that. As for me, personally, for example, I am not looking for fame. I am perfectly satisfied if my name is known by two hundred specialists in the world. Apart from that, contemporary technique is such that actually it is not always possible to determine who is the author of this or that technical production. The epoch of Edison has come to an end. The time of separate great inventions has passed. Now we have general technical progress. Who is building Boulder Dam? Six companies—and that's that."

"But in the U.S.S.R. engineers and workers enjoy great popularity. Newspapers write about them, magazines print their portraits."

"That's because you are carried away by construction. It is playing too big a role with you now. Later you will forget about it and will stop proclaiming the fame of engineers and workers."

We talked for quite a while about fame; or rather, about the right to fame. It seems to us that we did not convince each other of anything. Mr. Thompson's position was clear to us. Capitalism had denied him fame—or rather, had stolen his fame—so this proud man did not even want to hear of it. He gave his bosses knowledge and in exchange received a salary. He felt that they were quits.

Standing on the summit of one of the most beautiful constructions of our age, about which it is only known that it is not known who built it, we spoke about fame in the United States.

Fame in that country begins with publicity. And publicity is given a person only when it is to somebody's advantage. Who in America really enjoys the greatest, all-national fame? People who make money or people with the aid of whom somebody else makes money. There are no exceptions to this rule. Money! All-national fame is enjoyed by a boxing champion or a football champion, because a match with their participation garners millions of dollars. A motion-picture star enjoys fame, because her fame is of use to her producer. He can deprive her of this national fame at any time he so desires. Bandits enjoy fame, because it pays newspapers and because with their names are associated figures with many zeros.

But who could utilize and need to create fame for Thompson or Jackson, Wilson or Adams, if those people merely build machines, electric stations, bridges, and irrigation systems? Their bosses find that it is even unprofitable that they should be famous. They would have to pay a large salary to a famous man.

"Seriously," Mr. Adams told us, "do you really think that Ford is famous in America because he created a cheap automobile? Oh, no! It would be foolish to think that! It is simply because throughout the country automobiles run around with his surname on the radiator. With you, Ford the mechanic is famous; with us, Ford the merchant."

No, perhaps Thompson is right when he waives American fame. Fame in America is merchandise. And like all other merchandise in America it brings profit not to him who has created it, but to him who trades in it.

PART IV
THE GOLDEN STATE

30
Mrs. Adams Sets a Record

ON THE BORDER of California we were stopped at the inspector's station, around which small cactuses were planted, and our automobile was searched.

It is forbidden to transport fruit or flowers into California. Californians are afraid that bacteria which cause plant diseases may be carried into their state.

The inspector pasted on our windshield a label portraying unnaturally blue vistas and green palms, and we found ourselves in California, in the Golden State.

However, after we passed the inspector's bungalow we did not find any palms at all. The desert continued as grandiose and beautiful as in Arizona, Nevada, and New Mexico. Only the sun became warmer and more and more cactuses appeared. A whole forest of cactuses jutted out of the sand on either side of the road. The cactuses were large, the size of an apple tree. Their branches, as thick as the trunk itself, looked as if they had been injured in torment, looked like outspread arms cut off at the elbow.

Thus half a day passed. We lunched on bananas, like monkeys. The road passed from one plateau to another, rising continually. Cactuses disappeared just as suddenly as they had appeared. A grated tower appeared on the horizon, then another, then a third. They looked like the fighting machines of Martian warriors. We were crossing the high-pressure line built for transmitting current from the Boulder Dam station to California. The electricity marched in measured step across the sands and hills of the desert.

"Gentlemen," asked Mr. Adams, "is there a ringing in your ears? Confess!"

We listened. There actually was a ringing in our ears. Mr. Adams was greatly elated.

"This is rarefied air," said he. "Don't let it astonish you. Unnoticeably, we have climbed to considerable height. But I think this is the last mountain pass now."

As usual, Mr. Adams was right.

Soon we began to descend, down the beautiful winding road, to a new desert. We saw it from a great height. It did not at all look like those deserts to which we had become accustomed in the course of the week. Wrapped in a light rising mist, it disclosed itself gradually with every new winding of the road. We drove carefully lower and lower. After a considerable interruption, life began again: a ploughed field, irrigation canals, green winter crops, long brown vineyards disappearing in the misty horizon, and oil derricks of the city of Bakersfield. It was December. Palms appeared, trees, girls in skirts and girls in trousers. The girls in the long and wide trousers of thin wool, and with a light kerchief around their necks, were a sign that Hollywood was near by. This is the motion-picture style—to go around in trousers. They are comfortable and roomy.

This part of California is an irrigated desert. If California were to be deprived of irrigation for one week, it would return to what it had always been: a desert. If flowers are not watered here for one day, they perish.

"California," cried Mr. Adams suddenly, "is a remarkable state. As a matter of principle, there is never any rain here. Yes, yes, precisely as a matter of principle. You will simply insult a Californian if you tell him that rain is possible here. If on the day of your arrival it rains anyway, the Californian will be very angry, will shrug his shoulders, and say: 'This is something incomprehensible. I have been living here for twenty years. One of my wives died here and another fell ill. Here my children grew up and graduated from high school. This is the first time I have seen rain.'"

The Bakersfield oil well derricks, in distinction from those of Oklahoma, which were of metal, were made of wood. These are the older oil wells. And again, side by side with the derricks, we saw pathetic hovels. Such is the law of American life: the wealthier the place, the more millions are pumped out or dug out of the earth, the poorer and shabbier are the hovels of the people who dig out or pump out those millions.

As a matter of fact, the oil is not pumped only by large companies. It is pumped, so to speak, individually as well, by local residents, the owners of the little houses and the little Fords. They make an opening side by side with the oil-bearing lands of the company, right in their own small garden, in their own garage, in their own parlour, and pump a few gallons a day for themselves. This method of mining Americans call "wildcatting."

Only its palms distinguished Bakersfield from the hundreds of other Gallups we had seen. But this is an appreciable difference, for a Gallup with palms is considerably more pleasing than a Gallup without palms.

Trade and advertising assume a much more lively character here than in the desert. After endless and monotonous "Drink Coca-Cola" signs, we found here a certain New York flair in the advertiser's concern about the consumer. The owner of a small petrol station on the outskirts of Bakersfield hung over his establishment a funny man made up of empty automobile oil cans. The man rocked in the wind, clattered and groaned like a lonely ghost forgotten by all. And in his groans one could clearly hear: "Buy only Pennsylvania Oil. This oil is from the Quaker State. The Quakers are good people. Their oil cannot be bad."

And farther on, over an automobile repair station (a "service station") hung such a fancy placard that Mr. Adams, who was the first to notice it, loudly clapped his hands and shouted: "Becky! Stop here!"

"Yes, gentlemen!" he said to us. "You must think deeply about this placard if you want to understand the American soul."

On the placard was written:

Automobile service. Here you will always be met with a friendly laugh.

That is right. American laughter, generally good, loud, and lively laughter, occasionally does irritate.

Let us suppose that two Americans meet.

FIRST AMERICAN (smiling): . . .

SECOND AMERICAN (showing part of his teeth): . . .

FIRST AMERICAN: How are you? (Laughs.)

SECOND AMERICAN: Very well, thank you! (Shows all of his thirty-two teeth, among which are three gold ones.) And how are you?

FIRST AMERICAN: Very well! Fine! (Laughs loudly.) How is business?

SECOND AMERICAN: Good! (Laughs uproariously.) And yours?

FIRST AMERICAN: Excellent! (Laughs wildly.) Well, good-bye, regards to your wife!

SECOND AMERICAN: Thank you! Ha, ha, ha! Regards to yours! (Emitting an entire waterfall of laughter, he slaps FIRST AMERICAN on the shoulder with all his might.) Good-bye!

FIRST AMERICAN (shaking with laughter slaps SECOND AMERICAN on the shoulder): Good-bye! (Each goes to his automobile, and they part, driving off in different directions at a terrific speed.)

There is a possible variant to that conversation, which, as a matter of fact, scarcely alters the case:

FIRST AMERICAN (smiling): How's business?

SECOND AMERICAN (laughing): Very bad, very bad. How's yours?

FIRST AMERICAN (laughing uproariously): Disgusting! I lost my job yesterday.

SECOND AMERICAN (bursting with laughter): How's your wife?

FIRST AMERICAN: She's quite dangerously ill. (He tries to make a serious face, but vigorous, joyous laughter breaks out again.) Yesterday we called . . . ha, ha, ha . . . Yesterday . . . oh, I can't bear it . . . yesterday, we called the doctor.

SECOND AMERICAN: Really? Is that so? Oh, what a pity! I'm sorry for you, my friend. (And laughing uproariously, slaps FIRST AMERICAN on the back.)

Americans laugh and never stop showing their teeth, not because something humorous has happened to them, but because laughter is their style.

America is a land that loves explicitness in all its affairs and ideas.

It is better to be rich than to be poor. So, instead of wasting time on thinking of the causes of poverty and eliminating them, the American tries in every possible way to acquire a million dollars.

A billion is better than a million. So, instead of retiring from business and enjoying the million of his fondest dreams, he sits in his office in his shirt sleeves and sweats at making a billion.

Sport is better for health than reading books. So, he devotes all his free time to sport.

It is necessary at times to be entertained, to rest from work. So he goes to the cinema or to the burlesque, where he is not compelled to think about the slightest problems of life, because that would prevent him from resting completely.

It is better to laugh than to weep. So, he laughs. No doubt, in the past he forced himself to laugh, just as he forced himself to sleep with windows open, to indulge in gymnastics, and to brush his teeth. Subsequently these things became daily habits. And now laughter rattles in his throat, irrespective of his circumstances or his wishes. If you see a laughing American, it does not mean that something strikes him as comical. He laughs only because an American must laugh. Let the Mexicans, Slavs, Jews, and Negroes whine and grieve.

We drove out to an excellent four-lane road, a highway between Los Angeles and San Francisco, and again found ourselves in the automobile whirl from which we had been unaccustomed in the desert. The highway, divided by white lines, was black, the colour of pitch, shining greasily from the constant drip of oil. Advancing upon us, their windshields gleaming, automobiles whisked by in the opposite direction. From the distance they seemed very high, for the road reflected their wheels. Buicks, Fords, Chryslers, Packards, raced ahead. Countless machines roared and snorted like tomcats. There is constant movement on American highways.

California is notorious for its automobile accidents. More and more frequently along the road we came across bill-boards pleading with chauffeurs to drive more carefully. They were beautifully executed, laconic and horrifying. A huge policeman holding the corpse of a little girl in his left arm, pointed his right hand at us. Under it was the inscription: "Stop these murders!" On another bill-board was portrayed a distraught man who had lost his reason, a child's corpse in his arms, and the inscription read: "What have I done!"

"No, Becky, I don't want anyone to greet us with friendly laughter," said Mr. Adams. "Do you want our mutilated car greeted with friendly laughter? Becky, you must keep to forty miles!"

Mrs. Adams made an attempt to argue, but the bill-boards made such a strong impression on us that we seconded Mr. Adams, and our adventurous driver submitted.

"Becky!" exclaimed Mr. Adams. "Do you really want to hold my heavy corpse in your arms and shout for all of California to hear, 'What have I done!'"

Then Mr. Adams buried his nose in a map and, concentrating on his grumbling, began to draw over it straight and crooked lines.

Finally he said, "We must drive into Sequoia Park. It is not far from here. At the town of Delano we shall have to turn to the right. It's a bit out of our way—about sixty miles, no more. We'll drive over for five minutes, return to the highway and then drive straight to San Francisco. No, don't say anything to me. It would simply be foolish not to drive into Sequoia Park. We should be real travellers!"

Now we are very grateful to Mr. Adams for insisting upon our going to Sequoia Park. But then we were too fatigued by the journey through the desert, too full of impressions, and too eager to reach San Francisco to agree at once to taking this step.

We held a quick council, at which Mr. Adams, always most circumspect, behaved like Suvorov.

It was decided to drive over to Sequoia Park for five minutes.

By the time we reached Delano two hours had passed. On the right appeared mountains. We turned toward them. These were the Sierra Nevadas, a mountain chain which stretches for five hundred miles between the Colorado Plateau and the California Valley.

Again before us were stern mountain vistas, again Mrs. Adams, raising her arms in exaltation, would put her head out of the window and cry "Look, look!" and we pleaded with her to put her hands back on the steering wheel and keep her eyes on the road, swearing to her that at dinner-time we would describe all the beauties to her in the most artistic manner. But it was too long to wait until dinner-time.

The rise on the scenic highway began among small cliffs, streams, and a thick coniferous growth which gleamed in the sun. What joy it was with every turn to rise higher and higher into the blue sky, to the point where on a height beyond our reach we could see the snow-clad peaks. Below, on almost sheer green inclines could be seen narrow strips of the roads we had passed an hour before, while the streams were no longer visible. Soon even the sun appeared below us.

"Where are the sequoias?" we kept asking monotonously.

"Don't talk to me about sequoias!" Mr. Adams replied quite distractedly. "The sequoias will soon be here."

"But it's already dinner-time," remarked Mrs. Adams, looking at her watch and at the same time making a dizzying turn.

"Now, Becky, you must not talk that way; it is already dinner-time! It hurts me to hear you talk like that!"

We thought that we would drive in for five minutes, but here four hours had already elapsed.

Then suddenly appeared an entrance booth of the national park, and we, sighing with relief, surrendered a dollar apiece. However, another hour of travel passed before we saw the first sequoia.

"Look, look!" cried Mrs. Adams, stopping the automobile.

At first we could not notice anything. On a level with the road immovably stood an entire forest of coniferous tree-tops, the trunks of which grew out of the sheer inclines below our level. But one tree-top mixed in with them was somehow distinct from the others. Looking closely, we noticed that the needles of this conifer were darker and some-what differently shaped. Cautiously we looked down. While the trunks of the other trees ended quite close, growing crookedly into the inclines, this trunk, as thick as a tower, plunged straight into the abyss, and it was impossible to discover where it began.

"Well, what do you say to this?" Mr. Adams crowed. "Didn't you ask me where the sequoias were?"

"Look, look!" Mrs. Adams cried again.

But this time we had to look not down, but up. Right beside us, out of the earth, rose the trunk of another gigantic tree. It is not at all surpris-ing that we did not notice it at once. It was too great, too abnormal among the customary trunks of firs and pines that surrounded it, for an eye, trained to the natural difference between large and small, to be able at once to notice this phenomenon.

We drove slowly from tree to tree. We soon learned that the first two before which we stopped in astonishment were the very smallest of the species. Now we were driving through an ancient darkened forest, a fantastic forest, where the word "man" ceases to sound proudly and only one word sounds proudly, the word—"tree." Sequoias, which according to the restrained expression of the scientists, belong to "the family of the conifers," grow alongside of ordinary firs and pines, and astonish man as much as if he were suddenly to see among chickens and pigs a living pterodactyl or a mammoth.

The very largest tree is four thousand years old. It is called "General Sherman." Americans are intensely pragmatic. Near "Sherman" hangs a little sign which with the greatest precision informs you that out of one such tree it is possible to build no less than forty five-room houses and that, if you were to lay that tree beside a Union Pacific train, it would be longer than the train. But, looking at this tree, looking at all this trans-parent yet dark forest, we did not want to think of five-room houses and of Union Pacific trains. We wanted to pronounce dreamily the words of Pasternak, "cathedral darkness wreathed the forest," and tried as calmly as possible to envisage this "coniferous family" growing peace-fully before the world had seen not only Columbus but even Caesar and Alexander of Macedon and even the Egyptian tsar, Tutankhamen.

Instead of five minutes we spent nearly two hours in the forest, until the darkness became thicker than ever. We could not even think of dinner before returning into the valley. The best thing we could have done was to turn back without further delay. But at this point the Adamses suddenly looked at each other, and on their faces appeared two identical, ill-boding smiles. It was clear to us what our kind friends had in mind. In vain did we plead with them to bethink themselves, to consider their baby. But the Adamses were implacable. Taking each other by the hand, they went off to get information. It was our luck that they returned very quickly, since there was absolutely no place where they could get information, except perhaps from "General Sherman." The forest had been deserted long ago. It became very cold.

"Well, now, I'm glad of that. We'd better turn back to the old road."

"We'll have to go back," Mrs. Adams said with a sigh, starting the motor.

"It would be well," said Mr. Adams, "to find out whether there is some other road into the valley."

"Why do we need another road? We have the excellent road over which we have come here."

"A little additional information never hurts."

At this point, to our horror, we saw the figure of a warden. He had nothing to do, he was in an excellent mood, and he was whistling gaily. The Adamses pounced upon him like werewolves.

"How do you do?" said Mr. Adams.

"How do you do?" replied the warden.

And the questioning began. No less than fifty times the warden said: "Yes, ma'am," and the same number of times: "No, ma'am."

"Gentlemen!" exclaimed Mr. Adams, resuming his place in the machine. "We have found a new road. Right past 'General Grant.' It is near here, about fifty miles away."

"But it is already dark. We won't be able to see anything, anyway."

"Don't say 'we won't see anything.' You must not talk like that."

Before finally starting on our journey, Mrs. Adams decided to verify the correctness of the information she had received, and again called the warden over.

"So we must go straight ahead?" she asked.

"Yes, ma'am!"

"Until we reach 'General Grant'?"

"Yes, ma'am!"

"And then turn to the right?"

"No, ma'am. To the left."

"And not to the right?"

"No, ma'am."

"To the third crossing?"

"No, ma'am; to the fourth crossing."

"Thank you very much!" cried Mr. Adams.

And thus began the great campaign of the night, from the heights of the Sierra Nevadas to the California Valley. For nearly two hours we drove in complete darkness. We did not see what grew around us, and no doubt will never see it again. It is possible that "General Grant" was there and "General Lee," and maybe even a score of other generals of the North and of the South. At each turn the light of our headlights glided over smooth chalky cliffs. To the left was a deep black ravine. Far below a few lights were dimly gleaming. Suddenly our machine

G

tugged and the rear wheels began to slide. We remembered at once the day of mishaps, the Rocky Mountains, Gallup, and we held our breath. The automobile, losing direction, turned on its own hub for some distance, skidded backward, and finally stopped a few inches from the edge of an abyss.

"No, no," muttered Mr. Adams, trying to get out of the machine and striking his elbow on the window. "Be calm, calm. . . . Yes, yes, yes. . . . It's all over now!"

We stepped down into the road and saw that we were standing on ice.

One cabin was in order. We put it on, and carefully began to push our machine. Mrs. Adams opened up skilfully and the automobile gingerly moved ahead. It had become a habit with us when suffering heavily on the road to maintain a proud silence. We were silent on this occasion too. Only Mr. Adams whispered passionately:

"Becky, Becky! No more than five miles an hour! No, seriously. You must understand that it is no joke to fall off the Sierra Nevadas!"

Among the tree-tops of the firs hanging over the abyss a large red moon appeared.

The descent down the icy road continued for a long while. We lost all sense of time while our stomachs lost all conception of food. Finally the icy stretch ended. But a new misfortune confronted us. The red column of the meter which indicated the level of the petrol in the tank went down to the limit and was scarcely noticeable.

"Our petrol has gone to the devil!" Mr. Adams exclaimed in elation and horror.

We drove for a short while longer, listening to the sound of the motor and trying to figure out how we would spend the night when the petrol would give out and the machine stopped.

Just then something happened which was appropriate in America, the land of automobile wonders. A petrol station appeared, a small station with only one pump, but how overjoyed we were to see it! Again service began! Life began! A sleepy man, muttering "Yes, ma'am" and "No, ma'am," filled our tank full of petrol. After twenty miles, we noticed that he had forgotten to screw on the cap. We drove to the very city of Fresno without a cap, afraid to throw cigarette butts out of the window, because we decided that open petrol might catch fire and our car would go to the devil, and along with it, of course, we too would go to the devil.

For a long while we travelled along a highway planted on both sides with palms.

The city of Fresno, famous, as Mr. Adams told us, because many Greeks live there, was asleep. There was not a soul on the streets. Only one extraordinarily tall policeman walked slowly from store to store, stopping at each one to make sure that the lock was intact. The American Greeks could sleep in peace.

When we drove up to the hotel it was twelve o'clock—midnight.

The speedometer showed that that day we had travelled three hundred and seventy-five miles. Mrs. Adams had sat behind the wheel for sixteen hours on end. It was a real record. We wanted to shout "Hurrah!" But we could not. We had lost our voices.

31
San Francisco

ABOUT FIFTY MILES away from San Francisco travellers become witnesses of a struggle between two competing organizations, the owners of the San Mateo Bridge and the owners of the ferry. The point is that to reach San Francisco from the Oakland side one must pass across the bay. At first you meet small modest bill-boards along the road. On one of these the bridge is advertised, and on the other the ferry-boats. So far travellers do not understand anything. As the bill-boards become wider and higher, the voices of the owners of the ferry begin to sound more persuasive.

"The shortest and cheapest way to San Francisco is across San Mateo Bridge," shout the owners of the bridge.

"The quickest and pleasantest journey to San Francisco is in the ferry! A first-class restaurant! An enchanting view of the Golden Gate!" shout the ferry owners at the top of their voices.

At the point where the roads branch out the bill-boards attain idiotic dimensions. They shut out the sky and the sun. Here the traveller must finally decide on his direction.

We chose the ferry, evidently out of a sense of contradicting the owners of the San Mateo Bridge. We saw several machines turn decisively in the direction of the bridge, apparently because of a feeling of dislike for the ferry owners.

Having passed Oakland, the petrol-asphaltish appearance of which confirmed once again that we were in America, we stopped at the ferry dock. A small line of automobiles was already waiting there. We did not have to wait long—about ten minutes. A bell rang out, and a broad-nosed ferry, with two thin and high stacks side by side, came to the dock. The sailors dropped a gangplank, and one after the other several score automobiles drove off the ferry. We did not see a single pedestrian passenger. The machines drove past our motorized column, in the direction of Oakland. Immediately the bell rang again and it was our turn to drive one after the other to the warm places still smelling of petrol and oil. The entire operation of unloading and loading the ferry took no more than two minutes. The automobiles were disposed on the lower deck, on either side of the engine-room, in two rows on each side, and the ferry pulled away.

"I don't think we have to lock our car," remarked Mrs. Adams, looking at the passengers, who, carelessly leaving the doors of their cars open, went to the upper deck.

"But I'll take the key to the motor with me in any case," said Mr. Adams. "You must remember, Becky, that caution is the traveller's best friend."

We went above. Over the engine-room was an open space with wooden benches, two pinball games, automatic chewing-gum machines, and a small restaurant. Forward and aft were decks reserved for promenading, while on either side, over the automobiles, were several bridges with two lifeboats at each end. Astern the star-spangled banner snapped in the wind.

Here was the old steam-boat world, with the smells of seaweed and hot machine oil, with the taste of salt on the lips, with peeling enamel on the rails, with whistles and steam, with a fresh Novorossiisk wind and Sebastopol seagulls that, crying, floated on the wind above the stern. The bay was so wide that at first we could not make out the opposite shore on the horizon. At that point the width of the bay is more than five miles. We seemed to be going out into the open sea.

"I surmise, gentlemen," said Mr. Adams, "that you do not expect to feast your eyes on the Golden Gate?"

We said that that was precisely what we intended to do.

"In vain, sirs! The Golden Gate is very much like your Muscovite Myasnitsky Gate, in the sense that it does not exist at all. It is simply an exit from the bay into the ocean, which, by the way, cannot be seen from the ferry-boat."

"But the ferry-boat advertised down the entire length of the road a view of the Golden Gate!"

"You ask too much of the joint stock company of the San Francisco ferries," Mr. Adams said. "You acquire the right to ride across the bay. You receive harbourage for your car. You can obtain chewing gum from an automatic machine. Yet, in addition, you expect to see the Golden Gate! Truly, you must take pity on the owners of the ferry. If even now they can scarcely manage to exist because of competition with the San Mateo Bridge, what will happen to them in another two years when that thing over there is finished, in fighting which they spent a million dollars?"

Mr. Adams pointed with his hand to a construction which from a distance looked like cables stretched across the bay.

So that's what it was—this world-renowned technical wonder—the famous suspension bridge! The nearer the ferry came to it, the more grandiose it seemed. To the right, almost on the horizon, could be seen the contours of another bridge being built across the bay.

The Empire State Building, Niagara, the Ford plant, the Grand Canyon, Boulder Dam, sequoias, and now the suspension bridges of San Francisco—they were all phenomena of the same order. American nature and American technique not only supplement each other in order jointly to astonish the imagination of man, but to squelch him. They gave expressive and precise conceptions of the extent, the dimensions, and the wealth of the country, where everything, no matter what it might be, must be the tallest, the broadest, and the most costly in the world. If it's an excellent road, then it must be a million miles long. If there are automobiles, then there must be twenty-five million of them. If it's a house, a building, then it must be a hundred and two stories high. If it's a suspension bridge, then it must have a main span a mile long.

Now Mrs. Adams could freely cry: "Look! Look!" Nobody stopped her. And she took full advantage of her right. The ferry passed a barred pylon which rose out of the water. It was broad and high, like "General Sherman." From its top our ferry must have seemed as small as a man at the bottom of the Grand Canyon. Half of the pylon was painted an aluminium colour. The other half was as yet covered with red lead.

From this point we could already have a good view of San Francisco, which grows out of the water like a little New York. But it seemed pleasanter than New York. A gay white city coming down to the bay in an amphitheatre.

"Here, gentlemen," said Mr. Adams, "you don't know what this bay really is! Seriously! The fleets of all the governments of the world can find room here. Yes, yes. It would be well to gather them all here, all of those fleets, and sink them all."

Chatting gaily, we admired now the bridge, and now the city.

"Where are you from, folks?" we suddenly heard a flagrantly Volga basso say.

We looked around. Before us stood a sailor of the ferry-boat in a uniform which disclosed the striped sweat-shirt common to all the sailors of the world. On the black ribbon of his blue cap we made out the name of the ferry-boat: *Golden Gate.* He had a broad red face, grey temples, and blue eyes.

"Are you really from Russia?"

"From Moscow."

"Oh, my God!" exclaimed the deck hand of the ferry *Golden Gate.* "Really from Moscow! Don't you worry, now; I'm no enemy of yours. Well, how is Russia? How is Moscow? Have you ever been to Siberia?"

And without waiting for a reply to any one of his questions, he hastily began to tell us about himself. Evidently he had been dying to talk for a long time, and he talked rapidly, glancing now and then at the approaching shore.

"And you have never been at Blagoveshchensk? That's a pity, because it's my home town! The devil only knows me! I pulled out in the year 'nineteen, at the time of Kolchak. It isn't that I ran away, but you know . . . And yet, to tell the truth, I did run away . . . I am disgusted with myself when I recall it. I have three brothers navigating on the Amur. They're all like me, only a little bit wider. All three of them are captains, each in command of a steamer. And I, too, you know, used to be a captain. Everyone in our family was a captain. We were a family of captains. And here, now . . . ekh, the devil! A common sailor! And where? On a ferry-boat! And I have to be thankful that they took me on . . ."

"How did it all come about? You would have been a captain now!"

The whistle resounded. The ferry was rapidly approaching the shore.

"But I have comforts!" He pronounced the word English fashion. "I have comforts," he said.

We do not understand to this day whether he was speaking seriously or bitterly, with irony, about his comforts on a ferry-boat.

"Well, good luck to you!" he cried. "I've got to run! My job!"

We hurried down, arriving just in time, because the gang-plank was being dropped from the ferry and all the automobiles except ours were already sputtering impatiently.

"Quick! Give me the key to the motor!" cried Mrs. Adams to her husband.

From the rapidity with which Mr. Adams began to dig in all his pockets, we understood that a catastrophe would occur immediately. Not finding the key in his vest, he began to look for it in his coat.

"Well, what's the matter with you?" Mrs. Adams urged him on.

The first machines had already driven to shore.

"Right away, Becky, right away!"

An impatient signal sounded behind us.

"You lost the key!" cried Mrs. Adams.

"Oh, Becky, Becky!" muttered Mr. Adams, digging in his pockets and bringing up some folded pieces of paper to his eyes. "Don't talk like that: 'you lost the key!'"

But we were already enveloped in the honking of automobile horns. The machines behind us roared, and the machines awaiting their turn on the shore did likewise. A group of sailors ran up to us.

"Quick, quick!" they cried.

Deafened by the outcries, Mr. Adams, instead of searching systematically, began to go through utterly incomprehensible motions. He rubbed his eyeglasses and looked under the automobile, then he looked at the floor, lifting each one of his legs, then he made an attempt to run to the upper deck.

But it was simply impossible to wait any longer. The sturdy sailors, among whom we noticed our Amur captain, quickly put us into the machine, and with a cry which sounded very much like "Veeraah," began to push us to the dock.

"I'm very, very sorry!" muttered Mr. Adams, bowing to either side like a President. "I'm terribly sorry! I'm terribly sorry!"

To the sound of the uninterrupted blaring of the ferry-boat, the honking of automobile horns, and the taunting laughter of chauffeurs, the sailors rolled us out on the rocky dock, and ran back to the ferry. Mr. Adams was left to face his angry wife.

"I'm terribly sorry!" Mr. Adams continued to mutter, still bowing.

"Well!" exclaimed Mrs. Adams. "How long are we going to stand here on the dock?"

"Oh, Becky, don't talk like that!" said Mr. Adams, regaining his composure. "It hurts me to hear you talk like that!"

"Well, all right, I only want to know what we are going to do here on the dock? What have you done with the key?"

Interrupting each other, we tried to recall how Mr. Adams took the key and how he told us at the time that caution is the traveller's best friend.

"Well, now, try to remember, try to remember where you put it!"

"Oh, Becky! How can I tell you where I put it? You talk like a little girl! You must not talk like that!"

"Let me do it!" Mrs. Adams said decisively, and, sinking her two fingers into her husband's waistcoat pocket, she immediately pulled out the key. "What is this?"

Mr. Adams was silent.

"I'm asking you: what is this?"

"Becky," muttered Mr. Adams. "Don't talk like that: 'what is this?'! It's a key, Becky. You can see perfectly well for yourself."

A minute later we were rolling over the streets of San Francisco.

This is the most beautiful city in America, apparently because it is in no way reminiscent of America. Most of its streets rise from hill to hill. An automobile journey through San Francisco looks more like a sideshow called "American Mountains" and presents the passenger with a number of strong sensations. Nevertheless, in the centre of the city is a piece which looks like the flattest Leningrad in the world, with its squares and broad avenues. The other parts of San Francisco form a remarkable seashore mixture of Naples and Shanghai. The resemblance to Naples we can certify from personal experience. The Chinese find the resemblance to Shanghai. There are many Chinese in San Francisco.

Among the triumphs of the city is the fact that its principal street is called neither "Main Street" nor "Broadway," but simply "Market Street." We sought in vain for uptown and downtown. No, in San Francisco there is no upper town and no lower town, or rather there are too many of them, several hundred upper and lower parts. No doubt, the denizen of Frisco, as the city is called in friendly familiarity by the sailors of the entire world, might take offence at this and tell us that San Francisco is no worse than New York or Gallup and that the denizen of Frisco knows very well where his uptown and where his downtown are located, where business is carried on, and where people rest after business in their family circles, and that it's no use our trying to isolate San Francisco and tear it away from its family of other American cities. Possibly, it is so. But to our foreign view San Francisco looked more like a European than an American city. Here, as everywhere else in America, was limitless wealth and limitless poverty standing side by side, shoulder to shoulder, so that the faultless dinner jacket of the rich man touched the dirty blouse of an unemployed stevedore, but wealth here did not seem as depressingly monotonous and dull, while poverty was at least picturesque.

San Francisco is one of those cities one begins to like from the very first moment and continues to like more and more every day thereafter.

From the height of Telegraph Hill opens a beautiful view of the city and the bay. Here a broad platform has been constructed with a white stone balustrade surrounded by urns.

The bay, gleaming in the sun, is crisscrossed in all directions by white ferries. In the harbour stand large ocean steamers. They belch smoke, ready to go off to Yokohama, Honolulu, and Shanghai. From the aerodrome of the military encampment an aeroplane rises and, its wings gleaming in the sun, disappears in the translucent sky. In the middle of the bay on Alcatraz Island, which from the distance looks like an antiquated armoured cruiser, one can make out the building of the federal prison for particularly important criminals. There sits Al Capone, the famous chieftain of a bandit organization which had terrorized the country. Ordinary bandits in America are placed in the electric chair. Al Capone has been sentenced to eleven years' imprisonment, not for bootlegging and not for robbery, but for non-payment of income tax on the money he acquired through robbery and bootlegging. In prison Al Capone writes anti-Soviet articles which the Hearst newspapers print with pleasure. The famous bandit and murderer (something like the cabman Komorov, only much more dangerous) is concerned about conditions in America, and while sitting in prison composes plans for saving the country from the spread of communist ideas. And Americans, great lovers of humour, do not see anything funny in that.

On Telegraph Hill is a high tower from the top of which, we were told, opens a broad view of the city. However, we were not allowed to go to the top. We learned that in the morning an unemployed young man had flung himself from the tower and was crushed, and so for that day it was decided to forbid admission to the tower.

San Francisco Bay is separated from the ocean by two peninsulas, which jut out from the northern and southern sides of the bay and end in high cliffs that form the exit into the ocean. That is the Golden Gate. The northern peninsula, full of cliffs, is covered with a wild forest. San Francisco lies on the southern peninsula, facing the bay.

We drove toward the Golden Gate. On a high cape at the exit into the ocean is a beautiful park and in it a museum of fine arts with numerous reproductions of famous European sculptures. Here ends Lincoln Highway, the autostrada between New York and San Francisco. American technicians are people of amazing modesty. The end of their concrete masterpiece which unites the Atlantic and the Pacific oceans they have marked with a memorial column only three feet high, on which are the letter "L," a small bronze bas-relief of Lincoln, and the inscription: "The Western End of the Lincoln Highway." The names of the builders of the road remain unknown. What of it! The people who a year from now will be driving across the bridges of San Francisco Bay will not know who planned and built them.

Thanks to the kindness of the bridge builders we were granted permission to look at their work. We got into a naval cutter, which waited for us in the harbour, and departed for Yerba Buena Island, located in the middle of the bay. The little island is in charge of the War Department, and one must receive special permission to visit it. The San Francisco-Oakland Bridge, eight and a half miles long, consists of several bridge spans of different types. Especially interesting is its western suspension part, which is 10,450 feet in length. It joins San Francisco with Yerba Buena Island and consists of suspension spans connected by a central stabilizer. On the island the western part of the bridge meets with the eastern part, which connects the island with the land. That part consists of a cantilever span, which stretches for 1400 feet, and several other spans, which are overlapped by latticed girders.

The main work on the island, which is almost completed, is a wide and high tunnel drilled through the cliffs. It is this tunnel which connects both parts. The tunnel and the bridge will be two stories high. On the upper story automobiles will move in six rows. The pedestrians have not been forgotten either. There will be two sidewalks for them. On the lower story in two rows will pass trucks, and between them an electric railway. By comparison with this bridge, the greatest European and American bridges will seem small.

Now they were finishing the spinning of the steel cable on which the bridge will hang. Its thickness is almost a metre in diameter. It is that which, when we were approaching San Francisco, looked to us like thin wires dangling over the bay. The guy, which before our very eyes was being spliced in the air by moving machinery, reminded us of Gulliver, whose every strand of hair was tied by the Lilliputians, each to a little peg. That cable, hanging over the bay, is safely provided with a wire net for the workmen to walk on. We ventured to make a short journey along the cable. We felt as if we were on the roof of a skyscraper, with only this difference—that there was nothing at all under our feet except a thin wire net through which the waves of the bay were visible. A strong wind was blowing.

Although the journey was quite safe, we clutched the cable with desperation.

"How thick it is," said Mrs. Adams, trying not to look down.

"A beautiful cable," confirmed Mr. Adams, without letting the upper steel support out of his hands.

The cable is woven out of seventeen and a half thousand thin steel wires, our guide explained to us.

We went into transports of rapture over this figure, and hung on to the cable more firmly than ever.

"And now let us go higher," the guide proposed, "to the very top of the pylon."

G*

But it was impossible to tear us away from the cable.

"What a cable!" Mr. Adams exclaimed. "Just see how thick it is. How many wires did you say?"

"Seventeen and a half thousand," said the guide.

"I simply don't want to go away from it," Mr. Adams remarked.

"But we don't have to go away from it. We will go up alongside the cable," the guide said naïvely.

"No, no. In this particular place the cable is especially good! This is a magnificent cable! Just look how faultlessly thin it is and at the same time what durable workmanship!"

Mr. Adams looked down by chance, and instantly shut his eyes.

"An excellent, excellent cable," he muttered. "Write that down in your little books."

"Wouldn't you like to look through the console span of the eastern part of the bridge?" the guide suggested.

"No, no, sir! What a thing to say! No, this is an excellent cable! I like it very much. This is a perfect, a superior cable. It would be interesting to know from how many wires it is made up."

"From seventeen and a half thousand," our guide said sadly.

He understood that we would not go anywhere else and suggested that we go down. The entire way back we walked without letting the cable out of our hands and admiring its unheard-of qualities.

Only when we found ourselves on the hard rocky surface of Yerba Buena Island did we understand the meaning of the heroism of people who, whistling gaily, were splicing the cable over the ocean.

32
American Football

ON THE fifth day of our life in San Francisco we noticed that the city began to suck us in, just as long ago—thousands of cities, a score of deserts, and a score of states ago—we had been almost sucked in by New York. Our notebooks were filled with a multitude of notes, signifying the dates of business appointments, of business luncheons, and business cocktail parties. We were leading the life of businesslike Americans, without having any business at all. Our days were tremulous with the fear of being late for an appointment. Cursing, we crept around the room, looking for the lost collar button. Like Chichikov, we paid a visit to the mayor of the city, a very charming Italian by the name of Rossi, a bald-headed gentleman with black eyebrows. He showed us a letter from Honolulu which had been sent only the day before. The letter had been brought over by the *China Clipper*, a flying boat of Sikorsky's. For exactly five minutes we praised the city of San

Francisco to the mayor and he treated us to excellent cigars. It was our
luck that San Francisco really is a fine city and we were not obliged to
lie to Mr. Rossi. We walked out of the City Hall with pleasant smiles
on our faces and with apprehension in our hearts. It was high time to
break through the ring of business appointments and really begin a
business life—that is, wander aimlessly through the city.

For the first time we circled a high cape at the Golden Gate and drove
out on a quay. Along the quay stretched a beach on which the waves
of the Pacific Ocean broke with thunder: it was a sunny but windy
December day. The swimming season was over, and the entertainment
establishments which faced the quay were empty. Here San Franciscans go
out to enjoy themselves on warm Sundays. Here one may test his strength,
ride on electric automobiles that bump into one another, for ten cents
receive a portrait of one's future wife with a description of her character,
play pinball games, and, on the whole, secure a brimful measure of the American entertainment ration. But how beautiful this place was! The quay
seemed no less sweeping than the ocean—there was no end to either of them.

At the "Topsy" restaurant—which specialized in roasted breaded
chicken, and, therefore, had its roof decorated with a cockerel's head and
its hall with the portrait of hens—we saw how a San Franciscan in
moderate circumstances has his "good time." For fifty cents he gets a
portion of chicken, and, having eaten it, dances until he is on the verge
of collapsing. After he is tired of dancing, he and his girl, taking no
pity on his Sunday-best trousers, ride down a polished wooden chute
placed in the hall especially for entertainment-seeking chicken eaters.

It may be due to the influence of the ocean, the climate, or the sailors
from all parts of the world who crowd each other here, but in the
restaurant business of San Francisco one notices a play of mind not
customary in America. In Bernstein's Restaurant, somewhere in the
centre, near Market Street, we were served fish courses exclusively. The
restaurant itself was built in the shape of a ship, and the food was served
by people in the uniforms of captains and sailors. Everywhere hung life
preservers with the inscription "Bernstein." That, of course, was no
evidence of a very artistic imagination. But after a drug-store lunch No. 3,
this was much more satisfactory, especially since it did not cost any more
than a visit to a drug-store. Not far from the harbour was a quite remarkable food establishment, an Italian restaurant called "Lucca's." Its
owner impressed us as a magician and benefactor. The magician's charge
for a dinner is, to tell the truth, not so very little—a dollar—but then here
for the same price one has the right to ask for additional helpings of any
course one finds to his special liking. However, the main surprise is still
ahead. After dinner, when the visitor is putting on his overcoat, he is
given a package of pastry neatly tied with a ribbon.

"But I did not order any pastry!" the visitor says, turning pale.

"This is free," the waiter replies, looking at him with burning Italian
eyes. "It is a gift."

But this is not all. The visitor is also given a ticket. The ticket entitles him to come the following morning into Lucca's pastryshop for a roll and a cup of coffee. At the moment the visitor's overwhelmed brain cannot grasp that the price of the pastry and the coffee and roll entered into the honestly paid dollar, and that all of this extraordinary commercial reckoning of Lucca's is based on the supposition that many of the visitors will not come the next day for their coffee and roll, since they will not have the time for it. Here, as they say, was a plain case of diamond cut diamond.

Having relieved ourselves of visits, we felt cheery and buoyant, like students after an examination. The fact that we had seen real Rodins in Paris and in Moscow saved us from the necessity of looking at the copies of Rodin at the museum, so we wandered over the city without plan or purpose. And since our entire journey had passed quite wisely and had been subjected to Mr. Adams's strict plan, we regarded these free hours of wanderings as a well-deserved rest.

We don't understand why and how we found ourselves in the "Tropical Swimming Pool"—that is, in a winter basin. We stood there, without taking off our top-coats, in a huge, old, white wooden dwelling where the air was as oppressive as in a hothouse; here and there bamboo poles and drapery protruded, and, after admiring a young couple in swimming-suits who very busily played ping-pong and a fat man who floundered in a large box of water, we noticed several pinball games and an automatic machine for chewing gum, so went on, to the Japanese garden.

This garden was a gift to the city from the Japanese empress. In it everything was small. Hunchbacked bamboo bridges, midget trees, and a Japanese house with sliding paper doors. In it lives a Japanese who, if the visitors like, will brew real Japanese tea for them. We sat in a midget bamboo pergola and drank fragrant green hot water, which the polite host served noiselessly. When we felt ourselves on the blessed islands of Nippon, our fellow travellers told us that this Japanese had recently destroyed his wife. He had tormented her so that she had poured kerosene and set fire to herself.

From the Japanese garden we went to the Chinese city. It was picturesque and rather dirty. Everything in it was Chinese—its denizens, its paper lanterns, and the long pieces of cloth with hieroglyphics. But in the store sat only Japanese who sold kimonos, robes, wooden slippers, coloured photographs and Chinese trinkets with the stamp "Made in Japan."

Our free day was finished by a visit to a football match. The teams of two universities were playing: Santa Clara and Texas Christian.

But before passing to a description of this event which, to some extent, helped us to understand the nature of America, it is necessary to say a few words about American football in general.

Football in America means this: the very largest stadium, the very largest congregation of people and automobiles in one place, the very loudest noise that can be emitted through the oral cavity of a certain creature with two hands, two legs, one head, and one hat put on aslant; it means the very largest appropriation of money, a special football press and a special football literature (stories, novelettes, and novels of football life). A big football match in America is an event of much greater significance than a concert by a symphony orchestra under the direction of Toscanini, a cyclone in Florida, a war in Europe, or even the kidnapping of a famous millionaire's daughter. If a bandit wants to become famous, he must not commit his sensational crime on the day of a football match between the Army and the Navy, but must find for it a more suitable and quieter time. Mussolini, for example, found a very convenient moment for attacking Abyssinia. On that day there was no football game in America, so the Duce received good publicity on the first page of all the newspapers. Otherwise, he would have had to move over to the second or maybe even to the third page.

The match which we saw in San Francisco cannot be regarded as one of the big games. However, it was not such a very small game either, and we would not advise Gigli or even Jascha Heifetz to give a concert on that day in San Francisco.

The grandstands of the stadium, filled in the centre, were almost vacant on the ends. Still, there were approximately thirty thousand people there. At first the play seemed incomprehensible and, therefore, not interesting.

American football has nothing in common with European football. These games resemble each other so little that when in New York in a newsreel theatre a portion of a football match between two European teams was shown, there was laughter in the audience.

And so, for some time we could not understand what was going on in the field. People in leather helmets, looking a little bit like sea divers, some of them in red, others in white, stood facing each other, their heads and backs bent, and for several seconds kept standing without a move. Then a whistle blew and these people dashed frantically away from their places. The reds and the whites got mixed up, as it seemed to us, seizing each other by their legs. Such a commotion occurs in a chicken coop when a polecat appears. It seemed to us that we even heard the flapping of wings. Then they all fell on top of each other, forming a large pile of bodies in motion. The audience rose and shouted lustily. The referee whistled. The football players resumed their places and everything began all over again.

The first few minutes we did not even see the ball: that is, we noticed it, but only for a second or two, and then again we lost sight of it. Gradually we learned to follow the ball and to estimate the situation. By the end of the first quarter we began to understand a little about American football and by the end of the second quarter we were already great experts, repeated the names of the best players, and yelled with all the other onlookers.

In broad outline, American football is somewhat like this: There are two teams; each team has its goal with a crossbeam. The grassy field is marked off by white crosswise strips, and each of these strips is occupied by assault. We will not describe the rules of the game in detail. They are too complicated. The important thing is how it is played, what is done with the ball. The ball is made of leather; it is not round, it is oblong. This, it seems, makes it possible to hold on to it more firmly and more conveniently, pressing it to the stomach. When the teams take their places, bending over and facing each other, three players stand behind. The central player throws the ball back between his legs, which are spread apart, to one of his teammates at the back. The opponent does not see at once who caught the ball, and therein lies the advantage of the team that begins the play. The man who receives the ball either kicks it or throws it far ahead, on the calculation that one of his running team-mates will catch it, or he passes it as unnoticeably as possible to a partner from hand to hand. In either case, the man who finally receives the ball presses it to his stomach and runs ahead. Everyone has the right to push him, to catch him by his legs, to trip him up. Sometimes (this happens rarely and calls forth ovations from the stadium) the player manages to elude all attacks and carry the ball to the extreme end, into the territory or camp of the opponent. However, more frequently he is caught and thrown to the ground. If at that time he let the ball drop out of his hands, the next turn, or, if you like, the next paroxysm, of football begins from the spot where the man fell with the ball. Occasionally the man who receives the ball, if he is a good runner, makes a wide circle in order to elude his enemies. But the enemies quickly discover him who holds the ball and run across to cut off his way. He passes the ball to another, that one to the third one, but it is difficult to break through, it is almost impossible, and the man with the ball is sometimes thrown to the ground farther away from the goal than at the moment when the turn began, and thus several feet are lost. Between the turns of play the team which has the ball holds a conference as to further tactics. By tradition this team goes a little to the side, and, forming a circle—so that only the bent backs and outspread legs are seen, while their heads, almost touching each other, form the centre—whispers. Finally, the terrible plan is thought up, the players peer ahead warily, and a new overwhelming brawl begins.

The Santa Clara and Texas Christian teams were almost evenly matched. The Christian young men of Texas were a trifle stronger. In almost all the skirmishes their tactics consisted in having the player who had the ball fling himself headlong into the very thickness of the Santa Claraites and thus attempt to gain at least an inch of ground. He was felled at once. A new skirmish began and again an inch was gained. This reminded us of the attack on the western front at the time of the World War, when after a three-day artillery preparation the armies managed to move a hundred yards ahead. Slowly and implacably the

Texans moved toward the goal of the Santa Claraites. The tension increased more and more. The young men in slanting hats shouted louder
and louder. Now our entire attention was drawn to the public.

On the grandstands of the stadium, facing each other, sat the students
of the respective universities, "suffering" for their teams. On our side
sat several thousand Santa Claraites, in red caps, with their own band.
Opposite us, the entire centre of the grandstand was occupied by the
Christian young men in white caps, likewise with their own band, who
had especially journeyed here from Texas.

When only about twenty feet remained before the last line of the
Santa Claraites was reached, the Texans rose from their seats, took off
their white caps and, rhythmically waving them in the direction of the
opponent's goal, began to cry under the command of the band leader:
"Go! Go! Go!"

In exact translation this means "proceed!" But it should be understood rather as: "Forward! Forward! Forward!"

The band also rose and, raising the horns to the very sky, blared forth
intact the cacophonic sounds: "Go! Go!"

The Santa Claraites in their red caps were downcast and silent. By
the time of the intermission, Texas Christian was ahead. A new disgrace
fell on the heads of the poor students of Santa Clara. By tradition, the
band of the victors played during the intermission. But now, while the
players, spitting out the grass and pulling it out of their nostrils and
ears, were restoring themselves into fit condition for the next half, the
drums resounded, fanfares bayed, and parading into the field marched
the white orchestra of Texas Christian. Ahead of them walked the drum-
major, executing fancy dancing steps and waving his baton like a
virtuoso. The band played its university march. All that time the Santa
Clara band, sitting idly, must have suffered the torments Wagner experienced while listening to the hateful sounds of *Traviata*. Moreover, the
contemptible band of the opponents played and played and played. Now
the musicians were playing fashionable fox-trots and songs, marching
one after the other down the field, coming together, walking apart,
executing various marching figures. The band leader wriggled his body,
tap-danced, and on purpose made all sorts of impudent body movements
in order to irritate and humiliate his defeated enemies.

The second half began.

Beyond the walls of the stadium we could see the houses of San Francisco ranged up and down. Close together and fresh and green were the
trees of the gardens. The square of lawn shone in the sun, while the
light odour of seaweed, oysters, youth, and happiness, which came from
the ocean, mingled with the disgustingly drug-storish stench of whisky.
The public, in order to warm up its enthusiasm and in fond memory of
Prohibition days, pulled out flat pocket flasks and drank right out of the
bottle while in the grandstand.

Again an interesting skirmish began. This time Santa Clara did not

begin so badly. The line of combat came closer and closer to the goal
of the Christian young men. Now red caps were lifted and the Santa
Clara boys began to work up their football players.

"Go! Go! Go!" they cried in ringing youthful voices.

The Santa Clara band, jumping to their benches, launched such a
bedlam of music that this alone should have turned the accursed and
impudent Christian young men into ashes. With every new whistle of
the referee the line of the game moved toward the goal of the Texans.
The Santa Claraites literally broke their way through with their heads,
capturing inches and feet of green grass. Urged on by yells, they fought
tooth and nail, and like bucking goats plunged headlong into the wall
of enemy stomachs.

"Santa Clara!" some young men over our heads shouted desperately.
"Santa Clara! Go! Go!"

Their eyes were popping. Their mouths were wide open. Forgotten bits
of chewing gum stuck to their teeth. The hour of reckoning was at hand.

And suddenly something frightful happened. Something happened
which compelled both warring grandstands to rise and to emit one heart-
rending cry, in which was everything, including triumph and pride and
horror. In a word, it was a universal cry, the very loudest cry thirty
thousand throats can muster.

The best football player of Texas Christian unexpectedly caught the
ball and raced to the goal of Santa Clara. He had to cross the entire
field. Men ran to intercept him. Men chased after him. They tried to
tackle him. The most desperate defendants of Santa Clara flung themselves headlong under his feet. But the little football player, pressing
the ball to his stomach, kept running and running and running. It was
a remarkable miracle. At first he ran along the edge of the field. Then
he turned sharply into the middle, leaving behind those who ran to meet
him on the side. He jumped over a Santa Claraite who flung himself
under his legs and cleverly skipped away from a score of other arms
stretched out toward him. It is difficult to convey the excitement of the
public. Finally, this player ran across the last line and stopped. That
was all. Texas Christian had won. Our grandstand was disgraced. The
grandstand opposite exulted stormily.

33
Russian Hill

WE RETURNED from the football game in excellent spirits and, interrupting each other, began to tell the Adamses our football impressions.
The Adamses did not go with us to the football game; they went instead
to the post office.

"Don't talk to me about football," Mr. Adams said to us, "it is a horribly barbarous game. Seriously, it hurts me to hear you talk about football. Instead of studying, these young men do the devil only knows what. No, let's not talk about that nonsense."

Mr. Adams was worried about something. Before him lay a long piece of paper covered all over with figures and with all kinds of other markings, and a small parcel.

"In other words, Becky, the hat has not arrived in San Francisco. And yet, we sent directions to Santa Fé for them to send the hat directly to San Francisco."

"Are you sure that it was San Francisco?" asked Mrs. Adams. "For some reason, it seems to me that the last time you asked that the hat be sent to Los Angeles."

"No, no, Becky, don't talk like that. I have it all written down."

Mr. Adams took off his spectacles and, bringing the paper close to his eyes, began to decipher his notations.

"Yes, yes," he muttered, "there! According to the last notations the hat was sent from Detroit to Chicago. Then to St. Louis. But since we didn't go to St. Louis, I wrote them to send the hat to Kansas City. When we were in Kansas City the hat had not yet come there . . ."

"Very well," said Mrs. Adams. "That I remember. In Santa Fé we forgot to go to the post office for some reason and you wrote them a letter from Las Vegas. Remember? At the same time you sent the key to the Grand Canyon. Didn't you get the addresses mixed up?"

"Oh, Becky, how *could* you think anything like that?" Mr. Adams moaned.

"Then what is this package?" exclaimed Becky. "It is so small that there cannot possibly be a hat in it."

The Adamses had come from the post office a little while ago and had not yet had time to open the parcel. It took them a long time to open it. They opened it very carefully, talking at the same time about what it could contain.

"But suppose it is my watch from Grand Canyon?" Mr. Adams suggested.

"How can it be your watch from Grand Canyon when the box was mailed in Santa Fé?"

Finally, they opened the parcel. In it lay a key with a round brass disk on which was hammered out the figure "82."

"Just as I thought!" exclaimed Mrs. Adams.

"What do you mean: 'just as I thought,' Becky?" Mr. Adams asked ingratiatingly.

"Just as I thought! This is the key of our room in Grand Canyon which you sent by mistake to the Santa Fé post office, while the directions for shipping the hat you evidently sent to the Grand Canyon, to the camp. I think that the request to return your gold watch, which is a gift from me, instead of going to Grand Canyon went to Santa Fé."

"But, Becky, don't talk so rashly," Mr. Adams muttered. "Am I to blame for everything? Becky, I appeal to your sense of justice. Especially, since it is so easy to correct it all. We shall write . . . Yes . . . Where shall we write?"

"First of all, we will have to return this key and this plaid blanket, which you took by mistake in Fresno."

"But, Becky, I left my binoculars in Fresno, and I should think they're more expensive than the blanket."

"All right, that means that the key goes to the Grand Canyon, the blanket goes to Fresno, and we write to Santa Fé for the watch. That is, no, we write to Grand Canyon for the watch, but before all, we write an apology to Santa Fé. Then . . ."

"But what about the hat, Becky?" Mr. Adams asked sweetly.

"Now, wait a minute, you! Yes, the hat. This is what we'll do with the hat . . ."

At that moment there was a knocking at the door, and into the room came a man of immense proportions—with broad thick shoulders and a large round head on which sat a small cap with a little button.

This man, evidently sensing the hugeness of his body, tried to take very short steps and to walk as quietly as possible. Nevertheless, the hardwood floor creaked under him, as if suddenly a grand piano had been rolled into the room. Having stopped, the stranger, speaking in a thin voice, said in excellent Russian:

"Good day! I have come to you from the Molokan community. Forgive my intrusion. It is a custom of ours, when anyone comes from Russia . . . We extend our welcome to you and ask you to come and have tea with us. I have an automobile here, so don't worry about that."

We had heard a lot about Russian Molokans in San Francisco, torn away from their homeland, who, like the Indians, preserved their language, their habits and customs.

In five minutes Mr. Adams and the messenger of the Molokan community were friends. Mr. Adams showed good knowledge of the subject, and not once did he get the Molokans confused with the Dukhobors or the Subbotniks.

On the way to "Russian Hill," where the San Francisco Molokans live, our guide told us the history of their migration.

Long, long ago the Molokans lived on the Volga. They were oppressed by the Tsar's government, which sent priests and missionaries to them. The Molokans would not yield. Then they were moved to the Caucasus, somewhere in the region of Kars. There, too, in the new place they did exactly what they had done for ages. They raised grain. But it became more and more difficult to live. The persecutions became increasingly cruel. So the Molokans decided to forsake their native land, which had become a stepmother to them. Where could they go? People went to America. So they, too, went to America—five hundred families of them. That was in the year 1902. How did they come to San Francisco? In one way or another. People were going to San Francisco. So they, too, went to San Francisco. Our giant who guided us seemed to be about forty years old. That meant that he had come to America as a six-year-old boy. Yet, he was so decidedly Russian that it was impossible to believe that he could talk English. In America the Molokans wanted to raise grain, as was their custom. But they did not have enough money to buy the land. Thus they began to work in the port. From that time on the San Francisco Molokans have been stevedores, the purest kind of proletarians. In the city the Molokans settled apart, on a hill, gradually built small houses, built a small prayer-house which they solemnly called the "Molokan Church," built a Russian school, and the hill began to be called "Russian Hill." The October Revolution the Molokans greeted not as Molokans but as proletarians. In the first place it awakened the stevedores in them, and only after that the Molokans. For the first time in life, these people felt that they have a homeland, that it stopped being a stepmother to them. At the time of collectivization, one of the respected Molokan elders received from his nephews in the U.S.S.R. a letter in which his advice was asked about the advisability of joining a collective farm. They wrote that another Molokan elder in the U.S.S.R. tried to tell them not to enter a collective farm. And the old man, who had become less of a Molokan preacher and more of a San Francisco stevedore, in replying, advised them to join the collective. This old man told us with pride that now he frequently receives grateful letters from his nephews. When Troyanovsky came to San Francisco, and later Schmidt, the Molokans met them with flowers.

We drove through the city for a long time, rising from hill to hill. It seems that we passed through Chinatown.

"And here is Russian Hill," said our mighty driver, shifting gears into second. The machine rattled and began to climb up the cobbled roadway.

No, there was nothing here reminiscent of San Francisco. This street looked more like the end of Old Tula or Kaluga. We stopped near a small house with a portico and went in. The first room, where on the wall hung old photographs and pictures cut out of magazines, was crowded with people. Here were bearded old men in spectacles. Here were men somewhat younger in coats that disclosed Russian shirts. It was just such clothes that prerevolutionary Russian workers wore on a holiday. But the strongest impression of all was made by the women. We wanted to rub our eyes, just to make sure that such women could exist in the year 1935, and not only somewhere in some old forsaken Russian hole, but in the petrol and electric San Francisco, at the other end of the world. Among them we saw Russian peasant women, white-faced and pink-cheeked, in good holiday waists with puff sleeves and full skirts, the cut of which had years ago been brought from Russia and without any changes had become petrified in San Francisco, and we saw large old women with weird prophetic eyes. The old women wore calico kerchiefs. It was hard enough to accept that. But where did they get calico print in this polka-dot design! The women spoke softly and roundly, in chanting voices, emphasizing "o's" and, as it should be, offered their hands spade-fashion.

Many of them could not speak any English at all, although they had lived almost all of their lives in San Francisco. The gathering reminded us of an old village wedding at the point when all the guests are on hand and the celebration is about to begin.

Almost all the men were as tall and broad-shouldered as the one who had brought us here. They had tremendous arms and hands, the arms and hands of stevedores.

We were asked to come downstairs. Down there was a very spacious basement. A long narrow table was laden with pirozhki, salted pickles, sweet bread, and apples. On the wall hung the portraits of Stalin, Kalinin, and Voroshilov. Everyone took his place at the table, and a conversation began. We were asked about collective farms, about factories, about Moscow. They served us tea in glasses. Suddenly the very largest of the Molokans, a rather elderly man in steel-rimmed spectacles and with a greyish little beard, deeply inhaled a goodly quantity of air and began to sing in a voice so extraordinarily sonorous that at first he seemed to be not singing but shouting:

> "Exhausted I am by sorrow,
> The accursed viper!
> Burn to the end, my matchwood!
> I, too, will burn down with you."

The song was caught up by all the men and women. They sang in full voices, just like their choir leader. There were no nuances in their singing. They sang fortissimo, only fortissimo, with all their might, trying to outshout one another. It made a strange and a somewhat unpleasant first impression. The singing did become a little more composed as it went on. The eardrums soon became accustomed to it. Despite its sonorousness, there was something sad in it. Particularly good were the voices of the women, who brought out the high notes almost hysterically. Such sad and penetrating voices had resounded across the fields at twilight after haying, ringing tirelessly, quieting down slowly, and finally intermingling with the chirrup of the crickets. These people had sung this song on the Volga, later among the Kurds and Armenians near Kars. Now they were singing it in San Francisco, in the state of California. Were they to be driven off into Australia, into Patagonia, into the Fiji Islands, they would sing that song even there.

That song was all that was left to them of Russia.

Then the man in spectacles winked at us and began to sing:

> "All of us have come from the people,
> Children of labour are we.
> Brotherly union and freedom—
> Such is our slogan for war."

Mr. Adams, who had wiped his eyes several times and was now even more profoundly affected than during conversation with the former missionary about the manly Navajo Indians, could not contain himself any longer and began to sing in chorus with the Molokans.

But here a surprise awaited us. The Molokans introduced their own ideological correction when they· came to the words: "The dark days are over; the hour of deliverance has struck." They sang it thus: "The dark days are over; Christ has shown us the way." Mr. Adams, the old atheist and materialist, did not make out the words and continued to sing loudly, opening wide his mouth.

When the song was over we asked why they had changed the text.

The choir leader again winked at us significantly and said:

"We have a songbook. We sing according to the songbook. Only this is a Baptist song. We sang it especially this way for you."

He showed us a badly thumbed book. In its preface it said:

"Songs.may be solemn, sad, or middling."

"Christ Has Shown Us the Way" was evidently a middling song.

In order to please us, the Molokans with great inspiration began singing Demian Biedny's song entitled "How My Own Mother Saw Me Off." They sang it in full, line by line, and for a long time after that they sang other Russian songs.

Then again we talked. We talked about various things. They asked us whether it would be possible to arrange for the return of the Molokans to their native land.

Two old men who sat beside us got into an argument.

"All the slavery under the sun has come from the priests," said one old man.

The old man agreed with this, but he agreed contentiously.

"For two hundred years we haven't paid the priests anything!" exclaimed the first old man.

The second one agreed with that, too, but again in a contentious tone of voice. We did not intervene in this two-hundred-year-old argument.

It was time to go. We bade our hospitable hosts farewell. Toward the end, already standing, the Molokans repeated for us the song "How My Own Mother Saw Me Off," and we went out into the street.

From Russian Hill there was a good view of the lighted city. It spread far and wide on all sides. Below seethed American, Italian, Chinese, and simply sailor passions, wonderful bridges were being built, on the little island of the federal prison was Al Capone, while here in a kind of voluntary prison were people, with their own Russian songs, Russian women and Russian tea, sitting there with their Russian nostalgia, huge people, almost giants in size, who had lost their homeland, but who remembered it every minute, and who in remembrance of it had hung a portrait of Stalin.

34
Captain X

WE WERE very sorry to leave San Francisco. But the Adamses were implacable. The entire journey had to be consummated within two months and not one day more.

"Yes, yes, gentlemen," said Mr. Adams, beaming. "We must not torment our Baby more than sixty days. Today we received a letter. Last week Baby was taken to the zoo and she was shown the aquarium. When Baby saw so many fish at once she cried out 'No more fish.' Our Baby is lonesome. No, no, we must go as soon as possible."

Full of compassion and regrets, we drove for the last time across the picturesque hunchbacked streets of San Francisco. In this little square we could have sat on the bench and did not sit. On this noisy street we could have promenaded but we had not been there even once. And in this Chinese restaurant we could have had a wonderful lunch but for some reason we did not have lunch there. And the dives, the dives! We forgot the main thing: the famous dives of Old Frisco, where skippers smashed each other's thick heads with bottles of rum, where Malayans danced with white girls, where quiet Chinamen go insane smoking opium! Oh, we forgot it, we forgot it all! And there was nothing more we could do about it: we had to go!

We were going farther and farther from San Francisco down a road that ran along the ocean. The day before we had been at the University of California. We had seen the professor of Russian literature, Mr. Alexander Kaun, and he, holding in his hands a book of Leo Tolstoy's stories in the Tatar language, told his students about the U.S.S.R. policy of nationalities, about the culture and development of the minority nations. Small, grey, and elegant, the professor interspersed his lecture with witticisms, while a hundred-odd students listened attentively to his speech about a distant land with a new and amazing tenor of life. We spent the evening in the professor's house on the shores of San Francisco Bay, near Berkeley. Mr. Kaun had invited about fifteen of his best students. The fireplace glowed, the young men and girls sat on the floor, chattered, cracked Chinese nuts. From the bookshelf loomed the bronze head of Maxim Gorky, made by Valeria Kaun from life, while her husband was working on Gorky's biography at Sorrento. One of the girls rose, went somewhere, and about ten minutes later returned, her hair wet and flowing, like a naiad's. She had been swimming in the bay. In a large wooden box in the kitchen slept six newborn puppies. The professor would go there frequently and, his hands folded touchingly, look at the puppies. Then we went to the shore of the bay, and, under the light of the moon, wandered along the sandy beach. The young men arranged themselves in a circle and sang several student songs in chorus. They began by rendering their fighting song, "Our Sturdy Golden Bear," directed against Stanford students, sworn enemies of the University of California in the football field. The students of the University of California call themselves "Bears." Having sung their fill (they sang quite tunefully but rather weakly—the voice of one Molokan could have drowned them all out), they told us that a student eighty-four years old was enrolled at the University of California. He is moved not merely by an extraordinary love of knowledge. There is still another consideration. Long long ago, when this exceedingly old student was a youth, he received a bequest from an uncle. According to the literal meaning of the will, the beneficiary might utilize the income from the enormous capital so long as he did not graduate from the University. After that the inheritance was to pass to charity. Thus the businessman uncle wanted to kill two rabbits with one shot—give his nephew an education and placate before God his sins, which were inescapably connected with rapid enrichment. But the nephew proved to be no less a businessman than his uncle. He enrolled at the University and ever since then he has been listed as a student, enjoying the income from the capital. This outrage has been going on now for sixty-five years, and the departed businessman of an uncle still cannot move from Hades to Paradise. In a word, an amusing incident in the history of the University of California.

All of that was yesterday. But today, blown by the ocean wind, we raced down the length of the Golden State toward Los Angeles. Passing the town of Monterey, we saw near one wooden house a memorable sign: "Here lived Robert Louis Stevenson during the second half of the year 1879." We drove on a road which was not only comfortable and beautiful, but even somewhat flamboyant. The bright bungalows and the palms, their leaves gleaming as if covered with green enamel, and the sky, so clear that any expectation of the flimsiest cloudlet upon it was patently absurd—all of it seemed like flaunting to us. Only the ocean thundered and rolled like an ill-mannered kinsman waxing boisterous during a birthday celebration in a respectable family.

"Gentlemen," said Mr. Adams, "you are driving through one of the few places in the United States where people retired from business live on their incomes. America is not France, where such people are met in every city. Americans almost never stop when they accumulate some previously agreed upon sum of money. They continue to acquire and to acquire more and more money. But occasionally you find some queer fellows who suddenly decide to retire. More often than not, they are not very rich people, because a rich man can arrange a little California all his own even in his New York house. California attracts because of its cheapness and its climate. Look, look! In these little houses which we are now passing live the petty *rentiers*. But not only *rentiers* live in California. Occasionally you find here representatives of a special human breed—American liberals. Gentlemen, our radical intellectuals are good, honest people. It would be foolish to think that America is all standard-ized and that it consists only of dollar-chasing, only of bridge games or poker. Please remember the young gentleman with whom we recently spent an evening."

The "young gentleman" was an old friend of Adams's who came of an aristocratic family. His parents were very wealthy. He received a splendid education, and ahead of him was an easy, refined life, without care or thought, with three automobiles, golf, a beautiful and devoted wife—in fact, everything that only wealth and descent from a pioneer family, whose ancestors had disembarked from the *Mayflower* several centuries ago, can secure in America. But he spurned it all.

We came to him late one evening (that was in a large industrial city). He had rented an apartment which consisted of one large room with a gas fireplace, a typewriter, and a telephone, and was almost without furniture. The host and his wife, a German communist, were pale in an un-American way. Theirs was the pallor of people whose working day is not regulated and too frequently goes beyond midnight, of people who have neither the time nor the money needed for indulgence in sports, of people who eat any old way, any old place and devote themselves completely to their chosen cause.

Convinced of the injustice of the capitalist order, the young man did not limit his reading to uplifting books, he drew the necessary inferences, and carried on to the bitter end—abandoned his rich papa and joined the Communist party. Now he is a party worker.

A half-hour after we came, another guest arrived. He was the secretary of the district committee of the party. There was not enough furniture, so our host sat on the floor. Before us were two typical representatives of American communism—a worker communist and an intellectual communist.

The secretary was a young man with high cheekbones who looked like any young Moscow communist. It seemed that the only thing lacking to complete the resemblance was a cap with a long peak that hangs over like a cornice. He was a dockworker, and at the moment was leading a strike of stevedores at the port.

"We have already lost several people. They were shot. But we'll fight to the bitter end," he said. "Last night the police tried to bring strike-breakers to the ships. They began to crowd our pickets, took their revolvers out, started firing. The police flooded the place where the fighting was going on with searchlights. Many workers were threatened with arrest. Then one of our fellows broke through to the searchlight and threw a rock into its lens. The searchlight was snuffed out. In the dark the workers managed to protect their positions and not let the strike-breakers through. It is hard to carry on this strike, because we do not have trade-union unity. While the stevedores strike, the sailors work! On our coast a strike goes on, but on the Atlantic coast there is no

strike. Of course, the bosses take advantage of this and send their freight
to the Atlantic ports. It costs them more, but at the moment money
doesn't matter to them. They've got to break us. Nevertheless, we
work hard to establish trade-union unity, and we hope for success."

He suddenly became thoughtful and said:

"If we could only get hold of some kind of automobile, even as old
as can be. I have a tremendous district. When I have to go some place
on party business, I go out on the road and raise my thumb. A thumb
is all the means that has been allotted to me for transportation. It
wouldn't be bad if American communists had only one-millionth part
of that Moscow gold about which Hearst writes in his papers every day."

He began to talk about the thirty dollars which are needed in order to
begin the fight against the medieval exploitation of Mexicans and Filipinos
on onion plantations. But he couldn't get hold of that thirty dollars.
And he had to get that money.

Certain party workers live on two dollars a week. A funny figure for
a country of millionaires. But what could you do about it? With their
pathetic little bit they manfully began a fight with the Morgans and are
succeeding. The Morgans, who have billions, in spite of their powerful
press, are afraid of them and detest them.

Mrs. Adams and the wife of our host had long ago gone somewhere
and only now returned with bread and sausage. While we were finishing
our conversation, they were making sandwiches on a shaky little table.
Here was a spectacle of the kind we know only from museum pictures
which portray the life of Russian revolutionists on the eve of 1905.

"Yes, Mr. Ilf and Mr. Petrov, I see you recall those good people," continued Mr. Adams. "Americans know how to be carried away by ideals.
And since in general they are business people and know how to work,
they are just as efficient in the revolutionary movement, when they also
attend to business and not to a lot of talk. You saw the secretary. He
is a very businesslike young man. I advise you, gentlemen, to stop in
Carmel. You will see there even more interesting people. In Carmel
lives Lincoln Steffens. He is one of the best people in America."

The road now came close to the ocean, now drifted away from it. At
times we passed through long lanes of tall palms. At other times we
drove up small hills in green orchards and summer resort houses. In the
small quiet town of Carmel we lunched in a restaurant on the walls of
which were hung autographed photographs of famous motion-picture
actors. Here was already the odour of Hollywood, although it was still
about two hundred miles away.

The streets of Carmel, overgrown with greensward, descend to the
very shore of the ocean. Here, as in Santa Fé and in Taos, live many
famous painters and writers.

Albert Rhys Williams, the American writer and friend of John Reed,
who had travelled with him through Russia during the Revolution, a
large grey-haired man with a young face and good-natured squinting

eyes, met us in the yard of his little old house which he rents by the month. His house looked like all other American houses only in that it had a fireplace. Nothing else in it looked like the rest of them. Here was a Bohemian couch covered with a rug, many books, on a table lay pamphlets and newspapers. At once one thing struck the eye—in this house people actually read. In his workroom Williams opened a large reed basket and a trunk. They were full of manuscripts and newspaper clippings.

"Here," said Williams, "is the material for my book about the Soviet Union, which I am now finishing. I have several other baskets and trunks filled with material. I want my book to be completely exhaustive, and I want it to give the American reader a full and precise idea of how life is organized in the Soviet Union."

Williams has been several times in our country, and on one of his journeys lived a whole year in a village.

With Williams and with his wife, the scenario writer, Lucita Squier, we went to call on Lincoln Steffens. Lucita Squier wore a homespun linen Mordovian dress with cross-stitch embroidery.

"I am wearing this in remembrance of Russia," she said.

We were walking along the shore of the ocean and did not tire of admiring it.

"The Black Sea is better," remarked Lucita Squier.

We praised Carmel, its houses, its trees, its tranquillity.

"I like Moscow better," remarked Lucita Squier dryly.

"Don't listen to her," said Williams. "She is simply frantic. She is always thinking of Moscow. She doesn't like anything in the world except Moscow. After being there for a while she has come to prefer everything Russian. You have heard her speak! She said that the Black Sea is more beautiful than the Pacific Ocean. She is even capable of saying that the Black Sea is bigger than the Pacific Ocean, only because the Black Sea is Soviet."

"Yes," said Lucita stubbornly. "I say it and I shall continue to say it. I want to go to Moscow! We should not stay here another minute!"

Conversing thus, we walked up to the home of Lincoln Steffens, which was not visible from the street because of its thick greenery.

Steffens is a famous American writer. His autobiography in two volumes has become a classical work in America.

Heart disease would not let him get out of bed. We went into his room, where a white iron bedstead stood with its head against the window. On this bed, resting against pillows, reclined an old man in gold spectacles. A little lower than his chest, on the comforter, stood a low bench on which was a portable typewriter. Steffens was finishing an article.

Steffens's illness was incurable. But like all doomed people, even those who understand their situation, he dreamed of the future, talked about it, made plans. As a matter of fact, he had only one plan for himself—

to go to Moscow, so as to see before his death the land of socialism and to die there.

"I can no longer remain here," he said quietly, turning his head to the window, as if the free and easy nature of California were choking him. "I cannot bear to hear any longer this idiotic optimistic laughter."

This was said by a man who all his life had believed in American democracy, supporting it with his talents as writer, journalist, and orator. All his life he reckoned that the social structure of the United States was ideal and might secure for the people freedom and happiness. And no matter what blows he received on the way, he remained ever true to it. He was wont to say: "The whole point is that in our administration there are not enough honest people. Our social system is good, what we need is honest people."

But now he said to us:

"I wanted to write a book for my son, in which I would tell the whole truth about myself. And on the very first page I had to . . ."

Suddenly we heard curt, dismal sobs. It was Lincoln Steffens weeping. With his hands he covered his thin and nervous face, the face of a scholar.

His wife raised his head and gave him a handkerchief. But, no longer embarrassed by his tears, he continued:

"I had to disclose to my son how difficult it is to regard yourself all your life as an honest man, when as a matter of fact you have been a bribetaker. Yes, without realizing it, I had been bribed by bourgeois society. I did not understand that the fame and respect with which I was rewarded were only a bribe for the support I gave to this iniquitous organization of life."

For a long time we discussed how best to transport Steffens to the Soviet Union. He could not go by train, because his weak heart would not allow that. Could he go by boat from California by way of the Panama Canal to New York, and from there through the Mediterranean to the Black Sea coast? While we were making these plans, Steffens, exhausted by the conversation, lay in bed, his hands resting on the typewriter. Having calmed down now, in his white shirt with its sailor collar, thin, with his little beard and his thin neck, he looked like the dying Don Quixote.

It was already dark when we walked back to Williams's house. Behind us walked Mr. Adams, arm in arm with Becky; and sighing, he muttered:

"No, no, gentlemen, it would be foolish to think that there are few remarkable people in America."

We passed the evening at the home of a certain Carmel architect where the local intellectuals gathered to spend an evening.

In a quite large Spanish hall, with wooden beams under the ceiling, a lot of people assembled. The host, as little as a doll, shaven, with long artistic hair, was respectfully offering to those who had gathered cooling drinks with syrups. His daughter walked up to the grand piano with a look of determination and sonorously played several pieces. Everyone listened with extreme attention. It reminded us of the dumb scene in *Inspector-General*. The guests stopped in the same positions as when the music found them, some with glass raised to the lips, others with their body bent in course of conversation, still others holding a plate on which lay the skimpy pastry. Only one little fellow, whose shoulders were equal in breadth to his height, did not evince sufficient delicacy. He was telling something out loud. His ears, overgrown with flesh and flattened, betrayed the boxer in him. Mr. Adams led us to him. He was presented to us as a former champion of the world, a Mr. Sharkey, a wealthy man (three million dollars), who had forsaken his affairs and was resting at Carmel among the radical intellectuals, with whom he keenly sympathized.

Mr. Sharkey joyfully stared out of his palish little eyes, and at once let us feel his muscles. All the guests had already felt Mr. Sharkey's muscles, but still he could not rest and was constantly bending his short and mighty arms.

"Let's have a drink," Mr. Sharkey said suddenly.

With these words he led away with him about fifteen people who were the guests of the architect, including his musical daughter and us, with the Williamses and the Adamses.

The champion of the world had a fine little house, the windows of which directly faced the Pacific Ocean, which rolled its moon-illuminated waves right up to it. Sharkey opened a closet from which appeared rums, gins, various sorts of whisky, and even a Greek *mastika*, that is, everything that was the very strongest ever prepared by the world's alcohol distilleries.

Having made some hellish mixtures and distributed the glasses among the guests, Mr. Sharkey opened his pale eyes wider than ever and began to lie at a great rate.

In the first place, he declared that he was convinced of the innocence of Bruno Hauptmann, the murderer of Lindbergh's baby, and he could even appear as a witness in this case, if he were not afraid to expose his connection with bootleggers.

Then he told us how once, while in command of a three-masted schooner, he got down to the South Pole, how the schooner was caught by ice and how the crew wanted to kill him, but he alone suppressed the mutiny of the whole crew and safely steered the ship into warm latitudes. This was too colourful, too corsairlike a tale, to refrain from having one more drink to celebrate the occasion.

Then Mr. Sharkey informed us that he admired radical intellectuals, and that in America it was necessary to make a revolution as soon as possible. Therefore, he led us into his bedroom and showed us three daughters sleeping in their three little beds. Here he told us quite a romantic tale of how his wife had run away from him with his own butler, how he ran after her, caught up with her and, revolver in hand, compelled the treacherous butler to marry the woman he had seduced. He taught his little girls to march, regarding that as proper upbringing.

In short, Mr. Sharkey did not let his guests be bored for a single minute.

He led his guests into the gymnasium, took off his shirt, and naked to the waist, began to raise himself on the parallel bars. In conclusion, he put on his boxing gloves and challenged any and all comers to a friendly bout.

In Mr. Adams's eyes lit that little spark, that glint which we had seen before, when he had sat down in the electric chair and had sung spiritual hymns with the Molokans. That man had to try everything.

Someone put leather gloves on his hands, and, with a boyish whoop, he flung himself headlong at the champion of the world. The retired champion began to hop all around Mr. Adams, shielding himself in make-believe fear. Both fat men hopped around and whooped hysterically with laughter. In the end Mr. Adams fell on a bench and began to rub his slightly injured shoulder. Then the guests drank another glass and went home.

In the morning, after bidding farewell to Lincoln Steffens, we departed for Hollywood.

Half a year later we received a letter from our friend, Mr. Adams. The envelope was full of newspaper clippings, and we learned much news about Carmel. Rhys Williams finished his book about the Soviet Union but now, with the publication of the project of the new constitution, he again resumed his work in order to enter into the book the necessary additions.

The kind Mr. Sharkey, as naïve as a child, captain of a schooner and bootlegger, champion of the world, Sharkey proved to be a police agent connected with a fascistic ex-soldier's organization, and besides that—an old provocateur who at one time had betrayed Big Bill Haywood, the famous leader of the Industrial Workers of the World. And he was not at all Mr. Sharkey. He was also Captain Boxy, *alias* Berge, *alias* Forester. At the time of the war, when he betrayed Bill Haywood in Chicago, he was the famous Chicago racketeer who bore the name "Captain X."

And a month later we read in the papers that in the city of Carmel, the state of California, in the seventieth year of his life, the writer Lincoln Steffens died.

And so it was not fated for him to die in the land of socialism.

He died from paralysis of the heart—at his typewriter. On the paper which stuck out of it was an unfinished article about the Spanish events. The last words of that article were the following:

"We Americans must remember that we shall have to wage a similar battle against the Fascists."

35
Four Standard Types

IT IS TERRIBLE to say it right out, but Hollywood, whose fame has gone around the world hundreds of times, Hollywood, about which in the last twenty years more books have been written than in two hundred years about Shakespeare, the great Hollywood, on whose firmament stars rise and fall a million times faster than astronomers have told us about it, Hollywood, of whom dream hundreds of thousands of girls in all ends of the terrestrial globe—this Hollywood is dull, hellishly dull. And if a yawn continues several seconds in any small American town, here it stretches into a full minute. And there are times when one simply cannot muster enough strength to close his mouth. There you sit, your eyes squinting with boredom, your mouth wide open, like a trapped lion.

Hollywood is a correctly planned, excellently paved, and finely lighted city in which live three hundred thousand people. All these three hundred thousand either work in the motion-picture industry or serve those who work in it. The entire city is occupied with one business—it makes pictures, or, as they say in Hollywood, it "shoots" pictures. The noise of the photographing apparatus is much like the noise of a machine-gun, and it is from that resemblance the term "shoot" is derived. All this honourable community "shoots" in one year nearly eight hundred pictures—like all other figures in America, a grandiose figure.

The first stroll through Hollywood streets was sheer torment for us. Strange! Most of the passers-by seemed familiar. We could not rid ourselves of the thought that we had met these people somewhere, that we were acquainted with them, and that we knew something about them. But where we had seen them and what we knew about them—you could kill us, but we could not remember!

"Look, look!" we cried to each other. "Why, this one here, with the light hat and fashionable narrow ribbon, surely we have seen him somewhere. It is impossible to forget those impudent eyes! Where, then, did we meet him?"

But after the man with the impudent eyes came hundreds of others—old men who looked like composers but who whistled falsely the fashionable song "Cheek to Cheek" from the picture *Top Hat*, and old men who looked like bankers but who dressed like small bank depositors, and young men in the most ordinary leather jackets who reminded us of gangsters. Only the girls were, on the whole, all of one face and that face tormented us, was unpleasantly familiar, just as equally familiar were the physiognomies of young men with gangster features and of respectable old men who were either bankers or composers or God only knows what. Finally, it became unendurable. It was only when we realized that we had seen all these people in motion pictures, that all of them were actors or dumb performers, of the second- and third-rate people. They were not so famous that we could remember their faces and names, but at the same time in our memory was embedded a dim recollection of them.

Where had we seen this handsome fellow with the Mexican sideburns? It may have been in a picture called *Be Mine Alone*, or maybe it was in the musical *Meet Me at Midnight*.

Drug-stores in Hollywood are sumptuous. Nickel-plated and glassed, provided with a well-trained personnel in white jackets with chevrons, these establishments have attained such operating perfection that they remind one rather of the machine rooms of electrical stations. This impression was aided by the hissing of taps, the light thunder of little motors that whip malted milk, and the metallic taste of sandwiches.

Over the city shone a strong Christmas sun. Solid black shadows fell on the asphalt ground. There is something unpleasant about the climate of Hollywood. There is nothing sunny in the sun. It resembles a hot moon, although it warms very strongly. In the air one senses constantly a kind of sickish dryness, while the odour of worked-over petrol which permeates the city is unendurable.

We passed under the street lamps on which were placed artificial cardboard firs with electric candles. This decoration was made by the merchants on the occasion of the approaching Christmas. Christmas in America is a great and bright holiday of commerce which has no connection whatever with religion. It is a grandiose clearance sale of all the old merchandise, so that, with all our lack of love for God, we cannot indict Him for participating in this unsavoury business.

But before telling about God, about trade, and Hollywood life, we must say a few things, first of all, about American motion pictures. It is an important and interesting subject.

We, Moscow theatre patrons, are somewhat spoiled by American cinematography. That which reaches Moscow and is shown to a small number of cinema specialists at nightly previews is almost always the best that Hollywood creates.

Moscow has seen the pictures of Lewis Milestone, King Vidor, Reuben Mamoulian, and John Ford: cinematographic Moscow has seen the best pictures of the best directors. Moscow theatre audiences have admired the little pigs, the penguins, and the Disney mouse, and were delighted with the masterpieces of Chaplin. These directors, with the exception of Chaplin who releases one picture in several years, make five, eight, ten pictures a year. But, as we already know, Americans "shoot" eight hundred pictures a year. Of course, we naturally suspected that the remaining seven hundred and ninety pictures were not anything to write home about. But we had seen only good pictures and we had only heard about the bad ones. All the more depressing, therefore, was the impression American cinematography left with us after we became acquainted with it in its own native land.

In New York we went to motion-picture theatres almost every evening. On the way to California, stopping in large and small towns, we visited motion-picture theatres not almost every evening, but simply every evening. Usually two feature pictures are shown during one performance, in addition to a short comedy, an animated cartoon, and several newsreels, all taken by different motion-picture companies. Thus, we must have seen more than a hundred feature pictures alone.

All these pictures are below the level of human dignity. It seems to us that it is degrading for a human being to look at such pictures. They are designed for birds' brains, for slow-thinking human cattle of camel-like lack of fastidiousness. A camel can do without water for a week, and a certain kind of American motion-picture spectator can look at senseless pictures for twenty years on end. Every evening we would enter a motion-picture theatre with a vestige of hope and departed with the feeling of having eaten in all its details the famous lunch No. 2, of which we were duly sick and tired. However, the spectators, the most ordinary American garage mechanics, salesgirls, storekeepers, liked these pictures. At first we wondered about it, later we were worried about it, and then we began to understand how it all came about.

Those eight or ten pictures which are nevertheless good we never managed to see even once throughout the three months of visiting motion-picture theatres. Good pictures were shown to us in Hollywood by the directors themselves, who selected several out of hundreds of films made in the course of several years.

There are four main standard types of pictures: musical comedy, historical drama, a film of bandit life, and a film featuring some famous opera singer. Each of these standard types has only one plot, which is varied endlessly and tiringly. American spectators see one and the same thing year in and year out. They have become so accustomed to it that if they were presented with a picture that had a new plot they would undoubtedly burst into tears, like the child from whom his favourite toy had been taken, though it was old and broken.

The plot of a musical comedy consists of a poor but beautiful girl becoming the star of a variety show. On the way she falls in love with the director of the variety show (a handsome young man). The plot is, after all, not so simple. The point is that the director is in the clutches of another dancer, also beautiful and long-legged, but with a disgusting character. Thus, a measure of drama or conflict is indicated. There are, of course, also other variants. Instead of the poor girl, a poor young man, a kind of ugly duckling, becomes a star. He performs with his comrades; together all of them constitute a jazz band. It happens also that the stars are at the same time both the young girl and the young man. Naturally, they love each other. However, their love takes only one-fifth of the picture, the other four-fifths being devoted to the variety show. In the course of an hour and a half bare legs flash by and the gay theme of the song which is compulsory on such occasions is heard. When a lot of money is spent on a film, then the best legs in the world are shown to the spectators. When the film is cheaper, the legs are a little worse, not so long and not so beautiful. That has nothing to do with the plot. In either case, the plot has not yet startled anyone with the sheer complexity of its inventiveness. The plot is unravelled like a tap-dance number. The public dotes on tap-dance plays. They are box-office successes.

In historical drama the events are of various kinds, depending on who is the principal character of the drama. They are divided into two categories: ancient Greek or Roman, and the more contemporary Musketeer plays. When the cock-o'-the-walk in the picture is Julius Caesar or, let us say, Numa Pompilius, then Greek or Roman fibre-made accoutrements are brought out into the light of day, and the young men whom we saw on the streets of Hollywood "hack" each other frantically with wooden poleaxes and swords. When the main acting person is Catherine the Second or Marie Antoinette or some long lanky Englishwoman of royal blood, then that is already in the Musketeer category—that is, there will be waving of hats and sweeping of floors with ostrich feathers, countless duelling without any particular warrant for it, pursuits and hunts on fat-rumped little racing horses, also a grandiose platonic and boresome connection between the young impoverished nobleman and the empress or queen, accompanied with strictly timed kisses (the Hollywood censorship permits only kisses of a definite film length). The plot of such a play is whatever God sends. If God sends nothing, the play goes on without a plot. The plot is not important. Important are duels, executions, feasts, and battles.

In films of bandit life, the heroes from beginning to end shoot out of automatic pistols and machine-guns, portable and stationary. There are frequent pursuits in automobiles. The machines never fail to swerve off the road as they turn a corner, which constitutes the chief artistic detail of the picture. Such films require a large cast. Scores of actors are eliminated from the list of characters at the very beginning of the play. They are killed by other dramatis personae. It is said that these films resemble life itself very much except for one thing: real gangsters who raid banks and abduct the children of millionaires have never even ventured to dream of profits as large as those garnered from films of their life.

Finally, there is the film with the participation of an operatic singer. Here, you must understand there is no reason whatever for embarrassment. Who would ever think of expecting an operatic singer to act like the elder Coquelin! The singer does not know how to act and does not wish to act. He wants to sing. And that legitimate desire must be satisfied, especially since the spectators themselves want the famous singer to sing as much as possible. Thus, here, too, the plot is of no moment. Usually, a story somewhat like this is unfolded: A poor young man (you'd want him, of course, to be handsome, but here you have to take into consideration the appearance of the singer—a bit of a paunch, pouches under the eyes, short legs) is studying singing but has no success.

H

Why he has no success it is impossible to understand, because at the beginning of his training he sings just as remarkably as at the zenith of his fame. But then appears a young and beautiful Maecenas who brings the singer out. At once he lands in Metropolitan Opera, and has a colossal, incredible, dizzying, miraculous, and supernatural success, the kind of success which even Chaliapin did not dream of at the zenith of his career. There is only one variant of this: the success may be attained not by a man singer but by a woman singer, but then, in accordance with Shakespeare's laws of the drama, the role of the Maecenas is played no longer by a woman but by a wealthy and attractive man. Both variations are accepted by the public with equal joy. But the main thing is popular arias, which are rendered as the action proceeds. It is best that the arias be from *Pagliacci, La Bohème,* or *Rigoletto.* That's what the public likes.

In all the four standard types unity of style is preserved. No matter what the Hollywood actress plays, whether it is the sweetheart of a Crusader, the bride of a Huguenot or a contemporary American girl, her coiffure is always in the very latest fashion. Horizontal permanency lies equally on the Huguenot and on the medieval head. In that Hollywood refuses to compromise. One may yield to history on any other point—if you insist on poleaxes or halberds or anything else like that, you shall have your poleaxes or halberds and the like. But curls must be arranged as called for in the current year. That's what the public likes. The Middle Ages are numerous, so it does not pay to change the coiffure for their sake. But, of course, if it should change during the current year, then it will be necessary to rearrange the hair according to the fashion of that year.

All the historical dramas portray against a variety of backgrounds one and the same frigid American love. At times against the background of conquering the Holy Sepulchre, at times against the background of the burning of Rome by Nero, at times against the background of cardboard Scandinavian castles.

Besides the main standard types, there are several secondary ones, as, for example, pictures with child prodigies. That is all a matter of chance. It is necessary to find a talented child. At the moment there happens to be such a gifted child, the little girl Shirley Temple. There is only one children's plot—the child brings happiness to the grown-ups. So, the five- or six-year-old girl is forced to be photographed in several pictures in order to bring happiness to her parents, who with their daughter earn as much as if she were an oil well that suddenly began to spout.

Besides, occasionally there are pictures of working-class life. In that case, it is some utterly vile Fascist concoction. In a little town of the South, where the trees rustle idyllically and the street lamps shine peacefully, we saw a picture called *Riffraff.* In it was portrayed a worker who went against his boss and the boss's company union. The impudent worker became a tramp. He fell quite low. Later he returned to his boss, a giddy and prodigal son. He confessed the errors of his ways and was accepted with open arms.

The cultured American does not recognize his native motion pictures as an art. More than that, he will tell you that the American motion picture is a moral epidemic, no less harmful and dangerous than scarlet fever or the plague. All the superior attainments of American culture—schools, universities, literature, the theatre—all of it has been hurt and stunned by motion pictures. If you believe him, one may be a fine and clever boy, study well in school, pass through his university course brilliantly—yet after several years of regular attendance at motion-picture theatres turn into an idiot.

We felt all of this even on the road to Hollywood.

When we returned to our hotel after our first stroll (we stayed by strange coincidence on Hollywood Boulevard, in Hotel Hollywood, located in the city of Hollywood—one surely could not think of anything more Hollywoody), we stopped at the window of a pet shop. Here, in a litter of finely cut newspaper, ugly and kindly puppies were playing. They rushed at the window, barked, embraced each other, and in general gave themselves over to their little canine joys. In another show window, in a cage, sat a tiny monkey with an even tinier newborn monkey in its arms. The mother was slightly bigger than a cat, while the baby was quite microscopic, pink, naked, evoking pity. Mamma tenderly licked her child, fed it, stroked its head, did not take her eyes off it. She paid no attention whatever to the spectators. Here was the epitome of motherhood.

Nevertheless, never in our life had we seen a more vicious caricature of mother love. All of it very much resembled what people do, but at the same time, for some inexplicable reason it was so unpleasant that the large crowd which gathered at the show window did not utter a single word. On the faces of all were peculiar, embarrassed smiles.

It was an effort for us to turn away from the monkey show window.

Then we acknowledged to each other that, looking at the monkey with the child, we thought of the American motion picture. It looks like real art even as monkey love for its offspring looks like human love for children. It looks like it, yet at the same time it is unendurably disgusting.

36
The God of Potboilers

THE WINDOWS of our room looked out on Hollywood Boulevard. At one corner of the street crossing was a drug-store, on another was a bank. Beyond the bank loomed a new building. The entire façade of that building was covered with the electric letters: "Max Factor."

Many years ago Max Factor, a young man in torn trousers, came from the south of Russia to America. Without much ado, Max Factor began to make theatrical make-up and perfumery. Before long, all the forty-eight united states noticed that the production of Mr. Factor began to conquer the market. Money flowed to Max from all sides. At present Max is incredibly wealthy and likes to regale his visitors with the enchanting story of his life. And if the visitor happens to be from Yelizavetgrad, Nikolayev, or Kherson, then he may be sure that the happy host will make him take as a souvenir a large jar of face cream or a set of artificial eyelashes which have the best recommendation of Marlene Dietrich or Marion Davies. Not long ago Factor celebrated some kind of anniversary —it was either in honour of the twenty years of his fruitful activity on the make-up front or an annual celebration of his successful landing on American soil. The invitations for that celebration were the most complex and the richest constructions of vellum paper, splendid and shining cardboard, high-grade cellophane, and steel springs. They were thick albums, the pretentious text of which announced to the addressee that they have the honour to invite him and that he has the honour to be invited. But at the last moment the hospitable Factor was evidently doubtful whether he would be understood. Therefore, on the cover he printed in large letters: "Invitation."

Under our windows for eighteen hours out of the twenty-four, young newsboys were shouting. One in particular was distinguished, a fellow with a loud and penetrating voice. Never in the world can anyone with such a voice go astray. It undoubtedly belonged to a coming millionaire. Once we even put our heads out the window to take a look at this young marvel. The young marvel was hatless. He wore a Hollywood leather jacket and "everlasting" canvas trousers. Selling the papers, the marvel bellowed so that one preferred to die rather than listen to these terrible sounds. We wished he would earn his million as soon as possible and calm down. But two days later this respected boy and all of his companions, newsvendors, roared louder than ever. Some famous cinema actress was found dead in her automobile, and her mysterious death was a sensation for four or five days. The Hearst *Examiner* devoted itself solely to that.

However, more frightful than the desperate vendors of newspapers proved to be a timid woman who stood opposite our windows. She wore the uniform of the Salvation Army, a black hood with wide ribbons tied under her chin, and a black satin, loose overall. Early in the morning she placed at the corner a wooden tripod stand from which on an iron chain hung a bucket covered with a grate, and she began to ring a bell. She was collecting for a Christmas tree for the poor. The contributions had to be dropped into this home-made bucket. But the heartless Hollywoodites, preoccupied with their potboiling, paid no attention to this woman in the hood and did not donate any money. She did not annoy the passers-by, did not ask them to contribute their widows' mites, did not sing religious songs. She acted with more persuasive means—she rang her little bell, slowly, calmly, uninterruptedly, endlessly. She had a short intermission only in order to go off and eat. At times we wanted to run out of the hotel and give this person all our savings if it would only terminate the ringing of the bell, which was driving us crazy. But we were deterred only by the thought that the woman, overjoyed with the success of collecting donations, would then come to our corner earlier than ever and depart later than before.

Of all the advertising methods we had seen, of all the ways of pressing things upon people, of reminding them, and of persuading them, this little bell seemed to us the most convincing and the surest of all. And really: why beg, argue, or persuade? None of it is necessary. All that it is necessary to do is to ring the bell—ring for a day, for a week, for a year—ring until the burgess, debilitated, tormented by the ringing, reduced to hallucinations, yields his last remaining ten cents.

A few days later we felt easier. We began to examine the motion-picture studios. What we call cinema factory bears in America the name of studio. We would leave the hotel early and return late. We almost did not hear the ringing of the bell. But in its place a new problem appeared. Each time we returned and took the key at the counter, the clerk of the hotel would hand to us our mail for the day as well as messages of those who had telephoned us. And each time among the familiar names of friends and acquaintances appeared the following notation: "Captain Ivanov telephoned Mr. Ilf and Mr. Petrov." This continued for several days. Captain Ivanov kept telephoning right along. Later his messages became more detailed. "Captain Ivanov telephoned and left the message that he would like to see you." "Captain Ivanov telephoned again and asked that you set the day and hour when you can meet him." In a word, the captain displayed considerable activity. We were completely at a loss to guess who this Captain Ivanov might be and what he wanted of us. We ourselves became interested in him, asked the motion-picture people about him, but no one could explain anything sensible to us. The last note announced that the tireless captain had telephoned again, that he was very sorry that he could not find us in and that he hoped that we would telephone him when we had the time. From the attached address, it was evident that Ivanov lived in the same hotel with us. Then we sensed at once that we could not avoid meeting the energetic captain.

For several days we toured the studios. Of course, we did not attempt to penetrate the technical aspect of the matter, but the technique here is self-evident: it compels you to look upon it. Just as in all American enterprises that we had seen (except the Ford conveyors, where fever reigns), in the Hollywood studios people work, not in too great a hurry, but with assurance and skill. There is no agitation, no hair standing on end, no torments of creation, no perspiring inspiration, no screams and hysterics. All American work is reminiscent a little of a circus show—sure motions, everything calculated, a curt exclamation or order, and the act is done.

The average Hollywood picture is " shot " in three weeks. If it takes longer than three weeks to make it, then it represents a financial failure. There are exceptions, but the exceptions also bear an American character. The famous dramatist, Marc Connelly, was at the moment filming a picture after his famous play, *Green Pastures*. This is a charming production, on the theme of how a poor Negro imagines God's Paradise. Mr. Connelly worked under exceptional conditions: he was the author of the play, he wrote the scenario according to it, and he was producing it himself. In this exceptional case he was given the special privilege of filming his picture in a month and a half. His picture belongs to the Class A category. Pictures which are "shot" in three weeks belong to Class B.

Before the filming begins, everything is gathered to the last piece of string. The scenario is in order, the actors have been rehearsed, the stage sets have been prepared. So the "shooting" of the picture proceeds purposefully and uninterruptedly.

Marc Connelly was producing his *Green Pastures* in the Warner Bros. studios. We do not recall exactly at the moment how many pictures a year Warner Bros. make, whether it is eighty, a hundred, or a hundred and twenty. At any rate, they make a multitude of pictures. Theirs is a large, excellently organized factory of potboilers. *Green Pastures* is not a frequent recurrence for the enterprising "brothers." They seldom produce a picture according to a good literary scenario. We were told that recently a picture was slapped together in eight days, and it was no worse than other pictures in Class B—a neat, clean, and nauseating picture.

On the territory of the studio an entire city is built.

It is the strangest city in the world. From a typical street in a small American town with a garage and a five-and-ten-cent store, we walked out on a Venetian square. Right behind the Palace of the Doges could be seen a Russian inn, on the signboard of which were painted a samovar and a Caucasian astrakhan hat. All the decorations are made to look like the original. Several steps away you cannot believe that these monumental entrances into cathedrals, these coal mines, ocean ports, bankers' offices, Paraguayan villages, railway stations with half a passenger car, are made out of beaverboard, coloured paper, and plaster of Paris.

The strange phantom city through which we walked changed at every step: centuries, people, cultures—all of it was here mixed with an extraordinary and intriguing ease of manner.

We entered a large half-dark pavilion (stage set). At the moment no one was working there, but not so long ago a great feast of art had transpired here. One could judge of it by the tremendous frigate with many guns which occupied the entire pavilion. All over the place lay piles of weapons—cutlasses, grapnels, officers' swords, axes, and other piratical properties. Here people had not been fighting just for fun. The frigate was made so conscientiously that if it had been a whole ship and not only a half·of one, we have no doubt that one could have gone out

into the ocean in it without further ado and captured commercial ships
—to the glory of those great corsairs, the Warner brothers.

In the next pavilion we saw the effulgence of Kleig lights and the gilded
set of the "Musketeer standard" type. The famous cinema actor,
Fredric March, was standing in a camisole, stockings, and shoes with
clasps. His unusually handsome, lustreless face was luminous in the
shadows of the set.

This is what was going on in the pavilion at the moment—the light
was being fitted to Fredric March. But since every effort is made not to
fatigue a great actor, the light was being fitted to a stand-in. When everything is ready, then March will come forth to be photographed.

In another pavilion we saw the actress Bette Davis, whom our
audiences know by the picture *The Crime of Marvin Blake*. She sat in a
chair and in a low voice, but irately, was saying that in the course of ten
days she could not find an hour in which she could have her hair washed.
She had no time! The picture had to be "shot."

"I have to be photographed every day," she was saying in a tired voice
while the habitual grin of a dazzling cinema smile was on her face.

In the expectation of being photographed, the actress looked with dis-
gust, or perhaps rather with complete indifference, at the set, where under
Kleig lights in front of the camera walked a man with a familiar face that
tormented us. Where had we seen this second-rate actor—in the picture
Kidnappers (machine-guns and pursuits), or in the picture *The Love of
Balthaʒar* (catapults, Greek fire), or was it in *Mene Mene Tekel,
Upharsin?*

From the face of Balthazar, who was now being photographed in a top-
hat and swallow-tails (picture of the type of *Child of Broadway*), it was
evident at once that the work did not rouse the slightest vestige of
enthusiasm in him. He was bored and disgusted with it.

This was exceedingly typical of every Hollywoodite who thinks at all.
He disdains his work, thoroughly realizing that he plays nothing but
trash. One cinematographist, showing us the studio in which he works,
literally poked fun at all his pictures. Sensible people in Hollywood, and
there are not a few of them there, simply moaned at that defilement of
art which goes on there every day and every hour. But they
have nowhere else to go, and there is nothing they can do about it. They
curse their work, be they scenarists, directors, actors, or mere technicians.
Only the bosses of Hollywood remain in good spirits. With them it is
not art that matters, but the box office.

In the very largest pavilion was being photographed the scene of a
ball aboard ship. Several stand-ins were crowded on a platform. The
place that was being photographed was amazingly lighted. Hollywood
studios have at their disposal a great quantity of light, and they are not
stingy about it. An intermission came in the photographing, the light
was decreased, and the stand-ins, breathless from their dances, ran off into
the half-lighted corners of the pavilion to rest and to talk. Girls in naval

uniforms with medals and the epaulets of admirals now began to chatter loudly about their feminine affairs. Young men in white naval uniforms, with the stupid eyes of motion-picture lieutenants, were walking up and down the pavilions, stepping over the electric cables lying on the floor.

Oh, those resplendent motion-picture lieutenants! If grateful humanity were suddenly to think of placing a monument to the god of potboiling, it could not find a better model than the motion-picture lieutenant. When in the beginning of a picture the hero appears in a white tunic with a naval cap, set cockily on his head, it is safe, without a single qualm, to walk out of the theatre. Nothing sensible or interesting will happen in such a picture. He is the god of potboiling himself, joyful and empty-headed.

While we were looking over the decorations and the extras, suddenly we heard behind us a Russian voice—such a good Russian voice, juicy, aristocratic—say:

"What do you say, Kolya, shall we go somewhere today?"

The other voice, in a junior captain's timbre, replied:

"And what shall we use for money, Kostenka?"

We turned around quickly.

Behind us stood two gentlemen in swallow-tails. The brownish make-up covered their quite haggard faces. The stiff collars forced them to hold their heads up proudly, but there was despondency in their eyes. Alas! Kolya was no longer young, and even Kostya looked oldish with his numerous wrinkles. They have grown old here in Hollywood, these two who seemed apparently Vladivostok emigrants. It was no fun at all to play a nameless steamship gentleman in a dancing picture about the life of young idiots. Soon the light will be turned off and they will have to return these swallow-tails and the stiff collars to the local storeroom. All their lives they had to deal with storerooms, and so will it evidently be unto death itself.

A signal sounded, and the blinding light was on. The girls, the lieutenants, and the swallow-tailed gentlemen hurried to the stage.

We walked out of the studio, and half an hour later were slowly rolling along with the automobile flood which was making its way to Santa Monica to breathe the ocean air. The great motion-picture capital smelled of petrol and fried ham. Young girls in bright flannel trousers were busily walking the sidewalks. All the girls of the world congregate in Hollywood. Here the very freshest merchandise is needed. Crowds of those who had not yet become rising stars, beautiful girls with unpleasant, spiteful eyes, fill the city. They want fame and they are ready to do anything for it. Probably no place else in the world is there such a number of determined and unattractive beauties.

The cinema stars of both sexes (in America men also have the title of star) live on streets which lead to the ocean. Here we saw a man whose profession is in all probability inimitable. He alone represents this remarkable means of earning money. This man sat under a large striped umbrella. Beside him was placed the following bill-board:

Houses of motion picture stars.

From 9 A.M. until 5.30 P.M.

He would not show you the inside furnishings of these houses and not Gloria Swanson at her morning tea (they will not let him inside), but just on the outside, from the street. Here is the house where Harold Lloyd lives—and here is the house where Greta Garbo lives.

Although the business day was at its height, no one engaged the guide, and on his face was expressed an irrepressible disgust for his foolish profession and for American motion pictures.

Farther on, we saw a young man standing in the middle of the pavement. On his chest hung a placard which read:

I am hungry. Give me work.

No one walked up to this man either.

The vastness of the ocean, the steady wind that blew toward the shore, the tranquil pounding of the surf, reminded us that in this world there is still a life that is real, with real emotions, which do not necessarily fall within a set quantity of footage filled with tap-dancing, kisses and gunshots.

When we entered the lobby of our hotel, a mighty figure rose from a divan and came to meet us. Leaning on a cane, the figure came close to us, and in a stentorian voice said:

"Allow me to introduce myself. Captain Ivanov, a former White Guard."

The captain had a large, smiling face. He looked at us in a friendly manner with his little boarish eyes, and at once declared that he had not been engaged in politics for a long time, although as a matter of fact we had heard nothing about the captain even when he had been presumably occupied with them.

The captain seized us by our hands, sat us down on the divan, and at once, without wasting a single minute, began to talk. In the first place, he told us that it was he who had been entrusted with bringing to Siberia the famous Order of Denikin in which the latter placed himself under the command of Kolchak. Since we happened to recall a name other than his, we did not express any special surprise, in spite of the fact even that the captain was picturesquely telling us how he had carried the order around the world.

"You see, I raced in express trains! From the train to the ship! From the ship to the train! From the train again to the ship! From the ship, and again to the train! Through Europe, the Atlantic, America, the Pacific, Japan, the Far East . . . I arrive, as wet as a wet hen, but Kolchak is no longer there. They have made short shrift of him. So I tore back from the train to the ship, from the ship to the train, from the train again to the ship. Bang! While still in America, I learn it's all over with Denikin, he had transferred his command to Wrangel. The devil take it!

H*

Again I go from the train to the ship, from the ship to the train. I arrive in Paris—but it is all over with Wrangel too. Well, I thought to myself, all of you can go wherever you like, while I myself backed up to America. Now I am a traveller and a lecturer . . ."

The captain took out a fat cigarette-case and began to treat us to Russian cigarettes with mouthpieces.

"I fill them myself," he said. "I import the cigarette wrappers from Bulgaria. I refuse to put this American trash in my mouth."

And right there and then, without the slightest transition, he informed us:

"Do you see the skin on my face? A remarkable skin, isn't it? Amazingly smooth and pink. Just like a milk-fed porkling's. I'll tell you a secret. In 1916, at the front near Kovel, a gun explosion tore the skin off my face to the devil's mother! Shshsh . . . They had to graft some skin from my behind. Ah! How do you like that? Well done! A marvel of medicine! Remarkable skin! What? Of course, I never tell a word of it to the ladies, but to you, as writers and psychologists, I have told about it. But, please, not a word of it to anybody!"

Then he compelled both of us in turn to hold his cane.

"Splendid! What?" he cried eagerly. "Twenty-two pounds of pure iron. I was ill, was forbidden to engage in sports, so I carry this cane, that my muscles shouldn't weaken."

In farewell he informed us that not so long ago, before departing for South America, he had to have seven of his teeth filled at one time.

"I simply didn't have the time! You see, I was so preoccupied prior to my departure, so tired, that I fell asleep in a dentist's chair. I awakened an hour later, and what do you think? All the seven teeth were filled, and I didn't even know anything about it. A marvel of medicine! What?" ·

When we were going up the stairway, the captain was loudly shouting after us:

"Now, please, gentlemen, not a whisper to the ladies!"

Saying this, he pointed to his pink cheeks and in farewell waved his twenty-two-pound cane.

37
Hollywood Serfs

WE WERE SITTING with one of the American motion-picture folk in a small Hollywood café decorated, like many of them, in something like Baghdad style. It was a sultry December evening and the entrance doors of the café were wide open. The dry wind rattled the leaves of the street palms.

"You want to know," the motion-picture man was saying, "why, with all our remarkable technique, with all our excellent actors, with our directors, among whom are the best artists of the world, why we, who now and then, but very rarely, make excellent films, why we spend day and night preparing our revolting, idiotic pictures, which little by little stupefy the spectator? You want to know that? Let me tell you, then."

The motion-picture man ordered a glass of sherry.

"You have to remember who used to be the villain in the old American motion-picture drama. He was almost always the banker. In those cinema plays he used to be the villain. Now look at thousands of films made in Hollywood during the last few years and you will see that the banker has disappeared as a negative personage. He has even become an attractive type. He is now the kindly sympathetic businessman who helps the poor or the lovers. This has happened because bankers, big capitalists, have become the bosses of Hollywood. They, as you can readily see, will not permit that they be portrayed as villains in their films. I'll tell you more. American motion pictures are perhaps the only industry into which capitalists have come not for profit alone. It is no accident that we make idiotic films. We are told to make them. They are made on purpose. Hollywood systematically stuffs the heads of Americans, befogs them with its films. Not one serious problem of life will be touched in a Hollywood film—I'll guarantee you that. Our bosses will not allow it. This work of many years has already yielded a frightful harvest. American spectators have completely unlearned to think. Today any motion-picturegoer stands on an unusually low level. It is very hard for him to sit through something more significant than a tap-dancing film or a pseudo-historical play. He will not even bother to see an intelligent picture, but will rather take his girl and go to the neighbouring motion-picture theatre. Therefore, European films, in which after all there is more sense than in the American ones, enjoy a pitiful distribution here. I am telling you horrible things, but such is the actual state of affairs. It would take many years of hard work to restore to the American motion-picture fan his proper taste. But who is going to do that? The bosses of Hollywood?"

The man we were talking to spoke sincerely. Evidently this subject continually tormented him.

"We have not a single independent man except Chaplin. We serve our bosses and do everything that they tell us to do. You will ask me, how is it then that occasionally appear a few good pictures made in Hollywood? They appear against the will of the boss. They are an accidental success, a concession by the boss to a servant whom he values highly, to keep that servant from foolishly giving up his job. Occasionally it is necessary to hide a good film from the bosses, so that they will not have an opportunity to spoil it. Do you know Lewis Milestone? When he was making *All Quiet on the Western Front*, being afraid of his bosses, who have the habit of coming in during the filming to offer their advice, he spread the rumour that there were constant explosions during filming that were a menace to life and limb. The bosses were frightened and left the wily Milestone in peace. But even then he did not succeed in hiding everything to the end. Once he was called out by his worried and excited boss and asked:

"'Listen, Lewis, they say there's an unhappy ending in your film. Is that right?'

"'Yes, that's so,' Milestone admitted.

"'But that's impossible!' cried the boss. 'The American public won't go to see a film with such an ending. You must attach another ending.'

"'But we're taking the film according to the famous book by Remarque, and there the ending is unhappy,' replied Milestone.

"'I don't know anything about that,' said the boss impatiently. 'I never read that Remarque, and it has nothing to do with me. It's enough that we paid a lot of money for filming rights. But I repeat to you, the American public will not go to see a picture with such an ending.'

"'All right,' said Milestone. 'I'll make another ending.'

"'Now that's fine!' said the boss, overjoyed. 'How is it going to come out now?'

"'Very simple. In Remarque's book the French win, as it actually happened. But since you insist on changing the ending, I'll make it so that the Germans win the war.'

"It was only with this witty rejoinder that Milestone saved his picture. It had a tremendous success. But that happens rarely. Usually even a well-known, even a famous director is compelled to do everything that he is ordered to do. At this particular time—it happened only a few days ago—one of the cinema directors who is famous throughout the world received a scenario that he liked. For several years he has been looking for something significant to produce. Can you imagine his satisfaction and joy when he finally found it? But in that picture the Hollywood star, Marlene Dietrich, had to be filmed. She read the scenario and decided that the roles of the other artists were too big and too well turned out and that they would interfere with her starring in the picture. And so the inimitable Marlene demanded that these roles be cut. The play was irretrievably spoiled. The director refused to work with the scenario in this mutilated form. You can well imagine that the director I am telling you about is so great and famous that he dares to refuse a job that does not please him. There are only a few such people in Hollywood. But the star won, because for our bosses the star is the main thing. The American public goes to see the star, not the director. If the advertisements bear the name of Marlene Dietrich, or Greta Garbo, or Fredric March, the public will bring its millions to the box office, no matter what nonsense these remarkable artists might portray. It all ended very simply. They called in another director, who did not dare refuse anything for fear of losing his job altogether, and they commissioned him to produce the spoiled scenario. He cursed his pathetic fate and began to 'shoot' the picture.

"Maybe you think that we are being managed by some enlightened capitalists? I regret to say that they are the most ordinary, stupid money-makers. Their studios release a mass of pictures every year. Let me tell you a story about the boss of one such firm.

"Once he came to his acquaintances and announced with joy:

"'You know, my wife has such beautiful hands that they are already sculpting a bust of them.'

"They say that one of his actresses, to whom he was paying ten thousand dollars a week (stars receive a dizzying, swinish honorarium, but there is no philanthropy here—a star who receives ten thousand dollars a week brings her boss at least as many thousands of dollars a week of clear profit), invited him for lunch at her castle, which she had purchased in France. Before lunch the building was shown to the old man. He conscientiously felt the silk wallpaper, touched the bed, tested the resilience of the mattresses, attentively examined the turrets. But he was especially interested in the ancient sundial. When it was explained to him how it worked, he was greatly elated and exclaimed:

"'Well done! What are they going to invent next!'

"You see, we have to deal with people who are so ignorant that they think the sundial is the latest invention. Such is their level of knowledge, their cultural level. And these people do not confine themselves merely to giving money for the production of a picture. No, they interfere in everything, suggest corrections, change plots. They tell *us* how to make pictures. Well, I have told you so many sad things that I guess it will last you for a while. You know what, let's get into the machine and go for a ride, freshen up a bit."

We drove out of the city to an alternate reservoir which assures Los Angeles of a water supply in case of damage to the water-transmission station. The night was black. In the stillness of the darkness we actually rested up and recovered from the frightful tales of Hollywood.

On the way back to the city our companion asked:

"Have you seen in the Warner Bros. studio the house of Marion Davies, the famous star? Hearst brought that house over, stone by stone, from somewhere thousands of miles away—maybe even from Europe!"

Returning to our Hollywood Hotel, we slept a cast-iron sleep, devoid of visions, rest and calm—well, in a word, of everything that makes sleep wonderful.

38
Pray, Weigh Yourself, and Pay

THE PREPARATION for Christmas assumed greater and greater proportions. Millions of turkeys and turkey cocks were killed, dressed, and displayed in stores, enchanting Hollywoodites with the yellowish subcutaneous fat and the lilac stamps of the sanitary inspection placed on the turkey breasts.

We have already remarked that an American Christmas is a holiday that has nothing in common with religion. On that day it is not the birth of the Lord God that is celebrated. This holiday is in honour of the traditional Christmas turkey. On that day the Lord, smiling bashfully, retreats to secondary importance.

The worship of the turkey is connected also with one other strange custom—the presentation of gifts to one another. An advertising campaign of many years, cleverly organized by the merchants, has brought matters to such a pass that the presentation of gifts has been transformed for the population into something in the nature of a duty from which commerce derives unheard-of profits. All the old stock, which accumulates throughout the year in various stores, is sold in several days at higher prices. The stores are full of people. The customers, having gone stark mad, grab anything they see. Every American presents gifts, but not only to his wife, his children, or his friends. The main thing is to present gifts to your superiors. The motion-picture actor presents gifts to his director, film operator, sound operator, and make-up man. The office girl presents gifts to her boss, the writer presents gifts to his publisher, the journalist presents gifts to his editor. Most of the gifts go from the lower ranks up the social ladder, and sometimes bear the rather frank aspect of a bribe.

Gifts also pass on the descending line—from superiors to inferiors—but that is a thin stream by comparison with the mighty fountain of love and respect which beats from below upward.

The actor presents his make-up man with two bottles of good champagne, figuring that for the rest of the year the latter will make him up especially well; a gift is presented to the director, to maintain a friendship that is useful, to the operators, that they may remember to film him at the best angles and record his voice as well as possible.

The selection of the gift is a subtle matter. It is necessary to know exactly what gift should be made, and to whom; otherwise, instead of gratitude, the gift may yield a grudge. The gift fever causes Americans a lot of trouble, costs them a lot; but then, it does present the merchants with paradisiacal moments and weeks.

People present each other with cigars, wines, perfumes, scarves, gloves, trinkets. Delivery boys fly all over the city, bearing gifts wrapped in special Christmas paper. Trucks distribute nothing but gifts. Preceded by orchestras, in the handsome uniform of generals, red-nosed Santa Clauses with a cotton beard, wrapped in a naphthalene storm, ride through the city. Boys run after this god of gifts. The grown-ups groan at the sight of the Christmas grandfather, and with an effort remember to whom else they must bear offerings. God forbid that they should forget someone!—or for the rest of the year important business relations would be spoiled.

As a matter of fact, it is only on such occasions, during the feverish pre-Christmas days, that the name of God is mentioned. But God has no bearing whatever on Christmas itself. He is not even allowed to come near it.

In America there are many religions and many gods. Millions of people want to believe in something, so scores of mighty church organizations offer them their services.

The old and, if one may say so, the European religions, suffer because of a certain abstraction. Let them stay in Europe, on that old and decrepit continent. In America, side by side with skyscrapers, electric washing machines, and other attainments of the age, they somehow pale into insignificance. Something more contemporaneous, something more effective, and, let us speak honestly and frankly, something more business-like than eternal bliss in heaven for a righteous life on earth is needed.

In that respect, the most Americanized is a sect which calls itself Christian Science. It has millions of adherents, and essentially is something in the nature of a colossal hospital, only without doctors and medicines. Christian Science is great and wealthy. In many towns and cities remarkable temples with beautiful banklike porticos belong to it.

Christian Science does not ask that people await an endlessly long time for reward in heaven. It transacts its business right here on earth. The religion is practical and convenient. It says:

"Are you ill? Do you have rupture? Believe in God and your rupture will pass!"

Christianity as a science, as something which brings immediate benefit! The average American understands that, it reaches his comprehension, which is befogged by years of unendurable and hurried work. Religion which is as useful as electricity. That's good. One can believe in that.

"Well, all right! But suppose the rupture does not go away?"

"That means that your faith is insufficient, that you have not sufficiently given yourself to God. Believe in Him—and He will help you in everything."

He will help you in everything. In New York we happened to go into one of the Christian Science churches in the centre of the city. A small group of people were sitting on benches, listening to an elderly gentleman dressed in a good tailored suit (in America, a made-to-order suit is a sign of affluence).

Mr. Adams, who accompanied us on that excursion, pricked up his ears and, bending his head, listened attentively. He made a sign to us to come closer. What we heard was very much like the scene in the New York flophouse which we saw on our first evening in America. With this exception: there paupers were being persuaded, while here the rich were being persuaded. But they were being persuaded in absolutely the same manner—by means of living witnesses and incontrovertible facts.

"Brothers," the elderly gentleman was saying, "twenty years ago I was poor and unhappy. I lived in San Francisco. I had no job. My wife was dying. My children were starving. I could turn nowhere for help, except to God. And one morning the voice of God said to me: 'Go to New York and get a job in an insurance company.' I forsook everything and made my way to New York. Hungry and in tatters, I walked through the streets and waited for the Lord to help me. Finally, I saw the sign of an insurance company and understood that God had sent me to that place. I entered the huge and shiny building. In my tattered suit they did not want to let me see the manager. I nevertheless went to him and said:

"'I want to get a job from you.'

"'Do you know the insurance business?' he asked me.

"'No,' I answered in a firm voice.

"'Why, then, do you want to work for an insurance company?'

"I looked at him and I said:

"'Because the Lord God sent me to you.'

"The director did not say anything in reply to me. He called out his secretary and told him to give me a job as an elevator operator."

Having reached this point, the narrator stopped.

"What happened to you then?" one of his auditors asked impatiently.

"You want to know what I am now? Now I am the vice-president of that insurance company. It was God who did that."

We walked out of the church somewhat dumbfounded.

"No, gentlemen," Mr. Adams said excitedly. "Have you heard? If one businessman can in all seriousness tell another businessman, to the sound of calculating machines and telephone bells, that God sent him there to him to get a job, and this recommendation by God is actually taken into consideration, then you can see for yourself that this is a very useful, businesslike God. That is the real American God, of offices and business, not some European chatterbox with a penchant for useless philosophy. Even Catholicism has acquired special attributes in America. Father Coughlin has built himself his own radio station and he advertises his God no less frantically than Coca-Cola is advertised. Seriously, European religions do not suit Americans. They are predicated on an insufficiently businesslike basis. Besides, they are too clever for the average American. He needs something simpler. He must be told which god to worship. He cannot decide for himself. Besides, he has no time to make the decision; he is a busy man. I repeat, he must have a simple religion, telling him definitely what advantages a given religion yields, how much it will cost him, and in what way this religion is better than others. But whatever you say, do say it concretely. The American cannot endure vagueness."

Once, when we were sitting in our Hollywood Hotel, hard at work, the Adamses ran into our room. We had never before seen them in such a dither. Mr. Adams's coat hung on only one of his shoulders, just as it had hung on Pushkin before the duel. He emitted inarticulate cries, and minute by minute his face turned redder and redder. Mrs. Adams, meek Mrs. Adams, who never lost her presence of mind and her composure, even while we were crossing the icy mountain passes, was running around the room and exclaiming from time to time:

"Why didn't I have a revolver with me? I would have shot her like a dog!"

"No, Becky, *I* would shoot her like a dog!"

We were frightened.

"What's come over you? Whom are you going to shoot like a dog? Why like a dog?"

But more than ten minutes passed before the Adamses calmed down and were able to begin the story of what had so incensed them.

We learned that early that morning, not wishing to wake us, they departed for Los Angeles to hear a sermon by a well-known woman in America who had created a new religion, Aimee McPherson.

After quibbling about who should tell the story, Mr. Adams, as usual, won out.

"Gentlemen, it is simply incredible!" he cried in a stentorian voice. "You have missed a lot because you were not with us. Write it down in your little books that we all lost out. And so, Becky and I went to the temple of Aimee McPherson. In spite of the fact that it was still a whole hour before the sermon was to begin, the church was full. More than a thousand people were sitting there. All of them were good, simple people. The ushers evidently decided that we were important people, so they placed us in the first row. Very well. We sit and wait. Yes, yes. Of course, in the meantime we got into conversation with our neighbours. Excellent people. One of them, a farmer from Iowa; another, had also journeyed here especially for this. He has a small ranch in Nevada. Good, honest people, who want to believe in something, who long for spiritual sustenance. They must be given something without fail! They need something, gentlemen! Finally, we hear music. A flourish of music blares forth, and, just as in a circus, Aimee McPherson appears, marcelled, all in curls, with a raspberry manicure, in a white cape, all primped up and rouged. No longer young, but still good-looking. Everybody is elated. And why not? Just think of it, gentlemen! Instead of a dull preacher, a handsome modern woman comes out. And do you know what she said? It was frightful!"

"If I only had a revolver," Mrs. Adams interposed. "I would have..."

"No, no, Becky, you must not be so bloodthirsty. And you must not interrupt me. And so, gentlemen, I will not bother to repeat to you the nonsense she talked. In Europe it would have called forth laughter, even from the most ignorant people. But we are in America! Here you must say only very simple things. My word of honour, the good people who filled the church were in raptures. The spiritual food which Aimee McPherson offered to them would not have suited even a canary, if a canary needed religion. Crude charlatanism, manured with pathetic witticisms, and a considerable quantity of eroticism in the form of a chorus of young women in transparent white dresses. But the main thing was

still ahead! We learned that Aimee McPherson needed a hundred
thousand dollars to repair the temple. A hundred thousand dollars,
gentlemen, is big money even in rich America. And I must tell you that
Americans do not like to part with their dollars. You understand yourself that if she had merely asked the assembly to contribute money for the
repair of the temple, she would not have collected much. But she thought
up a trick of genius! The orchestra, which was shaking the joists, became
silent; and, marcelled, like an angel, Sister McPherson again turned to
the crowd. Her speech was truly inspiring. Gentlemen, you missed
everything because you did not hear that amazing speech. 'Brothers,' she
said, 'money is needed. Not for me, of course, but for God. Can you
give God one penny for every pound of your body's weight which He has
given to you as a gift of His unutterable grace? Only one penny? It isn't
much! Only one penny God asks of you! Will you refuse Him that?'

"And right away the attendants ran down the aisles, distributing
leaflets on which was printed:

"'Pray, weigh yourself, and pay!'

"'Only one penny for each pound of your live weight. Weigh yourselves! Weigh your relatives! Weigh your friends!'

"You know, gentlemen, to think that up is a work of genius! It takes
a subtle knowledge of the peculiarities of American character. Americans
love figures. It is easiest of all to convince them with figures. They
would not have given money just like that. But a penny a pound—
there's something boundlessly convincing and businesslike in that!
Besides, it is an engaging occupation. The farmer will return to Iowa,
and all through the week he will be weighing his neighbours and his
relatives. There will be a lot of laughter!

"Yes, yes. The attendants again ran down the aisles, this time with
large trays. They collected trayfuls of money in a few minutes. The
average American weighs about one hundred and eighty pounds. My fat
neighbour from Nevada gave two dollars. Yet he was clearly not rich.
He was convinced with the aid of idiotic arithmetic. I tell you quite
seriously, the religion of all these sects is somewhere halfway between the
multiplication table and the music-hall. A few figures, a few old
anecdotes, a little pornography, and quite a lot of gall. Write that down
in your little notebooks, gentlemen!"

39
God's Country

AIMEE McPHERSON exceeded the limits of Mr. Adams's patience.

"No, seriously, gentlemen," he was saying to us, pacing up and down
our hotel room. "Becky and I decided to go away. No, no, I under-

stand you excellently. You are writers, you want to learn all you can about American motion pictures. It is very necessary for you. But Becky and I have nothing to do here. We shall go to Mexico."

With these words Mr. Adams spread on the bed a large map torn at the folds and fell on it with his stomach.

"We shall go to Mexico and rest up at the seashore. Becky and I have already gone to the Chamber of Commerce and have got information there. Besides, we shall go at once to the A.A.A., and there we shall get more information. Is that right, Becky? Right near the American border is an excellent place, the village of Encinada—a marvellous beach, a good road. Then, later, we shall meet in San Diego. From there our return trip to New York will begin. What do you think of it, gentlemen?"

Although the journey had been a great source of pleasure to the inquisitive Adamses, they now began to fear that we might not return to New York on time. They were homesick without their baby. Days on end they would seek out little children, press them in tight embraces, stifle them with kisses. The delay in Hollywood beyond the schedule frightened them.

"If we start from San Diego by the twenty-sixth of December, we shall manage to return home on time," Mr. Adams was saying, drawing with a red pencil on the map our return journey. "Along the Mexican border we shall travel to El Paso, then by way of San Antonio we shall reach New Orleans, and, there, cutting across almost all of the Black Belt states, we shall make our way to Washington."

Regrettable as it was to part with our fellow travellers, we were obliged to do it, because getting acquainted with Hollywood required a few more days. We did not wish to torment Mr. Adams by making him tag along with us to various studios. It would have been too inhuman. We agreed to meet on the twenty-fifth of December in San Diego, a city situated on the shores of the Pacific almost on the Mexican border. In case we should not arrive by that date, the Adamses were to proceed on the journey without us, and we would have to catch up with them by train. We had become so accustomed to the Adamses that, standing at our newly washed car shining with freshness, we bade farewell time without end yet could not really part from them. As a matter of fact, at the very last minute the Adamses again disappeared in the Chamber of Commerce for additional information and did not reappear for so long that, unable to wait for them any longer, we set off on our own affairs.

We met numerous people in Hollywood and learned much that was interesting. But one sin lies on our conscience. We were in Hollywood and did not meet Chaplin, although that could have been arranged and we desired it fervently.

It all happened because the meeting with Chaplin was undertaken by a person who simply could not do it even if he had worked on it a whole year. To our regret, we lost many days before we learned that. When we undertook the matter from another end, Chaplin had finished the music for *Modern Times* and had gone away for a rest. Then came that cheery commercial holiday—Merry Christmas. Then we had to leave. And thus our meeting with Chaplin came to naught.

Conversations with Milestone, Mamoulian, and other directors, among the ten best, convinced us that these excellent craftsmen were sick and tired of the senseless plays which they had to produce. Like all big men in art, they want to produce significant things, but the Hollywood system will not let them do it.

We saw several Russians of the many found in Hollywood. They work a lot, are sometimes successful and sometimes not successful, but feel themselves guilty because they stick around here instead of being in Moscow. They don't say anything about it, but it is evident by every indication.

When the Art Theatre was in America, one very young actor decided to remain in Hollywood for a while to work in films. He stayed behind for three months, but has been there more than ten years. He is one of those who are successful. His affairs are constantly improving.

What is the nature of his success? He receives five hundred dollars a week. He has a seven-year contract with his firm. Don't think that a seven-year contract is a great streak of luck. The essence of such a contract is that the actor who signed it is actually obliged to serve the studio with which he is connected for seven years. The studio itself, however, has the right every half-year to reconsider the contract and to decline the actor's services. Thus, it is a seven-year contract for the employee, while for the employer it is only a semi-annual contract.

He has a lot of work. Early in the morning he drives out to be filmed, and returns home late in the evening. He is filmed in one picture, gets a week's rest, and then he begins filming in another picture. There is no stop. He has time only to change his make-up. Since he is a foreigner and does not speak very pure English, he plays foreigners—Mexicans, Spaniards, Italians. All he has to do is to change his sideburns from Spanish to Italian. Since he has a stern face and black eyes, he plays mostly villains, bandits, and the most primitive boors.

"It's a fact!" he cried to us. "The interval between one picture and another is so short that I almost have no time to learn my role. Word of honour!"

Having shown us his house (a good American house with electric appliances, gas heat in the floor, and a silver Christmas tree), his automobile (a good American car with cigar lighter and radio), and his wife (a good Russian wife with grey eyes), the actor turned to what evidently concerned him most of all.

"Well, and how is it in the Union?"

Having received a substantial answer as to how it was in the Union, he asked with even greater interest:

"Well, and how are things in Moscow?"

Having received a no less substantial reply about that too, the actor cried out:

"And at the Art Theatre, how is it? How is it in our theatre?"

We told him about that too.

"Mishka Yanshin is an honoured artist of the Republic?" he groaned joyously. "But Mishka is a mere boy! We played together in silent roles. And Khmelev? Is it possible that he is playing *Tsar Fedor*? Simply miraculous! But Khmelev and I . . . we were children in 1922! It's a fact that we were children! Well, I know everything about Ilyinsky! He's become a famous artist, yet we studied in the studio together. It's a fact that we studied together! Igor and I!"

He could in no wise become accustomed to the thought that all of our Yanshins and Khmelevs had already grown up and had become great artists. He could not get accustomed to it, because he measured them by Hollywood standards. Essentially, nothing at all had happened to him in the course of thirteen years. True, he received more money and had his own automobile, but he did not become a famous actor. Only recently, literally a month ago, they began to place his name in the list of players. But before that he did not have even that distinction. They simply used him—some anonymous motion-picture genius with Mexican sideburns and sparkling eyes. Yet he is a very talented actor!

Late that night, accompanying us through the hushed Hollywood streets, he suddenly became excited and began to curse everything.

"Hollywood is a village!" he cried in a passionate voice. "It's a fact! A wild village! There is nothing to breathe here!"

And for a long time after that his rich Russian voice was heard throughout California:

"A village! I assure you, it's a village! It's a fact!"

This wailing in the night was the last thing we heard in Hollywood. In the morning we left by train for San Diego, by way of the Santa Fé Railway.

To do this we first went to Los Angeles, which is separated from Hollywood . . . as a matter of fact, it is not at all separated from Hollywood, but merges with it, just as Hollywood itself unnoticeably passes into Beverly Hills, Beverly Hills passes into Santa Monica, and Santa Monica into something else.

Los Angeles in translation means "city of angels." Yes, it is a city of angels, smeared in oil. Here, as in Oklahoma City, the oil was found in the city itself, and entire streets are occupied by metal derricks—they tap, pump, make money.

Los Angeles is a ponderous city with large buildings, dirty and populous streets, iron fire escapes which stick out of the façades of houses. This is a California Chicago—brick, slums, the realest kind of poverty and the most revolting wealth.

Just before our departure we saw a long line of people standing before the entrance to a restaurant. A piece of cloth over the regular sign announced that here the Salvation Army was giving away free Christmas dinners to the unemployed. The doors of the restaurant were closed. It was still a long wait for the dinner hour. The queue represented all kinds and types of American unemployed—from the tramp with cheeks and chin long unshaven to the tractable clerk who had not yet cast aside his necktie and who had not yet lost the hope of returning to respectable society. Here stood youths—they who had already grown up at the time when jobs vanished, they who had never worked, do not know how to do anything, and have no place to learn a trade. No one needs them, who are full of strength, who are capable young men. Here stood old men, who had worked all their lives, but who will never work again. Fathers of families, honest toilers, who during their toiling lives had enriched more than one boss—they, too, are no longer needed by anyone now. They still hope for something, but nothing will happen.

Upton Sinclair, whom we had met several days before in Pasadena, a small and beautiful California town, said to us:

"Capitalism as a system for bringing to people profit and wages, as a system for giving people means of livelihood, has long ago come to an end in America. But I regret to say that the people have not yet realized it. They think that this is a temporary mishap, of the kind that happened before. They do not understand that never again will capitalism give jobs to fifteen million American unemployed. Since 1930, when it began, the depression has lightened considerably, business is considerably better, yet unemployment does not decrease. People have been replaced by new machines and by the rationalization of production. The richest country in the world, 'God's country,' as Americans call it, a great country, is capable of assuring its people neither jobs, nor bread, nor lodging."

And this great passionate man who all his life had rushed about in search of truth, who had been a liberal and a socialist, and the founder of his own social theory, under the flag of which he had been nominated for governor of California on the Democratic party ticket and even polled nine hundred thousand votes, wearily dropped his head. We sat in his house, a darkish, old-fashioned, dusty house, which did not look livable. The house, too, was old and tired. His attempt to make of California an isolated state where there would be no unemployment came to nothing. Sinclair was not elected governor. But nothing would have come of it even if he had been elected governor.

"I am through with that," Sinclair told us in farewell. "I am returning to my literary work."

Sinclair has a handsome silver head. He was in a grey flannel suit and summer shoes, woven out of narrow strips of leather. In his hand he held a gnarled and crooked stick. He has thus remained in our memory—an old man, standing in the door of his modest old house, lighted by a California sunset, smiling and tired.

The streets of festive Los Angeles were unusually quiet. The railway station seemed empty. At the kiosk were sold newspapers, coloured postcards, five-cent packages of candy. These round candies have a hole in the middle, and they look like a corn plaster. Their taste confirms their visual impression.

Some railroad official snored behind his partition, having pulled his service cap with its lacquered visor down his nose. We entered a Pullman car and sat down on the movable velvet chair which had an antimacassar on its back. The Negro porter soundlessly brought in our suitcases, soundlessly placed them on the baggage rack, and departed without a word.

Right outside the city appeared orange groves. Their bright fruit peeked out of shaggy bearlike foliage. Scores of thousands of trees stood in even rows. The soil between those trees was ideally cleaned, and under each tree stood a kerosene stove. Ten thousand trees and ten thousand stoves. The nights were quite cool, and the oranges needed warm air. After all, winter was on. The stoves produced a greater impression on us than even the orange groves themselves. Again we saw faultless and grandiose American organization.

Unnoticeably orange orchards were supplanted by oil orchards. These were not even orchards, rather thick jungles of oil derricks. They stood on the ocean beach and marched even into the ocean itself.

Then everything was jumbled. Orange and oil groves succeeded each other and into the window at the same time broke the aroma of oranges and the heavy smell of crude oil. Finally, the production of man's hand disappeared from view and before us opened the ocean, vast, proud, and calm. It was the hour of ebb tide and the ocean had retreated far from the shore. The wet bottom of the sea reflected the setting sun. Both suns (the real and reflected one) ran at full speed after the train. The sun descended quickly on the horizon, turned redder than ever, became flat, folded up, lost its shape. Now it was a listless luminary devoid of all splendour. But the ocean continued to run along with the train, rolling a light greenish blue wave without bustling and without pressing for our attention.

The passengers rustled their newspapers, dozed in chairs, walked into the smoking-room, where one could also have a Bacardi or Manhattan cocktail or something else of that kind, talk with a neighbour, chant the ever-recurring "Sure!" or simply doze on velvet divans.

It was already dark when we reached San Diego. At the station we were met by the glad wailing of the Adamses. They were full of Mexican impressions and they simply could not wait to share them with us.

"Gentlemen!" exclaimed Adams before we had a chance to step out on the platform. "Do you know who was the first man we saw on Mexican soil? The first man we met on the way? Yes, yes, he was a Cossack from the Terek! The most genuine Terek Cossack, gentlemen! Speaks excellent Russian. But not a word of Spanish!"

The Adamses led us to the "California Auto Court" (an automobile inn which was also a camp) in which they had been living since the day before, had become friends with its owner, had spent the whole day with him, and had learned from him all the San Diego news—about this year's harvest of oranges, about the oil business, whether the flow of tourists had increased, and many other useful bits of information indispensable to every thoughtful traveller.

The owner of the camp met us as if we were his favourite relatives. We must suppose that the Adamses had presented us in the most favourable light. After glad and lengthy effusions we left our belongings in the room assigned to us and went off to have dinner.

San Diego and San Pedro, which is located a hundred miles north, are the bases of the Pacific fleet of the United States. Sailors strolled about the streets. Solemn, lanky, and taciturn, they escorted their girls arm in arm. The happy little chits clung to their cavaliers, chattering and laughing.

We circled in our automobile around the restaurant we had selected, without finding a place where we could park our car. All the sites were occupied. There was no end of automobiles. Looking for a place to park, we drove farther and farther away from our restaurant, migrating from street to street. But the city was so full of automobiles that we could not find a place for just one more little, respectable, mouse-coloured automobile. It was one hell of a situation!

We drove to the very end of San Diego, where even the noises of the city did not reach, and in the darkness we heard only the roar of the ocean. Here we finally parked and went to the restaurant. We had to walk a half-hour to it. This is what happens occasionally in a country where there are twenty-five millions automobiles.

In the restaurant, holding on the fork a large piece of pale Christmas turkey, Mr. Adams solemnly exclaimed:

"Now, gentlemen, we have come to the very end of the United States. We cannot go any farther. From now on, no matter what we do, no matter where we go, we are going home, to New York! Let's eat this turkey to our health! We have already driven six thousand miles! Hurrah!"

PART V
BACK TO THE ATLANTIC

40
On the Old Spanish Trail

THE GENEROUS December sun poured its light on the gay city of San Diego, on its bright yellow bungalows built in the Spanish style with iron balconies and wrought-iron grilles over windows, on mowed lawns before houses, and on the decorative trees with their thick dark-green leafage at the entrance doors.

In the sheen of the clear morning stood the fleet in its roadstead. The torpedo boats were side by side, four abreast, as close together as bullets in a revolver clip. The bright grey lines of the old cruisers and battleships stretched to the edge of the horizon. The warm winter somnolence shackled the bay, and the high thin masts of the naval boats stood motionless in the pale blue sky. There were no dreadnoughts and none of the newest boats in sight. Perhaps they were at the moment standing in San Pedro, or maybe they had gone into the ocean for manœuvres.

On the way to the ocean we saw beautifully cut streets with wide asphalt pavements, with sidewalks, with street lamps painted in aluminium paint. We saw a whole town, with canalization and water system, with gas and electricity brought to every part of the city; in a word, we saw a city with all its conveniences. But without houses. There was not a single house in this little town, where even the streets had been named.

This is how building lots are sold in America. Some large company buys the land where it supposes a new residential section or town will arise, brings it into the state we have just described, and sells the lots at a profit. Another company, which is occupied with the building of houses, will rig up for you in two months a wonderful Spanish house with striped awnings, with a bathroom on the first floor, with a bathroom on the second floor, with balconies, with a lamp before the house, and a fountain behind it; it will do everything; give them only your ten thousand dollars, if you have it. You don't have to pay cash; you can pay on the instalment system. But the great American God forbid that you lose your job and stop making payments!

"Gentlemen," Mr. Adams was saying solemnly, "you must remember that all the plants you see here—palms, pines, apple and lemon trees, every blade of grass—have been planted here by the hand of man. California was not at all a paradise; it was a desert. California was made by water, roads, and electricity. Deprive California of artificial irrigation for one week, and it will be impossible to repair this misfortune for years. It will again become a desert. We call California the Golden State. But it would be more correct to call it the state of man's remarkable labour. In this paradise it is necessary to toil endlessly, uninterruptedly; otherwise it will turn into a hell. Remember that, gentlemen! Water, roads, and electricity!"

At the ocean itself stood a lovely villa. On its doors shone a brass plate cleaner than the California sun: "Headquarters International Theosophist Society."

"No, no, gentlemen," cried Mr. Adams, "don't be surprised at that. Where you have water, roads, and electricity, it is easy to live. As you see, theosophists are not at all fools."

Opposite the beautiful beach which stretched for many miles stood long rows of cabins. Even now, in the winter, some of them were occupied. On their porches girls were sunning themselves, girls with insouciant faces, touchingly wild women who had run off to nature from their strait-laced and wealthy parents, from the madness and the clatter of large cities.

At the Old Spanish Mission we turned back toward the east, homeward.

A high brick cross stands here on a hill in honour of the Spanish monk whose name was Junipero Serra. At one time he had seized this land "for the glory of God and the king of Spain." From this hill one can see the entire city and the bay.

We drove over the Old Spanish Trail. Concrete, asphalt, and gravel have changed the old road considerably. We dare say, the conquistadores would not recognize these spots today. Where the feathered arrow of the Indian had whistled stands a petrol station, and the compressor breathes heavily, forcing the air into the automobile chamber. And where the Spaniards, breathless under the weight of their leather and steel armour, dragged themselves along the scarcely noticeable trail now stretches the usual American highway, a road of high calibre, veering at times on turns.

Although we were now moving toward the east, the sun was becoming smaller each day. Again we saw the distant mountains, blue and lilac on the horizon. Again the evening twilight of the road came down and night began and the headlights gleamed. It was rather late when we arrived at El Centro.

The nasty little town of El Centro lies in the Imperial Valley. The entire valley is thirty by thirty miles in size. Lemons are picked here three times a year, oranges twice a year. In December and January vegetables, which do not grow anywhere else in the United States, are grown here. Now they were beginning to harvest lettuce, later they would harvest melons. In this paradisiacal valley, where large pale grapefruit ripen, in the valley permeated throughout with the opiating odour of lemons and oranges, in this valley goes on the most cruel exploitation of Mexicans and Filipinos in the entire world. And more than for its lettuce and oranges, this valley is known for its brutish treatment of strikers, of the unhappy, pauperized, always hungry Mexican seasonal workers and their numerous children. It is only twelve miles from here to Mexico.

Las Palmas Camp, where we stopped, was something of a cross between a camp and a hotel. It already had a hall with decorative plants in tubs, with swings and soft divans. This made it resemble a hotel and justified the traveller's filling his heart with pride. (Remember? "Let your heart fill with pride when you utter the name of the hotel in which you stopped!") On the other hand, the price of the room was not high, which made it clear that Las Palmas was, after all, a camp. In short, it was a convenient haven. Its owner was an Austrian German who thirty years ago had come to America in a third-class cabin. Now, in addition to the camp he owns also the California Hotel, a four-story building with a café and a table d'hôte. Therefore, the optimistic American smile, which makes him kin to Mr. Max Factor and other fortunate ones, never leaves his face.

El Centro with its cracked sidewalks and brick arcades, El Centro, depressing city of exploitation and big business, was still in California. Benson, which we reached on the evening of the next day, was three-quarters of the way across Arizona.

To Benson we drove past huge fields of cactus. This was giant cactus. It grew in groups and singly and resembled cucumbers enlarged a thousand times and placed end up. They were filled with cooms, just like Corinthian palms, and with hair, like monkey paws. They have fat stubby little hands. These appendages make these giant cactuses extraordinarily expressive. Some of them pray, having raised their arms to high heaven, others embrace each other, still others nurse their children, and others simply stand in proud tranquillity, looking down on the travellers who pass them by.

The cactuses live just as at one time the Indian tribes lived. Where one tribe lives, there is no place for another. They do not mix.

The cactus desert was succeeded by a sand desert, a real Sahara with dunes striped by shadows or pockmarked, but an American Sahara. A splendid road crossed it with oases, where, instead of camels, automobiles rested, where there were no palms, but, instead of a spring, petrol streams flowed.

Benson has a population of eight hundred and fifty people. What do they do here in the desert? Why did they convene on this particular spot of the globe?

We learned that here was a DuPont powder factory. DuPont is one of the real masters of America, the same DuPont who makes such remarkable celluloid films, combs, and explosives!

What can people do here in this ordinary American small town, with several petrol stations, with two or three drug-stores, and a grocery store where everything is sold ready-made—the bread is sliced, the soup is cooked, the crackers are wrapped in cellophane—what can people do here, if not go mad?

In the store where we bought sliced bread, prepared soup, and a cheese which had already been eaten (at any rate, it looked like it), we were told that business had improved, that there was no unemployment in the city, because the powder factory had begun to work full speed.

When Mr. Adams, seizing the owner of the store by the lapel of his coat, began to find out from him what people did in Benson, the owner answered:

"You know what they do—they smoke Chesterfields, they drink Coca-Cola, they sit in the drug-store. They have money. Somebody needs powder."

Somebody needs powder, somebody needs copper, the munitions industry has improved.

The next morning we arrived in Bisbee, a town in the hills. Here are the copper mines of Arizona. The houses are located on steep inclines. Long wooden stairways lead to them. In the square of the city stands a red monument to a worker made of crude copper, a monument to the unknown worker who made big money for the owners of the mines. In a drug-store on the tables are displayed sugar bowls beaten out of thick red copper. Right outside the city is a gigantic crater seemingly made by nature. As a matter of fact, it has been dug out by people. This is the place where the old copper mines used to be.

Later we found ourselves in a desert populated by cactuses of a kind we had never seen before. Out of a large ball of pins a long blooming branch shoots up. When we passed this desert we found ourselves in another one, where telegraph poles were grown and nothing else. Another day passed, and from the desert of telegraph poles we passed to a desert overgrown with advertisements, bill-boards, announcements, and all kinds of written, drawn, and printed pleadings about a town called White City.

Every two miles, and then more frequently, bill-boards hysterically invited travellers to White City. The bill-boards promised such joys that even if White City were the pseudonym for Nice or Sochi it could not justify the insane enthusiasm of the pleas, demands, and prayers that the little town be visited.

Overwhelmed by such insistence, we swerved from the course of our journey. From Arizona we passed into the state of New Mexico, and the nearer we approached to White City the more shrill became the advertisements. Finally, we learned that White City was founded by the famous cowboy, Jimmy White, who discovered the even more famous Carlsbad Caves.

Twenty years ago Jimmy White, who had not yet founded the city that now bears his name, noticed that thick smoke was rising through a cleft in the earth. Drawn to it, he went up closer and saw that this was not smoke but an incredibly large flight of bats emerging from somewhere under the earth. The cowboy bravely ventured into the crevasse and discovered under the earth colossal stalactite caves. Soon thereafter the caves were declared to be national property, and efforts were made to prepare them for convenient surveying. The caves were entered on the list of national parks of the United States. As for Jimmy White, he was not satisfied with the fame of a discoverer and a geographer, so right near the caves he himself founded a camp of several houses under the proud name of White City, and filled space for hundreds of miles around with announcements and pronouncements about his city.

For hundreds of miles around was desert, a real rattlesnake desert. We were certain that we would have to crawl underground on all-fours. Therefore, when we drove up to the caves we were amazed at what we saw. Remarkable, indeed, was this vision of two elevators, two excellent elevators, with beautiful cabins, which, emitting a pleasant city drone, dropped us seven hundred feet underground. On top were stores where Indian souvenirs were being sold, and an excellent information bureau, with rest rooms which would have done credit to a first-class hotel. Here was a bit of desert that was ultramodern, electric, with a loud-speaker.

It takes a whole day to inspect the caves. But we were late, so we took part only in the second half of the excursion. We went down in elevators to the very bottom of the caves, where we found an underground restaurant. The luncheon was not in any way remarkable, but one must take into consideration the fact that produce is brought here from afar. Nevertheless, here was a luncheon which included hot coffee in thick cups, tasteless bread wrapped in cellophane, sandwiches and California-tasting oranges—that is, not too tasty—a real American luncheon in a place located several hundred feet under the surface of the earth.

Then we were all assembled, stood up in a long line, and the guide, dressed in the green semi-military uniform of a national park employee, went ahead. The procession was closed by another employee, whose duty it was to see that no one was lost on the way.

As we moved on, passing from one cavern to another, ahead of us electricity was lighted and behind us it was put out. Everywhere the light was masked, its source hidden and so disposed that it illuminated the caverns to the best advantage.

Before us opened grandiose decorations—Gothic arches, small cathedrals hidden in niches, lacy many-toned stalactites hanging from cupolas. The caverns were larger than the largest theatre in the world. The stalagmites formed curly miniature Japanese gardens, or rose shining monuments of lime. The stalactites hung in huge rocky mantillas with folds. Here stood chalky Buddhas, the models of stage decorations, petrified mirages and aurora borealis—all that the human imagination can muster was here, including even a small stalagmite which looked like a machine-gun.

The excursionists walked, stretched in a chain, looking like a procession of monks in a Max Reinhardt production.

Before emerging from the caves, the guests were seated on a stalagmite barrier formed in one of the caverns, and our guide in green uniform read a three-minute lecture interspersed with figures. A few figures in support of the wonders of nature we had just seen—that is something Americans always appreciate. The lecturer informed us how old the stalactites were, how big was the biggest of them, and how much it cost to build the elevator ($175,000). After that he announced the territorial composition of the excursion. Today, seventy-two persons participated in it. Of those, four were from the state of Montana, two from North Dakota, fourteen from New Mexico, nine from California, and so forth. Almost all the American states were represented. We had already noted that at the entrance to the caves. The automobiles parked there bore blue, green, yellow, brown licence-plates, thereby disclosing that they hailed from various states. The lecturer finished his speech with the information that among the excursionists were two Russian gentlemen from Moscow. Since of the four of us the Adamses appeared to be the most venerable, all eyes turned on them.

Then another employee, the one who brought up the end of the procession, went into the adjoining hall, put out the light and in the darkness sang a sad song in order to demonstrate the acoustics of the caves. The employee sang four hundred feet away, but we heard even his breathing—so amazing are the acoustics.

Tired, we got into our trusty automobile, which again raced off with us. We were driving to El Paso, a city on the Mexican border. The quiet roar of the motor and the measured roar of the gravel under our fenders lulled us to sleep. We drowsily shook our heads, and even Mr. Adams became thoughtful.

We awakened from the silence that suddenly overtook us. The machine was standing. Mr. Adams was looking at us quizzically. We discovered that a hitchhiker was asking us to take him. We took him, and were sorry at once. He talked like a drunkard. In spite of that, he proved to be quite sober. Such was unfortunately his original impediment of speech. He told us his views on life quickly and willingly. They were as battered as his old grey coat and his decrepit black trousers covered with fuzz.

"War is coming," he announced, stuttering uninterruptedly, swallowing phrases and syllables. "The young people want to fight; they've got to have something to do. They need some kind of work, work and fame. There is no work, the machines have taken it away from people. It wouldn't be a bad thing to destroy at least a part of those accursed machines."

We had heard this many times by now. To set things right, it was a good thing to kill part of the people in war and to destroy a part of the machines. Then everything will again go smoothly.

When we were driving past the Mexican hovels, with their broken windows and their torn blankets hanging on ropes, our pauper fellow traveller cast a contemptuous glance at a group of Mexicans assembled on the porch of one of these hovels. They were dressed in worn-out mackinaws, made of tent canvas, with sheepskin collars.

"Mexicans," said our fellow traveller in his drunken voice, "like to live in dirt. No matter how much money they earn, they will always be dirty. That's the kind of people they are. Give them five dollars a week, give them even five dollars a day, it will do no good."

It was easy for our hitchhiker to live with such views. Everything was easily solved. Part of the people must be killed, part of the machines must be destroyed. And if there are any poor people, it's because they are a special kind of people—they like to live in poverty—all these Mexicans, Negroes, and Poles.

"Pay them even six dollars a day," he repeated with the stubbornness of a drunkard. "They will live like this anyway—like paupers. They like it."

41
A Day in Mexico

EL PASO, a city on the south-western tip of Texas, impresses one as a kind of trick. After a desert of incredible size, after endless and peopleless roads, after a silence broken only by the roar of our motor, suddenly a large city, a hundred thousand people at once, several hundred electric signs, men dressed just exactly as they dress in New York or Chicago, and girls so painted as if beside them instead of the desert was an entire continent full of motion-picture theatres, manicuring establishments, lunchrooms, and dancing academies.

Yet we had just crossed this desert! Although we raced across it at the rate of fifty miles an hour, it took us several days to cross it, so vast is it. We yielded to its enchantment, and at times muttered under our nose something about "the desert harks to God." But in El Paso we did not even think about the vastness of the desert. Here people were busy with their affairs. Here was the rattle of cash registers and calculating machines, here flashed advertising lights, and the radio cooed as plaintively as a dove whose tail has been set on fire.

Having refreshed ourselves in the first restaurant with fat little pieces of meat called "baby beef," we went on foot to Mexico. It was located right there, on the outskirts of El Paso. It was necessary only to cross a bridge over the Rio Grande, which was half dry because it was winter, and there was Mexico—the city of Juarez.

We were afraid to go to Mexico. Because of this: On our passports was a one-year visa for staying in the United States issued to us by Mr. Ellis A. Johnson, the American vice-consul in Moscow. But every visa ends automatically as soon as you leave the country. What would happen if upon returning from Mexico to the United States we should be·told that the government of the States regards its duty of hospitality fulfilled and no longer insists that we remain its guests? Horror possessed us at the very thought that the remainder of our days we should have to pass in the city of Juarez, located in the Mexican state of Chihuahua. On the other hand, we wanted very much to be in Mexico. In such trepidation of the soul we arrived at the bridge which connects El Paso and Juarez, and entered the dwelling of the border customs.

The proximity of Mexico made itself known by the depressing odour reminiscent of carbolic acid or formalin with which the small customs house was permeated. The immigration official, shifting a cigar from one corner of his mouth to the other, looked at our passports for a long time with interest. It must be supposed that Soviet citizens appear very rarely on the El Paso border point.

The official unexpectedly became quite gracious. Just as unexpectedly can such an official be quite pedantic. You never can tell about them! This is a profession which seems to be entirely dependent on the emotions, moods, and similar elusive shadings.

Our official delivered a loud speech, from which we gathered that the two Russian gentlemen may venture without any apprehension into Mexico. Their visas will continue in force. The two Russian gentlemen need have no qualms about that at all. After that, he walked out with us on the bridge and told the man sitting at the booth:

"These are two Russian gentlemen. They are going to Mexico. Let them pass."

The cautious Mr. Adams asked whether our talkative benefactor would be here when we returned to the United States.

"Yes, yes," replied the official. "I shall be here all day. Tell the Russian gentlemen not to disturb themselves about it. I'll be here and I'll let them back into the United States."

We paid two cents of some sort of tariff, and a minute later were on Mexican soil.

On the Mexican side of the bridge was another border station, but there no one ever asked about anything. There, true enough, near a booth stood a saffron-faced man with a dirtyish neck, dressed in a dazzling uniform of dark-coloured khaki, with gold pipings. But on the face of the Mexican border official was utter contempt for the duties imposed upon him. On his face was sketched: "Yes, a sad fate has obliged me to wear this beautiful uniform, but I will not soil my graceful hands by looking over nasty scraps of paper. No! You will never live to see that done by the honourable Juan Ferdinand Cristobal Colbajos!"

We, who were not provided with Mexican visas because of the absence of diplomatic relations between Moscow and Mexico, were very glad that we had come across such an honourable hidalgo, and quickly walked down the main street of Juarez.

Having become accustomed after considerable time to the odour of petrol, which reigns in the United States, we were rather embarrassed by the odours of Juarez. Here were the smells of fried food, burned oil, garlic, red pepper—strong and heavy odours.

A multitude of people filled the streets. The idle unhurried pedestrians moved slowly. Young men with guitars passed by. Despite the glitter of their orange shoes and new hats, they appeared to be rather poor. Cripples begged loudly for charity. Fine-looking, black-eyed, and snot-nosed children ran after foreigners, begging for pennies. Hundreds of tiny boys ran with brushes and shoe-shining boxes. It seems to be a rule that the poorer a southern city is, the more importance is attached to shoes that shine like mirrors. A detachment of soldiers passed—ugly-mugged, spruced up, the leather straps of their fighting equipment creaking—a detachment of scandalously secure bruisers.

As soon as we appeared in the streets of Juarez an unhappy young man with sideburns on his thin face approached us. He wore green trousers and a shirt with an open collar. He asked that we buy from him cigarettes, tickets for today's bullfight, smuggled tobacco, and a thousand other articles. He offered to sell everything that a salesman could possibly sell to a customer. Noticing that we were yielding, he became busier than ever and led us to the building of the amphitheatre where the bullfight would take place.

The outer walls of the amphitheatre were covered with large advertisements of American whisky. We could not manage to get inside. At the moment there was in progress a meeting of a worker-peasant union directed against former President Calles, who was trying to seize power. The entire square around the amphitheatre was filled with people, red and green ribbons in their lapels (emblem of the union). Inside, an orchestra was playing, orators talked hoarsely, while at the entrance stood the military detachment we had already seen today. The cries that reached us, the crowd that listened to it, standing on an unpaved square, the wind which carried the hot prickly dust and straw, the determined and stupid faces of the soldiers—all of it created an alarming, explosive frame of mind.

We went to the market-place, where food was being fried, baked, and cooked, the kind of food the mere appearance of which produced unquenchable thirst. People sat at the stands. They took the food off the plates with their hands.

Then we visited a church. At its entrance crowded impudent paupers with the dirty, inspired faces of prophets and wise men. A service was going on in the church, and women in black wept over their bitter, unhappy, insecure Mexican life. The church was narrow and long. Several lighted candles scarcely dispelled the gloom. The women sat on wooden benches with high backs. A small organ bleated.

During Prohibition Juarez was an alcoholic oasis for the suffering Americans. Even now the city has several large restaurants built exclusively for foreigners. All of them are located right at the bridge across the Rio Grande.

I

The bullfight was set for three o'clock, but it began forty minutes late. Time and again we managed to examine the arena and the small crowd which gathered here. Judging by the deafening "Sure!" which from time to time resounded not far from us, there were several Americans in the audience.

The arena was surrounded by a beautiful but crudely built amphi-theatre without a roof. It was a simple public building utterly devoid of decoration. The spectators who were afraid to catch cold on the cement seats could rent flat straw pillows in striped covers. A large orchestra of boys dressed in dark coats, green neckties, caps with large peaks, and grey pantaloons with white stripes, blew Spanish marches loudly and falsely out of their horns. The round arena was strewn with clean sand.

At last a movement began behind the wooden gates, and about eight or ten people appeared. Ahead of them walked two girls in the costumes of toreadors. Today was an unusual fight. Of the four bulls indicated in the programme, two had to be killed by the two sisters who had come from Mexico City. The band thundered in full blast. After the girls came the men, likewise in shabby costumes edged with gold. They looked as if they knew their business, and replied to the greetings of the public with slight bows. The girl matadors were excited and bowed very low. The procession ended with a pair of horses in harness. The horses were there to drag away the slaughtered bulls.

Up and down the aisles walked salesmen, carrying in buckets, bottles of fruit water, and small flasks of whisky.

A meagre little black bull ran into the arena. The game began.

Right under our seats in a special wooden enclosure stood a very thin Mexican with a sword which he was wiping on a cloth rag. This sword is handed to the matador before the decisive blow. Not being experts or devotees of obloquy, we choose to refrain here from using special terms, particularly since they are unknown to us.

The first bull was a long time being killed, and badly.

The spectacle was tormenting from the very beginning, because at once the desire of the bull to get away from the arena became evident. He clearly understood that here someone wanted to do him harm. He did not want to fight. He wanted to go home, to his pen, his grazing field. He wanted to pluck the coarse Mexican grass and not to fling himself upon people.

In vain was he being irritated by means of hooks with coloured ribbons that were plunged into his neck. The bull had to be tormented a long time before his anger was aroused. And even when he finally became in-furiated, even then he quickly calmed down the moment he was let alone.

The most depressing part of this entire spectacle was the fact that the bull did not want to die and was afraid of his opponents. Nevertheless, he was roused to anger, and he attacked the girl. She scarcely managed to turn away, when the bull pushed her several times with a powerful side-swipe. The girl made grimaces of pain, but continued to wave the red cape before the bull's eyes. He pushed her with his horns, flung her on the sand, and passed over her. The bull's attention was diverted by calm and experienced men. In the meantime, the girl rose and, rubbing her injured spots, went off toward the enclosure, where the keeper of the sword was in readiness. Now we saw her closely. She breathed heavily. Her velvet vest had burst at its seams. On one cheekbone was a scratch. She took the sword from the hands of the Mexican, walked away from the barrier a bit, and, turning around to face the balcony where the officials of the city sat, took off her little hat. In the balcony someone waved a hand-kerchief, and the girl, taking a deep childlike breath, walked up to the bull.

The decisive moment had come. The girl aimed and shoved the sword into the neck of the bull, right behind his horns. The sword, when deftly aimed, enters sufficiently deep and kills the bull. It is said that it is a glorious sight. One blow, and the bull falls at the feet of his vanquisher! But the girl did not know how to kill the bull. She stabbed him weakly and incompetently. The bull ran away, carrying on his neck the swaying sword. The girl had to live through several humiliating moments when the banderilleros chased the bull in order to pull the sword out of him. That was repeated several times. The bull was tired, and so was the girl. A pink foam appeared on the bull's snout. He wandered slowly around the arena. Several times he walked up to the closed gate. We suddenly heard a peaceful pastoral mooing, distant, and foreign to what was going on in the arena. How did a cow get in here? Why, yes, the bull! He made a few more wandering steps and began to descend to his knees. Then a hefty man in civilian clothes appeared in the arena and killed the bull with a small dagger.

The girl cried with anguish, shame, and pain. The public was dis-satisfied. Only later, when the second sister was killing the next bull, the first one was given an opportunity to rehabilitate herself, and quite deftly she let the bull run past her an inch from her hip, having deceived him with the red cape. Applause broke out, the girl again blossomed forth and bowed to the crowd, making several ballet curtsies.

Rag in hand, the thinnish Mexican was busily wiping the blood off the sword which had been returned to him. The horses dragged off the dead animal, and a second bull was led into the arena. This one was as small and black as his predecessor, and this bull, too, knew that something bad was about to be done to him. He, too, was cut up painfully, tortuously long and clumsily, and finally was killed with a dagger. Frightful is the moment of passage from life to death! Suddenly the bull fell, something happened inside his coarse body, and his end came. It was shameful and terrible to gaze upon it, and we felt as if we had abetted a murder around the corner.

Perhaps a fight between ferocious bulls and a famous toreador has its sporting aspect—perhaps! But what we saw in a small provincial Mexican town was repulsive.

However, worse was still ahead. Three toreadors in clownish masks and costumes, protected from blows by pillowed breasts, sides, and behinds, made fun for half an hour of another bull. In the beginning it looked like an ordinary circus interlude, which usually ends with the clowns running away from the arena and then again appearing in order to bow to the public, remove their masks and show their real unpainted faces.

But here the interlude ended with the killing of the bull. This was so unexpected and horrible that we rose from our seats. We scarcely managed to reach the exit when we saw that the bull was being carried off. His noble black snout dragged heavily and disgracefully across the sand, while his blinded eyes stared intently and reproving at the mooing and neighing spectators. The public flung its hats at the toreadors, and the latter deftly threw them back.

It was already dark. We walked slowly through the badly lighted streets of the famous city of Juarez. Guitars tinkled. Young men plucked the strings, leaning against the peeling walls of the one-story huts. From the restaurant "Lobby No. 2" came a passionate Mexican song. Our hearts were gloomy.

Walking past Juan Ferdinand Cristobal Colbajos, who, as before, paid no attention whatever to us, and casting a last glance at Mexico, we crossed the bridge. To our surprise, and even to our dismay, the official who should have let us pass back into the States was not there. In his place stood another, who looked so forbidding that we did not expect anything good to happen. But no sooner did we present our passports than the forbidding official cried out:

"These are the two Russian gentlemen who this morning went to Mexico. Yes, yes, I have been told about them! I was told everything. The two Russian gentlemen may freely pass into the United States. They have nothing to worry about."

And he turned to the official in the booth:

"These are the two Russian gentlemen who are returning from Mexico to the United States. Let them pass!"

When we walked past the border stations, Mr. Adams said:

"No, gentlemen, this is an organized country. Our morning official went away, but he did not forget to tell his successor that in the evening two Russians would come from Mexico. After all, this is service, isn't it? And do you know what I want to tell you? I want to tell you that this is a country where you can calmly drink raw water out of a tap without catching typhoid fever—the water will always be perfect. This is a country where you need never look suspiciously at the linen in your hotel, for the linen will always be clean. This is a country where you don't have to think of how to drive by automobile from one city to another. The road will always be good. This is a country where in the cheapest restaurant you will not be poisoned. The food may not be to your taste, but it will always be of good quality. This is a country with a high standard of living. And this becomes especially clear, gentlemen, when you happen, as we did today, to visit another American country. No, no, I don't mean to say that the United States is a remarkable country, but it has its attributes and you must always remember that."

Before reaching El Paso, we had spent quite a long time in the United States and had travelled considerably through the country. We had become so accustomed to good roads, to good service, to cleanliness and comfort that we stopped taking any note of it. But after one day in Mexico we began to appreciate once again according to their deserts all the material achievements of the United States.

It is useful at times, in order to know a country the better, to leave it for a day.

42
New Year's Eve in San Antonio

IT WAS NEW YEAR'S EVE when our grey car drove into San Antonio, the largest city in the state of Texas.

"I know this city," said Mr. Adams, "I was here last year. I assure you, gentlemen, this is a fine city."

The city was unusually lively. After the desert its centre, with its several twenty-story buildings, seemed like real New York. The lights came from the thin gaseous pipettes of advertising signs and from the show windows of stores. Passing through the small American towns, we had become unused to crowds, so now like country bumpkins we gaped in surprise at sidewalks crowded with pedestrians. Among the ordinary soft hats and the short sideburns common in these places, we found occasional broad-brimmed hats and most impressive sideburns, indicating the proximity of Mexico and ranches.

We had been driving by automobile nearly two months. We wanted to rest and to have a good time. The lively crowd, the open fruit markets, the odour of coffee and tobacco smoke, all this strange, busy world filled our hearts with a lyric sadness and at the same time with a secret hope for a miracle. Suppose suddenly something remarkable should happen to us, something that never happened with ordinary travellers in a strange city where they do not know a single soul. On this New Year's Eve we felt keenly that we were unusually far from our native land, from Moscow, from friends and near ones. To tell the truth, we wanted to have a good swig of vodka, a bite of herring and black bread, we wanted to make merry and to declaim gay, senseless toasts.

"Yes, yes, gentlemen, in Moscow there is snow now, no doubt," said Mr. Adams, looking solicitously at our harassed faces.

The gentlemen groaned.

"No, seriously, we must properly celebrate New Year's Eve today, come what may. I have a plan. It is now only eight o'clock in the evening. I suggest that we drive directly to the Robert E. Lee Hotel: I gave the address of that hotel to my correspondents. There we will shave, get dressed, leave our automobile in a garage, and then sally forth. I know a fine little restaurant in San Antonio. It is not very far from the hotel. There poets and artists meet. San Antonio reminds one of Santa Fé and Carmel in that it is beloved by people of the arts. Yes, yes! In this little restaurant the food is excellent. . . . And on this day we will not be economical. We shall meet poets and artists, and we shall feast. Gentlemen, what do you think of that plan?"

And Mr. Adams smacked his bald head with the palm of his hand in the audacious manner of a hopeless roisterer.

We fell in enthusiastically with this plan. In less than an hour, cheery, washed, with traces of powder on our shaved cheeks and hope in our hearts, we went out into the street and mixed with the crowd.

"First we must send some telegrams of congratulation," said Mr. Adams.

The Western Union telegraph office was located in a small store divided into two halves by a wide oak stand, behind which sat a young man with a pencil behind his ear. At the entrance to the bureau waited two boy bicyclists, in leggings, caps, and tunics, with shoulder straps and bright buttons. It was their duty to deliver telegrams to various addresses. The bicycles, with broad handle-bars and thick tyres, were leaning against the street lamp-posts. The boys were proud of their uniforms and carried themselves importantly, yet they remained children and passed their time in the most carefree fashion. Inside the handle-bars of their bicycles they placed a firecracker, lighted it, and, running off to the door, watched the passers-by jump as soon as they came near the bicycles and heard a shot explode right over their very ears. When the shot was especially loud and the passer-by jumped with particular nervousness, the boys ran into the office and, choking with laughter, looked out into the street, while the young man with the pencil behind his ear waved a reproving finger at them. Then the messenger boys would get into a fight with a company of ordinary youngsters without leggings, without shoulder straps, and without bicycles. The warring sides attacked each other with firecrackers which resounded deafeningly.

The young man accepted our telegrams, pulled the pencil from behind his ear, and, quickly counting the words, said:

"Two dollars and eighty cents."

We pulled out our money.

"This telegram," said the young man, "will be delivered in Moscow today. But maybe you would like to have it delivered tomorrow morning? This is a telegram of congratulation, and I think the person you are addressing it to will be just as well satisfied if he receives it in the morning."

We agreed with that proposal.

"In that case, the price will be different."

The young man took a piece of paper, made a calculation, and said:
"It will cost you, all told, two dollars and ten cents."
Seventy cents of economy! We began to like the young man.
"But perhaps, gentlemen, you would rather send the telegram some other way. We have a special rate for telegraph letters. Such a telegram will not come much later and will cost you a dollar and a half, and besides, you have the right to add eight more words."
We spent nearly an hour at the Western Union Office. The young man scribbled figures over several sheets of paper, consulted information books, and finally saved another ten cents for us.
He behaved like a kind and cautious uncle who gives his light-minded nephews lessons in how to live. He was more concerned about our pocket-book than we were ourselves. On New Year's Eve, when one longs especially for home, and the job is especially trying, this clerk seemed more than ideally patient with his clients. He seemed a true friend, whose duty was not only to serve us but to protect us, to save us from vital errors.
"Seriously, gentlemen," Mr. Adams said to us, "you have travelled a lot through America and must understand the nature of American service. Ten years ago I made a round-the-world trip and went to a certain tourist bureau to get my ticket. My itinerary was very complicated. It came out too expensive. They sat with me in that bureau all through the day and finally, with the aid of some complicated railway combinations, they economized a hundred dollars for me. A whole hundred dollars! A hundred dollars is big money. Yes, yes. I ask you not to forget that the bureau receives a certain percentage from a deal and that actually, having made my ticket cheaper, it lessened its own earnings. Therein lies the cardinal principle of American service! The bureau earned less on me than it could have earned, but the next time I will unfailingly come to them and they will again earn a little on me. You understand it, gentlemen? Less, but more often! That is exactly what is happening here in the Western Union telegraph office. Truly, you simply do not understand, you do not want to understand the nature of American service!"
But Mr. Adams was mistaken. We had long ago understood the nature of American service. And if we admired the work of the young man with a pencil behind his ear, it was not because it seemed an exception to us, but because it confirmed the rule.
Throughout our journey, in one way or another, every day we used that service and we learned to prize it highly, although at times it made itself known in scarcely noticeable details.
On one occasion, in Charleston, South Carolina, we sat down in an empty street car which went across the main street with a thunder peculiar to this antiquated form of transportation. The motorman, who at the same time performed also the duties of the conductor, gave us our tickets.
"Ten cents a ticket," said he. "But if you buy four tickets at once there is a rebate. It costs you seven cents apiece, do you understand?

Seven cents apiece. Twenty-eight cents all told. Twelve cents of economy! You understand? Only séven cents a ticket!"

All the way down he turned around, showing us his seven fingers, as if we were deaf, and shouting:

"Seven cents. Understand! Seven cents a ticket!"

It was a pleasure to him to give us a rebate, to give us service.

We have become accustomed to having our laundry not only washed but also mended, and should we forget our cuff-links in the sleeves of a soiled shirt, they will be attached to the clean laundry in a special envelope, on which will be printed the advertisement of the laundry. We stopped noticing that in restaurants, cafés, and drug-stores there were pieces of ice in the glasses of water; that at petrol stations free information and road maps are given; while in museums catalogues and prospectuses are given free. Service is best in so far as it becomes as necessary and as unnoticeable as air.

In a New York department store called Macy's, behind the backs of the clerks hang placards addressed to the purchasers: "We are here to serve you!"

To store service belongs likewise the classical American adage: "The customer is always right."

Insurance companies, when their interests coincide with the interests of the insured client, perform wonders of service. For a small fee they give medical service to a man insured for life, since it does not pay them to have the man die. The man, on the other hand, wants very much to live and, getting well, he proclaims the fame of insurance service.

In America there is an interesting trade enterprise called "mail-order house." As a matter of fact, such establishments are known also in Europe, but they are not successful there and frequently go into bankruptcy. This is trade by mail. Here everything is built on service. Should the service be bad, neither the quality of the goods nor the sumptuous office of the head of the enterprise will do any good. A mail-order house serves principally farmers. The distinctiveness of such an establishment lies in the fact that everything, from a pin to house furnishings, is ordered by catalogue. The success of this business is built on the fact that any order is filled within twenty-four hours and not a second more, irrespective of what is ordered, whether it is a hundred cigarettes or a grand piano, and irrespective of where the order must be delivered, whether on Fifth Avenue or to a small house in the state of Dakota. If the thing is not to your liking, it can be sent back to the mail-order house and the purchase money is refunded, except for a small deduction for postage.

When an American finds that he has been well served by some worker or government official, he will write that very day a letter to the corporation or to the department, saying in his letter: "At such and such a time and in such and such a place I was splendidly served by Mr. So-and-so. Allow me to congratulate you on having such a fine employee." And such letters are not lost. The good worker or official is rewarded with promotion. Americans well understand that in order to have good service it is important to have more than just a "complaint book." This does not deter them from writing letters about bad service.

At times, in the desire to give everything and to receive something in return, service becomes comical and occasionally even vulgar.

There is a whole book of ready-made telegrams, of long and pretentiously composed telegrams, for all the occasions of life. It costs only twenty-five cents to send such a telegram. The point is that not the text of the telegram, but only the number by which it is indicated in the book and the signature of the sender are transmitted by wire. This is rather amusing and reminiscent of drug-store lunch No. 4. Everything is served here ready-made, and man is liberated from the unpleasant necessity of thinking and, besides that, he spends extra money.

There are congratulations for a birthday, for a house-warming, for New Year, for Christmas. The content and style of the telegram are adapted to every need and taste—congratulations for young husbands, for respectful nephews, for old clients, for sweethearts, children, writers, and old women. There are even telegrams in verse.

SMITH SYRACUSE TEXAS STOP
MERRY CHRISTMAS TO YOU OLD TOP
GREETINGS ALSO TO YOUR WIFE
HOPE YOU PROSPER ALL YOUR LIFE.

For dissipated students, there are particularly extensive, quite artistically composed and touching telegrams addressed to parents, requesting money ahead of time and threatening in case of refusal to commit suicide.

And all this pleasure for only twenty-five cents!

The country respects and values service, and that service is not only ability to trade and to derive some benefit. It is necessary to say once again: service has entered into the very blood of the people. It is an integral part of the national character. Essentially, it is a way of doing things.

This feeling of respect for service, like all other popular feelings, is played upon expertly by priests and bankers. It is considered here that priests render service to the people. True, the church performance is actually called "service," yet the church also likes to use it in the figurative, or main, sense of that word. The thought is pounded into the brains of people that the church serves the people.

Service is the favourite expression of the Wall Street robber. Openly robbing people, and not only single individuals but entire cities and countries, he will unfailingly say that he is a small man, a simple fellow, and a democrat, as much as are all good people, and that it is not money he serves, but society. He gives people service.

"And so, gentlemen," said Mr. Adams when we left the Western Union, "now we shall celebrate. I ask you to follow me. It is, I think, not far from here. Forward! Go ahead!"

"Go! Go! Go!" cried Mrs. Adams.

I*

Since it was already nearly ten o'clock, and all of us were quite hungry, we hastily moved forward.

"This is a marvellous restaurant," Mr. Adams was saying. "I suggest, gentlemen, that we order a large beefsteak and a couple of bottles of good California wine apiece. Although, since we are celebrating, we might as well celebrate right and take some French or Rhine wine. By the way, have you noticed that Americans drink very little wine and prefer whisky? Oh, oh! Didn't you really know that? This is very, very interesting and will be useful for you to know. This is a profound problem. I advise you to write it down in your little notebooks. You see, a bottle of good wine presupposes good conversation. People sit at a table and talk, and so one thing supplements the other: without good conversation wine brings no pleasure. But Americans do not like and do not know how to converse. Have you noticed it? They never sit around a table longer than necessary. They have nothing to talk about. They dance or play bridge. And they prefer whisky. You drink three glasses and you're drunk at once. So that there's no use talking. Yes, yes, gentlemen, Americans do not drink wine!"

We walked for quite a while down some broad street, with cottages on either side. The business centre was far behind us. We were in the residential part. Here there were no restaurants, no stores, not even any drug-stores. It began to rain. Over the hidden lights hung a placard: "Forty deaths as a result of automobile accidents in San Antonio during the past year. Drive carefully!"

"Hadn't we better turn back?" asked Mrs. Adams.

"Oh, Becky!" exclaimed the old man. "How can you talk like that: 'Let's go back!' It's quite near to the restaurant. I well remember the place."

We walked another half-hour in the rain, becoming gloomier every minute. We passed an automobile cemetery, then a vacant lot where second-hand machines were being sold. Going in the other direction, toward the centre of the city, several automobiles passed, filled with young people who shouted something and lighted firecrackers. At a crossing was a swing illuminated with electric lights. A couple having a good time were sadly swinging in a metal boat. Only here we noticed that the rain was beginning to come down in earnest. By electric light could be seen the thin streams of rain.

"Well, all right," said Mrs. Adams, with her customary reasonableness, "if you don't remember where the restaurant is located, we can ask a policeman."

"No, no, Becky," said Mr. Adams, "don't do that. The restaurant is somewhere around here."

"But, after all, where is it? On what street?"

"Becky, you must not talk like that."

"I'm going to ask a policeman right away," Mrs. Adams said with determination. "What is the name of your restaurant?"

"Why, Becky, I ask you, please, don't worry! No, truly, we must not bother a policeman."

"You have forgotten the name of the restaurant!" said Mrs. Adams.

Mr. Adams groaned, clutching his wet head.

Talking thus, we passed through the entire city and finally saw ahead of us what was evidently the wet desert.

We turned back and, stumbling, ran toward the centre of the city.

"If we could only find a taxi," said Mrs. Adams.

But we did not find a taxi. Evidently they had all been taken by people celebrating the New Year. It was getting on toward twelve o'clock. We ran in the rain, hungry, angry, and tired. The closer we moved toward the centre, the more frequently we met machines with hilarious young people. The centre of the city was full of people. Our nerves had gone altogether to pieces, we winced at every shot, and they resounded on all sides. There was an odour of gunpowder, as during street fighting. Everywhere rattles which emitted the noise of machine-guns were being sold.

"Gentlemen!" Mr. Adams cried suddenly. "Let's have a good time!"

With lightning rapidity he bought a rattle and gaily began to swing it. Some riotous youth struck Mr. Adams on his bald pate with a rattle, and Mr. Adams struck him back on the shoulder.

We went into the first drug-store and ordered sandwiches.

While they were being prepared for us, we sadly clicked our glasses of tomato juice and wished each other happiness. That very minute it struck twelve.

So we met the New Year in the city of San Antonio, in the state of Texas.

43
We Enter the Southern States

THE MORNING after the tempestuous greeting of the New Year we awakened in the Robert E. Lee Hotel with one passionate desire—to go on! To start as soon as possible, this very minute, this very second! In vain did Mr. Adams assure us that San Antonio was a fine city, that it would be unforgivable folly not to see it ("No, seriously, gentlemen"), that we did not understand anything and that we do not wish to understand. We, without previous agreement, repeated sadly one and the same thing:

"Yes, we do not understand anything, we do not wish to understand, and in all probability we will never understand. We gladly admit all that you say, that San Antonio is a wonderful city, but we want to go on! Besides, don't forget, Mr. Adams, that your baby is waiting for you!"

As soon as the baby was mentioned the Adamses began to make haste, and in half an hour we were driving over the same broad and long street where yesterday under a drenching rain we sought a restaurant without a name.

Before leaving San Antonio we drove around Breckenridge Park. Mr. Adams insisted on it.

"You must not think, gentlemen," he announced, "that San Antonio is a bad town. It is a good, well-planned city—and you must see Breckenridge."

The large fine park was empty. Only a few of its trees were naked. All the others, just as in summer-time, rustled with thick green foliage. The park was crossed in all directions by irrigation canals lined with rock. The water flowed with a quiet rustle from one canal into another located a little lower. We looked at a camel and some sea-lions, admired the boys who played football on an almost blindingly green lawn, looked at the tables and benches arranged for picnickers, and, having received considerable information from at least ten petrol stations, we moved on east to the border of Louisiana.

Each day we drove out of one city in order to reach another city by evening, having passed in the course of the day any number of large and small main streets, the Adamses in front, we two in the back seat, and between us some hitchhiker with a suitcase on his knees! But never before had we been in such a hurry. It seemed that the faultless motor of our car was fed not only by the petrol, but also by the impatience that beat within us—as soon as possible to get to New York, as soon as possible to board a ship, as soon as possible to leave for Europe! The second month of our automobile journey was coming to an end. That is a short time for such a large and interesting country. But we were already filled to the brim with America.

The Negro South was approaching. The last mile separating us from Louisiana we drove through forests. The sun looked out. It was warm and joyous, as in the spring-time in the Ukraine. More frequently we met towns, habitations, petrol stations, and horses running freely over fields, their manes flying.

Finally, we passed the little post with the inscription "State of Louisiana," and raced alongside reddish fields of harvested cotton.

The monumental churches of the East and the West were succeeded by wooden, white-washed little churches on poles instead of foundations, Spanish and Indian names were succeeded by French names, and at the petrol station where Mrs. Adams "got" information they replied to her not "Yes, ma'am!" but "Yes, mom!"

Passing through the town of Lafayette we saw a large placard stretched across the street with a picture of an unpleasant self-satisfied face, bearing this inscription in heavy letters:

Elect me sheriff. I am a friend of the people!

This plea of the police Marat from the state of Louisiana reminded us of the manner of the recently assassinated senator, Huey Long, who likewise regarded himself "a friend of the people," of all the people, with the exception of Negroes, Mexicans, intellectuals, and workers, and demanded universal participation in wealth, in all the wealth, with the exception of the five millions apiece which, according to the idea of the "friend of the people," had to be left to every millionaire.

Here in the South we saw what we had never before seen in America —pedestrians wandering along the highway. There was not a single white man among them.

An old bent Negro woman in thick yellow stockings, ragged dirty slippers, in apron and an old-fashioned hat with a bow, passed by.

We suggested to Mr. Adams that we would like to give the old lady a lift.

"No, no, no!" he exclaimed. "What are you saying? You don't understand the nature of the Southern states. To give a lift to an old Negress! She will never, never believe that white people want to give her a lift. She will think that you are making fun of her."

On the highway, in the midst of the automobiles, suddenly appeared a grey horse pulling a two-wheeled cabriolet with a coachman's box (we saw such specimens in the Ford museum). In the cabriolet sat a planter's wife and her daughter. The ancient equipage turned into a country lane, an ordinary cart road, if you please, with a strip of yellowish grass in the middle. From all the automobiles that passed on the highway people looked out and gazed at the cabriolet which drove off, swaying importantly on its springs, high and thin as spider legs. In just such curiosity farmers had looked thirty years ago at the smoky and sputtering automobile with its clumsy body in which passengers sat up, dressed in wolf coats with the fur on the outside and wearing huge automobile goggles. We drove up to a large river. In the twilight it gleamed like metal.

"Mississippi!" exclaimed Mr. Adams.

"This is not the Mississippi," said Mrs. Adams calmly.

"This is the Mississippi!"

"This is not the Mississippi!"

"Becky, it depresses me to hear you say that this is not the Mississippi."

"Nevertheless, it is not the Mississippi."

Mr. Adams groaned. We drove across the bridge and found ourselves in Morgan City. Before going off to look for a night's lodging, we stopped at a restaurant called the "Blue Goose" to have our dinner.

"Sir," asked Mr. Adams of the proprietor, winking an eye, "what is the name of that river? I know what it is, but my wife would like to know."

"This is the Atchafalaya," replied the proprietor.

"How, how?"

"Atchafalaya."

"Thank you very, very," muttered Mr. Adams, backing out, "very, very."

That was the first occasion throughout the journey that Mr. Adams was guilty of a factual error.

Throughout the dinner Mr. Adams fidgeted in his chair and seemed distressed. Finally he produced a map and a guide book, looked into them for some time, and finally, without looking at his wife, he said timidly:

"I can inform you, gentlemen, of a very interesting detail. This accursed Atchafalaya is the deepest river in the world."

In order to fill up somehow a dull evening in dull Morgan City, we did what we usually did on such an occasion—we went to a motion-picture theatre. Usually, looking at the screen, Mr. Adams was not so much angry as he was ironical about the plot and the actors of the Hollywood production. But on this occasion he suddenly started a regular demonstration. Ten minutes after the beginning we noticed that Mr. Adams was not his usual self. He jumped up and down in his seat, groaned and muttered quite aloud:

"To hell, hell, hell with it!"

Suddenly he cried out: "To hell with it!" so that everybody in the hall could hear him, jumped out of his seat, and, muttering curses and sputtering, ran out into the street. Mrs. Adams ran after him. We remained to see the picture to the end, sensing that an important family battle was at that very moment being waged in the street.

When the show was over we did not find either of the couple at the entrance to the theatre. With great difficulty we found them in various parts of the city. Happily, the ends of the city were not at any great distance from one another.

Mr. Adams, without a hat (his hat was still cruising from city to city), the collar of his coat raised, was taking broad steps across the dark highway in the direction of the Gulf of Mexico, continuing to mutter: "To hell with it!"

"Seriously, gentlemen," he said to us piteously, "I cannot bear it any longer. These motion pictures will finally drive me crazy. In New York I never go to the movies, and it is very hard for me to bear it, because I am not used to it. No, truly, I wanted to shoot at the screen—with a machine-gun."

The couple quickly made it up and the evening ended with a heart-to-heart talk at the gas fireplace of the tourist home.

It was only a hundred miles to New Orleans. On a sunny morning we started on our journey. It was soft, almost summery weather. We drove along a new but rather narrow concrete road, along a quiet little river. On the other side stretched reddish fields of cotton, on which here and there could be seen pieces of white cotton tuft and fields of sugar-cane where Negroes in large groups were chopping down its dry stalks with machetes.

Frequently across the river were flung protuberant and narrow little suspension bridges.

In the course of several hours we met the monotonous and pathetic board huts of Negro farm workers. Here was the devastating monotony of limitless poverty, a kind of standard of poverty. In the doorless entrances, surrounded by wattles almost falling apart, one could see not only no cows, pigs, or chickens, but not even a wisp of straw. This was the very lowest stage of poverty, before which the picturesque poverty of the Indians may seem the height of well-being, even of luxury. This was in south United States, in one of the most fruitful places on the globe.

Before us again appeared a large, smooth and completely deserted river, which reminded us of the Volga, although perhaps it was not so broad.

"This is the Mississippi," said Mrs. Adams triumphantly.

Mr. Adams sighed heavily. He would have paid a high price that the river should bear some other name. But there was no doubt. There was the bridge, the famous new silvery bridge with its side roads for automobiles and its central part designated for trains. Again American nature and American technique met in a contest of strength. The longest river in the world was crossed by the longest bridge in the world resting on abutments. It was opened only five days ago, had been three years under construction, and cost fifteen million dollars. Beyond the bridge began the widest express highway, and cottages appeared. We were driving into New Orleans.

New Orleans might have been called the American Venice (after all, like Venice it has risen out of water), if its innumerable canals had not been hidden underground.

The city is widely spread on a low promontory between the Mississippi and Lake Pontchartrain. From the place where the Mississippi enters into the Gulf of Mexico to the city it was ninety miles. Closer to the Gulf, not another place could be found where a city might be built. But even where it has been built the soil is alluvial, slimy clay. The city has always suffered from floods and fevers. The water which brought it its good fortune at the same time brought it misfortune. In the course of its entire life the city has been fighting itself, fighting against the soil on which it is built and the water which surrounds it on all sides. It is fighting even now. But the main work has already been done. Pontchartrain is separated from the city by a concrete embankment which drops toward the lake step by step. The approaches to the city for many miles around are covered with a system of dams, on top of which pass faultless highways. In the long battle between man and nature, man has come out the victor.

The city is planned with extraordinary simplicity. The streets which go parallel to the river follow the bend which the river makes at that place, and assume the shape of a crescent. They are crossed by completely straight and very long streets. Under one of these, located approximately in the centre of the city, is hidden the largest canal. In honour of this unseen canal the street itself is called Canal Street. This is the main street. It divides the city into two parts—the French, which is as careless as old Paris, with its little streets, its small arches on thin wooden posts, its stores, its restaurants of unprepossessing appearance with first-class French cooking, its port inns, cobbled streets, and street stands filled with vegetables and fruits, the beauty of which stands out particularly, thanks to the proximity of dirt and slops thrown right out into the streets —and the new American part, which adds nothing to the character of the American cities already known to the readers.

At one time Louisiana belonged to France, and New Orleans was founded by Frenchmen. It is difficult to say to what extent the French spirit has been preserved in New Orleans, but on to Canal Street emerge the streets of the Dauphin, Toulouse, Royale, and there is even a Champs-Elysées, while in the old city in the Restaurant Arnot they serve the kind of filet that surely cannot be found anywhere else in America.

The city lies a little more than a metre below the level of the river. There is not a single dry spot in it where the dead might be buried. No matter where they try to dig the ground, they unfailingly find water. Therefore, people here always bury their dead in the manner of the ancient Egyptians, in sarcophagi, above the earth.

We went to the cemetery, which is located in the French part of the town, and for a while wandered through this white and tedious city of the dead. The quadrangular vaults are made of brick, and painted white. The coffin is placed in the front opening, which is then closed in with bricks. One vault is built on top of the other, and occasionally a third one on top of that. Its two-storied brick dullness makes the cemetery reminiscent of a small American town. It even had its Main Street.

From the cemetery we went to a photographer's supply store to have our camera repaired. While Mr. Adams was talking with the woman in charge about the prospects of the city's future development (the prospects were bad), and about trade (the trade likewise was bad), there entered a handsome young man with black eyes and a beaked French nose.

"May I see the manager of the store?" he asked.

"He is not here now," answered the lady, a thin, red-haired woman in spectacles, "but if you need anything, you may tell me."

"But I should like to talk to the owner," muttered the young man, looking appealingly at us.

"Is it a very important matter?" asked the lady.

"Yes . . . that is, it is not so important, but I thought . . . however, you also, of course . . . I can tell you what it is."

He came close to the lady and very quietly said:

"I should like to wash the show window in your store for only five cents."

The lady said she was very sorry, but she did not need that kind of work. The young man apologized, and, stumbling several times, ran out of the store.

We were silent for some time; then Mr. Adams ran out into the street. He returned ten minutes later.

"Gentlemen," he said, shaking his round head, "this is terrible! You can't imagine to what stage of pauperism he has descended. I caught up with him with difficulty, he ran so fast down the street. I had a talk with him. He is an unemployed artist. He has had no orders for a long time and he does not expect any in the future. The boy no longer counts on his profession. He is ready to do any kind of work, but this is also hopeless. Yes, gentlemen, that nice boy has been hungry for several years. He would not take a dollar from me for anything in the world. He was even angry with me."

"What? And you did not manage to give him . . ." .

"No, don't say I could not give it to him. It is simply foolish to think so. Let us not talk about it."

We had left the store some time ago, passed all the way down Canal Street, were coming to the Mississippi, and Mr. Adams was still muttering, as he groaned and moaned:

"No, gentlemen, let us not talk about it."

New Orleans is a beautiful city. It appealed to us. But the feeling of indifference and boredom, which overcame our automobile group after New Year's Eve in San Antonio, like a never-ceasing rain pouring constantly from an ever-cloudy sky, did not even think of leaving us. We had skimmed the cream off the journey. Man is not equipped to enjoy himself eternally. Therefore, all the beauty of New Orleans was appreciated only with our minds. The heart was speechless.

On a large square at the Mississippi it was quite deserted. Automobile ferries, the same kind as in San Francisco, were leaving the wooden docks for the other side. On a parapet, his legs hanging down toward the river, a Negro sat sadly, in a straw hat pulled over his nose. Beside him stood a crazy old man, a black coat flung around his shoulder, who directed the departing and approaching ferries. While doing this, he emitted cries of command. A street photographer came to us and, listlessly, as if he had seen us yesterday and the day before, asked in Russian whether we did not wish to have our pictures taken. He had arrived here twenty years ago from Kovno to become a millionaire, and one sensed such scepticism in his face and in the figure of this Kovno photographer that we did not even ask him how business was and what were his further prospectives.

Unexpectedly, from beyond the wooden dock moved a high long white structure which one could not at once recognize as a steamship. It went past us up the river. Quite close to its prow stood two high stacks, placed side by side across the deck, decorated in curlicues and looking like cast-iron poles of some monumental fence. The steamer was set in motion by the movement of one huge wheel placed astern.

"The last of the Mohicans," said Mr. Adams. "Now people ride on such ships only for rest and recreation, and that very rarely. Mississippi has come to an end!"

We looked at the river on which at one time floated barges with merchandise and slaves. It was on this river that Harriet Beecher Stowe introduced Tom to her readers. On it moved the raft of Huckleberry

Finn, who hid the Negro, Jim, from his pursuers. Now the river is dead, river transport having proved too slow for the United States. Trains and automobiles have taken possession of all the cargoes of the river. Speed —that is the slogan under which the economy of the United States has developed in recent years. Speed at any price!

And there are no longer any slaves in the United States. By law the slaves have become free men with equal rights. But let a Negro so much as dare to enter a Southern motion-picture theatre, a street car, or a church where white men sit!

In the evening, wandering over the old streets of New Orleans, we saw the Palace Motion Picture Theatre, over which was this lighted inscription:

Splendid Southern Theatre.
For Coloured Folks Only.

44
Negroes

THE FARTHER we moved through the Southern states, the more frequently we met with all kinds of limitations designed for Negroes. Sometimes they were separate comfort stations "for the coloured," or a special bench at an autobus stop, or a special section of the street car. Here even the churches were separate; for example, one for the white Baptists and another for the black Baptists. When the Baptist God several years hence returns to earth, in order to destroy Soviet atheists who help one another, he will be delighted with his establishments in the south of America.

When leaving New Orleans we saw a group of Negroes working on swamp reclamation. The work was carried on in the most primitive manner. The Negroes had nothing but spades.

"Gentlemen," said Mr. Adams, "this should be especially interesting to you. Common ordinary spades in the land of the greatest mechanization! It would be foolish to think that in the United States there are no machines for draining swamps. The labour of these people is almost thrown away. These are unemployed who receive a little relief. For that relief they must be given some kind of work, they must be occupied in some way. So they have been given spades. Let them dig. The productivity of labour here is equal to zero."

Our further route lay along the Gulf of Mexico, through the states of Louisiana, Mississippi, and Alabama. We passed through all these states in one day, and stopped in Florida. Then from Florida—to the shore of the Atlantic Ocean—into Georgia, then through South Carolina, North Carolina, and Virginia—to Washington.

The first part of our route along the Gulf of Mexico was made by us with great speed. American technique delivered a new blow to our imagination. It is hard to astonish people after they have seen Ford's plant, Boulder Dam, the San Francisco bridges, and the New Orleans bridge. But in America everything proved possible. The fight against water—this is what occupied technique here. For scores of miles, bridges and dams alternate. At times it seemed that our automobile was a motorboat, because all around, as far as the eye could see, there was nothing but water, and across it in some marvellous way a broad concrete road stretched. Then a bridge appeared, then again a dam, and then again a bridge. What effort, what money were needed to build it all! Most astonishing of all was the fact that twenty miles from here was an excellent parallel road, and there was really no pressing necessity for the road on which we were travelling, the construction of which was a technical wonder of the world and cost hundreds of millions of dollars. We learned that during prosperity this road was built in order to attract tourists to these places. The very shore of the Gulf of Mexico was covered with a quay that stretched for hundreds of miles. We regret that we did not write down the exact figure, but we do remember distinctly that it was several hundreds of miles. It is hard to believe, but we drove an entire day alongside the sea, which was separated from us by a solid and beautiful quay.

We spent the night in the small port and summer resort town of Pensacola, in Florida. Rain poured down all night. Our automobile stood under the open sky, and in the morning it was impossible to start the motor. Mr. Adams walked around the machine and, throwing his hands up in despair, said:

"Our battery has gone to the devil! Our battery has gone to the devil!" The rain annoyed and perplexed Mr. Adams, and he redoubled his usual automobile cautiousness.

It was our luck that our battery had not even thought of going to the devil. The wires had become a bit damp, and as soon as they dried out the motor began to work.

"Gentlemen," said Mr. Adams, looking at the murky sky, "I ask you to be as careful as possible. I suggest that we postpone getting out of here. Suppose the rain should start again."

"But suppose it doesn't start again?" said Mrs. Adams. "You don't expect us to stay here in Pensacola for the rest of our lives!"

"Oh, Becky, you don't know what Florida is. Here the climate is changeable and dangerous. Anything can happen here."

"Well, what can happen?"

"Seriously, Becky, you talk like a little girl. Anything can happen here."

"At the worst, if we should run into rain, we will drive in the rain."

All of us were so eager to get on our way that we paid no attention to Mr. Adams, and, taking advantage of a lull in the downpour, set out along the Gulf across the new dams and the new bridges.

An hour after driving out of Pensacola, we ran into a tropical storm (rather, this was a subtropical storm, but at the time it seemed so frightful to us that we regarded it as a tropical storm). Everything happened according to Jules Verne—thunder, lightning, and a Niagara pouring out of the skies. Now everything was covered with water. We moved ahead blindly. At times the water was so deep that we seemed to be driving along the bottom of the Gulf of Mexico. At each clap of thunder Mr. Adams jumped and muttered:

"Gentlemen, be calm . . . be calm . . ."

He was undoubtedly afraid that a stroke of lightning would hit our automobile.

We tried stopping and waiting for the storm to blow over, but we were afraid that the water would flood the motor and the battery would actually "go to the devil." We remembered with trepidation newspaper stories about hurricanes in Florida and photographs of gigantic trees pulled out by the roots and trains knocked off the rails.

At any rate, just as in Jules Verne, it all ended well.

We spent the night in the city of Tallahassee, and in the morning we were already in Georgia. The January day was almost sultry, and we forgot about our terrors of yesterday.

Georgia proved to be a forest country. For some inexplicable reason we had always imagined the Southern Negro states in the form of sheer cotton fields and tobacco plantations. And here suddenly we learned that besides plantations and fields, there are also thick forests. We drove through lanes over which, in the manner of goatbeards, hung down the hempen tails of a tree called "pecan," a kind we had never seen before.

We met Negroes more and more frequently; at times for several hours at a stretch we saw no white people. But in the cities the white man ruled, and if a Negro appeared at some moss-covered mansion in the residential part, he would invariably have a broom, a pail or a package, all of which pointed to the fact that here he could be only a servant.

The high American standard of living has not yet conquered the Southern states. It has, of course, penetrated considerably—there are Southern Main Streets, drug-stores, quadrangles of butter at dinner and luncheon, pinball games, chewing gum, petrol stations, highways, T-bone steaks, girls with the coiffures of movie stars, and advertising billboards in no way distinguishable from the Eastern, Western and Northern quadrangles of butter, girls, highways, and billboards. Yet the Southern states have something of their own, something peculiar and indigenous to them which is amazingly charming and warm. Nature? Perhaps it is partly nature too. Here are no self-conscious palms, no polished suns as in California. But then there is also no dryness of desert here, something that is felt over there. The Southern states are a land of village landscapes, of forests, and of mournful songs. But, of course, it is not only a matter of nature.

The soul of the South is its people; not its white people, but its black.

We stopped in Charleston, South Carolina. After looking over the city, we were returning home in the evening over the inevitable Main Street when we saw in a dark lane a Negro girl about twelve years old. The girl did not see us. She held a basket on her arm. The walk of the girl at first seemed strange to us, but, peering more closely, we saw that the girl was dancing. It was a talented improvisation, clean-cut and rhythmic, an almost finished dance which we should have liked to call: "A Girl from a Southern State." Dancing, the little Negress went farther and farther down the dark lane, glided, made turns, little hops, and gracefully balanced the light and empty basket. After the commerce of the day, the city was asleep. It was wrapped in utter darkness. It seemed to us that we heard the sounds of the banjo, so rhythmic and musical was her dance.

Negroes are talented people. True, the whites gladly applaud them, but at the same time continue to regard them as a lower race. Negroes are graciously permitted to be artists. Evidently, when the black is on the stage and a white man in a loge, the latter can look down on the black man, and his lordly pride does not suffer therefrom.

Negroes are impressionable people. The whites regard that ironically and figure that Negroes are fools. Indeed! For success in commerce there is no need of impressionability.

Speaking now of white people, we have in view Southern gentlemen, and not them only but also the gentlemen from the North who are likewise infected with the psychology of slave-owning. We also want to say that not all the people in the South regard Negroes as lower beings, but, to our regret, these are the majority.

Negroes possess a strong imagination. They love to bear the names of famous people, for example, and occasionally some porter, elevator operator, or farm labourer, whose name is Jim Smith, pronounces his full name thus—"Jim George Washington Abraham Lincoln Grant Nebuchadnezzar Smith."

"Why, of course," says the Southern gentleman, whose imagination day and night encompasses only the splendid vision of a million dollars, "he is an utter idiot!"

In all the motion pictures and vaudevilles Negroes are represented as comic personalities who are foolish but good-natured servants.

Negroes love nature. As is peculiar of artistic characters, they are contemplative. Southern gentlemen find their own explanation for this. The Negroes, you see, are lazy and incapable of systematic labour. At that point is inevitably recounted the case of a Negro, who, having earned five dollars, does not go to work the next day, but, instead, taking his black girl by the arm, goes off with her to have a good time in the woods or by the river. And then the profound conclusion is drawn which, in a way, serves as the theoretical justification for exploiting the black man.

"No matter how much you pay him, he'll live like a pig, anyway. Therefore, pay him as little as possible."

Finally, Negroes are expansive. Oh! Here the Southern gentleman is seriously disturbed. He is already reaching for a pulley, a rope, and a piece of soap. He is already laying out the fire. He suddenly becomes incredibly noble and suspicious. Negroes are sexual criminals. It is simply necessary to hang them.

Negroes are inquisitive. For this there are a thousand explanations. It's as clear as day that they are simply an impudent and hopeless people. They stick their nose into what does not concern them. They stick their black nose into everything.

In spite of all this, the Southern gentleman figures that Negroes love him very much. In motion-picture dramas about the life of the landed gentry there is always an old grey Negro who adores his master and is ready to give up his life for him.

Oh, if only the Southern gentleman, the kind-hearted spectator or the participant of a lynching-bee suddenly understood that in order to attain full one hundred per cent. humanity he needs what he lacks—namely, these very Negro characteristics which he derides! What would he say to that?

Negroes have almost no opportunity to develop and to grow. In the cities the careers of porters and elevator operators are open to them, while in their homeland, in the Southern states, they are farm labourers without any rights; reduced by oppression to the status of domestic animals; they are utter slaves there.

Nevertheless, if Negroes were to be taken away from America, the country would, of course, become somewhat whiter, but most certainly it would become at least twenty times more dull.

True to our rule to take into the automobile people waiting for the occasion on the road, at an isolated petrol station in North Carolina, we picked up an eighteen-year-old boy from a CCC camp near Washington. These camps had been built by President Roosevelt for unemployed young men, originally for six months. Roosevelt hoped to end unemployment in six months—but later, when it became clear that it was not so easy to end unemployment, the camps were left for an indefinite period. The boy had to drive eighty miles from his camp to his native town of Elizabethtown. Quite a cold rain was pouring. The young man shivered in his summer khaki shirt and his perforated, broad-brimmed felt hat.

Soon our last hitchhiker warmed up in the enclosed machine and began to reply to our questions. He did not add anything new to the impression we had acquired of American young men as a type—talkative, self-confident, and lacking in curiosity.

His story was ordinary. His father was a farmer. The old man's affairs were not so good. The boy graduated from a high school. He didn't have enough money to go to college. He set out to look for a job. He did not find it. He had to enroll in the CCC. There, together with other boys, he clears forests and digs fire-prevention ditches. They feed him not badly, clothe him, and give him thirty dollars a month (five in hand and twenty-five to his parents). Of course, this is a help. What will happen further is unknown. He knows only one thing: he is young, healthy, he has a white skin, he plays baseball. That means that everything will be well—"all right"—and will work out well. There is no fog in his consciousness. On the contrary, utter explicitness. He could give no answers to most of the questions we asked him. Then, with charming frankness, he would say: "I don't know about that." But then when he understood the question, he would reply at once, without thinking, with a ready-made formula, which was evidently firmly embedded in the family of his father, the farmer, and in the city of Elizabethtown.

"But, after all, don't you want to go to college?"

"Of course, although I do know lots of fellows with diplomas in their pockets who tramp through the country in search of work. But still, it is easier to make your way after going through college."

"Well, what studies interest you in college?"

"Well, what do you mean—what studies? Why, of course, those that they study there."

We were passing through a Negro village. It was the same standardized Negro poverty. It would have been just as unusual to find here a good Negro house as to find a bad road.

"You can tell a Negro house right away from a white man's house," our fellow traveller said with a smile.

"Is it possible that all Negroes live so poorly?"

"Of course, all of them."

"Well, now, you have grown up in the South. Tell us, do you know at least one wealthy Negro?"

The youth thought for some time.

"No, I don't know a single one," he finally answered.

"Why is it so? Are Negroes bad workers?"

"No, they know how to work."

"Maybe it's because they're dishonest people?"

"Why dishonest? I know Negroes well. Negroes are good people. There are some good football players among them."

"How does it happen then that all Negroes are poor?"

"I don't know about that."

"Is your father acquainted with any Negroes?"

"We know many Negroes."

"And you treat them well?"

"Of course!"

"Would you ask such a Negro to sit down at the table with your family?"

The youth laughed.

"No, that's impossible!"

"Why?"

"Because! Negroes and white folks cannot sit together at the same table."

"But why not?"

"You must be from New York," said the young man.

To the Southern mind, New York is the limit of freethinking and radicalism.

"Now tell us this. We have passed through several Negro states and occasionally we saw quite good-looking Negresses. Could you be fond of a Negress?"

"Why, yes, that can happen," said the young man after some cogitation. "Yes, that might happen. It's true that among the coloured there are some good-looking ones, especially mulattoes."

"But if you were fond of her, would you marry her?"

"Go on! That's out of the question!"

"Why?"

"That's impossible!"

"Well, but suppose you loved her very much? Or suppose a white girl fell in love with a Negro and married him?"

The youth waved his arms.

"No, I can see right away that you're from New York."

"I dare say such a Negro would be hanged. Right?"

"I think something of the kind might happen to him."

The young man laughed gaily for a long time.

This conversation is reproduced here with complete accuracy.

Not only here, but even in New York itself, about which the young boy from the South talked with horror, it is almost impossible to see a Negro in a restaurant, a motion-picture theatre, or a church, unless, of course, he is there as a servant or a porter. In a large New York hall —Carnegie Hall—at the concert of the Negro singer, Marian Anderson, we saw hundreds of intelligent Negroes who sat in the gallery in a quite separate group.

Of course, in accordance with American laws, and especially in New York, Negroes have the right to take any place among the white, to go into a white motion-picture theatre or into a white restaurant. But the Negro himself will never do it. He knows only too well how such experiments might end. He will not be beaten up, of course, as in the South, but his closest neighbours in most cases will at once demonstratively depart—that is indubitable.

By law, Negroes are free citizens of the United States, yet in the South under various pretexts they are deprived of the right to vote, and in Washington itself, and not alone Washington, but in the very building where the laws were written, the following occurred: a Negro by the name of DePriest was elected to Congress from the city of Chicago. To the disaffection of the white Congressmen, he sat beside them at the sessions of the House of Representatives. But that wasn't all. This black man with his black secretary went to eat in the Congressional dining-room. He could not be turned out, and he paid no attention whatever to the quiet demonstrations against him. Finally, they thought up an excellent way out of the situation. They closed the dining-room. They closed down entirely the Congressional dining-room, just so that the Negro would not be able to eat with white people.

"Yes, yes, gentlemen," said Mr. Adams, when, after letting off our young man from the CCC, we drove on, "I'll tell you a remarkable story about my friend from the Island of Trinidad. I knew an American family that lived there. They decided to come to New York. It so happened that I was obliged to leave New York for a year and decided to sublet my apartment to them. I recommended them to my landlord and went away. When I returned a year later the landlord flung himself at me almost with clenched fists. 'It's an outrage,' he cried. 'I never thought that you would play such a dirty trick on me!' I became frightened and began to wonder what I could have done to him that was so bad. 'I don't know what I did to hurt you,' I told the landlord. 'You settled Negroes in my house,' the landlord groaned. 'I beg your pardon,' I said, 'I settled in your house my friends from the Island of Trinidad. They are white people, just like you and me. They lived in the Islands for thirty years, and now return to America.' 'But why didn't you tell me at once that your friends lived in the Island of Trinidad? I wouldn't have let them in for anything in the world.' 'What happened?' I asked. 'This is what happened. All my tenants in one voice insist that your friends have a touch of Negro blood. They have a grandmother whose hair is too curly. That's definitely established. One of my tenants moved out. The others said that if I didn't get rid of these Negroes, they would break their leases and move out.' Seriously, gentlemen, it would be foolish to think that Negroes are well off in New York. Now, in our house there is a Negro elevator man. But, of course, that's a different matter."

It became cold in Northern Carolina and still colder in Virginia. The thin rain poured on the roof of our car all through the last day of our journey. It was only a few miles to Washington, but Mr. Adams feared that the water might begin to freeze. Bill-boards appeared advertising Washington hotels.

"Stop!" Mr. Adams cried suddenly.

The machine stopped.

"Gentlemen," he said solemnly, "do you want to know what is America?"

"We do," we replied.

"In that case, look!"

And Mr. Adams pointed to a bill-board we had almost passed.

We saw a large picture, exceedingly touching in content. On it was portrayed a fine young mother of the type of Greta Garbo with a fine young girl (of the type of Shirley Temple) in her arms. Behind them stood a wonderful guardian angel with the face of a Hollywood motion-picture lieutenant and with outspread wings.

. "The signature!" cried Mr. Adams. "The signature! Do you know what this guardian angel is telling the good mother? He advises her to place money in a bank to the credit of her child. The angel is so kind that he even explains to her in which particular bank she should place her money. Seriously, gentlemen, you don't want to understand what America is!"

As we were driving into Washington the speedometer of our car showed exactly ten thousand miles.

For the last time we shouted "Hurrah!"

45
American Democracy

ON A RAINY winter day a small freight boat came to the shores of England. A hatless man came down the wet gangplank to the pier. With one hand he held his wife and with the other he pressed his child to him. He was attacked from all sides by photographers, motion-picture operators, and journalists. The man walked right through, paying no heed to anyone. Only after he took his place in a taxi did he turn to look back at the crowd that followed him, and in his look was reflected hatred and fear.

That man had fled from America. He abandoned America at night, when the country was asleep, after eluding the vigilance of New York's fleetest reporters. In order to avoid persecution, he departed not on a comfortable passenger ship, but on an old shabby freighter, where there was not even a convenient cabin. And this man who had abandoned his native land was happy to be on a foreign shore.

That was Charles Lindbergh, one of the most famous men in the world, and his native land was the United States of America, the country of the greatest democracy, as Americans firmly believe.

All know, of course, the reasons that drove Lindbergh to the necessity of undertaking the most serious step in the life of any man—to abandon his native land. America was not able to protect the inviolability of personality of its national hero. It was unable to defend his domicile from the intrusion of bandits. It was unable to protect his family.

There is no doubt that Lindbergh loves America and that Americans adore Lindbergh. And if one will read carefully the text of the American Constitution, it is easy to discover there grandiose and equitable sections which would seem to guarantee the general welfare. Nevertheless, Lindbergh fled, while the Constitution in the capitalist country is merely a bronze tablet or a no less beautiful parchment preserved in the vault of a lawmaking institution.

From the story of the famous man let us pass to the story of an ordinary woman for whom as much as for Lindbergh were written the sonorous words of the Constitution of the United States.

That American woman had a seventeen-year-old daughter and a grown-up son. On one occasion the daughter did not return home. She did not come back all through the night, nor did she return the next day. The girl disappeared. The police looked for her and did not find her. The mother regarded her daughter as lost. A year passed. Then, in one way or another, a friend of her son's told him a horrible bit of news. He had seen the girl whom they all regarded as lost in a secret brothel. (Officially, there is no prostitution in America. As a matter of fact, there are any number of secret brothels there.) At once the brother, pretending to be a client, went to this den of iniquity. There he actually saw his sister. He recognized her with difficulty, so frightfully had the young girl changed. What she told him was even more horrible. She had been kidnapped and sold.

"I'm lost," said the girl, "and don't try to save me. The people who abducted me are so powerful that nobody can fight them. They will not hesitate to kill you or Mother."

Nevertheless, the fight began. The mother went to the police. But nothing came of it. Behind the backs of the bandits stood some unknown but extraordinarily powerful people. The mother appealed to the courts. The lawyer of the bandits proved that the girl was an old prostitute, and the menace to society were not the bandits who had abducted her but she herself. The superior court of the state likewise decided the case in favour of the bandits. A trip to Washington did not help the mother. Washington simply has no power over the court of the state. That's all there was to it. The girl remained in the brothel.

This happened in a country which has freedom of the press. The girl's mother had complete freedom, not only to speak but even to shout. She shouted, but no one heard her.

This happened in a country where freedom of the press has been declared. Yet not a single newspaper wrote a thing about this case. Where were all the resourceful, tireless, fleet-footed reporters from whose penetrating gaze not a single robbery can escape, or a single wealthy wedding, or a single step of a motion-picture star of even the fourth magnitude?

This happened in a country where inviolability of person exists. But a poor person sat in a brothel, and no power could free her from it. It seems to us that if Abraham Lincoln himself were able to rise from his grave, even he could not do anything about it. Not even the cannons of General Grant could help him!

For some reason, every time one begins to sift in his memory the elements of which American life is composed, one recalls bandits, and if not bandits, then racketeers, and if not racketeers, then bankers, which as a matter of fact is one and the same thing. One recalls all this human garbage which has polluted an excellent, freedom-loving, and industrious country.

What could be gladder tidings than free elections in a democratic country whose citizens according to the Constitution are guaranteed all the rights to "liberty and the pursuit of happiness"? In their Sunday best the electors go to the ballot boxes and gently drop into them ballots with the names of their favourite candidates.

As a matter of fact, what happens was what our Chicago doctor told us—racketeer politicians come and by means of blackmail or threats force a good man to vote for some crook.

And so, the right to liberty and to the pursuit of happiness is undoubtedly there, but the possibility of actually enjoying that right is exceedingly dubious. This right is in too dangerous proximity with the money vaults of Wall Street.

But, to make up for that, the outer forms of democracy are preserved by Americans with extraordinary meticulousness. And that, one must say in truth, is rather impressive.

Henry Ford, by virtue of his position in American society, is a figure almost unapproachable. Yet on one occasion he walked into one of the buildings of his plant where several engineers happened to be, shook hands with all of them, and began to talk about the business on which he came. Throughout the conversation old Henry looked very worried. A certain thought tormented him. He stopped several times in the middle of a word, evidently trying to recall something. Finally, he excused himself, interrupted the conversation, and walked up to a young engineer who was sitting in a far corner of the room.

"I am very sorry, Mr. Smith," said Mr. Ford, "but I think I forgot to say hello to you."

An extra handshake will not lie as a heavy burden on the balance sheet of the Ford automobile plants, while the impression produced was tremendous. Ford will never invite that young engineer to his home, but they are equals on the job, they make automobiles together. Ford knows many old workers in his plant and calls them by their first names —"Hello, Mike!" or "Hello, John!" And Mike and John address him: "Hello, Henry!" Here they seem to be equals; they make automobiles together. But old Henry alone will be selling them. And old Mike or old John, after they've worked themselves out, will be thrown out into the street, just as worn-out bearings are thrown out.

And so, after making ten thousand miles, we found ourselves in the capital of the United States.

Washington, with its comparatively low government buildings, its gardens, its monuments, its broad streets, looks somewhat like Vienna, somewhat like Berlin, somewhat like Warsaw, somewhat like all the capitals. And only automobiles remind one that this city is located in America. Here there is an automobile for every two persons, but there is not a single permanent theatre for the entire population of five hundred thousand. Having looked over George Washington's house in Mount Vernon, having visited sessions of Congress, and having been at the grave of the Unknown Soldier, we discovered that there was really nothing else to see. Only the President remained to be seen. In America that is not so difficult.

Democratism in relations between people, the democratism of daily intercourse, is quite strongly developed in America and reaches quite far at times.

Twice a week, at ten o'clock in the morning, the President of the United States receives journalists. We managed to come to such a reception. It takes place in the White House. We walked into the reception room. There stood a large round table made of sequoia wood. It was a gift made to one of the former presidents. There was no cloakroom, so the incoming journalists laid their overcoats on that table, and when there was no more room on the table, they began laying them on the floor. Gradually about a hundred people gathered. They smoked, talked aloud, and looked impatiently at the small white door, behind which, apparently, the President of the United States was sequestered.

We were advised to stand as close as possible to the door, so that as people were being admitted to the President we would find ourselves in front; otherwise, it might so happen that behind the backs of the journalists we would not see anything. With the skill of experienced street-car fighters, we pushed ahead. Before us were only three men. They were greyish and quite respectable gentlemen.

The reception hour struck, but the journalists were not yet admitted. Then the greyish gentlemen, at first quietly but then louder, began to rap on the door. They were knocking to be admitted to the President of the United States, just as some assistant director might rap on the door of an actor to remind him of his entrance cue. They knocked laughingly, but still they knocked.

Finally, the door opened and the journalists, crowding each other, rushed ahead. We ran with the rest of them. The cavalcade raced across the corridor, then passed through a large empty room. In that room we easily outstripped the panting grey-haired gentlemen and were the first to run into the next room.

Before us in the depths of a circular private study—on the walls of which hung old lithographs depicting Mississippi steamers, and in the small niches of which stood models of frigates—at a medium-sized writing-desk, a smoking cigarette in his hand, and Chekhovian pince-nez on his large handsome nose, sat Franklin D. Roosevelt, President of the United States. Behind his back twinkled the stars and stripes of two national flags.

Questions began. The correspondents asked them, the President answered.

All of this ritual was, of course, somewhat conditional. Everybody knows that the President will not disclose any particular secrets to the journalists. Certain questions the President answered seriously and quite extensively, parried some with a jest (it is not so easy, of course, twice a week to get off with a joke against a hundred pushing journalists), to still others he replied that he would discuss them the next time.

Roosevelt's large handsome face looked tired   Only the day before the Supreme Court had vetoed the AAA, Roosevelt's law regulating farmers' sowing of crops, one of the pivots of his programme.

The questions and answers took up half an hour. When a pause came, the President looked quizzically at the people gathered there. This was understood to be a signal for a general retreat. There resounded a helter-skelter "Good-bye, Mr. President!" and everyone departed. And Mr. President remained alone in his circular study among the frigates and the star-spangled banners.

Millions of people, old and young, who compose the great American nation, an honest, boisterous, talented people, who have a somewhat too great respect for money but who are hard-working, can do anything they like according to the Constitution, for they are the masters of the country. They can even take Morgan himself, John Pierpont Morgan himself, and call him out for questioning in a senatorial commission and ask him severely:

"Mr. Morgan, didn't you pull the United States into the World War because of the mundane interests of your personal enrichment?"

The people can ask that. But this is how Mr. Morgan answers—we heard him ourselves.

And on that occasion, too, everything was very democratic.

The entrance to the hall where the Senate Commission was sitting was free. Again you were free to do with your overcoat what you liked—put it on the floor, or shove it under the chair on which you were sitting.

At one end of a small hall were chairs for the public; at the other end, a table at which the questioning was proceeding. The table was covered with neither red nor green cloth. It was a long polished table. Everything was very simple. Right beside the billionaire, on the floor, lay his thick and no longer new brief-case. Morgan was surrounded by his lawyers and advisers. They were numerous. Grey and pink-cheeked, fat and bald-headed, or young with piercing eyes—they were all armed with facts, information, documents, folios, and folders. All this band of Morgan's braves felt quite unconstrained.

In the chair was Senator Nye, his face thin, inspired, almost Russian. (A Russian shirt would suit him very well.) The interrogation was carried on by Senator Clark, round-faced and gay. It was at once evident that he enjoyed questioning John Pierpont Morgan, Jr.

"Junior" was almost seventy years old. He was a huge and obese old man in a long dark coat. On the back of Morgan's apoplectic head was visible the grey fuzz of a chick. He was calm. He knew that nothing untoward would happen to him. He would be asked a question, he would look at his lawyers, the latter would begin to dig frantically in their books and would prompt the answer to him.

It was an amazing spectacle. Several score of advisers whispered something into Morgan's ear, shoved little papers to him, prompted him, helped him. It was not Morgan speaking, it was his billions speaking. And when money talks in America, it always talks authoritatively. After all, America's favourite saying is:

"He looks like a million dollars."

Indeed, a million dollars looks very good.

And Morgan, in his long dark coat resembling an old fat hawk, looked like several billions.

For being summoned to the Senate Commission, the person subpoenaed is entitled to daily pay, the normal government daily pay for expenses. John Pierpont Morgan, Jr., took that money. He took advantage of all the rights which a democratic constitution gave him.

Morgan received everything he was entitled to under the Constitution —even a little more. But what did the people get?

On the territory of the United States live more than a hundred and twenty million people.

Thirteen million of them have not had work for several years. Together with their families they make up one-fourth of the population of the entire country. Yet economists insist that on the territory of the United States right now, even today, it would be possible to feed a billion people.

46
They and We

OUR JOURNEY came to an end. Within two months we had been in twenty-five states and several hundred towns, we had breathed the dry air of deserts and prairies, and crossed the Rocky Mountains, had seen Indians, had talked with the young unemployed, with the old capitalists, with radical intellectuals, with revolutionary workers, with poets, with writers, with engineers. We had examined factories and parks, had admired roads and bridges, had climbed up the Sierra Nevadas and descended into the Carlsbad Caves. We had travelled ten thousand miles.

And throughout that entire journey we never once stopped thinking of the Soviet Union.

We had travelled over American highways but in our thoughts were Soviet highways. We spent nights in American hotels, but we thought about Soviet hotels. We examined Ford's factories, but in our thoughts we saw ourselves in our own automobile factories, and while conversing with Indians we thought of Kazakstan.

Through the tremendous distance that separated us from Soviet soil we envisioned it with especial incisiveness. It is necessary to see the capitalist world in order to appreciate in a new way the world of socialism. All the attributes of the socialist arrangement of our life, which man ceases to notice because of daily contact with them, seem especially significant at a distance. We understood the mood of Maxim Gorky when upon his return to the Union after many years of life abroad, tirelessly, day in and day out, he repeated one and the same thing: "It's a remarkable thing you are doing, comrades! A great thing!"

We talked constantly about the Soviet Union, drew parallels, made comparisons. We noticed that the Soviet people whom we frequently met in America were possessed of the same emotions. There was not a single conversation which in the end would not end up with a reference to the Soviet Union: "But at home it is like this," "but at home it is like that," "it would be well to introduce it at home," "we don't know how to do that yet," "that we have already adopted." Soviet people abroad were not mere travellers, not merely engineers or diplomats on a mission. All of them were lovers who had been torn away from the object of their affection and who remembered it every minute. It is a unique patriotism that cannot be understood, let us say, by an American. In all probability the American is a good patriot. If he were asked he would sincerely say that he loves his country; but at the same time it will be found out that he does not love Morgan, that he does not know and does not care to know the names of the people who planned the suspension bridges in San Francisco, that he is not interested to know why in America drought increases every year, who built Boulder Dam and why, why Negroes are lynched in the Southern states, or why he must eat frozen meat. He will say that he loves his country—yet he is profoundly indifferent to questions of agriculture, since he is not an agriculturist; to questions of industry, since he is not an industrialist; to finances, since he is not a financier; to art, since he is not an artist; and to military problems, since he is not a military man. He is a hard-working man who receives his hundred and thirty dollars a month, so he sneers at Washington with all its laws, at Chicago with all its bandits, and at New York with its Wall Street. He asks only one thing of his country—to let him alone, and not to interfere with his listening to his radio or going to the movies. Of course, when he becomes unemployed, then it's a different matter. Then he will begin to think about everything. No, he will not understand the patriotism of a Soviet man, who loves not his juridical native land which gives him merely the rights of citizenship, but a native land which is tangible, where to him belong the soil, the factories, the stores, the banks, the dread-noughts, the airplanes, the theatres, and the books, where he himself is the politician and the master of all.

The average American cannot endure abstract conversations nor does he touch upon themes too far removed from him. He is interested only in what is directly connected with his house, his automobile, or his nearest neighbours. He shows an interest in the life of the country once in four years, at the time of the presidential election.

We do not at all insist that this absence of spirituality is an organic attribute of the American people. There was a time, after all, when the Northern armies marched off to liberate the Negroes from slavery! It is capitalism that has made these people thus, and in every way it nurtures in them this spiritual lassitude. Terrible are the crimes of American capitalism, which with amazing trickiness has palmed off on the people the most trivial of motion pictures, radio, and weekly journalistic tosh, while reserving for itself Tolstoy, Van Gogh, and Einstein, but remaining profoundly indifferent to them.

Essentially there is in the world only one noble striving of the human mind—to vanquish spiritual and material poverty, to make people happy. Yet those people in America who have made it their goal to attain that— the advanced workers, the radical intellectuals—are at best regarded as dangerous cranks, and in the worst case as the enemies of society. The result is that even indirect fighters for human happiness—men of learning, inventors, builders—are not popular in America. They and their works, inventions, and wonderful constructions, remain in the shadows, while all of fame goes to boxers, bandits, and motion-picture stars. While among the people themselves—who see that with the increase in the number of machines, life becomes not better but worse—prevails even hatred of technical progress. There are people who are ready to break up machines, just like the drowning man who, in desperation to get out of the water, seizes his saviour by the neck and drags him down to the bottom.

We have already said that the American, in spite of his businesslike activity, has a passive nature. Some Hearst or some Hollywood shyster can manage to drag millions of good, honest, hard-working average Americans down to the spiritual level of a savage. But even these all-powerful men cannot divest the people of the notion that life must be improved. That notion is very widespread in America. But when it finally finds its expression in the form of political ideas, their level does not exceed the level of the average Hollywood picture. And such ideas have a colossal success.

All the political ideas which tend to the improvement of the welfare of the American people are inevitably presented in the form of easy arithmetic problems for students of the third grade. In order to understand the idea, the voter need merely take a sheet of paper, a pencil, make a quick calculation, and it's done. As a matter of fact, all of them are not really ideas but tricks, suitable for advertising purposes only. They would hardly bear mentioning, if scores of millions of Americans were not carried away by them.

How to save America and improve its life?

Huey Long advises division of wealth. A sheet of paper and a pencil appear on the scene. The voter, puffing, adds, multiplies, subtracts, and divides. This is a terribly interesting occupation. What a smart fellow this Huey Long is! Everyone will get a large sum of money! People are so carried away by this impudent arithmetic that it does not even occur to them to think about where these millions will come from.

How to improve life? How to save America?

There arises a new titan of thought, another Socrates or Confucius, the physician Townsend. The thought which has entered the thinking head of this respectable practising physician could have been born in any

K

small European country only in a psychiatric hospital in a ward for the tranquil, quiet, polite, and utterly hopeless madmen. But in America it has a dizzying success. Here it isn't even necessary to bother with subtraction and multiplication. Here everything is quite simple. Every old man and every old woman in the United States upon attaining the age of sixty will receive two hundred dollars a month under obligation to spend these dollars. Then trade will increase automatically and automatically unemployment will disappear. Everything takes place automatically.

We saw a sound newsreel of a meeting of the Townsend Committee under the management of the thinker himself. The meeting began with Dr. Townsend, a haggard old man with a freckled face, in spectacles and an old-fashioned coat, delivering a short speech on his plan.

"Ladies and gentlemen," he began, clearing his throat, "I spent many sleepless nights before I thought up my plan."

If Mark Twain could only take a look at this freckled old man, so methodical, so neat, and undoubtedly Godfearing! There is no doubt that it is precisely such an old man, coming out of Sister McPherson's ecclesiastical musical hall, weighs himself and weighs his entire family, in order to calculate how many pennies of live weight he must pay for, through the intercession of the esteemed sister, to the Lord God.

After Dr. Townsend the old men and women who filled the hall spoke. They came out on the stage and asked questions, to which the thinker replied.

"In other words, I will receive two hundred dollars?" an old man asked.

"Yes, if my plan goes through," the thinker answered firmly.

"Every month?"

"Every month."

"Well, thank you," the old man said.

And he vacated the place for the old woman who followed him.

"Listen, Dr. Townsend," she asked excitedly. "We are two old people—my husband and I. Will both of us really receive two hundred dollars each?"

"Yes, both of you," the thinker replied importantly.

"That is, all told, we will get four hundred dollars?"

"Quite right—four hundred dollars."

"I also receive a pension of seventeen dollars. They won't take that away from me?"

"No, you will likewise receive your pension."

The old woman bowed low and went away.

When we were leaving America the number of Townsend's followers was increasing at a frightful rate. Not a single politician dared to speak against this doctor of genius on the eve of elections.

But American capitalists understand that motion pictures, a radio broadcast, stories in weeklies, bill-boards about revolution "which can never happen in America," churches, and arithmetical plans may not prove sufficient, so there are already growing "American Legions" and "Liberty

Leagues," and little by little Fascist forces are trained, so that at the necessary moment they may be turned into the most genuine kind of storm troops, which will be ordered to stifle the revolutionary movement by force.

America is rich. But it is not merely rich. It is phenomenally rich. It has everything—oil, grain, coal, gold, cotton—everything that can only lie beneath the earth or grow upon the earth. It has people—the best workers in the world—capable, neat, efficient, honest, hard-working. America marched toward its enrichment at a quick rate of speed. The country reminds one of a man who has made a rapid career, who at first sells suspenders from a push-cart on the East Side, then opens his own store of ready-made clothes and moves to Brooklyn. Then he opens a department store, begins to play the stock market and moves to the Bronx. And finally he buys a railroad, hundreds of steamships, two motion-picture factories, builds a skyscraper, opens a bank, joins a golf club, and moves to Park Avenue. He is a billionaire. He had striven for that goal all his life. He bought and sold everything in any old way. He dispossessed people, speculated, sat at the stock exchange from morning until night, he toiled sixteen hours a day, he awoke with the thought of money, he fell asleep with the same thought, and now he is monstrously wealthy. Now he may rest. He has villas by the ocean, he has yachts and castles, but he becomes ill with an incurable disease. He is dying, and no billions can save him.

The stimulus of American life has been and is money. Contemporary American technique grew up and developed so that money might be made faster. Everything that brings in money develops, and everything that does not bring money degenerates and wilts away. Gas, electricity, construction, and automobile companies, in their chase for money, have created a high standard of living. America has raised itself to a high degree of welfare, having left Europe far behind. But precisely at this point it has become clear that America is seriously and dangerously ill. The country is now facing its own *reductio ad absurdum*. It is capable now, today, of feeding a billion people, and yet it cannot feed its own hundred and twenty millions. It has everything needed to create a peaceful life for its people, yet it has come to such a pass that the entire population is in a state of unrest: the unemployed fears that he will never again find a job; the employed fears that he will lose his job; the farmer fears a crop failure, because then prices will increase and it will cost him more to buy bread, but he also fears a good crop, because then prices will fall and he will have to sell his produce for a pittance. The rich fear that bandits will kidnap their children, bandits fear that they will be placed in the electric chair. Immigrants fear that they will be deported from America; Negroes fear that they will be lynched; politicians fear elections; the average man fears illness, because then doctors will take everything he owns; the merchant fears that racketeers will come and riddle his store counters with a machine-gun fusillade.

At the foundation of life of the Soviet Union lies the communist idea.

We have a definite goal, toward which the country advances. The slogan that technique decides everything was given by Stalin after that idea triumphed. That is why we, the people, by comparison with Americans of the average kind, are now already much calmer and happier than they, in the land of Morgan and Ford, of twenty-five million automobiles, of a million miles of ideal roads, the land of cold and hot water, of bathrooms, and service. That is why technique does not seem to us an evil spirit sprung from a bottle. On the contrary, we want to catch up with technical America and to outstrip it.

America does not know what will happen with it tomorrow. We know, and we can tell with definite accuracy, what will happen with us fifty years from now.

Nevertheless, we can still learn much from America. We are doing that. But the lessons which we learn from America are episodic and too specialized.

To catch up with America! That task which Stalin set before our people is immense, but in order to carry out this task we must first of all study America, study not only its automobiles, its turbine generators and radio apparatuses (we are doing that), but likewise the very character of the work of American workers, engineers, business people, especially the business people, because if our stakhanovists sometimes outstrip the norms of American workers, while the engineers are no worse at times than the American engineers (about that we heard frequently from Americans themselves), still, our business people or economists are considerably behind American business people and cannot compete with them in any way.

We will not discuss now the attributes of our economists, their loyalty to ideas, their devotion, their efficiency. These are the attributes of the Communist party, which brought them up. Nor will we touch upon the deficiencies of American business people, their lack of loyalty to ideas, their lack of principle, their chase after the dollar. These are the defects of the capitalism which brought them up. It is important for us right now to study their attributes and our defects, because it is necessary for us to learn from them. Not only engineers but also economists, our business people, must learn from them.

The American businessman always finds time for a business conversation. The American sits in his office with his coat off and works. He works quietly, unobtrusively, without making any fuss. He is never late anywhere. He never hurries anywhere. He has only one telephone. No one waits for him in his reception room, because an appointment is usually made with absolute accuracy, and not a single extra minute is wasted during the interview. He is occupied only with his business, exclusively with his business. When he holds conferences nobody knows. In all likelihood he holds conferences rarely.

Should an American say in the course of a conversation, even incidentally, "I'll do that," it is not necessary to remind him of anything at all in the future. Everything will be done. The ability to keep his word, to keep it firmly, accurately, to burst, but keep his word—this is the most important thing which our Soviet business people must learn from American business people.

We wrote about American democracy, which in fact does not give man freedom and only masks the exploitation of man by man. But in American life there is a phenomenon which should interest us no less than a new machine model. That phenomenon is democracy in intercourse between people, albeit that democracy, too, covers social inequality and is a purely outward form. The outward forms of such a democracy are splendid. They help a lot in work, deliver a blow to bureaucracy, and enhance human dignity.

We drove out of Washington to New York. In a few hours, and our journey over the American land would come to an end. We thought about America during those final hours. We think that in our book we have told everything that we have thought.

Americans are very angry with Europeans who come to America, enjoy its hospitality, and later scold it. Americans often told us about this with annoyance. But we do not understand such posing of the question: to scold or to praise. America is not the first night of a new play, and we are not theatre critics. We transmit to paper our impressions about that country and our thoughts about it.

What can be said about America, which simultaneously horrifies, delights, calls forth pity, and sets examples worthy of emulation, about a land which is rich, poor, talented, and ungifted?

We can say honestly, with hand on heart, that we would not like to live in America. It is interesting to observe this country, but one does not care to live in it.

47
Farewell, America!

THE WEATHER was crisp in New York. The wind blew. The sun shone.

New York is amazingly beautiful! But why does one feel sad in this great city? The houses are so high, the light of the sun lies only on the upper stories, and throughout the day one does not lose the impression that the sun is setting. Sunset begins in the morning. Probably that is why one feels so sad in New York.

We again returned to the city where live two million automobiles and seven million persons who serve them. Oh, it is a remarkable sight— automobiles driving on a promenade through Central Park! One cannot get rid of the thought that this immense park located in the middle of New York was built so that automobiles might breathe fresh air there. There are only automobile roads in the park—little place is left for pedestrians. New York has been captured by automobiles, and in the city the automobiles behave like genuine troops of occupation. They kill and cripple the natives, deal with them strictly, and won't let them complain. People deprive themselves of much in order to fill their oppressors with petrol, quench their eternal thirst for oil and water.

Besides automobiles, New York has still another frightful sovereign. He is Noise. Noise is manufactured here in enormous quantities. Underground bays the subway, overhead thunders the elevated railroad, hundreds of thousands of motors roar simultaneously on the streets. And at night, when the noise quiets down somewhat, one can distinctly hear the long and alarming sirens of the police, fire department, and gangster automobiles. The roar approaches, passes by, and is lost somewhere in the distance. Someone has been shot for love's sake, someone else out of hate, someone else simply for not sharing the spoils. Or maybe someone has hanged himself, or poisoned himself, or shot himself through his heart, unable to endure the life in the city of automobiles, noise, and headaches.

"Bromo-Seltzer," a drink for headaches, is sold everywhere, along with orange juice, coffee, and lemonade. Soon Bromo-Seltzer will find a place on the menu. The dinner will then be something like this: First, "Bromo-Seltzer"; in the second place, "chilli," which is a Mexican soup; in the third place, a fish called "sole"; and for dessert, again "Bromo-Seltzer." New York alone may have more telephones than all England, but undoubtedly in New York alone in the course of a day more headache powders are used than in all England in half a year. In the more quiet districts of New York apartments cost more, not because they are better, but because there is less noise there. In New York, quiet is an object of trade—and it is costly merchandise. It is in the same class with an English suit of clothes. It is expensive—but then, it is good.

In New York one can never be rid of a feeling of alarm. Down the busiest street there will suddenly drive an armoured bank car painted in bright red. The machine-guns of the armoured car are directed right at a crowd of young men in light hats who promenade with cigars in their teeth. Thus in New York money is transported. It can be carried only in armoured cars; otherwise, these same young men in light hats would make off with it. They seem to be smiling too suspiciously and anxiously, their hands in the pockets of their sleek overcoats.

It took us several days to bid farewell to our New York friends, streets, and skyscrapers.

On the day of our departure we went to Central Park West and up to the Adams's apartment. A Negress opened the door, disclosing shining African teeth that lighted up the vestibule.

In the dining-room we saw Mr. Adams pressing the baby to his chest. Beside him stood Mrs. Adams, who was saying:

"You have already held the baby for five minutes. It's my turn now!"

"No, no, Becky, don't talk like that! It hurts me to hear you talk like that."

On the table and on the floor lay unwrapped packages. Among the strings and wrapping paper lay a great variety of things: an old blanket, a plaid, binoculars, collars, several keys, with large hotel disks, and many other things.

"There, there, gentlemen!" said Mr. Adams, eagerly pressing our hands. "My things are beginning to come in little by little. All I have to do now is to return the keys to the various hotels and everything will be in order. Only my hat has not come yet."

"It would have been better to have got it in Washington, after all," Mrs. Adams said reprovingly, deftly taking the baby out of her husband's hands.

"But, Becky," Mr. Adams groaned, "you must not act like that! We have left instructions with the Washington post office to send the hat here. Let go of the baby! You have been holding her too long! It's harmful for the baby. Let her run around the room."

But scarcely had Mrs. Adams dropped the girl to the floor, when Mr. Adams with a cry caught the baby and pressed her to his chest.

A bell rang, and a postman came into the room with a package.

"This time it is the hat!" cried Mrs. Adams.

Yes, it was the hat. Mr. Adams solemnly pulled out of a box his old favourite hat and at once put it on his head.

"Let's go!" he cried in his ringing voice. "You are going away today, gentlemen, and until now you have not been on top of the Empire State Building! It would be foolish not to do that. If you want to know what America is, you must go up the Empire State Building!"

When the baby saw that her parents were again being led away by the unknown gentlemen who had already dragged them off for two months, she began to howl. She stamped her little feet and cried, tears flowing down her face, "No more trips!"

The parents swore to the baby that they were going away for only five minutes, but she continued to wail and to remind them that "that time they also said that they would go away for only five minutes and did not come back for a very long time."

We still heard the child's weeping while going down in the elevator. Papa and Mamma looked confused, but unquenchable curiosity lighted up their eyes.

"To go up the Empire State Building for the sixteenth time," muttered Mr. Adams, "is very, very interesting, gentlemen!"

For the last time we rode on top of a Fifth Avenue bus. Mannequins with pink ears looked at us out of the show windows. Between the automobiles passed three circus elephants who were inviting New Yorkers to visit an evening performance. Life proceeded apace.

We went to the top of the Empire State Building.

How many times, passing by, we could not contain ourselves, sighing and muttering: "Ah, the devil!—Well, well! That's something!" or words to that effect. Yet we went up only two hours before our departure from America!

The first elevator lifted us at once to the eighty-sixth story. The rise lasts only one minute. Naturally, one could not see here either stories or landings. We raced in a steel tube, and only the ears, which seemed to have filled with water, and a strange little chill around the region of the abdomen, made us aware of the fact that we were rising at an incredible rate of speed. The elevator did not clang or knock. It moved precipitately, smoothly, noiselessly. Only at the door tiny lamps flared, counting off tens of stories. At the eighty-sixth story landing we stepped out on somewhat weakened legs.

The second elevator brought the passengers to the roof of the building, and through large spyglasses we saw New York. It had snowed the day before. On the streets the snow had already melted. But on the flat roofs of the skyscrapers it still lay in pure, delicate white squares. The mountain air at the top of the buildings kept the snow from melting. An incredible city, winged with the comb of piers, lay below. The grey winter air was slightly golden from the sun. Over the black narrow streets crept tiny automobiles and the trains of the elevated railroad. The noise of the city reached here but faintly. One could not even hear the baying of the police sirens. All around, out of the midday twilight of the New York streets proudly rose the skyscrapers, their countless windows gleaming. They stood like the guards of the city, armed with glittering steel. At the pier of the Cunard-White Star Line could be seen a steamship with three stacks. The stacks were yellow, with black rings. That was the *Majestic*. Fifty-six thousand tons of steel, wood, rugs, and mirrors—the English steamer on which we were to depart that day. Yet, how small and helpless it seemed from the roof of the Empire State Building!

Two hours later we were on the steamer. The *Majestic* was making its last trip. After that this steamer, quite young yet, will be junked.[1] With the appearance of the *Normandie* and the *Queen Mary*, new colossal Atlantic steamers, the *Majestic* was too modest and too slow-moving, although it crosses the ocean in excellent time—six days.

The huge bulk of the *Majestic* had already left the walls of the pier, and we heard for the last time:

"Good-bye, gentlemen! Seriously, I hope that you have understood what America is!"

And over the heads of the people at the pier frantically waved the trusty old hat of Mr. Adams and the handkerchief of his wife, the manly driver, who twice drove us across the entire continent, the never tiring, patient, ideal fellow traveller of the road.

When the *Majestic* sailed past Wall Street, darkness fell and lights appeared in the skyscrapers. In those windows gleamed the gold of electricity, but perhaps also real gold. This last golden vision of America escorted us to the very egress into the ocean.

The *Majestic* gathered speed. The farewell light of a buoy flashed by, and a few hours later there was not a trace left of America. The cold January wind blew a large ocean wave.

[1] The *Majestic* was overhauled, and on April 23, 1937, it was launched as H.M.S. *Caledonia*, a training ship of the British Royal Navy.—C. M.

Printed in Poland
by Amazon Fulfillment
Poland Sp. z o.o., Wrocław

94849948R00170